CONTEMPORARY ASSESSMENT FOR EDUCATORS

CLINTON I. CHASE

INDIANA UNIVERSITY

LONGMAN

An imprint of Addison Wesley Longman, Inc.

New York • Reading, Massachusetts • Menlo Park, California
Harlow, England • Don Mills, Ontario • Sydney
Mexico City • Madrid • Amsterdam

Acquisitions Editor: Art Pomponio
Marketing Manager: Renée Ortbals
Project Coordination, Text Design, Art Studio, Photo Research, and Electronic Page
  Makeup: Thompson Steele Production Services, Inc.
Cover Designer/Manager: Nancy Danahy
Full Service Production Manager: Eric Jorgensen
Print Buyer: Denise Sandler
Printer and Binder: The Maple-Vail Book Manufacturing Group
Cover Printer: Coral Graphic Services, Inc.

Library of Congress Cataloging-in-Publication Data

Chase, Clinton, I.
    Contemporary assessment for educators/ Clinton I. Chase.—1st ed.
      p.   cm.
    Includes bibliographical references and index.
    ISBN 0-8013-1372-4 (alk. paper)
    1. Educational tests and measurements—United States. I. Title.
    1999
    371.26–dc21   98-25259
                                                     CIP

Copyright © 1999 by Addison-Wesley Educational Publishers Inc.

Please visit our website at http://longman.awl.com

ISBN 0-8013-1372-4

12345678910—MA—01009998

CONTENTS

CHAPTER 4
RELIABILITY: HOW CONSISTENT IS OUR MEASUREMENT 53

CHAPTER 5
ERRORS OF MEASUREMENT: HOW TO WORK WITH THEM 79

CHAPTER 11
DELIVERING CONVENTIONAL TESTS: PACKAGING; ADMINISTERING; DEBRIEFING   193

CHAPTER 12
ASSESSING STUDENT PERFORMANCE   211

CHAPTER 13
COMPUTER APPLICATIONS IN TESTING AND GRADING   245

SECTION III
UNDERSTANDING AND INTERPRETING PUBLISHED TESTS   259

CHAPTER 18
LEGAL AND ETHICAL CONSIDERATIONS IN TESTING   349

SECTION IV
REPORTING ON THE OUTCOMES OF EDUCATION   363

PREFACE

From years of visiting schools in several states, and having been one of the teachers who shared conversations in the lunch room, I have realized that teachers need more information on assessment than they normally receive. I believe that there are consistent deficiencies at the application level as well as in theoretical concepts that support applications. To this end this book provides basic skills and knowledge about assessment so that teachers can expand their ability to deal with appraisal problems in their own settings. I believe that educators can on a regular basis use every topic in this book, either in creating and managing their own classroom assessments, or in wisely understanding and interpreting the volumes of published materials with which they are bombarded.

The topics in this book emerge out of many years of observing teachers at work, in interacting with individual educators, of visiting schools, and working with officials in state departments of education. Every topic in this book has regularly appeared on the agendas of these encounters and in that regard their presence in this textbook is validated. Teachers want to be better at their craft. People who mentor them should not only help them be better but also expect them to be better.

There are many possible sequences in which the topics of this book could be arranged, and a collection of readers would support each of them. Ultimately one order must be selected, and I hope you will find the order of topics selected to be at least one of the more appropriate. In the text my intent is to present some advanced organizers to the reader before the actual topics are developed. I also refer to topics over several chapters because much of the information is applicable to many situations in teaching. I do not want teachers to think of any topic as being distinct from others, learning it *pro tem* and then disregarding it. Therefore, I occasionally refer the readers to a previous chapter, or cite a later chapter in which the topic will be discussed.

Traditionally, books like this concentrate all basic ideas around a given topic into one chapter. I have not always followed that plan. Instead, I have occasionally divided subtopics among several chapters so that the information can be placed at the point where it will be immediately applied. This sometimes means that a unit has been broken up into several segments that appear in different places in the book. This is especially true of statistical tools. I present correlation (at a conceptual and interpretational level) with validity, refer to it again with reliability, and at several later points. I present descriptive statistics just before standardized tests because they will be needed in understanding and interpreting scores from those tests. The scores themselves (e.g., grade equivalents) are not discussed until the chapter on achievement tests where they are first applied. This may not be a traditional presentation of statistics but I believe topics derive their greatest meaning for teachers in the context in which they are applied.

Several instructors advised me that statistics which involve calculations will not be learned by teachers, and my experience partially verifies this. I expect teachers to be able to do a few calculations. However, there are many statistical calculations that teachers will never be called upon to do, and I avoided calculations of this kind (or inserted them into the appendix for those who wish to use them). I have also included several shortcut methods of estimating statistics (standard deviation and correlation) that require very little calculation, and which are sufficiently accurate for most classroom work. I think we should expect teachers to be able to calculate statistics that will help them make more sense of their own classroom assessment. But if the topic is needed only to interpret a score or explain a student's position in a group, no calculations are needed—I discuss only the concept.

I have also put into the appendix a simple computer program that, once set up on a classroom computer, could provide valuable information for teachers' own tests with very little effort. I think this kind of facility in an increasingly computer literate teaching corps not only can be useful, but also should be readily available.

My intent in all chapters is to present the ideas in an easy flowing, near conversational style to keep the reading difficulty level out of the learning process. When you and I meet in the hall we speak in an informal style, and we use examples of real cases to elaborate our points. We do that in our classroom, also. This is the style that I have used in this book. To increase authenticity, the examples I use are based on situations I have actually encountered, sometimes depicted as they actually occurred and sometimes transposed to a different setting while retaining their essential content. The applications I make are not imagined; they are based on real situations I have observed. In this way I hope to make the book more meaningful to teachers who want answers to real problems in their classrooms.

I have provided several pedagogical procedures to help the reader grasp the ideas in each chapter. I have started each chapter with a scene that catches the reader's attention and leads to the topic to be discussed. I have listed the major points that will be covered in the chapter to give the student an overview of what is ahead and to serve as an outline for review. At the close of the chapter I have reviewed the content in a summary and listed the key terms that were learned in the chapter. In addition I have provided a manageable list of additional readings to expand the chapter.

As a further learning aid, I have inserted application problems within the text at appropriate times when students should be thinking about "What does this mean for my classroom?" and again at the end of the chapter. The latter aims at a review of the topics from the chapter overall. I have intentionally not developed an answer key for the problems. I believe such keys have disadvantages that I want to avoid. They insinuate that to each teaching problem there is one answer, when often several approaches would work. I want teachers to plan their own approach which may be discussed with their colleagues in groups or in class. In addition I have often observed students going to the answer key before attempting to solve a problem themselves, and then work from the answer back to the problem. I do not think this is an effective approach to learning. I want students to rely on their own knowledge and experience in providing a solution to the problems in the text. Occasionally, I have inserted a longer example which I have called a narrative. This narrative is designed to describe a real setting with a real problem to illustrate to teacher candidates that the information just presented has a genuine application. The narratives do not bring closure, allowing the student to become involved in the situation. The narrative is designed to put the subject matter into an actual educational setting that poses a problem.

Many people have contributed to the building of this book. I wish to thank a number of people for their contributions. Patricia L. Chase brought to the reading of the manuscript the experience of successful teaching and consistently useful suggestions on style and relevance of topics. She also tolerated my many hours at the computer, and indeed arranged events to make those hours possible. John Mathews provided a very large number of suggestions on style and content that have added greatly to the text. Suzanne Menzel checked my computer programming. Dr. Art Pomponio has given support and advice for moving the manuscript along.

The reviewers who teach courses in assessment across the country have been generous with their time and with their helpful suggestions. And above all, I am thankful to the very large number of students who posed interesting and challenging questions in my classes, and to the many teachers and administrators who have invited me into their schools to observe and interact with them. I hope this book faithfully represents to the next generation of teachers the demands and the possibilities for assessment in the many educational settings that profit from competent practice.

Clint Chase
August, 1997

SECTION I

PRINCIPLES THAT UNDERLIE COMPETENT ASSESSMENT PRACTICES

UNDERPINNINGS OF EDUCATIONAL ASSESSMENT
CONSTRUCTING MEASURABLE LEARNING OBJECTIVES
VALIDITY: WHAT DOES THIS TEST TELL ME?
RELIABILITY: HOW CONSISTENT IS OUR MEASUREMENT?
ERRORS OF MEASUREMENT: HOW TO WORK WITH THEM

In all professional work, the job begins with understanding the principles that guide the activities of the profession. No one designs an airplane without a grasp of the physics of aerodynamics. An accountant studies the general concepts of debits and credits. The effective teacher studies the psychology of learning.

In assessment too there are basic controlling principles that are relevant to all educational applications of the procedures. So that they may select and direct appropriate experiences for the class teachers must begin with the objectives they expect their students to achieve. Without objectives they will have no guide to decide what to assess to estimate how children are progressing. Assessments must be consistent so that teachers can depend on the result being a stable estimate of a child's behavior; and assessments must be an appropriate sample of the behaviors that are characteristics of the skill we are trying to assess.

In all assessment procedure there is some inexactness. This is called *error*, although by "error" we do not mean "mistakes." It is simply that the teacher's estimate of a child's ability does not correspond with that pupil's actual achievement. How shall we deal with this error? We need some guidelines to help us make appropriate judgments about children when we know that some error may occur in our assessment procedures.

The first chapters in this book deal with these basic principles because they pervade and enhance the meaning of the balance of topics discussed in this book. These are concepts you must apply to each of the successive chapters if full meaning of the work described there is to be grasped. Creating your own tests, scoring tests, completing observations of student performances, making out report cards, and many other tasks are most effectively performed when the following criteria are met: a) having clear objectives, b) having confidence that your assessments stably place children in terms of their actual achievement, and c) the conviction that your observations indeed reflect the behaviors that characterize achievement of the objectives. The skills presented throughout the following chapters, and the application of them in your own classrooms, will make most sense in the context of these basic principles.

CHAPTER 1

Underpinnings of Educational Assessment

It was 3:30 P.M. The children at Elm Heights School were spilling onto the sidewalk like marbles from a torn bag. I waited outside Ms. Morton's classroom while she talked with a student at her desk. The student soon left the room, her face curled into a frown, and I entered.

"I really am uncomfortable with assessment," Ms. Morton began, "and this student, Jessy, is an example of why. I just gave back tests and Jessy wanted to know why she got only half-credit on one of the short answer items on the test. How do you respond to a question like that? In my opinion she didn't have a good grasp of the topic, but it was my guess against hers. So what do you tell her? 'Because I say so!' isn't very convincing. I'd like it better if I could just teach, and not do any assessment. I'm a teacher, not some kind of a mind-meter."

Many teachers have felt like Ms. Morton during the assessment phase of instruction (Wise, Luken, & Roos, 1991). If you were to make a top-ten list of things teachers dislike about their jobs, testing would probably rank high. But in the best kind of teaching, assessment can help both students and teachers. It can identify students whose prior work has not prepared them to move on to the next concept to be presented. It can identify aspects of a concept students are not readily grasping and those which are well in hand. Assessment can show teachers where instruction has been effective and where it has not. Teaching without competent assessment will surely be less effective for both students and teachers.

What This Chapter Will Include. In this chapter you will find a discussion of the following topics that underpin all assessment activities.

1. Why teachers must be skilled in assessment
2. Assessment terminology—a first list
3. Basic concepts that direct assessment
4. Assessment in a contemporary classroom
5. An overview of the skills and knowledge presented in this book

The Need For Assessment Skills

The business of assessment in schools is an immense endeavor. The part of assessment that comes in the form of tests alone is almost unbelievably large. For instance, it is estimated that there are a quarter billion commercially published tests of achievement administered each year in kindergarten through grade twelve in the United States. Add to this the almost five billion tests that teachers make themselves for use in their own classrooms (Worthen, Borg, & White, 1993).

Beyond all this are the non-test assessments that are carried out by teachers, such as term papers, in-class essays, systematic observations of student projects, and other similar assessments that are a routine part of directing learning. The total involvement of educators in data collection is enormous and challenging.

Unfolding the curriculum to students requires teachers to make many decisions yearly, monthly, even hourly. Am I making progress toward the objectives I have set? Is Susan a better writer than she was when she came into my class three months ago? How well did I get that idea across in math class this week? To answer questions such as this teachers need concrete evidence that points to decisions, and for concrete evidence they need assessment. An impression, which may be distorted positively by Susan's sweet temperament or negatively by Karl's runny nose and unbrushed hair, is of little help in making decisions about their writing or mathematics skills. As a basis for making decisions teachers need records of pupil performances; and this requires assessment.

Teachers make decisions requiring assessment information at a rate of one every two to three minutes (Shavelson & Stern, 1981). To collect this information teachers can spend up to a third or more of their professional time in assessment activities of one type or another (Stiggins, 1991). In the face of this demand, teachers are often untrained or poorly trained in assessment techniques (Stiggins & Conklin, 1989; O'Sullivan & Chalnick 1991). No wonder they dislike the chores involved in assessment! They are facing very large tasks and often without the preparation to deal effectively with them.

Basic Concepts

In any discipline terms are devised to identify ideas or concepts. The same is true in assessment. We begin with the four basic terms used extensively throughout this book. Others will be discussed in later chapters, in the context where they are most often used.

Assessment

Assessment refers to the broad area of monitoring, or taking stock of, the performances of students or the impact of programs. It includes a variety of procedures, both quantitative and nonquantitative. The fifth-grade teacher who stops at a worktable and systematically observes a child's progress on setting up a science experiment is doing assessment. The high school history teacher who is giving a multiple-choice test on the colonial period in America is doing assessment. The fourth-grade teacher who judges the quality of social studies reports, following a list of features to note, is doing assessment. The commercially printed achievement test administered to the children in the Peach Orchard Elementary School is assessment.

The term assessment, then, is the umbrella that covers a variety of data collection procedures that are used in evaluating educational outcomes.

Measurement

Measurement is a system for observing a phenomenon, attribute, or characteristic and translating those observations into numbers according to a rule. We most often think of measurement in terms of equal-sized units that can be counted, such as inches on a ruler. Similarly, a child takes a spelling test and the teacher counts the number of correct answers; or a student in the clerical program takes a typing test and the instructor counts the number of words typed per minute. These do not have equal-sized units, but clearly 42 correct items on a test represents higher achievement than does 36. Numbers have been assigned here according to a procedure that applies equally to everyone, and the rule says that larger numbers represent greater skill than smaller ones.

Testing

A **test** is a set of specified, uniform tasks to be performed by students, these tasks being an appropriate sample from the knowledge or skills in a broader field of content. From the number of tasks done correctly in the sample, the teacher makes an assumption of how the student will perform in the total field.

For example, based on the first semester's work in Economics Mr. Dow and his class have made up a list of 76 subject-specific terms. From this list Mr. Dow selects a sample of 25 words representative of the list. Students are asked to spell each of these words as he reads them. Based on student performance on this exercise, Mr. Dow will make judgments about how they would do on the entire list. Students who score higher on the sample are believed to be better spellers on the entire list.

Evaluation

Evaluation is the determination of the worth or value of an event, object, or individual in terms of a specified criterion. Educators evaluate student progress by comparing student performance to the criteria of success based on instructional objectives. They evaluate a program in terms of how well children progress compared to how they might do in an alternative program.

In schools evaluation is typically done with the aid of assessment data of some kind. Consider this example. For the last two years the Jefferson School has been using a new system for teaching reading. It is now time to assess the results of this system. An evaluator lists the things children should be able to do as an outcome of the program; the list makes up the criteria of success. Then the evaluator, along with the teachers, collects assessment data to see how many of the students can perform at the criteria levels. The value of the program is determined by the number of students reaching the criteria of achievement.

As you and I journey together through the chapters ahead, many more terms will be presented. These terms are the names of ideas we will want to apply. The terms are best presented in the context where their application is most essential so as I present an idea, I will provide its name. For example, at this point the term "stanine" has no relevance to our discussion; however, in Chapter 16 where you will deal with some commercially published tests it has great relevance. Terms such as this are best presented in the section of the text where you will use them. Understanding these terms will contribute greatly to your grasp of the ideas in the remainder of the chapters. To assist you a list of some of the more important terms discussed is given for your review at the end of each chapter.

Axioms of Assessment

In the box below are some guiding axioms about devising and using assessments to improve instruction. Each of them describes a broad principle of assessment that deserves our further examination.

1. All assessment is based on samples of behavior, and all samples are likely to represent the skill with some inaccuracy.
2. Assessment must communicate to teachers how to make instruction more effective, and to students how to improve performance.
3. Schools have multiple purposes for assessment; no one procedure serves all purposes.
4. In devising and using assessment we must employ procedures at a high level of quality.
5. Assessment is not done solely to sort students for grade assignment but must also be used to promote instructional objectives.

Use of Samples

All assessments are based on samples of behavior, and all samples are likely to contain some imprecision in representing a student's skill. I have a pool of 200 words graded in spelling difficulty at the fifth-grade level. I randomly selected 20 words from the pool, and asked fifth-grader, Geraldo, to spell each of the 20 words as I pronounced it. He missed four, which gave him a score of 80 percent. Is Geraldo's spelling level at 80 percent for fifth-grade words?

I then repeated this process, selecting a second set of 20 words, and this time Geraldo got 17 words right, or 85 percent. My assessments suggest that Geraldo is a pretty good speller, but there is a little error in my samples or Geraldo would get the same score on each trial. With only two observations, the fact is that I do not know exactly what percentage of words in the pool Geraldo can spell.

Carefully prepared samples often provide a close estimate of a child's performance on the entire domain, but rarely match the total domain exactly. For this reason teachers must think of all assessments as having a bit of this "sampling error."

The more samples of a student's behavior the teacher has, the more accurate will be the conclusions about the student's skill. For this reason, assessments should be a regularly repeated operation within the context of instruction. Teachers need to see the student use skills in a number of circumstances to make stable conclusions. They need to see Sharon do her multiplication combinations several times and in different circumstances before deciding how well she knows them; they need to see Amad apply Newton's third law of motion several times before deciding if he can use this principle.

Assessments create the occasions for these replications. They should provide appropriately frequent samples of behavior so that the teacher can make a conclusion about what a student can do. For assessment to be a valuable part of instruction it must provide adequately large samples of the performances to warrant conclusions about the student's stage of progress toward the objective.

Assessment as Communication

Assessment provides information that helps teachers to direct, and redirect, their instruction. As we have discussed, it identifies the concepts on which the class is doing well, and provides diagnostic clues to concepts requiring additional work. Assessment may point to a need for change in instructional strategy, and it can identify students who have failed to grasp a given idea or procedure.

In many ways assessment actually leads instructional activities. It tells me where to begin instruction and indicates the strategy to use as instruction moves along. It shows students how well they are grasping the concepts, where their strengths are, and points to the topics on which they should improve their skill. In all the activity of the classroom—lectures, in- and out-of-class projects, discussions, and so on—assessment points the way for both teachers and students to direct their efforts.

Mr. Potter, the high school chemistry teacher, has just completed a unit on using the periodic chart in solving problems in which students combined an element and a compound which then released another element. In this exercise students made many errors related to the use of valences of elements, and it was clear to Mr. Potter that students did not understand the role of valences in solving the problems. Based on this information, Mr. Potter began planning some demonstrations of how polluting gases were formed in local manufacturing, demonstrations which involved more work with valences. Assessment information had clearly led to a redirection of instruction to remedy a learning problem.

At the same time in a local elementary school Ms. Wicker, a third-grade teacher, was reading reports from groups who had studied maps of different parts of the western hemisphere. In describing locations of countries by longitude and latitude, the children had made a number of errors in the location of certain countries. Ms. Wicker immediately began to plan more work and several concrete experiences to remedy the deficiencies noted in the reports. Both Ms. Wicker and Mr. Potter were better teachers because assessment had brought out valuable information for use in their instructional planning.

On the other side of the teacher's desk, appropriate use of assessment requires that students get information that will illustrate the learning areas and behaviors needing enhancement. After a class had worked on the structure of paragraphs, Maria failed to provide a topic sentences for her in–class essay. As she graded Maria's paper, the teacher illustrated how topic sentences work to guide the reader's thought. In these situations, wherein assessment exercises have been used to help students improve their performance, students learn how to be more critical of their work. Subsequently, students will be better prepared to assess the quality of their own performance, becoming more effective learners and more independent in guiding their own work.

Skilled assessment will improve the effectiveness of teaching by giving teachers a status check on the progress of the class and individuals in it, and provide students with direction for improving subsequent performance.

Multiple Applications of Assessment Data

No one procedure serves all the needs schools have for data. For example, a district-wide testing plan will not serve the purposes of the day-to-day assessments teachers perform in the classroom. District-wide testing of general achievement will probably occur only once a year, will likely include objective testing, and will produce scores that can be translated into broad ideas about how well the overall instructional plan is working. In contrast, classroom assessment involves multiple procedures, goes on continuously, and communicates to students and teachers how achievement of teacher-specific objectives are progressing.

For example, Ms. Wise has set up five learning centers in her classroom. Today students are busy at each of these centers. Ms. Wise walks from center to center, listening to the conversation, and reading over a child's shoulder the report that is in progress. On her return to her desk she makes some notes on the observations she has made—notes that will guide her in expanding her lesson planning.

Down the hall in the principal's office, Mr. Carson is looking over a report he is preparing for the school board. "Ms. Jefferson," he calls to the secretary, "I need those school-wide achievement test data from last spring to verify the results of our remedial program."

Here are two different assessment processes that serve school needs for information, one a less formal procedure, the other very formal. Ms. Wise, as she moves around her classroom, is monitoring behaviors, noting details on a list she will use to evaluate student progress toward objectives. This is **informal assessment.**

But the school district has data needs, too. The report being prepared in the principal's office points to a kind of information that is not available in Ms. Wise's notes. These school-wide tests will provide data that will be compared with other schools across the nation to see if the remedial program in the local school is producing improvement. This is **formal assessment.** It is used to support budgets and program and staff changes. The two procedures will be different, the objectives are different, but both are useful in carrying out the work of the school.

Schools support a variety of assessment operations because there are many kinds of decisions to make and defend with data. Since teachers have a stake in many of these decisions, they must be involved in assessment at several levels of school operation.

The Need for High Quality Assessment

In devising and using assessments teachers must implement procedures at a high level of quality. Quality assessment is shown in a number of features, the most central of which follow.

In instruction and assessment, objectives come first. Objectives not only guide instruction, they indicate the focus of the assessment the teacher will use. Objectives describe the skills that students should be able to perform at the end of a unit of work. They point to the behaviors the teacher will look for to confirm a child has acquired the focal skills. Objectives are vital to competent instruction and the assessment of student achievement. Because of this, objectives are the topic of the next chapter.

To ensure that assessment is done at a high level of quality, definite procedures have been devised for each appraisal technique. Out of the many years of experience and research on assessment, educators have developed various guidelines designed to increase the accuracy of their decisions about children. In utilizing any type of assessment teachers must follow these guidelines in order to increase the accuracy of their conclusions. When they evaluate a term project, assess a child's contribution to a group effort, examine a product, or administer a test, there are generally agreed-upon guidelines to follow. Many of these guidelines are discussed in subsequent chapters in this book. If guidelines are not followed teachers and students may suffer from the resulting imprecision.

Following guidelines will also increase the likelihood that your scores are **stable.** That is, if you do two observations on a student, the second look at the student performance will lead to the same conclusion as the first. (Stability is discussed in Chapter 4 and its consequences in Chapter 5.) Guidelines will also help the teacher focus on the list of performances that make up the broader skill the students are trying to acquire. This means that the sample of performances that are being observed appropriately samples the total skill area.

Here is an example. In teaching communication among people, one objective is to have them demonstrate the proper verb forms. There are several ways a teacher could assess the student's ability to use verb forms. An example is to request an essay from each student. In this case I must follow guidelines both in writing the instructions and reading the essay so as to maintain focus on the verb forms. Guidelines help me make an appropriate decision about the student's ability to deal with the objective.

Teachers must observe a child performing a skill in a variety of settings before concluding the level of skill a pupil achieved. You have already seen that the sample of behaviors you observe should be adequate to warrant the conclusions you wish to make about a child. It is also true that the variety of settings in which the child demonstrates these behaviors will increase your confidence in that conclusion. This speaks in favor of multiple assessment procedures.

Quality assessment makes every effort to control conditions that interfere with our focus on the objective behavior we intend to observe. For example, for years studies have shown that essays written in legible penmanship get higher scores than those written in poor penmanship (Chase, 1968) Quality of handwriting is neither a component of accuracy of composition nor of quality and organization of ideas, yet it tends to influence grades for nonpenmanship tasks such as demonstrating knowledge of chemistry. Grammar, which has nothing to do with chemistry, also is distracting to scorers. There are a number of extraneous conditions that attract our attention away from the original purpose of the observation. Quality assessment requires us to be focused on the objective and to resist interference from competing and distracting conditions.

Assessment, Grading, and Instruction

Effective assessment is not merely a scheme for sorting students for grading purposes; it has an important link to instruction. Grades have a long tradition in schools: Parents use them as guides to how well their children are progressing; some employers consider academic achievement when hiring; colleges and universities want student transcripts of course work before they make admittance decisions; and students themselves use grades as indicators of their own progress. Yet regardless of the interest in grading and the need for assessment in developing grades, it is the potential for improving teaching and learning that makes assessment necessary.

Mr. Shorter has just returned test papers to his geography class. He then ranked the scores from high to low and wrote the resulting ranking of scores (without names) on the blackboard. Next he drew four lines across the score range, and wrote letter grades between the lines. Scores from 30 to 42 were assigned A grades, from 23 to 29 were assigned B's, and so on. Without further comment he pulled down a map in front of the class and began an overview of the next topic, pointing to locations of special events in the next unit of instruction.

Mr. Shorter's assessment activity has fulfilled the grading function, but has not been related to his teaching nor used to aid students in learning. The test has been simply a device for sorting students into grade categories. Sorting can be a useful application of assessment, but assessment must do much more than this.

✎ Problems

1. In Ms. Sanchez's fifth-grade science class the students have bean plants growing under four different intensities of light. After three weeks of growing, in which amounts of water and temperature were controlled, the students who participated in this study each wrote a report on the experience. Ms. Sanchez, in reading the reports, noted that few followed the steps in the scientific method they had studied, that the order of events in the study was in error in most of the reports, and that about half of the group did not cite a conclusion based on the data. a) How should Ms. Sanchez use the assessment to guide her teaching in the next few days? b) How can the assessment help students to improve their procedures in the next experiment?

2. School systems have need for assessment data that is different from those of a teacher in the classroom. Describe at least four applications of assessment that serve the school system's need for information. How might a teacher be involved in each of these?

3. Mrs. Lukin, a Home and Living Arts teacher, scores her class papers. On a separate piece of paper she lists scores (no names) from high to low. Then she draws a horizontal line across the page to separate the A grades, the B grades, and so on. She duplicates these score ranges and attaches one to each student's paper. Then she returns the test papers to her class. She claims that the score report eliminates the need for discussion of the topics of the test, and therefore allows the class to concentrate on the instruction of the day. How would you respond to this manner of handling assessment? Explain.

Assessment in the Contemporary Classroom

Changes are common in education, but at no time in history has change moved ahead at quite the pace that it does today. The rapid increase in knowledge has changed the content in subjects taught in schools; there is public pressure for change; and changes in understanding how children mature and how learning occurs has led to changes in teaching methods. In addition, technology has brought new methods and vast amounts of information to the classroom, and has created new avenues for individualizing instruction. It follows, then, that there must be changes in the assessment procedures in education.

Here are some recent movements affecting the area of assessment of student skills. They include a) demands for concrete evidence to support decisions, b) greater emphasis on observations of performance of skills, c) greater emphasis on accountability, and d) statewide testing, and e) increased federal involvement in education. Let's take a closer look at each of these.

The Need for Concrete Evidence

More and more education professionals are seeking a base of concrete evidence for the decisions they make. This means controlled observations of performances, test scores, and anecdotal records. Legal decisions have encouraged this practice with the demand on school officials for justification of their decisions with data. Also, school boards, faced with budget restraints, want to see evidence that changes in programs have a positive ratio of cost to benefits. Parents are also pressing schools to provide justification for programs and for decisions about individual children. "Why did Jeremy get a B in science, and what evidence can you show me to support that grade?" Jeremy's father asks.

The Uniontown School has requested funds for a special remedial class for slow readers in the second grade. What data do they have to confirm the number of "slow readers"? Specifically, what skills seem to be lacking among these children? These are assessment questions whose answers will be required before the funds for the class are approved.

Many agents call for data, and as we have noted no one data source responds to all the educational questions. Education professionals seek out a variety of assessment procedures to support their own and the public's call for evidence for action. Teachers, the essential education professional, must be involved in building this database.

Emphasis on Performance

Another change in the classroom is in response to public demand that students be able to demonstrate skills in "real" settings. This trend has prominence among assessment tools used for performance assessment. (Basic procedures for assessing performances are discussed in Chapters 10 and 12.) Outcomes of instruction may be demonstrated by students in a variety of activities. And further, one student's project will most likely differ from that of another. To assess this diversity of evidence that students have progressed toward the objectives, teachers are pressed to utilize a variety of observational techniques (Perrone, 1991).

For example, teachers want students to write well. There are several activities in which students can engage in the development of writing skills, for example, writing a short story, doing a report on a series of interwoven current events, or doing a critique of someone else's writing. Each of these activities produce products that can be used to evaluate the children's progress in learning to write well. However, each outcome also requires an assessment procedure that fits the product. This often means that teachers apply several assessment procedures across a group of students. A test, for example, may be one appraisal activity, but is clearly not the only relevant one. Teachers require a wide range of assessment skills to complete their task.

Accountability

A substantial amount of money is spent on education in America. The taxpayers at the local and state levels want assurance that their tax dollars have resulted in the appropriate increase in skills for the children of their neighborhoods. In this regard schools are called to support their expenditures with evidence of student achievement. The extent to which schools can do this is called **accountability.** The public wants to see children improving in basic skills at a defined rate each year of school. Many state legislatures have demanded that schools attend to achieving specified results appropriate to each grade. These specified achievements are referred to as **minimum competencies.**

Pressure has been put upon schools to show that they are actually producing student achievement for the public money invested in education. Schools are asked to provide relevant evidence of student achievement that can be compared to a set of standards. Two standards are often used: 1) student scores are compared with those of a large sample of students in the same grade; this is called **norm referenced** assessment, or 2) scores are compared with a criterion of achievement, e.g., students in mathematics must do one digit multiplication with 95 percent accuracy to meet the criterion. This is called **criterion referenced** assessment. Whatever standard is used, accountability is on the minds of educators and their public.

Statewide Testing

Partly as an outgrowth of the accountability movement, most states now have statewide testing. A common test is administered at specified intervals (say, three or four times during the twelve years of school). These tests are designed to assess achievement in the basic skills. In some cases promotion, remedial work, and even graduation are based on scores obtained on the statewide tests. Consequently, these tests have enormously increased the concern teachers have for how tests are constructed, how content is selected, and how scores are interpreted.

There were several reasons for instituting state tests. First, the tests would emphasize to the public and to education professionals that the state was seriously interested in improving performance in fundamentals. Second, state education officers were faced with making plans with very little data to support a course of action. New state programs designed to facilitate instructional improvement in, for example, reading comprehension could not be evaluated because there was little usable data common to all school districts. A statewide test seemed to be the answer. Data from these tests are widely used to determine if local schools are meeting the state's minimum competencies and to support plans for altering funding and instruction. Teachers want to be involved in the creation of tests and their interpretation. To do so they must be skilled in assessment.

Federal Involvement in Education

In the program presented by the Department of Education and endorsed by the President, the nation set goals to be achieved by the year 2000. This idea went forth as the *Goals 2000: Educate America Act* (Earley, 1994). This act not only documents achievement goals for schools to be attained by the turn of the century, but also includes a great deal of assessment to monitor the nation's progress in achieving these goals. It not only has implications for instructional change, but also will regularly involve teachers in assessment and in its interpretation.

Some concern has arisen as a result of the President's plan. Diversity of programs has been a prized feature of local schools since the states were given jurisdiction over their own education systems. A system which assesses attainment of nationally prescribed skills, may well press schools to focus on those skills. If so, the federal government may be asserting unusual control over the local curricula. However, it may be argued that the standards being set in the various curriculum areas are not set by the government, but are typically provided by groups of specialists in history, the sciences, the humanities, and so on. Specialists are not governmental officials, but their work will surely be sanctioned by the federal government.

The National Assessment of Educational Progress (**NAEP**) is the testing operation which is providing achievement data from across America. Initiated in 1964, it originally planned to test selected age levels from nine through young adulthood and across ten subject areas. The states initially resisted NAEP because they feared unfair comparisons from state to state. In response to this concern, NAEP has carefully sampled students so as to minimize the effect of demographic characteristics that are different among states.

Because of its concern for standards, NAEP has unwittingly exerted some influence on public schools to improve the quality of performance among children. It has also increased the focus on assessment in education and the need for educators to be knowledgeable in assessment procedures.

Summary of Contemporary Assessment Trends.   In sum, changes in instructional styles, methodologies, and objectives involve more emphasis on student performances. This has, to a large extent, come about from increased pressure by state and national governments and the public interest in accountability. As a result teachers must become more versatile in assessment of student progress toward instructional goals. They must expand their repertoire of observational skills because assessment is more than a sorting of students for grading purposes. Rather, assessment is the beacon for instructional planning.

✎ Problems

1. In the last decade more educational establishments have moved toward accountability, and minimum competency standards. Give at least two reasons for instituting accountability, and two why a local district may oppose state wide standards.
2. Imagine that you are a teacher in a school that operated on achievement standards for accountability. How will these standards affect your plans for the year's instruction? In regard to the test that will be used to assess your class's skill, what would you be inclined to do?
3. What does it mean for a teacher to be more performance focused? What does performance focus mean in terms of how assessment techniques are applied?
4. How does the trend toward more emphasis on outcomes affect the skills that teachers must acquire in assessing the progress of the class?

How This Book Will Get You There

This book is intended to include the basic information that will allow educators to be capable of understanding the many aspects of assessment. The focus of the information will be on the topics teachers encounter. These topics were selected because they are central to assessment in classrooms and in the broader field of education.

The topics are laid out in four sections in this book. Section I identifies the underlying principles that pertain to *all* assessment procedures. To the extent that they have relevance and application for development of all assessment, it is especially important for educators to grasp these principles *first*. Incorporating these principles into your routine assessment can add appreciably to the dependability of your assessment data, to your skill in interpreting data, and most importantly, to the appropriateness of your conclusions about children.

Section II deals with developing and applying assessment procedures in the classroom. For competent assessment, teachers need a variety of skills. This part of the book provides the basic skills that teachers will be able to use on a regular basis. In a total assessment plan teachers need skill not only in developing objective tests, but also in ways to assess performance through observational techniques (Stiggins, 1989). A number of guidelines are given here for developing procedures that will make the results of your assessments more stable and increase the likelihood that they will represent the content of your instruction. Also, guidelines are given in this section that will set your course in developing a variety of techniques. You will find these guidelines valuable aids for creating dependable assessment procedures of all types.

Section III deals with commercially published tests. Schools have many data needs, one of which has to do with overall quality of programs. Here one tool is the *standardized achievement test.* Nearly everyone who has attended a public school in American has taken these tests, usually in the spring. They assess many basic skills, such as reading, mathematics, grammar and organization of writing, and sometimes science and social studies. Most of what you, as a teacher, will need to know about these tests will be found in Section III of this book.

And what about *aptitude,* that fundamental propensity to profit from experiences provided by schools? Every day, teachers must deal with children who have differences in aptitude. But how shall schools assess aptitude, what do scores on tests of aptitude mean, and how shall teachers help students profit from the information the scores provide? These questions are also dealt with in this section.

Section IV, the last section of the book, is about reporting to clients. Grading individual children, reporting to parents, and describing the effect of a school program to representatives of the public are all ways of reporting how well students are moving toward achievement outcomes. This section provides guidelines about carrying out each of these reporting techniques.

If you master all of the topics in these four sections, you will be prepared for assessment work in your school. Above all, in your teaching *do not select an assessment procedure just because it was used on you* when you were in public school. There are a variety of approaches to assessment described in this book. Select those that best fit your objectives. Use them wisely, mindful of their advantages, but also of their limitations.

SUMMARY

1. Assessment should not be used solely as a device for sorting students for grading purposes, but is most effective if also used by teachers to guide instruction and by students as an aid to learning.
2. Massive amounts of assessment data are accumulated in schools, and teachers many times each day make decisions that should be supported by these assessment data. However, teachers are typically not well trained in assessment procedures.
3. We have discussed several useful terms: measurement (systematic translation of observations into numbers), testing (assessing student skill by providing them with a common sample of the tasks involved in the focal skill and generalizing to all tasks in the field from which the sample came), evaluation (assessing a program or product in terms of a given criterion of worth), and assessment (the broad umbrella that encompasses systems and procedures for monitoring skill development).

4. All assessment is based on samples of behavior. Since samples may not precisely represent the total function of which they are a part, teachers must be aware of the possibility of sampling error in their assessments.
5. There are many purposes for assessment in education, and no one assessment procedure can serve them all.
6. High quality assessment is based on clearly presented objectives and carried out according to specific guidelines designed to improve assessment.
7. Recent trends that affect assessment are: the greater emphasis on students' performing skills rather than on knowledge alone; an increase in supporting educational decisions with concrete evidence; greater emphasis on accountability; the development of statewide assessment procedures; and the increased interest of the federal government on assessing common skills across all states.

PROBLEMS

1. If you were to compose a test right now in your major field, how comfortable would you feel about its quality? Would the test you create look pretty much like tests you have taken in the past? Why or why not?
2. What, if anything, would you build into your testing procedure that would help students become better learners? What else could you include in the assessment situation to help students?
3. One teacher was heard to remark, "Learning is learning no matter what changes come in teaching, so I still test what I always did." How would you respond to this?
4. Assessments of all kinds are only a sample of the content the class has covered during a period of study. You could sample work at the highest level, or a wide sampling across all levels of complexity, or on a specific subtopic, and so on. How would you go about sampling the content? Defend this procedure as though you were presenting it to your public school class.
5. Describe how the superintendent of schools will use assessment data in contrast to how a classroom teacher might use assessment. Will either of these people use assessment the same way a parent may want it used?
6. Contrast assessment, evaluation, and measurement. How are they alike and how are they different?

KEY TERMS

assessment	accountability
measurement	minimum competencies
test	norm referenced assessment
evaluation	criterion referenced assessment
formal assessment	Goals 2000
informal assessment	NAEP
stable	

ADDITIONAL READING

American Federation of Teachers, National Council on Measurement, and National Education Association. (1990). Standards for teacher competence in educational assessment of students, *Educational Measurement: Issues and Practices*, 9 (4), 30–32.

Herman, J. L. and Golan, S. (1993). The effects of standardized testing on teaching and schools, *Educational Measurement: Issues and Practices*, 12 (4), 20–25, 41.

Schafer, W. D. (1991). Essential assessment skills in professional education of teachers, *Educational Measurement: Issues and Practices,* 10 (1), 3–6.

Stiggins, R. J. (1991). Relevant classroom assessment training for teachers, *Educational Measurement: Issues and Practices.* 10 (1), 7–12.

CHAPTER 2

CONSTRUCTING MEASURABLE LEARNING OBJECTIVES

Objectives are the intended outcomes of instruction. They are fundamental to all phases of teaching and learning, but in this chapter the focus will be on writing and using objectives as guides for developing assessment procedures.

Mr. Watson, a seventh-grade teacher at Morningstar Middle School, is about to finish a unit on magnetism. Next he will take up a unit on electricity. He sits at his cluttered desk—books, papers and apparatus in disarray—and clears a space for the textbook his students are reading. He leans pensively over his book, brushes his hair back, and begins to turn pages in the chapter on electricity. He checks the topics the class will study and lists them on a sheet of paper.

For each topic, Mr. Watson scribbles several activities he will assign the class and indicates how many class periods he will allot to each activity. He reads the list again, sits back, and momentarily reconsiders each topic. "That should about do it, I guess," he mutters. Once more he scans the list, sets it aside, and writes a note on his calendar, "Check batteries in the storeroom!"

Mr. Watson now has his unit on electricity planned, using a procedure not unlike that used by many teachers anticipating the beginning of a new unit of instruction. Aside from its informality, one important feature is missing, i.e., What are the objectives Mr. Watson hopes to see achieved by his class? What will children be able to do when they have finished the unit? And what behavior will Mr. Watson observe to help him decide that the objectives are indeed achieved?

Most teachers, like Mr. Watson, have general goals in mind for everything they do in the classroom. "I want children to know their math," "Students should understand what our constitution tells us," "To function in this world everyone must understand basic science." These are the kind of statements teachers often make when asked about their teaching objectives, yet when supervisors hear them, they respond with, "Yes, but what will your children do to show us they have achieved your objective?" In order to assess the achievement of an objective, the objective must be stated in terms of behavior the teacher can see, measure, or compare with a standard. With behavior based objectives, the teacher can create situations (for instance research problems or test items) that should call out these behaviors so that an observer can see them and count (or otherwise record) their occurrence.

What This Chapter Will Include.   To help you write objectives, the attainment of which can be observed, this chapter will include a discussion of the following topics.

1. What behavior based objectives are about
2. The relationships between objectives, instruction, and assessment of skills
3. The distinction between, and relationship of, goals and objectives
4. A guide for creating objectives—Bloom's taxonomy
5. The simplified taxonomy of objectives used in this book
6. Writing objectives in behavioral terms
7. Using action verbs as the basis for observable objectives

Behavior Based Objectives

Teachers want children to read well. But what does a child do to show you she is reading "well"? Can you define "well" in terms of some things you want the child to perform? You could say, "She defines a given list of prefixes and suffixes, applies phonic word attack skills, and after reading a passage states the intent of the author." These are observable reading behaviors. Before I can determine what a child can do I must see it being done. Therefore, when I am assessing achievement my objectives must point to those things children perform, acts I can observe and record.

Teachers indeed have objectives for teaching a unit of student work. However, these objectives are often not stated, but are only implicit in the activities of the class. They are often broad, general, or informal, and their attainment difficult to observe. "I want children to read well" is an example of a broad, informal objective. General and informal objectives do not direct my observations when I want to see if a child is making progress. I need a set of specific behaviors on which to focus, behaviors that show me what a child can and cannot do. With such a set of **behavior based objectives** I will not only be a better teacher, I also will be able to develop more appropriate assessment techniques (Popham, 1987).

Objectives, Instruction, and Assessment

Objectives stated in terms of behaviors not only reflect what will be taught, but also what the assessment of student achievement will include. When teachers use an assessment procedure in their classes, they hope to see that their objectives of instruction are being met. What should teachers look for to reach their conclusion? If our objectives are in terms of things students can do, and our instruction has focused on learning these behaviors, our assessment procedures should require students to demonstrate the appropriate behavior. This shows the teacher that the students have acquired the skills and knowledge that were the expected outcome of the instructional activities.

The desired behavior based skills, knowledge, and attitudes are the objectives for the unit of instruction. Your instruction will develop the behaviors, and your assessments will create situations that call for their performance. Thus it is that objectives begin the instructional cycle, and they continue to control activities throughout the cycle. The cycle is illustrated below.

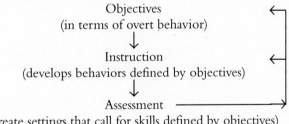

In many classrooms this model is not implemented properly. Imagine that you and I have just slipped into the back of the room where Ms. Brookings, a high school English teacher, is finishing work with her class on a unit on the short story. She has discussed the role of the short story in literature, worked on the development of the plot in short stories, and illustrated how characters emerge. Then she arranged class practice in the use of various descriptive procedures, and gave her students two days of class time to compose stories.

Although Ms. Brookings did not show us a list of objectives she used to direct her teaching, her activities *imply* certain general objectives she had in mind for the unit. You and I (and the students) assume, but with some lack of assurance, that objectives regulated the instructional activities for the class. These same objectives should also serve as a guide in determining the procedures and focus for the assessment of student achievement that will be applied at the end of the unit. But do we know what behaviors Ms. Brookings wants the class to demonstrate? Not specifically. There is an element of uncertainty inherent in this system because objectives were not specified.

Suppose Ms. Bookings invited you and me as senior faculty members to help her with her assessment tasks. We go to her class to create the assessment device for her. She has a unit outline that cites activities for every day of instruction, but it does not specify what students will demonstrate by the close of the unit. What behaviors would we look for in the students? At this point it would be difficult to know exactly what performances would be appropriate to ask from the students. We do not know what Ms. Brookings wanted students to be able to do as a result of instruction, nor what performances to observe at the end of instruction that show that students can do it.

The behaviors on which we could focus our assessment are not specified by Ms. Brookings, so what should we look for? To observe which students have learned what was expected, you and I need objectives that point to the behaviors to be developed by Ms. Brooking's teaching.

Likewise, we know that to assess their own achievement, students' need to know what specific behaviors they should perform for improvement. What will you tell a student who says, "I got a C on this short story! How come so low?" With no specific objectives, we will look at each other and shrug, and then come up with some general statement from our own experience that may improve that student's ability to write. But if students are to understand our assessment, they must know the behaviors that indicate achievement.

Let's analyze Ms. Bookings' procedures and discuss some ideas for improving the process. First, she should have explicitly stated her objectives. For example, she could have said, "We are now going to learn to write a short story" (her informal, general objective). "The elements you will learn to perform include steps in sequencing plot, using modifiers in developing characters, and three ways short-story writers deal with the conclusion" (her formal objectives). Ms. Brookings would then teach these elements to the class. Now the senior teachers could read the short stories written by the students, and see if they did indeed include the elements Ms. Brookings pointed to in the objectives. Formal objectives define the behaviors that will be observed in assessment.

You can now see why formal objectives are convenient aids to both instruction and assessment. These observable behaviors that we can record (and file for reference) are the teacher's guide to what instruction must take place. Moreover, the records of observation of the specified behaviors are the evidence of what a given student has, or has not, achieved. In sum, objectives are the foundation for assessing classroom achievement. But in all cases, teachers must designate the necessary behaviors that define the attainment of the objective. Assessment will then provide the occasion for the behaviors to occur so that we can observe them.

In teaching, objectives guide the content and methods of instruction. In assessment they indicate behaviors that verify that the instruction has been effective in guiding students toward attainment of the objectives. Objectives first, followed by instruction, and finally, assessment. (Please note, however, that this does not imply that in good teaching informal assessment does not accompany day-to-day instruction. It certainly does. In my design above, I am referring only to the major data collection point in a unit of teaching.)

✎ Problems

1. Mr. Jakes, a History teacher, has asked you to review his teaching of a unit on the colonial period in America. He began by outlining his objectives for the unit. These stated the learning of sequences of events and dates that led to the Declaration of Independence. His instruction a) emphasized the importance of causes of the war and their relevance to all wars, b) distinguished colonial leaders by assigning reports that included vignettes of these people, and c) illustrated the economics of revolution. He then took the textbook home over the weekend, reviewed the two relevant chapters, and devised test questions based on the book's version of events. He wrote 25 questions asking for dates of events and the names of people who initiated the events. How would you evaluate Mr. Jakes's procedures?

2. Ms. Althar, a fourth-grade teacher, has just finished a unit on the colonial period in history. She began by reading the "Things to Do" section of the *Teacher's Manual* that accompanied her textbook in social studies. Here she found several things she thought her children would enjoy—learning songs colonial children learned, writing a story using old English terms, in committees developing maps of different sections of the eastern seaboard, where colonies were located, and inviting a local member of the muzzle loaders' club to show children how the old guns worked (he would come in period costume). As a science project, the children would learn

what black powder is and where it came from in colonial times, and how lead balls and iron gun barrels were made.

But after Ms. Althar finished leading her class through these activities, she went to her textbook, picked out some facts of living in colonial times, and wrote a test based on these.

You, as the curriculum supervisor, review Ms. Althar's activities. How would you respond? What revisions to her procedures would you suggest?

Goals and Objectives

We can define objectives more precisely by differentiating them from goals. Let's begin by looking at the larger picture of a society and its educational system. Society has **goals** for its education system. These goals are *broad views* of how the educational system prepares students to make their way through life, as well as, take on economic and political roles that serve the national interests of a democratic society. Some examples of goals include the acquisition of skills, knowledge, and procedures needed to deal with the perplexities of complex social and economic environments, the wisdom for making political decisions, and personal fulfillment.

Goals are typically nonspecific and are intentionally general. Social agencies build institutions to assist the population in pursuing the broader goals. For example, a state goal is the education of youth. States establish school systems and appoint boards to develop programs to be promoted by schools. Local school boards translate the state programs into local instructional goals.

Societal goals are beliefs about what is "good" for individuals and society to achieve. Educators further define the goals in terms of specific skills students will acquire. Local teachers are each assigned a portion of these skills that are to be taught in the succession of classes. The defining of these skills in terms of specific tasks students should be able to perform creates the objectives for each class. Thus, educational **goals** proscribe the array of skills that define the broad boundaries, while local **objectives** define specific behaviors that will show movement of learners in the direction of the overall goals.

Here is an example. One overall goal of the state is to promote mathematics skills that will allow citizens to function in a complex social, political and economic system. To define this goal for schools, educators identify the succession of skills and understandings that politicians and social scientists accept as necessary for children to acquire. The local school system supports this goal by arranging the skills in a hierarchy of complexity, defining them in appropriate behaviors, and assigning to each grade level a subset of these skills and understandings at proper difficulty levels.

One state goal is that children should be able to do division of numbers. Consistent with this goal Ms. Kluzuski is teaching a unit on long division. Her objectives, stated in terms things children can do to show they have learned long division, direct her assessment. Goals have laid out the broad outlines for doing these mathematics processes; objectives describe for each grade level the behaviors (that can be taught and observed) that fill in the content of the state's outline.

Bloom's Taxonomy

If you ask teachers to cite their objectives for a class, they may tell you that they seek to have students learn basic factual content as well as develop skills in applying that knowledge in solving problems. However, if you look at assessment devices that have been used in these classes, they will likely require very little reasoning in the subject area. Most of the assessment deals with factual content, such as knowing the names of states and their capitols. This is not entirely an accident; it is much easier to construct and score tests for factual knowledge than reasoning ability.

Because in doing their assessments many teachers neglect the more complex mental processes, they need a framework that leads them to consider the more complex aspects of learning in a subject area. One such framework is **Bloom's taxonomy,** devised by Benjamin Bloom and his colleagues (Bloom, B. et al., 1956), who first defined the various types of mental operations students may learn to use as a result of an instructional experience, and then those operations were sorted into the following categories:

> Evaluation
> Synthesis
> Analysis
> Application
> Comprehension
> Knowledge

This hierarchy is based on the complexity of the mental process involved. It is believed that, at least for the lowest three categories, learning of the content in the lower level(s) supports the move into the next level (Krathwohl & Payne, 1971). The above levels are characterized as follows.

Knowledge, the lowest level of mental operation, deals with producing facts, terms, definitions, steps in a process, rules, and similar types of "self-contained" information. Material at this level is what some theorists call *declarative knowledge.*

Comprehension is demonstrated when a student carries a mental model across modes of expression, such as interpreting a formula into a declarative statement, translating or restating that shows understanding of an idea, and interpreting or extrapolating. For example, if students see the formula, $C = pi(D)$, they will say something such as, "That means if I want to find the distance around a circle (C), I will multiply 3.14 times the distance across the circle (D)."

Application is evidenced when students use knowledge to solve a problem, making use of the facts and comprehension skills they have acquired. For example, in applying the above formula, students are asked to find the amount of string it will take to reach around a barrel. The student will have to measure across the barrel and then apply the formula to get the correct answer. Application shows *procedural knowledge.*

Analysis disassembles an object or idea, showing how the totality of a thing is composed of related parts. It is basic to developing strategies.

Synthesis requires development of a whole by integrating parts. It constructs an idea, an object, a procedure—out of a group of parts (facts, objects) that are available.

Synthesis brings in creativity when the student's formulation of parts results in a unique assemblage.

Evaluation is evidenced when students monitor, regulate, reflect, or make judgments about the acceptability of an idea, object or operation, based on a preset criterion or set of criteria. For example, you have read a brochure on high octane gasoline. As a result you think it has some good features and are considering it for use it in your car. Based on the demands of the car's engine and the expense of gasoline (the criteria), is your decision to use high octane warranted? The answer to this question demonstrates the process of evaluation.

A Compact Hierarchy

The great contribution of Bloom and his colleagues has been to encourage educators to include the higher order mental functions in their tests along with the more concrete functions. However, from the outset researchers have not agreed that the categories are each verifiable or completely distinct from each other (Seddon, 1978). This is especially true of the higher order categories—Analysis, Synthesis, and Evaluation—and the two lower categories—Knowledge and Comprehension. Some recent work in cognition also suggests that cognitive processing probably does not warrant this much sorting of mental operations (Anderson, 1990).

Therefore, to make Bloom's categories a bit more manageable, I have broadened them as follows:

> Higher order processing
> Application
> Foundational content

Under the first level, foundational content, I combine Knowledge and Comprehension. Here I include into one category facts, rules (and other self-contained information), and their production into behavior such as reporting, restatement, interpretation, and translation. I call this category **Foundational Content.**

I leave **Application** as is. It shows us to what extent the student can take the basic content and utilize it when faced with a problematic situation.

Finally, I combine Analysis, Synthesis, and Evaluation into one category and call it **Higher Order Processing.** This category really hangs together because it is often hard to use one of the processes without the other ones. For example, students may wish to dismantle an idea (analysis) because they want to reconstruct parts or all of it into another one (synthesis). And when they do, they will sit back and say, "Now, this new idea is better than the old one because . . .!" (evaluation). The three processes—analysis, synthesis, and evaluation—seem to function quite well as mutual servants in the expansion of knowledge. Also, these skills do not appear to have the hierarchical order seen in the other categories. Skills in one category seem to be attainable without well developed skills in the others (Krathwohl & Payne, 1971 op. cit.). Putting all three operations into a single category makes sense.

Now that we have three categories into which to sort our instructional content, rather than six, the job of planning instruction and assessment utilizing a taxonomy seems somewhat easier.

Writing Objectives with Observable Behaviors

As teachers setting up objectives for our instruction, we begin with the compact hierarchy of Foundational Content, Application, and Higher Order Processing. To use these we will a) identify specific actions the student should perform that show achievement of the objectives of instruction, and b) sort our objectives into the three categories previously described. To further assist us, consider these guidelines for writing behavioral based objectives.

1. *First, our statements of objectives will be in terms of behaviors we, as teachers, can see happen.* Here is an example.

   The student will describe how an airplane wing provides lift for an aircraft.
   The instructor can observe the child's description and can judge if the child knows the concept. Description is something the teacher can see, hear, and evaluate for accuracy. But, what if the teacher had said our objective was "To know how an airplane wing provides lift." He or she would not have that advantage of pointing to action through which the student illustrates knowledge and by which the teacher sees evidence of the knowledge.

2. *Formal objectives should begin with words that have the fewest possible interpretations.* To achieve this we use an operating word (write, calculate, point to) that help us agree on what it is that the student should do. Here are some examples of words we might use.

Poor		*Better*
knows	states	produces makes a model of
understands	compares	creates
can	lists	sorts into
believes	solves	labels
appreciates	points to	
has a grasp of	writes	
develops an interest in		

   The first set leaves a wide range of possible interpretations of what it is the student should do. I do not know what Eugenio does when he "understands" the first amendment of the Constitution. I must see him do something before I can make a conclusion about his knowledge. Objectives should define what Eugenio should do.

   In the second list of words, above, you and I can come closer to agreeing on what constitutes evidence that the child has achieved our objective. When we see the student *point to* selected parts of an insect, we will probably all agree that this student has achieved the objective of learning insect anatomy. If a student *lists* the first five presidents of the United States, you and I can see, and agree on, the evidence of achievement. We should use these "seeable" behaviors in writing objectives for our instruction because they not only determine a criterion for having acquired the skill or knowledge, but also result in all observers sharing a single criterion for judging a child's achievement.

3. *A good behavioral objective should state, when possible, the level of skill the student must demonstrate* as evidence of having achieved success. Here is an example from a geometry class.

Given the following terms used in geometry, the students will
spell them with 95 percent accuracy. (followed by the list)

I can see this happen, or fail to happen, and we all agree that each student has met, or has not met, the criterion of success. Teachers know what they are aiming at in instruction and students know what they must achieve.

But suppose the objective was stated as: "Students will know how to spell the terms used in geometry." In this case what should I do as a test writer? The objective does not tell me what terms are to be learned, or how to observe the outcome, or at what level of proficiency. This objective is too broad, nonspecific, and does not give me a criterion to apply to show student success.

Subject matter areas—geography, mathematics, biology—have their own terms to describe items and events unique to their field, and in order to communicate in the field students need to spell the terms. The first objective above should provide a reasonable outcome to this end. Teachers can observe the process; they can prepare assessment events (tests, papers) in which they can observe the attainment of the outcome; and further, anyone shown the results will agree that it happened. That is the kind of statement of objectives we strive for because they reduce uncertainty in assessment.

There are circumstances, however, where use of a more general goal statement may be appropriate, provided that the teacher defines it with a list of behaviors, each of which is taken as evidence of the broader topic. For example,

Broad statement: Understands the number system

Behaviors I use to define this:

1. converts values from base 10 to base 2, and the reverse.
2. describes the relationship between addition and multiplication, between subtraction and division.
3. calculates with 95 percent accuracy problems of addition, multiplication, subtraction, and division with multiple digit numbers.

This list of behavior based objectives (though probably too short) demonstrates that teachers can use "hard to observe" achievements in their statements of objectives, but only if they follow them with clearly defined and observable outcomes.

✎ Problems

1. Indicate which of the objectives (listed at the top of page 28) convey observable or unobservable behavior. Rewrite those that do not indicate the act to be observed so that they point to the appropriate behavior.

1. To appreciate good literature
2. Does 100 basic one-digit multiplication problems with 98 percent accuracy
3. Lists the planets in the solar system
4. Understands how to use the periodic table
5. Comprehends what is read in the class' reading book

Using Action Verbs at All Levels of the Taxonomy

To write objectives that are in terms of observable behavior the objective must describe something students will do. That means that they must contain an action verb. You'll find that some action verbs work especially well at certain levels of the simplified taxonomy. Table 2.1 presents examples of verbs for each of our three categories of learning outcomes. Keep in mind that the items in the table are illustrative only; you will certainly add to them with time.

TABLE 2.1   Action Verbs for Three Categories of Learning Outcomes

Outcome Category	Some Verbs for Stating Objectives
Foundational Content	lists, labels, names, calculates, writes, orally reports, translates, interprets, summarizes, states in own words, states examples of, paraphrases
Application	solves, uses in, modifies to fit, transfers to
Higher Order Processes	differentiates, compares/contrasts, relates parts, designs, constructs, formulates, appraises, justifies

Here are examples of objectives at each of the three levels of learning categories. Let's begin with objectives at the Foundational Content level.

Writes examples of dangling participles.

Translates lines from the *Canterbury Tales* into modern English.

Reads atomic weights from a periodic table.

Given an unlabeled map of the U.S., writes the correct names on each state.

Writes sharps and flats for both treble and bass clefts for each of the major keys.

Consider these examples from the Application Level:

With 90% accuracy solves word problems involving complex fractions.

Uses complex fractions in relating national data to local problems.

Writes a paragraph on a given topic beginning with a topic sentence.

Given a Fortran language program containing three errors, finds the errors and runs the program.

Given the length and width of a parallelogram, calculates the area.

And finally some examples of objectives at the Higher Order Processes level:

> Constructs arguments for and against clear-cutting of forests, lists three criteria for maintaining forest areas, and justifies one maintenance procedure.

> Given a description of a section of depleted land, writes a plan for bringing it back to optimal production.

> Given a principle of physics (or poetic foot, or grammatical construction), identifies "real world" instances and non instances of it.

> Describes why plan B is superior to plan A in terms of dollar expenditure.

> Given a set of information about the operation of a small business, lists the elements that will become credits and debits.

> Describes the concept of molecular activity to show how a thermometer works.

Using Objectives in Constructing Assessments

Some practice with using action verbs will help teachers compose the objectives they will use to guide them when putting together a test. In their instruction teachers typically include work at all three levels of our classification system—Foundational Content, Application, and Higher Order Processes. Therefore, in their assessments they should be guided by objectives at each level. In the past the most prominent level found on teacher-made tests was that of Foundational Content (Pfeifer & Davis, 1965). However, for many teachers, Higher Order Processing is often the ultimate objective of their instruction. Procedures, such as tests, that assess student ability at this level are most difficult to write, but with practice will become easier. We will see in Chapter 7 that being able to write objectives at each of the levels will help us concentrate on item types.

✎ Problems

1. Read the following objectives. Classify each as Foundational Content, Application, or Higher Order Processes.
   a) List the names of the first five presidents of the United States.
   b) Restate in your own words the cited passages from William Shakespeare's *Romeo and Juliet*. (Citations follow.)
   c) Given two electrical circuits including wires, resisters, batteries, and switches, select the one in which the batteries will last the longest, and explain why.
   d) Given the length of the sides of a rectangular lot of land, calculate the length of the north east to south west diagonal.
2. Rewrite the following objectives using the action verbs found in Table 2.1.
   a) Children will understand the classics in literature.
   b) To increase the knowledge of historical events that shaped our country.
   c) Knows a well made product in shop from a poorly made one.

Objectives as a Labor-Saving Device

Teachers will make their work easier by writing behavioral objectives for all the course areas in which they teach. While this requires quite a bit of effort at first, when it is complete life gets simpler. As we have discussed, our objectives serve as a guide for teaching a unit of instruction, they point us at experiences children should have to produce the focal abilities, and provide a guide for assessment. Although some objectives may change with time, they will provide some standardization in our program from year to year.

Remember Mr. Watson at the beginning of this chapter? He was about to begin a unit on electricity and was skimming the textbook to see what he might include in the unit. With a set of behavioral objectives, he would no longer do this, because with the proper objectives, the textbook becomes a tool for imparting information, not the teacher's program director. Our objectives become the guide that leads us through the unit.

As the class moves through a unit of instruction, teachers need to assess the extent to which children have actually achieved the objectives the teachers have laid out. Now, rather than pick up the textbook and begin looking for points that may be grist for test items or reports, the teacher simply turns to the objectives and begins to construct assessment procedures (tests, observation schedules, or whatever best fits our plan) based on observations of the behaviors we were developing. In this we have simplified our lives as teachers.

By now you should have a basic grasp on what writing behavior based objectives is all about and the tools to write them. But it doesn't end here. Soon you will be creating different types of test items, and looking at alternative means of assessment. At that time we will again take a look at objectives, but in terms of more specific applications.

✎ Problems

1. From the following objectives, identify the ones that are observable and those that are not.
   a) Appreciates good literature.
   b) Knows the parts of a cell.
   c) Labels the parts of a diagram of an electric motor.
   d) Sees likenesses and differences in acrylic and oil painting techniques.
   e) Writes examples of dangling participles.
2. For each of the objectives in Problem 1 not stated in terms of observable behavior, rewrite it in terms of behaviors that can be seen, counted, etc. (Note verbs in Table 2.1.)
3. For the following goals, write three behavioral objectives. For example, for the first item below we might write, "Lists the provisions cited in each of the first ten amendments to the Constitution of the United States."
   a) Understands our heritage of freedom in America.
   b) Can function in a world requiring numerical skills.
   c) Can promote and maintain one's own health.

4. In your own teaching area, select a unit of instruction, determine the overall goal, and define it with at least five behavior based objectives.

SUMMARY

1. Objectives are the intended outcomes of instruction. They represent what teachers hope students will achieve as a result of instruction.
2. Behavior based objectives use specific behaviors that reflect not only skills students will be expected to perform, but that can be observed as evidence that the student has reached the objective.
3. Objectives assist students in assessing their own achievement as well as understanding the teacher's assessments.
4. Goals are more general than objectives; they are broad outlines of the achievement expected of students. In schools educators break down these goals into behaviors that define them.
5. Benjamin Bloom and his colleagues identified several categories of mental operations teachers may use as a guide for instruction, and that show how students may perform in response to instruction. Those categories are knowledge, comprehension, application, analysis, synthesis, and evaluation.
6. A compact version of Bloom's hierarchy consists of three categories: foundational content, application, and higher order processing.
7. Objectives should be stated in terms of behaviors teachers can see happen. They should contain words that have the fewest possible interpretations, and should indicate the level of skill the student must demonstrate.
8. Because an objective describes something students will do, it must contain an action verb (points to, writes, contrasts). Different verbs are used in writing objectives for different levels of mental operations.
9. An important application of objectives is in devising assessments that ensure that all levels of the hierarchy of mental operations are tested.
10. Written behavioral objectives makes teachers' work easier throughout a unit of instruction.

KEY TERMS

objectives
behavior based objectives
Bloom's taxonomy:
   knowledge
   comprehension
   application
   analysis
   synthesis
   evaluation

foundational content
application
higher order processing
goals

ADDITIONAL READING

Gronlund, N. E. *Stating Objectives for Classroom Instruction,* 3d ed. New York: McGraw Hill, 1981.

Mager, R. F. *Preparing Instructional Objectives,* Palo Alto: Fearon, 1962.

Metfessel, N. S., Michael, W. B. and Kirsner, D. (1975). Instrumentation of the Taxonomy of Educational Objectives in behavioral terms. In David A. Payne and Robert F. McMorris, Eds., *Educational and Psychological Measurement* 2d ed., Morristown: General Learning Press.

Pasch, M. et al., *Teaching as Decision Making,* 2d ed. White Plains, NY: Longman. Chapter 3.

Popham, W. J. (1987). Instructional objectives benefit teaching and testing, *Momentum,* 18, 15–16.

Woolfolk, A. E. *Educational Psychology,* 3d. ed. Englewood Cliffs: Prentice Hall, 1993. Chapter 11.

CHAPTER 3

VALIDITY

What Does This Test Tell Me?

Ms. Wilson furrows her brow as she looks at the academic aptitude test score on LaDonna's cumulative school record folder. "Hmm, 58th percentile rank." Ms. Wilson was about to place LaDonna in the accelerated writing group, but this academic aptitude score suggests she is slightly better than an average student. "How good a decision will I make if I base her placement on this aptitude score?" she wonders. In the machine shop Mr. Sturgis has written a test on the mechanical skills students must have to begin the metalwork class. A group of students who wish to begin metal work this fall have taken the test and Mr. Sturgis scans the list of scores. "I wonder how accurately these test scores tell which students are ready to begin the class?" he asks himself. Both of these teachers are wondering if the test score will help them make accurate decisions about students. This question goes to the heart of validity—how do I use test data to make better decisions than I would if I did not have these data?

What This Chapter Will Include. In this chapter you will learn the following:

1. What validity is in an assessment procedure.
2. How we determine the validity of an assessment
3. Some tools used in validation such as a taxonomy of learning outcomes and the interpretation of correlation procedures
4. Where to find information on the validity of a commercially published test
5. How to apply validity information in elementary and in secondary school programs

What Is Validity?

Questions such as those posed by the teachers discussed above deal with the quality of observations we call **validity.** In school settings we make inferences about children: Susan knows her multiplication combinations; Coral has above average reading speed; Harold is a slow learner. Educators want these inferences to correspond with a child's ability to perform in a given skill area. Tests and other assessment procedures are designed to increase our accuracy in making these inferences.

A test is *valid* to the extent that it helps educators make an appropriate inference about a specified quality of a student. The academic aptitude test is valid to the extent that it helps Ms. Wilson make an accurate decision in placing students in the accelerated group; a foreign language aptitude test is valid to the extent that it assists the French teacher in placing students at the appropriate level of learning demand in a language class; a mathematics test is valid to the extent that from it a fourth-grade teacher's inferences allow him more accurately to place children in number activities that are challenging but not baffling.

Validity is a quality of all assessment procedures educators use. It is discussed in detail in the manuals that accompany commercially published tests, but also applies to the assessment devices that teachers, themselves, make and use in their classrooms. If teachers are involved in assessments of any type that lead to decisions about students, validity of those assessments is important. The test that Mr. Sturgis made to begin his metal shop must have validity if it is to help him make more accurate decisions about his class. The commercial test that Ms. Wilson consulted to help her decide about LaDonna's placement in a special writing group must have validity or her decision could be in error. When a fourth-grade teacher collects a portfolio of student work, the evidence must help that teacher make an accurate decision about the student's achievement.

Validity is not an either/or situation. Rather, tests have varying degrees of validity ranging from essentially none (where the assessment does not help a teacher make a decision about a child's skill) to a high degree of validity (where the assessment helps make a fairly accurate decision).

For example, an achievement test in spelling may help a teacher make a decision about Jose's writing skill with more accuracy than if no score is available at all, but an essay on an expository problem could help significantly more. Both tests have some validity for the purpose of judging Jose's writing skill, but the spelling test has a lower level of validity than the essay because spelling does not deal with some of the essentials of communication, such as organization of ideas, structure of sentences, and supporting statements with data. The essay test will have a higher degree of validity because it is a sample of the very skill about which the teacher is to make a decision. Because of this, it will allow her to predict with some accuracy how Jose will do on other writing tasks. To demonstrate validity test makers, both publishers and teachers, should develop assessment procedures that ask students to perform acts that are as similar as possible to the skill about which educators are making a decision.

It is important to realize that tests are not valid or invalid as they stand. They are always valid relative to a designated skill, aptitude, or personality trait. For example, the Stanford Achievement Tests (which assess status in the basic academic skills) have a level of validity for making decisions about the academic skill levels of given children but are not valid as indicators of paranoia. When you and I talk about validity, we must refer to the *specific trait* about which a test score will help us make an appropriate decision. Tests do not have general validity.

Evidence of Validity

There are standard procedures for determining the level of validity of an assessment. Although the focus here is on tests, the same ideas apply to all assessment procedures.

Test makers use three procedures to illustrate the level of validity of their tests. These procedures are designed to provide data that show a) how precisely the test samples a specified body of knowledge, b) how closely the test's results correspond with a defined criterion of performance, and c) how closely the test relates to behavioral characteristics described by a psychological theory. An overview of these three procedures is given in Figure 3.1.

We will discuss each of these procedures, but our focus will be on content-related evidence for validity. This is the procedures that educators use most often.

Content Sampling

Many tests, both published and teacher made, achieve validity from planned sampling of the content of a specified instructional program. For example, Mr. Drothe, a Physics teacher, has just finished a unit on magnetism. He has stressed certain qualities of magnetic fields; he has illustrated a number of applications of magnetism, and he has led the class in problem solving in the area of magnetism. He is now ready to see how well the

Type	What it tells us	How shown	Example
Content validity	The extent to which the test content is a sample of the total subject matter content.	Comparing test content with text books, study guides or teacher lesson plans.	Relating the arithmetic problems for fourth-graders to the content of the fourth-grade arithmetic book.
Criterion related validity	How closely test scores correspond with people's rankings on an out-of-test performance of interest to us.	Comparing scores on tests with another measure of performance.	Correlating college aptitude test scores with grade point average.
Construct validity	The extent to which test results correspond with predictions based on a psychological theory.	Classify people according to a theory of behavior, then see if test classifies them the same way.	A psychiatrist groups children into three groups—good, fair, poor—according to a theory of adjustment; a scale of adjustment should sort children into same categories.

FIGURE 3.1 Types of Test Validity

class has acquired the knowledge and skills he has defined as his instructional objectives. He is ready to make a test.

What goes into his test? To be valid the test should reflect the instructional objectives in the unit relative to the emphasis in teaching it. The validity of Mr. Drothe's test is determined by the extent to which its content *samples* the content in his instruction.

Professional test publishers use a similar technique. Their tests of achievement will be used in many schools across the country. Therefore, they look for instructional content that is common to large numbers of schools, and then build their tests to be a sample of that content. Like classroom teachers, professional testmakers try to match their tests to instruction so they can claim validity by virtue of test content that mirrors the topics and emphasis of that instruction.

Matching Content With Objectives.   When designing a house an architect develops a drawing or blueprint of what the structure will look like. The blueprint defines the structure and shows the parts in relative proportion to the whole. The builders then create the physical structure to correspond with the blueprint.

The same concept is the foundation of testmaking. All testmakers, whether classroom teachers or professional testers, need a blueprint to specify the parts and relationships between parts in the instructional unit. They can then create the test to correspond to the blueprint. The blueprint serves as our guide in making the test match the instruction in the unit so that we can judge the evidence of content validity.

When we teach a unit on the formation of the earth's crust, or the use of the passive voice in English composition, or solving linear equations, there are certain performances we want students to demonstrate afterwards. We want them to be able to produce a collection of facts about the topic; we want them to be able to apply the content to solving problems, to take more complex situations and break them down to see how components relate to each other, and we want them to be able to assess the reasonableness of a plan of action based on the material we have just studied—performances found in our objectives for the unit.

If objectives list behaviors we have taught students to perform in the instructional part of a unit of study, the same objectives should also be represented in the test over the unit. But instruction involves a broad range of topics. Tests, and all assessments, are only samples of this broad range. We cannot include in a test everything we worked on in instruction. However, we want this sample to be representative of this broader instructional landscape.

To ensure that we allow students a chance to demonstrate behaviors we have developed in the instruction, we need a guide for sampling and for creating test content. There are several of these guides available, but the one most commonly used in education follows Bloom's taxonomy, which, as we discussed in Chapter 2, categorizes objectives according to levels of complexity. This is the guide we will use to illustrate a blueprint for making a test for academic skills.

Applying Bloom's Taxonomy.   The categories in Bloom's taxonomy can be used as a guide, not only for devising the objectives but also for teaching the unit of subject matter. In addition, these categories direct teachers to topics, their levels of complexity, and the behaviors to observe when assessing student progress. If a test is to be a valid representation of the content of instruction, the entries in the test should follow the goals of teaching, creating a "snap shot" of the instruction.

In Chapter 2 we condensed Bloom's categories into three levels: Foundational Content, Application, and Higher Order Processes. We will build our assessment activities into these three categories to match the content of our instruction.

Table 3.1 is one teacher's application of a blueprint for assessing children's achievement after a unit in biology. The cognitive production categories are listed across the top of the table. The unit topics are listed in the left-hand column. The numbers in parentheses refer to the number of test items (or observations) that will be devoted to a particular topic. The teacher will construct three items at the Foundational Content level dealing with the classification of the one-celled animals; three more will deal with the classification at the Higher Order level, and so on. The numbers at the bottom of the table show how many items will be written around different cognitive operations. In all, twenty-four items will be created following this table of specifications. By adding together the numbers in parentheses across the table we can find out how many items there are on each topic. For example, for the Medical topic seven items will be constructed. These numbers are derived from the instructional emphasis devoted to each of the listed topics.

Now imagine writing the test (or making a schedule for observation) with this table before you. Instead of trying to recall topics one by one and devising questions for the unit of instruction, the outline for the test is in the blueprint. I have seen teachers

TABLE 3.1   Specifications for a test on a unit in biology

The Amoeba	Cognitive productions		
Topic	Foundational knowledge	Application	Higher order processes
Classification	Phylum, other members in phylum. (3)		Given parts of animal classify as protozoa or not (3)
Structure	Know cell parts, functions (5)	Relate environment to development of structures (2)	
Reproduction	Steps in fission, factors influencing (2)		Given factors, create optimum combinations for amoeba growth (2)
Medical	Diseases due to amoeba (2)	Solve medical problems associated with the amoeba (2)	Given situations decide how to reduce danger from amoebic disease (3)
Items in category	12	4	8

write out a list of questions for a test by simply paging through the textbook for topics. When we look at the list of objectives and the instructional methods used in the unit, we often find that there are too many test items in the Foundational Knowledge category, and not enough in the others (Marso & Pigge, 1992). It is much more efficient to construct a test following a guide such as Table 3.1 than to write items without a guide. Most importantly, by using the guide teachers will also be building content validity into their assessment by including all levels of the classification scheme.

It should be emphasized that the table of specifications is not etched in stone. It provides a general layout for developing a test so that it fits the objectives of the instruction and serves as a guide for creating an assessment device that will have content validity, but may need adaptations consistent with the instruction in the unit.

In sum, a test must correspond with the content of instruction, sorted into levels of complexity that match those provided in the teaching. Bloom's taxonomy, in its condensed form, is a useful aid in making that match. If the sample of behaviors that will be observed in the assessment matches the original instructional objectives, the assessment procedure has achieved **content validity.** Now the teacher's decision about a student will relate to the student's achievement in an assessment exercise involving an appropriate balance of all instructional objectives.

Other Options for Sorting Content.   Bloom's format for developing test content is only one of several. For example, cognitive psychologists (Anderson, 1990) have proposed that instructors sort content into *declarative, procedural,* and *strategic* knowledge. Declarative knowledge represents content somewhat like that found in Bloom's first two categories—knowledge and comprehension. Procedural knowledge involves knowing what to do with content. For example, how do I manage what I know about mathematics in solving a "real life" problem in which I must find an unknown quantity from a known one? Strategic knowledge has to do with merging information into a new idea, developing a plan of action, or assessing alternatives and selecting a direction when alternatives are not clear. Skilled test writers could use these three categories to build a blueprint.

Tittle, Hecht, and Moore (1993) have argued that assessment should be organized on a framework based on "psychological constructs" (propositions about how learning takes place) and classroom activity settings. They assert that "psychological constructs that appear in active areas of subject matter research are best assessed in the context of activity settings, in order to link them to classroom instructional planning" (p.18). The intent is to place assessment at the scene of the actual learning activity, not in abstract categories developed out of a matrix similar to Bloom's.

You may use Bloom's format, as test writers have for some years, or you use an alternative. Most important is that teachers use a guide to increase the probability that the content samples used in assessment appropriately match all facets of instruction, thereby producing content validity for their tests.

When to Consider Using Content Validity

The idea of content validation is of special importance to classroom teachers. It is the foundation for the observational procedures (tests, problems sets, constructed products) that teachers develop for their own classes. It should be given attention every time a test or other assessment device is created by teachers for use in their own classrooms. These tests must fit the instructional objectives at the appropriate cognitive levels in order to have content validity. Classroom assessments of all kinds get their credibility from this match of objectives with instruction.

Content validity must also be considered for tests other than school achievement. It is given serious attention when buying commercial achievement tests like those taken by most American children during elementary and secondary school years, as well as the statewide tests that are in use in most states now, and the national research tests that are planned to assess achievement across the nation. Each of these test types is appropriate for your school only to the extent that their content fits your instructional objectives.

Face Validity

Face validity is a rudimentary type of validation that arises out of content validation. It is reflected in statements such as "I skimmed over some of the problems in this test, and they look like they test what we want." No actual matching of the content of the test with objectives has taken place, yet a subjective decision is made that the test is appropriate. The name—face validity—is derived from a cursory review that ended with the conclusion that a test looked valid on its "face." No one knows how many tests are bought on this basis, but my experience with schools indicates that it is a very large number.

Face validity does not substitute for a careful review of the test, wherein test content is matched with instructional goals and activities, yet it does have a role in test selection. To solicit motivation on the part of test-takers a test must look like it is measuring the right variable. For example, if I show you an inkblot and say I am going to measure your intelligence, you would not believe me and your effort would be half-hearted at best. The inkblot has no face validity for measuring intelligence. But if I show you a test that is made up of abstract number problems, vocabulary usages, and reordering of objects in space, you would be more convinced that I am assessing intelligence, and would probably work a bit harder on the test. Face validity is relevant from a motivational perspective.

Relating a Test to a Performance Criterion

This chapter began by citing three types of procedures educators use to validate tests. We have already discussed the first type, the content match between the test and the instructional program. The second type of test validation procedure is called **criterion related validity.** In this situation evidence of validity is found by first creating an assessment procedure that asks a student to perform a task like that required for a specified job. For example, suppose I made a test to use with laboratory assistants. I included a section on names of laboratory equipment, its uses and misuses. I also included a section on hazards in the laboratory. The next job is to show that this test really sorts out capable assistants from those who are not. To do this, scores on the test are held up against some other measure of job skill, for example an instructor's rating of assistants after a four-week trial period. If capable assistants score high on my test, and those less capable score low, the test is showing pretty good validity. Therefore scores on this test will help me make good decisions when selecting laboratory assistants.

Similarly a test anxiety scale could demonstrate validity in a manner much like the laboratory test. The test publisher might compare scores on the anxiety scale with a second measure such as a psychologist's rating of a student's feeling of anxiety when faced with examinations.

In criterion related validation, the test (the first measure) is presumed to predict status on a specified performance (the second measure), and if we can show that it does, the test can be used to rank people on the second measure. If the test does this, using the test can be both a time and money saving process.

The Concept of Correlation

In criterion related validation it would be handy to have a number series—like 1 to 5—that shows how close the test ranking of students fits the job ranking. This number series would be a very good way to communicate how well the test predicts the job ranking. (For example, 1 = no relationship, 2 = some, but low relationship, etc.) One number series similar to this is based on a process called **correlation.** In assessment correlation is used to show how closely test scores correspond to the ranking of the skill the test is designed to predict.

Correlation as noted, is a statistical procedure that shows how closely students' scores on one measure correspond in rank with scores on another. For example, how does height correspond (or correlate) with weight? Intuitively you know that as people grow taller they tend to get heavier; that indicates a correlation between the two measures. Correlation is represented by a *correlation coefficient,* a number that shows how closely the two sets of data correspond. These numbers run from .00 to 1.00 (positive correlations) and from .00 to -1.0 (negative correlations). Most educators will not find an occasion to actually calculate a correlation coefficient, but most will encounter and wish to interpret them. Consider the following example which shows how to interpret these numbers.

Suppose students with high scores on a clerical aptitude test tend to get the high scores in typing speed, and those with low scores on the test tend to get low scores in speed. This arrangement would show close correspondence between a score on the test and rank in speed. In this case, the test and the measure of speed have a high correlation.

The highest correlation one can get is 1.00. In the example above, if the correlation is 1.00, the student with the highest test score would also have the highest typing speed, the one with the next highest test score would have the next highest speed, and so on. A student's status on one measure will correspond exactly with status on the other if the correlation is 1.00. This is illustrated in Table 3.2, column X. The scores on the two measures do not have to be equal; the rank of the score in the group is what we look at. For example, in group X student A has the highest rank on both measures; student B has the next highest rank on both scores, and so on.

But sometimes students' scores on one test tell us nothing about their scores on the other test—there is simply no correspondence between students' scores on the two

TABLE 3.2   Data Showing a Positive Correlation (X), a Near Zero Correlation (Y), and a Negative Correlation (Z)

Student	Test score	Speed (words per minute)	Student	IQ	Shoe size	Student	Social class	Percent graduate
	X			Y			Z	
A	21	75	A	130	7	A	1	75
B	18	69	B	122	10	B	4	63
C	14	53	C	105	5	C	7	38
D	10	49	D	105	12	D	10	20
E	8	36	E	95	8	E	18	14

tests. For example, knowing one's shoe size tells us nothing about IQ. In this case we have essentially zero correlation. A zero correlation (or nearly so) is shown in the data in Table 3.2, column Y.

Most relationships of interest to educators show correlations below 1.00 but above .00. IQ and grades in high school, grades in high school and grades in college, or scores on Forms A and B of a test are examples of sets of data that are not perfectly correlated but are on the positive (plus) side. That is, the correlation will be less than 1.00, but larger than .00, showing a positive relationship. Students with higher IQs tend to get the higher grades, but some do not. The correlation is somewhere between 1.00 and .00. Most of the situations in which correlation is used in measurement are similar to these examples.

In a few circumstances students with low scores on one test tend to get high scores on a second measure, while the high scorers on the first test tend to be low performers on the second measure. An example of this might be number of days absent from school (the first measure) and grades (the second). Students who miss the most days of school tend to get lower grades. In this instance we have a negative correlation, such as −.62. If the relationship was a perfect negative—students with the highest scores on one test have the lowest scores on the second measure; students with the next highest scores on the first test will have the next lowest on the second measure, etc.—the correlation would be −1.00. An example of this is given in Table 3.2, column Z where scores (1 being the highest) show social class and the percent of students who graduate from high school.

In the social sciences, correlations that approach 1.00 or −1.00 are nonexistent. Most of the correlations I have seen based on data relevant to teachers run between about .25 and .80. For example, the correlation between grades in high school and grades in college is about .50, and mathematics aptitude test scores and grades in mathematics classes correlate at about .60. These are typical of correlation coefficients we will find in measurement data used by schools.[*]

[*]A brief description of how to calculate both a quick estimate of a correlation coefficient and the traditional method can be found in the appendix.

How Teachers Interpret Correlation Coefficients

Teachers read manuals provided by test publishing companies. These manuals contain data from studies the publishers have done to illustrate the relationship of their test to school variables, an indication of criterion related validity. They also contain data to show, for example, how closely Form A of the test correlates with Form B. Correlations also appear in journals, such as *The Reading Teacher* or *School Science and Mathematics,* where reports of curriculum studies involve test data, including correlation coefficients.

To be competent test users teachers should be able to interpret correlation coefficients. To help with your interpretations consider the following table of correlation coefficients and what they tell us about the relationship of two sets of data collected on the same group of students.

Correlation coefficient	Extent of relationship
.85 to 1.00	High correspondence (between the test and the performance)
.70 to .84	Moderately high correspondence
.50 to .69	Moderate correspondence
.30 to .49	Moderately low correspondence
.00 to .29	Low correspondence

We interpret negative and positive correlations in the same way; that is, $-.30$ to $-.49$ shows moderate correspondence. However, in all negative correlations as test scores get higher, performance scores get lower. For example, the number of assigned class projects that are incomplete and one's grade in a class are no doubt negatively correlated. We would expect that the larger number of incomplete projects, the lower the grade for the unit or course. If so, this would result in a negative coefficient, such as $-.45$, a correlation that indicates the correspondence between having incomplete projects in one's class and grades is moderately low. As the number of incompletes gets higher the grade tends to get lower.

However, it is important to note that there is not a one-to-one correspondence in that trend. With a coefficient of $-.45$, some people with quite a few incomplete projects will get moderately good grades, while some with most of their projects complete will receive mediocre grades. Therefore, the correspondence is less than perfect, but the trend toward correspondence is there.

Error in Prediction.   It is also important to note that the degree of accuracy in predicting one test score from another varies with size of the correlation coefficient. Accuracy is not a straight-line relationship. As the correlation coefficient gets larger the increments of accuracy in the prediction of one variable from another get larger.

Predicted scores typically do not hit the actual ability of a student, but are likely to be a little above or below it. This distance between actual ability and the predicted score is called error. The table below shows how as correlations increase (get closer to 1.00) the amount of error in our prediction decreases, and the accuracy of our prediction gets better. (The data are for predicting GPAs only and assume a grade point range from 0.0 to 4.0, with about ⅔ of the students having GPAs between 1.25 and 2.75.)

Correlation coefficient	Range of error (+/−)	Decrease in range of error over previous
.30	.71 GPA points	—
.50	.65 GPA points	.06
.70	.54 GPA points	.11
.90	.33 GPA points	.21

These data show four correlation coefficients, each .20 larger than the last. Note however that the reduction in the range of error in predicting GPA from the test is not the same across the four correlations, nor does the error in prediction decrease in a constant amount as we move from .30 to .50 to .70 to .90.

Because test users do not notably begin to reduce the error in prediction of a student's score on test A from test B until the correlation between A and B gets above .50, the range which is labeled as showing only a moderate correspondence begins at about .50 and extends well above, up to .74. We can now see that in correlation coefficients, **in terms of accuracy of prediction,** the mid-range between 0.00 and +1.00 does not occur at .50. Statisticians find that moderate correspondence between test scores and another test or performance measure appears at a larger value than .50.

The range of error works like this: First, assume you've estimated Jessie's GPA at 2.5. Then add the range of error to 2.5 and subtract it from 2.5—we can make errors by over- or underestimating. Now suppose that college grades correlate with our aptitude test at .30. For Jessie we would add 2.5 + .71, and 2.5 − .71. (The .71 is the amount of error in GPA values shown in the above table for a correlation of .30.) Jessie would probably have a GPA somewhere between 3.21 and 1.79. Therefore, if a counselor predicts Jessie's GPA to be 2.5, it will most probably be in that 1.79 to 3.21 range.

Using the same procedure we could see that if the correlation between the aptitude test and GPA was .90, the range of error for a GPA of 2.5 would be from 2.83 to 2.17. This is a much smaller range of error because the correlation between the test and GPA is higher in this case. We now know that as correlations between a test and a performance get higher, that is approach 1.0, the more accurate the test is as a predictor of the performance.

✎ Problems

1. Mr. Ferris, a Machine Shop teacher, is looking over a manual for a test that claims to predict success in machine shop. The section on test validity says that for 348 eleventh-graders the test correlated at .43 with final test grades in a machine shop

class. How would you interpret this correlation coefficient? Is the test likely to accurately predict performance in the class? Why or why not?

2. Mrs. Henry, a French teacher, is looking over a test of grammar which is touted as being a good predictor of success in foreign languages. For one group of 137 high school sophomores the correlation between the test and final grades in French was .69; in a second group of 86 juniors it was .73. Based on these correlation coefficients is the grammar test likely to be a good predictor of grades in French? Why or why not?

3. Following are several correlation coefficients between tests and grades in various classes. Interpret these correlations by indicating how close the correspondence is (high, moderately high, etc.) between the test and school grades:

a. .32 _____   d. .25 _____   g. .36 _____
b. .87 _____   e. .46 _____   h. .64 _____
c. .29 _____   f. .55 _____   i. .73 _____

On which of the above correlations between a test and school grades will we make the smallest errors in prediction?

Application of Correlation to Criterion Related Validation Methods

Now that you have some basic understanding of correlation methods we are ready to return to criterion related validity. In criterion related validation we have a test that we hope will predict where a student will rank in a given performance area. For example, suppose I wish to select 20 students for an advanced mathematics class. I give them a mathematics aptitude test and I hope the high scorers on this test will be the successful ones in my class.

If the test will appropriately place students in my class, it will be a time and money saver. I can save hours of faculty time in interviewing students and reviewing their previous work in mathematics. It is this kind of savings I want from my test.

However, the test must have evidence of fairly high correlation with the criterion to claim adequate criterion validity for this job. To find out how valid the test is for my purpose I look in the test manual for correlations of the test and performances similar to the one I want to predict. It is important to interpret these correlations correctly. We hope to find correlation coefficients somewhere above .50. This is not to say that we must discard all tests with validity data below that, but clearly we will make larger errors in selecting the best students if we have lower correlations.

It is our intention in using a test to get a ranking of students by test scores that will show how these same students rank on the performance in which we are interested. If we get a ranking on the test that closely matches the ranking on the performance, the test correlates well with the performance measurement. But if the test and performance measurement do not correlate well, giving the test will be of little use in ranking students on the performance. These correlations between a test and a performance in which we are interested are the evidence for criterion related validity. The test manual should give its readers the correlation data they need to judge the ability of the test to rank their students appropriately.

Construct Validation

Thus far we have discussed two procedures for determining validity: creating assessments that are a sample of the actual instructional material, and relating a test to a performance criterion, such as rating of skill on a job. A third procedure involves evaluating the correspondence between how a test assesses a trait and how a psychological theory, or construct, says it should assess it. The outcome of this process is **construct validation.** Like all other methods, construct validation holds test scores up to a second assessment of some kind. In this case, that second assessment is a complex theory (or construct) of the trait being assessed. For example, intelligence is a construct, as are test anxiety, hypochondria, and acrophobia. When testmakers hold the test up to a theoretical framework of a trait to see if the test content reflects the construct, they call this construct validation.

Construct validation begins with the development of a detailed theory of a trait. Our test is valid to the extent that it classifies people the way the theory says they should be classified. For example, Mr. Gruenbalm has a scale that is designed to sort people on the submissive-dominance dimension of personality. Does the test actually categorize people in the way independent psychologists trained in dominance theory would rank them? To the extent that it does, the test has validity for assessing the submissive-dominance characteristic of personality.

Construct validation is an umbrella for all types of validation. Construct validity assumes that the content of a test is that which is defined by the testmaker's concept of the instructional area. The closer the tasks in the test are to the operations that characterize the concept, the more appropriate the test content is (content validity). Similarly, the closer the tasks in the test are to those in the domain of the performance educators want to predict (criterion related validity), the more likely the test is to assess what the theory says it should assess. Thus, construct validation may be seen to subsume both content and criterion related evidence of validity.

Though the test manuals read by teachers will seldom mention construct validation, counselors should have a detailed understanding of it. Therefore in dealing with counselors and school psychologists, teachers should always ask questions about the validity of test data collected on a particular child. In this respect construct validity is important to teachers as well as to specialized school staff.

Finding the Validity of Published Tests

There are several sources where validity data can be found for published tests. The most prominent are the publisher's test manuals and the *Mental Measurements Yearbook*.

All competent test publishers develop manuals to accompany their tests. These manuals contain reports on how the tests were developed and how well they have fared when tried out. If teachers are looking for content related evidence of validity, the details of test development are essential. To determine if a test fits the local curriculum educators must know the source of the test content, how that content was selected, and how it was used in building the questions and problems in the test. Then teachers can more precisely compare the test content with their curriculum.

Test publishers should also report results of field trials for their tests. They should tell potential users who took the tests in the field trials and how many people were involved. (At least one thousand cases should be included if possible, and several thousand for the standard achievement tests.) For criterion related tests, such as mathematics aptitude, the test manual should also report correlation coefficients showing how well the test ranked students in terms of their success in the desired performance, such as success in mathematics. More than one such study should be reported in the manual to demonstrate the variety of situations in which the test has been tried, thereby allowing test users to look for a situation most like the one in which they will use the test.

The *Mental Measurements Yearbook* is a multivolume set of reports on published tests of all types. Each volume updates reports on tests that have been revised or reports on new ones that have appeared since the last volume. (You may have to look through several volumes to find the test you are interested in.) In the yearbook you will find a short description of the test and usually a review written by an independent specialist in the area of psychometrics and/or the curriculum or trait area for which the test was devised. The following is a sample of a report on a test listed in the *Mental Measurements Yearbook*.

Occupational Aptitude Survey and Interest Schedule, Second Edition—Aptitude Survey.
Purpose: Designed to measure career development of students.
Population: Grades 8–12.
Publication Dates: 183–91.
Acronym: OASIS-2 AS.
Scores, 6: General Ability, Verbal Aptitude, Numerical Aptitude, Spatial Aptitude, Perceptual Aptitude, Manual Dexterity.
Administration: Group.
Price Data, 1994: $98 per complete kit including 10 test booklets, 50 answer sheets, 50 profile sheets, and manual ('91, 38 pages); $29 per 10 test booklets; $28 per 50 answer sheets; $19 per 50 profile sheets; $26 per manual.
Time: 35 (45) minutes.
Comments: May be used in conjunction with the OASIS-2 Interest Schedule (264).
Author: Randall M. Parker.
Publisher: PRO-ED, Inc.
Cross References: See T4: 1862 (2 references); for reviews by Rodney L. Lowman and Kevin W. Mossholder of an earlier edition, see 10:243.

TEST REFERENCES

1. Levinson, E.M., Rafoth, B.A., & Lesnak, L. (1994). A criterion-related validity study of the OASIS-2 Interest Schedule. *Journal of Employment Counseling, 31,* 29–37.
2. Parker, R. M., & Schaller, J. (1994). Relationships among self-rated and psychometrically determined vocational aptitudes and interests. *Educational and Psychological Measurement, 54,* 155–159.

Review of the Occupational Aptitude Survey and Interest Schedule, Second Edition—Aptitude Survey by LAURA L. B. BARNES, Assistant Professor of Educational Research, Department of applied Behavioral Studies, Oklahoma State University, Stillwater, OK:
The Occupational Aptitude Survey and Interest Schedule, Second Edition—Aptitude Survey (OASIS-2AS) is intended to provide students with information "regarding their relative strengths in several aptitude areas related to the world of work" (p.1). The Aptitude Survey was developed basically as a shorter version of the U.S. Department of Labor General Aptitude Test Battery (GATB). Through factor analytic studies of the 12 GATB subtests, five factors were deemed to be responsible for a significant portion of test score variance. These five factors...

Truncated sample from the *Mental Measurements Yearbook*. Conoley, J. C. & Impara, J. C. (Eds.), (1995). The *Twelfth Mental Measurements Yearbook*. Lincoln, NE, Buros Institute of Mental Measurements.

Applying Validity Information

It is not enough simply to be aware of validity. Teachers must make practical use of information about validity to become more intelligent assessment designers and users. In this section we'll discuss several examples of how teachers apply validity.

An Elementary School Application

In this first example we'll focus on content validation, the most common type of validation used by teachers. Ms. Nimero has been working on multiplication with her students and now wishes to see how well they are acquiring the concepts and skills which are her objectives. Of course, she has informally observed skill levels as she works with individual children, but now wants a formal assessment common to all children in her class.

The mathematics textbook publisher has conveniently provided Ms. Nimero with a teacher's manual which contains unit tests at the end of each chapter, at first glance a handy way to assess the skills she has been teaching. But how well have these tests been validated? That is, through what effort and by what means has the text publisher compared the test content with the textbook material? Ms. Nimero has not followed the textbook exactly. She has some ideas of her own and has integrated some unique procedures into the daily lessons, so her instruction has not matched the text precisely. How has this affected the content validity of the test in the teacher's manual?

Several weeks ago Ms. Nimero made out a table of specifications to serve as an instructional guide. Now she takes out this table and looks it over carefully, noting that in her teaching she has followed it quite closely. She next reviews the publisher's test, question by question, and compares it to her table. She decides that of the 30 items on the test 24 fit her table and 6 do not. Also, the test contains a larger proportion of problems on the use of zero in multiplication than she had listed on her table of specifications.

To what extent does the test have content validity for Ms. Nimero's class? It appears to have some content that squares with her table of specifications and some that does not. She therefore decides to develop her own test utilizing the appropriate items from the publisher's test and creating some of her own. These additional items will cover her original ideas and those unique procedures she integrated into the instruction. She also adjusts her test for the difference in emphasis on the use of zero. Ms. Nimero now has a test which closely matches her table of specifications, and hence, in her judgment has content validity.

A Secondary School Application

Procedures like those illustrated above are not limited to elementary classrooms, but are also applicable in making classroom tests in high school. However, here is a different example that may illustrate a validity application often seen in secondary education.

At Floodtown High School the teachers have decided that they have a number of students would benefit from more intense instruction in the sciences. The Science

Department chair, Ms. Fortace, has called the teachers in the department together to discuss how they will select students for the program. After agreeing on a set of general criteria for the selection procedure (such as applying the same criteria to all applicants, admitting no more than 20 students, ranking in importance the several selection criteria they will use), they turn to the matter of choosing an aptitude test.

Ms. Fortace has obtained copies of two published tests that claim to assess general science aptitude. The manual for the first test states that the test scores made by 413 high school seniors have been compared to grades averaged across at least two science areas. The test correlated with averaged grades at .46, an indicator of criterion (in this case grades) related validation. On the second test the teachers find that it has been matched with content in five of the most widely used textbooks in chemistry, physics, and biology. A general table of specifications in the manual showed how many test items were from each topical area, the testmaker's evidence for content validity. The teachers looked over the table and decided it was at best only a modest fit to their objectives.

In addition the testmakers correlated test scores with teacher's ratings of 52 students on a list of characteristics showing science aptitude. The correlation was .57. The testmakers had attempted to develop a test that reflected teachers' perceptions of aptitude in their students, so as to demonstrate the construct validation of the test.

Following their review of the manuals, the teachers discussed the relative merits of each test. Each test used different procedures to collect data on validity. Now the teachers have to decide how relevant these procedures are to the job they want the test to do. The correlation coefficients between the test and the second observation are evaluated. Neither coefficient is high but both indicate that the test provides some modest ability to predict the criterion the publishers have used. Not entirely satisfied, the science teachers decide to explore other publisher's test catalogs to see what additional tests are available.

Guidelines for Evaluating Test Validity

To this point we have discussed those types of validation for assessments. Now we want to decide which procedures shown in test manuals or journals are done well. Here are three questions that guide our decision.

Guidelines for Evaluating Validation

1. Does the validation procedure fit the use to which the test will be put?
2. How well was the validation carried out?
3. Does the evidence reported for the validation support the use of the test?

Let's take a closer look at these guidelines.

Does the validation procedure fit the use to which the test will be put? When I wish to assess the achievement of my class with a test, whether teacher made, purchased by the school, or received from the state in a statewide assessment program, the content should closely match the objectives promoted in class. These tests require that content validation procedures be applied to them and I must ask were they indeed validated this way? Before I come to a conclusion about any student we must note how well the content sample in the test squares with the instruction.

However, if I am using the test to predict a performance, such as selecting persons who will be successful in a special program, then I need to find criterion related validity. In this case the criterion is very important: The criterion performance on which the test was validated must match the performance I will wish to see in my special program. If I am using a test to predict success in a school program, the testmaker must provide evidence of criterion related validity.

How well was the validation carried out? It is not enough to see that a validation procedure is appropriate, it must also have been properly carried out. Was a table of specification carefully developed for content assessment? Does the table fit my instructional objectives? In criterion related validation, how carefully did the testmaker define the criterion against which the test was compared? Are the tasks in the criterion very similar to the tasks we hope to see in our program develop? Each of these questions must be asked and answered. The adequacy of procedures here must be recorded and decisions should be based on this evidence.

Does the evidence reported for the validation support the use of the test? Although the validation procedure may have been appropriate and may have been done well, the results may or may not warrant the use of the test. A test publisher may have carefully created a table of specifications for an achievement test that matches several of the widely used textbooks in the field of teaching reading, and the test content may reflect this table closely. Although this looks like good procedure for content validation, if the test content does not match your objectives in teaching reading the test is probably not a good one for you to use.

Or perhaps the publisher has matched test problems with tasks required for success on a given job, but has found the test correlates at .25 with the measure of job performance, a very low correspondence between test scores and job performance. The procedure looks right for collecting criterion related data, but the correlation coefficient of .25 tells us the test is not very useful in selecting students who will be trained for the job local teachers have in mind.

In sum, the inferences teachers make, such as "John can write the multiplication table," "Caroline can apply the Periodic Table in solving problems about chemical compounds," or "Jeff has not learned to spell at the third-grade level," must be based on evidence from tests and other assessments and not on casual impressions. But assessments are useful in making inferences only if they have a sufficient level of validity. Therefore validity must be a primary consideration in selecting a test from a publisher or in making assessment devices for our own classroom use. Further, if the test is to aid us in making good inferences from its data it must be built on an appropriate procedure that is properly carried out.

SUMMARY

1. Validity is one of the most important aspects of assessment procedures of all kinds.
2. A test is valid to the extent that it helps teachers make an appropriate inference about a specified student characteristic. Validity of a test must be stated in terms of the specific trait in which we are interested—assessments do not have generic validity.

3. One way of determining validity is to judge how precisely a test samples a specified body of knowledge. This is referred to as content sampling, the key component of content related validity.

4. The categories in Bloom's taxonomy of learning outcomes, or similar outlines for categorizing content, can be used as guides in designing tests for assessing achievement that match our instructional objectives.

5. To the extent that the sample of behaviors observed in an assessment matches the instructional objectives, the assessment procedure has achieved content validity.

6. Face validity is determined by a scan of what the test appears to assess.

7. Criterion related validity is shown in the relationship of outcomes of an assessment device (e.g., a test) to a performance criterion (a job skill) the relationship is typically shown by correlation procedures.

8. Correlation is a statistical procedure that shows how closely scores on one measure correspond in rank with scores on another. A correlation is represented by a number known as a correlation coefficient, which ranges from 0 up to +1.0, and down to −1.0.

9. When interpreting correlation coefficients we note that in predicting student performance from a test score the range of error in predicting becomes smaller as correlations become larger (i.e., closer to 1.0).

10. Construct validation involves evaluating the correspondence between what a test assesses and what a psychological theory, or construct, of a trait says it should assess. Construct validity typically subsumes the two other types of validation.

11. Evidence of validity for published tests can be found most commonly in the publisher's test manuals and the *Mental Measurements Yearbook*.

12. Some questions to ask in considering the validity of a test are (a) Does the validation procedure fit the use to which the test will be put? (b) How well was the validation carried out? and (c) Does the evidence reported for the validation support the use of the test?

13. Without a reasonable amount of validity the assessment procedure is of very little use to educators.

A REAL CASE NARRATIVE

The salesman from Electra Publishing House had just talked to the faculty at Monroe Township High School. The publisher had brought a general academic aptitude test onto the market and the salesman pitched the presentation toward developing high anticipation among teachers for utility of this test.

The expression, "ranking students according to ability to achieve," and "placing students exactly with the subject matter they can best master," kept coming up in the presentation. These were intriguing promises for teachers in any school. No data were presented, because they would only "confuse" the listeners. Instead the faculty heard terms like "according to our studies . . ." and "the research shows that. . . ." Examples were given of students who "blossomed" after having their learning problems diagnosed by the test. There were also testimonies from teachers who found the test an invaluable adjunct to preparing appropriate lesson plans.

During the question period an English teacher inquired "I see that in the Exeter School Study the correlation between test scores and student achievement as judged by a team of teachers was .34. This is validity data, isn't it, and if so, isn't it a bit low?" The salesman smiled broadly, and asked, "How many of you understand the correlation business, anyway? Let's see your hands!" No hands went up. "And now let's see how many of you know this validity thing this young lady is referring to." No hands went up. "In that case, let's not take these people's time to discuss it," said the salesman.

As they walked down the hall after the meeting Ms. Barker and Mr. Hull discussed the presentation. "The test sounds like a very useful tool," said Ms. Barker. "I mean, haven't you had kids you just can't seem to reach, and wondered if you are not adapting the work to their level? I know I do, all the time!"

"Yes, but didn't you feel put down by that comment on correlation and validity?" Mr. Hull began. "I surely did! If this guy is legit he would have explained it to us rather than brush it off that way, and maybe we should know enough about it so we can challenge guys like that."

"Yes, I agree!" Ms. Barker replied. "Why don't we know about that stuff anyway?"

What is your response to the above conversation? How would you react to the salesmen? And what is your position on the last two remarks of the teachers?

_____

_____

_____

PROBLEMS

1. For each example identify the type of validation being illustrated—content, criterion related, or construct.
   a. Ms. Jackson has a table of specifications, which follow Bloom's taxonomy of educational outcomes, to help her work her way through a unit on complex fractions for her fifth-grade class. She writes the examination for her class to match the outcomes on the table of specifications.
   b. The Kennedy Elementary School first-grade teachers are preparing a remedial reading section for children who are not progressing well in acquiring a basic sight vocabulary. They decide to select a published test to use as information along with teachers' evaluations on children. They collect several publishers' tests and review them. The first test has a correlation of .55 with teacher ranking of children in the first four months of the first-grade. The second test has compared the test content with the instructional objectives found in two popular reading book series.
   c. A college admissions test company has correlated scores on the test with first semester grades for college freshmen.
2. For ten years Mr. Lommacher, a high school Earth Science teacher, has collected a file of tests he has found in various earth science textbooks. When he completes a

unit in class he looks through the file and selects questions for various tests that appear to touch on the topics covered by the class. Based on this method of test construction, how valid do you think the tests will be? Explain.

3. Interpret each of the following correlation coefficients relative to the relationship between the test and the performance with which we are correlating it. Use terms such as low relation, moderately high relation, etc.

   a. .67 _____   f. .36 _____
   b. .91 _____   g. .55 _____
   c. .25 _____   h. .84 _____
   d. .45 _____   i. .22 _____
   e. .75 _____   j. −.89 _____

4. Mr. Dodge, who teaches Auto Mechanics, has had his budget cut and therefore must lay off his assistant instructor. This means he must also reduce the number of students who can be admitted to his class. The principal has suggested he pretest all applicants for mechanical aptitude to find those most likely to profit from the training. Mr. Dodge's training has been in mechanics, not in a teacher-training program, so he asks you (a master teacher) how to go about selecting a test that will do the job of finding the "right" students. How would you advise him?

5. Mr. Dodge, who believed you gave him good advice in selecting a test for admitting students to his class in auto mechanics, has finished a unit on carburation. He will now give a test and again comes to you for advice. The test must be constructed so as to accurately reflect his objectives in teaching the unit (i.e., it must have content validity). What procedures would you suggest Mr. Dodge use?

KEY TERMS

validity   correlation
content validity   correlation coefficient
face validity   range of error
criterion related validity   construct validity

ADDITIONAL READING

American Psychological Association, *Standards for Educational and Psychological Testing.* Washington, D. C.: APA, 1985.

Cronbach, L. J. *Essentials of Psychological Testing,* 4th ed. New York: Harper & Row, 1984. Chapter 5, "Validation."

Hambleton, R. K. Validation of test scores. In R. A. Berk, ed., *A Guide to Criterion Referenced Test Construction.* Baltimore: Johns Hopkins University Press, 1994.

Messick, S. (1989). Meaning and values in test validation: The science and ethics of assessment, *Educational Researcher,* 18, 5–11.

Tenopyer, M. L. (1977). Content-construct confusion, *Personnel Psychology,* 1, 1–10.

CHAPTER 4

RELIABILITY

How Consistent Is Our Measurement?

The reliability of a test is demonstrated by the consistency with which it ranks individuals in the same order on two (or more) occasions. Ms. Holsman, a school nurse measured the height of twenty children entering the first-grade. Afterward, she used her measurement to line the pupils up starting with the shortest and ending with the tallest. "I'm in the wrong place," complained Jeanene. "So am I," added Dan. To check the consistency of the assessment Ms. Holsman measured their height again to see if her second measurement ranked students the same as the first.

Ms. Holsman is looking for consistency of her two measures. If her two measures completely agree, she has perfect reliability in her measurement but if her measurement produces more and more disagreement between the rankings of children on the first and second measures, the reliability of her procedure decreases. Consistency of outcomes on two or more observations is the essence of reliability. Without it scores will not help us make better decisions about children because we cannot depend on a score to give us a stable ranking of any child.

What This Chapter Will Include. In this chapter you will learn the following:

1. Why reliability is applied to assessments used in schools
2. Different ways in which reliability of a test or other assessment is demonstrated
3. How to interpret reliability data so as to make more appropriate decisions based on test results
4. Reliability of criterion referenced tests
5. Factors that affect the reliability of a test

Defining Reliability

As you and I noted above, reliability of assessments tells us the consistency of our observations. By consistency I mean two (or more) observations having similar results. Two comparable tests would place each child at, or nearly at, the same point on the score range. If John gets a score of 15 on a test, a comparable test should also put him at, or very near, 15. This general quality of consistency is called **reliability.** It tells educators to what extent a test will provide placements of a given child that are the same between two observations, and hence dependable.

The science textbook that Ms. Jones is using with her eighth-grade students includes several forms of tests for each chapter in the book. After completing the first chapter, Ms. Jones administered one of the tests to her class. For a number of children the scores seemed inconsistent with her estimate of their achievement, so the next day she administered another of the tests provided for the first chapter. The ranking of the students on the first test was quite different from the ranking on the second test. She pondered these differences with some frustration. The test results were inconsistent, that is they had little reliability. Therefore Ms. Jones knew that the tests would also be of little use in making decisions about the achievement of students based on the objectives of the first chapter in the textbook.

Before measuring anything—test anxiety, intelligence, reading comprehension—the initial consideration must be: Will the measure be consistent? That is, to what extent will successive observations agree as to the status of a given individual on a specific characteristic? If I have a score for Bessie on Form A of a beginning algebra test I must feel confident that a second testing with Form B would show a similar score. If I have that confidence the test score may be useful, but if the score fluctuates widely from test to test, I cannot be sure of Bessie's skill level. The scores are not reliable. Somewhere along this continuum is Bessie's true algebra ability. A reliable test will place her near that point.

Reliability and Validity

Reliability differs from validity. The measures of a given human trait can have very high reliability, but have almost no relationship to the decisions we make about achievement. For example, when Ms. Holsman measured the children's height she may have good reliability, but will have essentially no information that will help her place these students into remedial, average, and accelerated reading groups. The height measure is reliable but has no validity for placement in reading skill. Reliability is verified by the consistency of the observation of an outcome; validity tells me the relevance of an observation for making a decision I want to make.

It is important to note that reliability in your scores does not guarantee validity of the test. It indicates only that the scores are consistent from one assessment to the next. However, without reliability you can say very little about the test's validity. Since the primary purpose of assessment is to assist teachers in making decisions about children, validity is the sine qua non of assessment. But as we've demonstrated, without reliability, validity is likely to be problematic.

Reliability: A Variable Characteristic

Test scores are reliable to the extent that they are consistent with themselves. However, reliability is not an all or nothing quality of a measurement, that is, it is not true that observations have or do not have reliability. Reliability appears in varying amounts. Test scores can have no reliability—scores on the first test may tell me nothing about the rank of a student on the second comparable test. A test can also have perfect reliability—the first test ranks students in exactly the same order as the second. Most tests fall somewhere between these extremes.

Reliability in Educational Testing

Educational assessments are like any other measuring device. Teachers want to have confidence that their assessment of a given child is an accurate measure of that child's ability. Teachers want to know that the assessment is reliable. We know that if we use a given device and cannot get two observations that agree, the assessment results cannot be given much credibility. We cannot accurately determine a child's status from looking at inconsistent scores. This is a conclusion that applies to all assessments, whether test results, scores on essays, observational procedures, or any other type of assessment.

True Scores and Errors of Measurement

A test that measures with complete consistency would place each child at the exact same position on the score range on two successive administrations (assuming no practice effect). Test users often assume the test is providing a "true" measure of the trait for every child, but in fact the test score typically includes some error or degree of imprecision. The extent to which a test misses the mark, that is, deviates from the true score, is called **measurement error.** Therefore, it is often useful to think of a test score as having two components, one based on the child's actual ability and one based on errors of measurement.

Suppose that instead of using a yardstick Nurse Holsman had measured student height with an elastic tape. The stretch of the tape would make it difficult to get two consistent measures. If Nurse Holsman stretches the tape taut on some measurements but not on others she will sometimes overestimate the height of a child, while on others she will underestimate it. Errors of this accidental nature are called **random errors.**

Why Do Teachers Need to Understand Reliability?

Teachers continually make observations of children's behavior but only a few of them are made with formal tests. The idea of reliability applies not only to tests, but also to all types of assessments. For example, after a class of oral exercises Ms. Messorde decides that Julie knows none of the multiplication combinations the class has been studying. But now we know we must ask, "Will the same conclusion stand if Ms. Messorde provides another similar class exercise?" This is the reliability question we teachers face every day.

What about the reliability procedures used by professional testmakers? Do teachers need to understand them? Indeed they do! Teachers are themselves testmakers and their tests must be reliable. Also, teachers serve on test committees and participate in the selection of tests, and they use results of commercial and statewide testing programs. How reliable are the data from these tests? What procedure was used to determine the test's reliability? Was that procedure appropriate for the use to which we want to put our tests? These are questions teachers must ask, and to do so they must understand the relevance of these questions to the credibility of test (and other observational) data.

✎ Problems

1. Mrs. Jones is reviewing a test, and as she pages through it decides, "This test does not seem to sample the content I have taught in the last few months." Does her statement point to reliability or to validity? Explain.
2. The teachers in the second-grade of Elm Grove School are looking over their children's test results of their statewide testing. "Some of my class took both Forms A and B of the arithmetic test," one teacher notes. "The students' ranks on Forms A and B do not agree at all." With what characteristic of a test is this teacher concerned?
3. Looking over the scores for his class, another teacher from Elm Grove observed, "Some of the students did better on Form A of the test, while others did better on form B." You and I recognize this as a problem of error of measurement. What do test users call these errors? Are they more troublesome when users are looking at the group average or when they are making plans for a single child? Why?
4. A third teacher at Elm Grove noted the reliability of the test was reported by the State Superintendent of Schools to be high. The Superintendent had stated, "I guess we can be sure that the test is measuring knowledge of arithmetic." Is the Superintendent's conclusion about "knowledge of arithmetic" correct? Explain.

How Do Testmakers Determine Reliability?

Test publishers know that reliability is determined by how well two measurements of a given trait agree with each other in the ranking of each student. Therefore, publishers typically have to measure a group of people more than once and compare the results of two (or more) measurements in order to determine reliability. They then correlate the two sets of scores to see how well the sets agree with each other.

Reliability and Correlation

The job, then, in determining the reliability of scores from our measuring procedure—a yardstick, a test, or a controlled observation plan—consist of two basic steps:

1. Using two comparable assessment procedures, for example two 20-item tests of one-digit multiplication, get two assessments of a skill on all persons in a group.
2. Using correlation procedures compare the position of each student in the group on the first assessment with the student's position on the second of these two assessments.

In the last chapter you learned about correlation. You wanted to see how closely student ranking on your test correlated with a different measure of the skill. With reliability the basic procedure is similar, but what you correlate is different. In this chapter the correlation procedure we'll discuss will compare a student's score on one test, not with a score on a different measure, but with a second score on the same (or an equivalent) test used to get the first score.

Reliability coefficients—that is, correlation coefficients for reliabilities—resemble those for validity. They can range from −1.00 to 0.00 to +1.00, but in reliability studies most will be between .60 and .90. Educators look for reliability coefficients to be at least .80 for commercial test, because this indicates that a student's score on one form of the test is much like that person's score on the other, that is, the score is reliable.

For teacher-made tests it would also be useful to get reliability coefficients as high as .80 or higher, but the fact is that they often run a little lower than those for commercial tests. Educators who specialize in assessment like to see reliability coefficients on teacher made tests to be no lower than .65, but preferably higher.

Methods for Determining Reliability

The data you will see reported in the test manuals published by commercial testmakers are based on one of four standard methods of determining test reliability. These methods typically involve getting two measures on the same group of people. The four methods are:

1. Give the same test to the same people on two occasions—this method is called the **test–retest** method.
2. Prepare two tests that sample the same content (Form A and Form B) and give both tests to the same group of people—this is called the **alternate forms** method.
3. Give one long test to a group of people. Then sort the items from this long test into two shorter tests (often the odd numbered items—1, 3, 5, etc.—make up the first test, the even numbered items—2, 4, 6, etc.—make up the other*) so that each test now contains half as many items as the whole tests. Get the first score from one of the short tests and the second score on the other short test and correlate the two half-test scores. Then adjust the correlation for a test as long as both halves are put back together again. This is called the **split–half** method.
4. Calculate the extent to which students perform the same way on item 1, item 2, item 3, and so on across the whole test. This shows the extent to which test-takers perform consistently across all items in the test. In a sense each item is treated like a separate small test, and the procedure determines how consistent the test-taker is across all those small tests. This procedure is called the **internal consistency** method.

---

*Tests are never sorted by basing the first score on the first half of the test, and the second score on the last half. This could mean that practice on the first half of the test could affect achievement on the second half.

TABLE 4.1   Procedures for Determining Test Reliability

Method	Procedure
Test–retest	One test is administered to the same people on two different occasions.
Alternate forms	Two separate forms of the test are made and both administered to the same group of people.
Split-half	One test is split into two halves and scores on one half are correlated with scores on the other half.
Internal consistency	All test items are compared with each other to see how consistently test takers performed from item to item

Table 4.1 above summarizes these procedures. Although each method is discussed in some detail in the paragraphs ahead, Table 4.1 gives us a broad overview. It shows how scores obtained using each method demonstrate the reliability of a test. Note that these methods are applicable for all types of assessments—achievement, controlled observations, job aptitude, and even the tests teachers make for their own classes.

The Test-Retest Method.   The most obvious way to get two measurements of a given characteristic for each person in a group is to measure everyone twice with the same test. For example, suppose a test publisher gives the School and Community Achievement Test (a fictitious test) to a group of 100 high school students on January 10, and gives it again to these same people on January 30 (see Figure 4.1). The two sets of scores are correlated using standard correlation procedures.[*]

FIGURE 4.1   A Depiction of Data Collection for Test-Retest Reliability

[*]These procedures were discussed in Chapter 3, and the calculation, if desired, can be found in Appendix C.

Or suppose you give a test anxiety scale to a group of high school students on May 10. On May 20 you give the same scale to the same students and correlate the first set of scores with the second. Both of these examples include getting two scores for each student, using the same test each time, and comparing the two score sets using correlation procedures. This is the test-retest method.

Problems With the Test-Retest Method.   An important problem with the test-retest method is that it assumes the first and second measurements are independent of each other when they may not be. On the second testing students may recall how they dealt with many of the items the first time they took a test and if answers to questions on the test are very likely to be recalled, the nature of the test has been changed. A test that was originally a problem-solving test might become in the second session partly a memory test.

Even if students do not recall the exact answers they gave on the first test they may have learned a test-taking procedure. If so, this procedure could improve scores on the second testing. If the first testing provides an advantage for the second testing, this advantage will likely not be equal for all students, even those with the same ability. In any case, some students surely will profit more from the experience than others will, producing more disagreement between ranking of students on the two tests and increasing the errors of measurement. As a result reliability will be lessened. That is, the reliability coefficient will be smaller than if practice effect had been an equal influence on all students.

These difficulties for test-retest methods can be reduced by allowing more time to elapse between the first and second testing sessions. Students will tend to forget more of the procedures for and answers to problems in the test. However, a test user cannot let too much time go by or children, through normal learning and maturation, will change enough to cause disagreement between their first and second test scores.

The Alternate Forms Method.   In the alternate forms method testmakers receive two scores for each person by making two equivalent tests that assess the same behavior domain. Let's call them Form A and Form B. When equivalent forms are created, no problem on one test appears on the other even though the tests sample the same behavior domain. If two forms of a test are equivalent they will be equally difficult, and the spread of scores from lowest to highest will look very much alike.

To establish the level of test score reliability with alternate forms we administer each of the two forms to the same group of students, get one score for each person on Form A and one score on Form B. (This procedure is illustrated in Figure 4.2.) We then correlate these two sets of scores to see how closely the two measurements correspond. Again we have a reliability coefficient that reflects the degree of consistency between the two assessments.

If your score on Form A is very close to your score on Form B, and this is true for most of the other students who took the two forms, the test scores are probably quite reliable.

Many test publishers will have constructed two (or more) forms for a test they are selling. The test forms will each have questions and problems that cover the same

FIGURE 4.2   A Depiction of Data Collection for Alternate Forms Reliability

domain, for instance reading comprehension, but the items on one form will be different from those on the others. The publisher will give all forms of the test to a large number of children and correlate the scores to determine how well scores on Form A agree with scores on Form B. The correlation of the two sets of scores will be reported in the test manual as reliability coefficients.

Alternate Forms and Assessment of Student Gains.   Alternate forms of a test are often used to assess gains after a period of instruction. The first form is given as a pretest to see how the students perform in a given skill area. After a period of weeks the second form is given to determine student ranking at the time the learning period is completed.*

It is at this point we become most concerned with reliability. Before we can make any conclusions about gains from instruction we must be convinced that changes in scores from one testing to another are not due to inconsistencies in the way one test measures compared to the alternate form. A large reliability coefficient will tell us that without instruction a student will make a score on Form A that is very much like the one on Form B. If we then see changes between the first test and, after weeks of instruction, the second test it might be due to the instruction we gave students between the two test sessions.

If teachers are to have some assurance that changes from pretest to post-test are due to instruction, and not inconsistencies between tests, the reliability of the alternate

---

*With this procedure there are some hazards of a more complex statistical nature than are covered in this text. Interested persons may wish to consult R. L. Thorndike and E. P. Hagen, Measurement and Evaluation in Psychology and Education, 4th ed. New York, NY: John Wiley & Sons, 1977, p. 198 ff.

forms should be fairly high. When reviewing a test publisher's manual it is appropriate for a teacher to look at the reliability of equivalent forms before ordering the test.

Consider this second situation in which using equivalent forms is very useful. If a teacher has a large group of students to test, supervising the students—watching for errors in procedure or for exchanges of information among students, and so forth—is quite difficult. However, if students who are seated side-by-side have different forms of the test, the opportunity to copy from a neighbor will be reduced as will be the amount of supervision required.

Problems With Alternate Forms Reliability.   With the alternate forms method the items in the first form are different from those in the second. Therefore, memory of answers from one testing to the next is not as problematic as it is with the test-retest reliability method. We cannot, however, dismiss practice effects altogether.

As in the test-retest procedure it is possible that a student will learn test-taking skills in the first testing that will be useful in the second. For example, he or she may learn a technique for solving a given problem that may be useful in solving all problems of that type. If so, even though Form B has different items on it than Form A, students may have learned something on the first testing that will help them solve problems on the second. Since there are different test items on Form A than on B, test publishers expect that this transfer effect will be very much minimized.

Split-Half Procedures

Suppose you have only one test and can administer it only once. Some commercial tests are like this, as are virtually all teacher-made tests. With one test and one set of scores for everybody how can you get two scores to compare to see if one measure corresponds with another?

Suppose you have an arithmetic problem-solving test of 50 items. You give it to a group of people and get their responses to the items on the test. To get the necessary two scores for each person you now treat the test as though it is two 25-item tests. You use a semirandom procedure and sort the 50 items into two sets of 25 items each. You get the first score from one set of 25 items and the second score from the other 25 items. Instead of the 50-item test you now have two tests of the common trait, but each test is just half as long as the original test.

But wait! Which 25 items go into the first test, and which go into the second test? If you take the first 25 items for the first score, practice effect from that group of items may unfairly influence scores on the second 25 items. Practice effect cannot be eliminated, but it can be equally distributed across both halves of the test.

Two ways of sorting a test's items into two separate groups have been widely used. One method is to randomly assign items to two halves of the test; the other is to count the odd-numbered items (1,3,5, etc.) as one test and the even-numbered items (2,4,6, etc.) as the other test. (See Figure 4.3 for an example of odd-even scoring.) With each of these procedures, the items that make up either half-test will come from all sections of the test—some from the beginning, some from the middle of the test, and some from

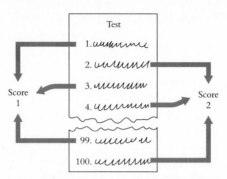

FIGURE 4.3   Split-Half Procedure—Odd-Even Scoring

the end—so that practice acquired at different stages of the test-taking process should affect one test about the same as it does the other.

The Spearman-Brown Split-Half Procedure.   Suppose you are faced with a child about whose arithmetic ability you know nothing. You have the option of asking the child either five or ten questions about arithmetic. Which option will give you the best picture of the child's ability to do arithmetic? The longer one will. It allows for a wider sample of topics and levels of skill, a generalization that applies to testing of all kinds. The longer test typically is a more appropriate behavior sample and consequently it is likely to be more reliable.

Let's return to the test you split into two parts. The two 25-item tests are only half as long as the original 50-item test and are likely to be less accurate as a sample of the behavior domain. That is, the correlation between the two sets of scores, each based on 25 items, is likely to be lower than the correlation between two equally well-constructed measures using 50 items. Therefore, you might expect that splitting the test will produce two shorter tests that are less reliable than the one long test was.

Luckily, you can still split our 50-item test into two 25-item tests, score each half and correlate these scores, and come out with the reliability coefficient for the 50-item test. This is done by using the Spearman-Brown prophesy formula which reads:

$$r = \frac{2r_h}{1 + r_h}$$

where r is the reliability coefficient for the total, unsplit test and r_h is the correlation between the two sets of scores, each based on a 25 item half of the test. The result is the reliability based on the 50 item test.

Teachers will not likely be called upon to calculate reliability using the Spearman-Brown procedure. However, they may well see it cited in test manuals and will wish to know what it is. To help you better understand the formula, consider this a "walk through" example. Suppose a published 80-item test is administered to a college fresh-man class in psychology. The 40 odd-numbered items are scored to get one half-test score on everybody in the class; for each student the 40 even-numbered items are scored to get the other half-test score. The publisher now has two scores (one on odd numbered items, one on even) on all students in the class.

Next the publisher gives these data to a statistician who calculates the correlation (r_h) between the odd and even test scores. She reports that this correlation is .88. Putting this figure into the Spearman-Brown formula the publisher gets .94, the reliability for the 80-item test. The data for the "walk through" example follows.

Student*	Odd	Even	
Abe	14	12	$r_h = .88$, the correlation
Bess	17	14	of two half-scores
Cal	29	26	$r = \dfrac{2(.88)}{1 + .88}$
Don	21	25	
Eli	20	21	$= .94$, the reliability of the
Flo	18	17	80 item test

*This is too small a group on which to do this analysis, but it serves for the purpose of illustration.

Now if you see in a test manual that the publisher used the Spearman-Brown approach to reliability, you will recognize it as a split-half procedure with the reliability extended to the full length of the test.

What does split-half reliability tell us? It indicates the extent to which scores based on one sample of behavior from a given domain (as assessed by the test) correlate with scores on a second sample of behavior for the same group of people. This is essentially what the other reliability coefficients indicate. If there is a considerable consistency between scores on one-half of a test and scores based on a second half, some test users say the test is "internally consistent," that is, one-half of the test is measuring like the other half. If such agreement does occur, as shown by a relatively large correlation coefficient, we can have considerable confidence in the reliability of the total test.

Internal Consistency Procedures

We have just seen that a test can be divided into two groups of items and that these two parts can be taken as separate measures of a common behavior domain. Each is scored, the score sets are correlated, and the Spearman-Brown formula is used to boost the correlation up to what will be expected for the original full-length test. This coefficient indicates the extent to which one part of the test is consistent with another.

Now suppose that instead of dividing the test into two parts, you divide it into four and think of each part as a separate form of the test. If the items belonging to each fourth of the test were selected on the basis of a random (or similarly unbiased) method, you may expect the parts to be separate tests of a common skill and their scores to correlate well. Of course, since the tests will be much shorter than the original test, the parts will be less accurate than the total test.

Now go to the extreme in dividing your test into subtests and treat each item as a separate measure of the common domain. Just as a correspondence is expected between odd-item scores and even-item scores in split-half reliability procedures, so do testmakers expect a correspondence among scores from item to item, provided all items assess the same behavior domain.

Psychometricians call this correspondence among items internal consistency reliability. Internal consistency, like other reliability techniques, provides a reliability coefficient. If all item scores correspond well with each other, internal consistency coefficients will be larger than .80, probably in the .85 to .90 range. If the item scores do not correspond well with each other, indicators of internal consistency will approach zero, maybe in the range of .20 to .40. Many internal consistency reliabilities will range between .40 and .85. As with other forms of reliability, a value of .80 or higher is desirable, but as with other forms of reliability, some use can be made of tests with reliabilities below the desired value if educators can tolerate small errors in placement of children for every group that takes the test.

Where do these coefficients of internal consistency come from? Several procedures for computing a coefficient of internal consistency have been developed by Kuder and Richardson (1937). Two of these procedures are most widely used: **Formulas KR 20 and KR 21.** KR 20 is the most commonly used because its assumptions are most likely to fit data we find in real testing situations.

A third, quite generalized procedure for computing internal consistency was developed by Cronbach (1951). It is known as **alpha,** which under certain assumptions can be shown to be equal to both the split-half and Kuder-Richardson procedures.

The actual computation of internal consistency coefficients, though not complex, is not within the scope of this book. However, as test consumers we will inevitably see internal consistency procedures cited in test manuals and in the periodical literature and may use them in making decisions about what a test will really do for us. To this end understanding them is important.

✎ Problems

1. Below are data taken from one version of a popular achievement test (junior high level). Note the reliability of the subtests in a skill area and compare these with the total of the skill area. What does this say about reliability of longer tests?

	Variable*	Reliability coefficient
1.	Reading Vocabulary	.90
2.	Reading Comprehension	.92
	TOTAL READING	.95
3.	Arithmetic Reasoning	.84
4.	Arithmetic Fundamentals	.93
	TOTAL ARITHMETIC	.94
5.	Mechanics of English	.92
6.	Spelling	.83
	TOTAL LANGUAGE	.93

*Number of cases equals 200.

2. Remember that internal consistency procedures produce a coefficient that is often interpreted as indicating the extent to which the test items are assessing a common trait. For the tests listed below, the manuals say that the KR 20 procedure was used to find the reliability. Is this the procedure you would have used? Why or why not?

> Arithmetic Reasoning   Spelling
> General Science Test   Test Anxiety Scale

3. Look again at the tests listed above. Each of their reliabilities was calculated using the Spearman–Brown formula. Suppose teachers consult the scores from these tests after a year's time. What reliability procedure would you like to see reported instead of S-B? (If the answer to this question is not evident, see the next section below.)

Making Use of Reliability Data

We have just discussed four techniques for determining the reliability of a test: test–retest, alternate forms, split–half, and internal consistency. The use of one or the other of these techniques is not an arbitrary matter. The four procedures speak to different aspects of the idea of reliability and tell the user slightly different stories about what the test can be expected to do.

Test-Retest Reliability

When we have only one test, split–half or test–retest procedures are two appropriate ways to assess its reliability. However, if we are interested in referring to a single student score over time, we must use the test–retest procedure. It will give us an indicator of **stability.** That is, it will tell us how well scores based on an administration of the test today correlate with scores we get from the test administered at some specified date in the future. This tells us how consistent scores are over a time period. We cannot tell, however, how much of the correlation is due to consistency of the test or to skillful recall of test content on the part of the student.

Consider this a real example of test–retest application. Suppose that Windfield Elementary School has academic aptitude tests on file for its students. This test is given in the third- and again in the sixth-grade. The third-grade score must be used by counselors and teachers for three years. To refer to that third-grade score over a period of several years, school professionals must have some confidence that the status of a boy tested in the fourth- or fifth-grade would be about the same as it was in the third-grade. The quality of the test providing that confidence is stability. People who are on the school testing committee, or those who will look at the child's record each year and use the score for placement of a child in a program, must be knowledgeable of the test–retest reliability. It will be reported in the manual of any reputable test publisher.

Alternate Forms Reliability

If you have more than one form of a test the alternate forms procedure is appropriate. With alternate forms we have two tests that call for behavior samples from the same skill area, even though the test items on one form are different from those on the other. Educators prefer alternate forms because we want children to perform a designated skill in any situation calling for that skill, and with alternate forms we have two samples of tasks that represent the skill area instead of one.

However, we want to be sure that one set of behavior samples correlates with the other before we can make a statement about how well one sample is equivalent to the other. This type of reliability is called a **coefficient of equivalence.** If this coefficient is high, say .80 or higher, we have some confidence that students will be ranked similarly by Form A and Form B. If so, we have an advantage over the one test, test-retest method because we know that the practice effect of having taken the test once has been a minor factor in the scores of the second testing. A score on either form then can be expected to provide a fairly accurate placement for a child.

With two forms of a test we can impose a time period between Form A and Form B. When the two forms are correlated over this time period we have a **coefficient of stable equivalence,** which is an indicator of both stability and equivalence.

Consider this application of alternate forms in assessing gains in student achievement over a period of time. Imagine that my school has an experimental program for teaching reading comprehension. I plan to give a test to see how much the children's reading comprehension skills have changed over the year. I give Form A at the beginning of the year and the alternate Form B at the end. Then I compare the average beginning score for my students with their average end-of-the year scores to see if the students in the experimental program have made more gains than expected. The test data must be stable over the time periods, and the two forms must be equivalent in order to compare data across the two tests. The design for this application is laid out in Figure 4.4.

There is no reason to believe that every test that shows a substantial coefficient of equivalence will also show good stability over larger segments of time. Therefore, tests that show only equivalence data should be used to assist in making only short-term decisions, for example, "What is the child's status in reading comprehension at present?" However, tests that show stable equivalence may be useful for both short- and long-term decisions and consequently have more versatility than tests that show only equivalence. Test manuals should discuss short- and long-term use if in fact the publisher has developed the appropriate data.

Using Internal Consistency. When do testmakers use an internal consistency approach to reliability? If all the items in a test are presumed to assess a common, unitary trait, number skill for example, internal consistency procedures may be useful indi-

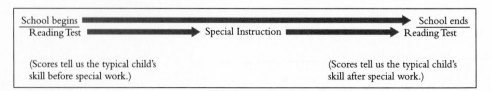

FIGURE 4.4

cators of reliability. Internal consistency reliability for a test that claims to measure verbal skill might be determined by use of the Kuder–Richardson formula 20 discussed earlier. If the KR 20 coefficient is high, testmakers believe all the items in the scale assess a common trait, in this instance number skill.

However, sometimes the total score is found by summing across several independent factors, for example spatial ability, number skill, and verbal aptitude. In this case items on the test are not aimed at a common behavioral trait. Internal consistency coefficients for the entire test are likely to be modest, say .50 or so. But if our test items all assess a single, common trait like number ability, then the internal consistency coefficient could be higher, perhaps .80. Due to this fact, internal consistency reliabilities if high may indicate that a test assesses a single trait.

Internal consistency methods are often used with the subscales in a vocational interest inventory where scores from these subscales may represent specific job interests. When aptitude tests are broken into subscales, in which each subscale is believed to assess a single trait like numerical reasoning or verbal comprehension, internal consistency reliabilities are often used with each subscale. If in each of these test types internal consistency reliability is high for a subscale, then the subscale is assumed to assess a single mental function. Internal consistency may be seen as less appropriate for achievement tests where subtests may involve not only a given subject matter, but also reasoning, verbal, and other skills.

Some Applications of Reliability Data

Let's take a look at some additional examples of the application of different types of reliability. Ms. Base, a Chemistry teacher, is about to start the New Universe Science Program. The literature that is sent out with the program states that students need at least a minimal knowledge of four science principles before the program is instituted. In the fall, before any instruction takes place, Ms. Base administers to the class the tests of the four principles. The purpose of this testing is to find out if the students have the skill level to begin the program.

Ms. Base has one class at 10 A.M. and one at 1 P.M. and does not want the morning students discussing the test problems with the afternoon students. To avoid this she uses alternate forms—Form A in the morning, Form B in the afternoon. In this case, we look in the test manual for a coefficient of equivalence for alternate forms given to a group of students with a very short time interval between testings. We find that the manual for the New Universe Science Program states that: "Form A and Form B correlate at .87 in a sample of 265 high school students who took the two forms one week apart."

This coefficient of equivalence looks pretty good. Ms. Base therefore decides to administer Form A in the morning and Form B in the afternoon with confidence that a student's score on one form of the test would be similar to the score achieved if the other form had been taken.

Another application of reliability is found in the school counselor's use of an aptitude test. In advising students about classes the counselor may use the intelligence quotient (IQ) or general aptitude score on the students' record cards. (General aptitude is discussed in Chapter 15.) Because these indicators of learning aptitude must remain stable over several years, the counselor will want a test that uses a stability approach to reliability. She will look for test–retest data with a long period (a year or more?) between

TABLE 4.2   An Overview of What Reliability Procedures Tell Us

Procedure	What it tells us
Split-Half	Equivalency of scores on half-tests; indicates present status
Test-retest	Equivalency over short time period, stability over long period
Alternate forms	Equivalency over short time period, stable equivalence over long period
Internal consistency	Extent to which all items assess a common trait

tests, or an alternate forms reliability administered by the testmaker with a long interval between testings.

Yet another application has to do with internal consistency. Internal consistency coefficients (such as KR 20 or alpha) reveal the extent to which the items in a test assess a common trait. If you and I wish to be sure that the test reflects a "pure" trait and not a collection of traits, then internal consistency coefficients are useful.

For example, in selecting students for my advanced mathematics class I want to assess the students' aptitude in numerical skills and in reasoning ability. One test should center on management of numerical relationships, the second on abstract reasoning. Because tests of this kind intend to assess only a single, unitary trait of the test taker each of the tests I use should show high internal consistency. If I find a KR 20 coefficient for the number test, and another for the reasoning test, I can judge the homogeneity of content for each test. The higher the reliability coefficient, the more homogeneous the content is expected to be.

After locating the tests in a publisher's catalog I find the KR 20 for the number test is .88 and the KR 20 for the reasoning test .64. Clearly, the number test has good internal consistency. The reasoning test scores would be better than a guess as to how students rank on this trait, but has too much inconsistency to suit me. If a school is planning to buy tests of this type teachers should check the test catalog or manual for indices of internal consistency.

In sum, noting the different kinds of information provided by different reliability procedures, test-users should, in evaluating a test, keep in mind the use to which the test will be put. (See Table 4.2 for an overview of these procedures.) If present status of a behavioral characteristic is being assessed, look for coefficients of equivalence. If a single test score is to be referred to, representing a person's status on a given variable at successive points over time, look for a coefficient of stability or stable equivalence. And finally, if an educator is dealing with a unitary trait, all items in the test should assess that trait, and if so internal consistency results are what we should look for.

✎ Problems

1. My fourth-grade colleague and I have made a 50-item test of one-digit multiplication, but we have only one form of the test. We have now asked the testing office in our district to find the test's reliability. Describe three methods we might legiti-

mately use to determine the test's reliability. What characteristic of reliability (stability, etc.) would each method reveal?

2. I have a general aptitude test which I will administer in grade three. I will not give another until grade six, so the grade three score will also be used in grades four and five. The test manual reports split-half reliability coefficients. Is this satisfactory? Explain.

3. The manual for a test of clerical aptitude says that "the internal consistency estimate of reliability was .78." How was the reliability determined? What does such a reliability coefficient tell the user?

4. A general achievement test indicates how well children are doing in various academic skills at a given point in time. The manual for an achievement test given to children in our school states that reliability has been calculated by a split-half method. Is this appropriate for an achievement test? Explain.

Using Reliability Data in Schools

The decisions teachers make about children based on classroom assessment procedures are very important and therefore all of their assessment activities should be reliable. The more carefully teachers plan and prepare their own observational procedures, the more reliable these tools are expected to be. This applies to all kinds of educational assessment techniques.

Almost all schools use commercially produced and/or statewide achievement tests. All teachers will see achievement test data and will make judgments about their students based on the tests. As we've noted, our ability to make these judgments depends partially on the reliability of the test scores.

At the sixth month of the fourth-grade, Jimmy was placed (4.6) in arithmetic on a published achievement test. Can you and I depend on this placement? If the test has a substantial equivalence reliability coefficient we can have some confidence that successive measures would also place Jimmy near 4.6. However, unless the test's reliability is quite high, we cannot have confidence and the score, therefore, is of very little use in planning instruction for Jimmy. Teachers and their students will benefit from appropriate interpretations of these scores, and basic to these interpretations is the understanding of reliability.

Sources of Reliability Data for Commercial Tests

Where do we find evidence about the reliability of a given test? We have already cited the test manuals. Credible test publishers will provide full data in the manuals that accompany their tests. Responsible users of test results should always consult these manuals for information about reliability before the tests are purchased and certainly before any attempt is made to use the scores in decision making.

The section in the publisher's manual that covers reliability will probably have a table of correlation coefficients. It should also state how many children took the test to provide these data and what procedure—split-half, test-retest, etc.—was used to calculate the coefficients. As noted, the type of reliability that is appropriate for you depends on how you use the test data. The narrative below illustrates how one educator used data from the publisher's manual to match her application of the test.

Choosing a Test From Its Reliability Data

Ms. West, a department chair at Idlerun Junior High School, was puzzling over a test the school was using. She had no data on reliability so she called the publisher who agreed to send her the test manual by overnight express mail.

The next day the publisher's packet arrived. She ripped it open and scanned the Table of Contents for the manual and found the table reproduced below. "Hmm," she mused, "Look at these numbers! I didn't think it would be this easy!"

She pressed the manual flat on her desk and began to study the data. "Let's see now, I want to use two forms of the test, and our teachers will refer to the scores only once, so I need an indicator of equivalence. I guess that means alternate forms. Let's see, which of these table entries is the one I need?"

Look at the data. Which reliability is appropriate for Ms. West's use?

Procedure	Verbal	Non–Verbal	Total
Split-half (Spearman-Brown)	.88	.89	.92
Test-retest (one week) Form A	.89	.87	.90
Test-retest (one year) Form A	.75	.74	.76
Alternate Forms (two weeks) Form A, Form B	.82	.83	.88
Alternate Forms (one year) Form A, Form B	.72	.71	.76

If you chose alternate forms (administered within a two-week period) with Form A given first followed by form B you are correct.

In Chapter 2 you saw that reviews of tests, including reliability data, are given in a reference book called The Mental Measurements Yearbook. You may need several editions to find what you want to know because if a test was reviewed in one edition it is unlikely to appear in later editions until changes have been made in the test. The yearbook is often found in libraries in the school system's central office, in larger public libraries, and in college libraries. If your school does not have one, why not request a copy be made available?

How Large Should a Reliability Coefficient Be?

As Ms. West sat in her room looking over the list of reliability coefficients, she recalled that reliability coefficients can be any size from .00 to 1.00. She wondered how large a coefficient should be before a test is useful in making decisions about children. Here are some points that may help Ms. West and other teachers as they look at test manuals.

In Chapter 3 you saw a listing of correlation coefficients with descriptions of how large the relationship is at each ranking level. That set of descriptors is a good place to begin in interpreting reliability coefficients. The question now is, "How large should a test reliability coefficient be to be useful?" Is .55 good enough? Or .75? Must all tests have reliability coefficients above .90? No single answer can be given here. The appropriate size of the reliability coefficient depends on how much random error (or inaccuracy) you can tolerate in your measurement. The larger the reliability coefficient, the less error of measurement.

Test scores need not be as accurate in making some kinds of decisions as for others. When you apply tests to making decisions about groups of people, you can tolerate lower reliabilities because your errors, being random, should average themselves out over the scores of individuals who make up the group. That is, because errors are random a characteristic for one person will be underestimated while for another it will be overestimated. The group's average score for all test-takers will be a fair estimate of the status of the group for this characteristic. For this reason, if I am looking at group averages I can work with reliabilities as low as .60 to .65, although all users of assessments would prefer higher values even for decisions about groups.

However, when test-users are dealing with an individual they cannot average errors of measurement because an individual student has only one score. As a further complication, no one can tell if a given person's score is likely to be an underestimation or overestimation. Therefore, when applying test results to making decisions about an individual person, reliability coefficients of .80 or higher are desirable. Luckily, many published tests have reliabilities this high and higher, but educators should always check test manuals to be sure the tests they use have reliability coefficients in this vicinity.

Teachers can use test scores with reliabilities lower than .80, but in doing so they must recognize that with these scores the placement of a child will be open to greater and greater error as the reliability coefficient gets smaller. You must also note that just because a test is on the market does not mean that it has high reliability.

Reliability and Criterion Referenced Tests

In Chapter 1 you saw that for some tests teachers set a minimum passing score and pitch the test items at the difficulty level required for minimal acceptable performance. This application is called **criterion referenced testing,** in which the focus is on the pass or fail status of each child. For example, suppose in the local arithmetic program teachers agree that all children must pass the 100 basic multiplication facts (such as $2 \times 4 = 8$, $6 \times 3 = 18$) with 90 percent accuracy in order to move to multiplication of fractions. This is an application of the criterion referenced approach to assessing basic multiplication. The critical information is pass (90 percent or more) or fail (below 90 percent).

In criterion referenced tests, as for any test, users should look for reliability. As before, two scores are needed for each student. In this case however, the meaning of reliability is a little different. For criterion referenced tests reliability refers to the consistency of placing a child in either the pass or fail category. If a test is reliable, the two assessments of a child should put them into the same category (pass or fail) in both measurements. If a test does this for all or most of the class, it is quite reliable. But if quite a few of the children who passed on the first test fail on the second, and quite a few who failed on the first test pass on the second one, the test is inconsistent or unreliable. It simply does not provide a consistent placement for students.

Test manuals that report the consistency of criterion referenced tests use two statistics to convey the reliability—**Kappa** and **P_O** (called "p sub owe"). Both range up to 1.0 and typically take two testings to calculate. They are often referred to as **indices of consistency of classification.** Kappa and P_O are not equivalent statistics. In P_O statisticians do not take into account a student's getting into a pass or fail category by chance, whereas in Kappa they do consider chance. Hence Kappa is typically somewhat lower than P_O. Calculation of these statistics is beyond the scope of this book. However, when you read about criterion referenced tests you will see these figures reported in test manuals or in journals, and you will know that they refer to the consistency of classification of students in criterion referenced tests.

For local use a simplified estimate of the index of consistency of classification for criterion referenced tests can be used. It involves two applications of the test. First, count the number of students who passed the criterion on both applications (passers). Next, count the number who failed to reach the criterion on both applications (failers). Now add these two numbers (passers + failers) and divide by the total number of children who took both tests. In shorthand the procedure looks like this"

$$\text{Index of Consistency} = \frac{\text{Passers} + \text{Failers}}{\text{Total taking both tests}}$$

Here is an example of its computation. If you gave two forms of the same criterion referenced test and 17 of your 35 students passed it on both administrations and 12 failed it on both administrations, the calculation of the index would be:

$$\text{Consistency} = \frac{17 + 12}{35} = .83$$

This value indicates a fairly high level of consistency of classification.

Factors That Affect Reliability

There are several factors that should be managed by teachers because they affect test reliability. In most cases test-users can at least control a part of the influence of these factors. Because the conditions involved apply to both the tests you create as a teacher, as well as to commercially published tests, you should attend to them with some care. Here are some important factors to note:

▼

Factors That Affect Test Reliability

1. Length of test.
2. Pressure of time limit.
3. Heterogeneity of the group taking the test.
4. Level of difficulty of the tasks required by the test.

▲

Let's look at each of these factors in detail.

Test Length and Reliability

We have already seen that length of the test influences reliability. The Spearman-Brown procedure utilizes this idea. As tests get longer they tend to become more reliable. We assume, of course, that the test is increased in length by adding good items that sample the same behavior domain as the original test items. Relatively short tests tend to be less reliable, often because they do not take enough samples of the required behavior to adequately represent a person's performance in the area. (Please look back at the content sampling procedures in Chapter 3. These procedures should give you an adequate sample of the content, and can also show you how long your test is likely to be if it covers the content of your instruction.)

Adding to a test's length does have diminishing returns, and each additional set of new items adds less to reliability than did the previous addition. A test twice as long as the original probably will increase reliability, but it will not double it or even come close to doubling it. Nevertheless, longer tests are expected to be more reliable than shorter ones. This conclusion about reliability and length of tests generalizes to all types of classroom assessment. Observations are more reliable if the teacher involves more "data points" in the check list, and essays are more reliably evaluated if more features that reflect quality are listed on the guide for scoring. In classroom assessment it's best to make your tests and other assessment devices "long."

Pressure of Time Limits and Reliability

Another variable that we must consider in assessing the reliability of a test is the extent to which the time limit of the test puts pressure on students in their effort to complete the test. This feature is sometimes referred to as **speededness** of the test. Do all students have sufficient time to try every item on the test, or is the time limit so short that many students have difficulty getting it all done? Tests that are highly speeded, that is, tests with working time limits so short that only a few people finish, tend to produce higher reliability coefficients than do the same tests given under generous timing conditions, and here is a reason why.

Many tests have short time limits, and to the extent that rate of work is a factor in getting through the items, scores will partly reflect rate of work and partly the skill being assessed. Rate of work is very consistent behavior, so to the extent that scores depend on rate of work, reliability coefficients will be inflated by the speed factor.

You may wish to use this information in situations like the following. You buy an arithmetic computation test, and in the manual you read that the 50-item test has a limit of 10 minutes of working time. This you decide is a rather short period in which to complete the 50 items. In fact you judge that only a very few exceptional students could even approach finishing the test in the allotted time. Students who integrate speed and accuracy have the best chance of getting a good score. Students who may have the knowledge and skill to get a good score but do not work at a high rate of speed, will not have a chance to try all problems and hence will not have a high score.

You continue reading the test manual and find that the reliability coefficient, calculated with a split-half and Spearman-Brown procedure, is .86. At first glance this appears to be an adequate level of reliability. However, when you consider the possibility that the coefficient is spuriously high because of the speed factor, you are not so confident that the reliability, in terms of a test of arithmetic ability alone is as appropriate as it originally seemed.

The fact that a test is timed does not mean it is a speed test. If the time limit is such that the great majority of test-takers (say 90 percent) can attempt all items, then speed is not an important factor. Speed is a feature for serious consideration only when the working time is so short that only a few rapid workers get the chance to attempt all of the items.

The conclusion about the effect of speed on reliability is that when looking over a test manual—or at tests you have made yourself—it is important to note whether or not the test was administered under speed conditions. Many tests reported in test review books and other sources have been administered under speed conditions, and therefore their reliability coefficients must be suspect.

Heterogeneity of the Group and Reliability

Another factor that affects the size of the reliability coefficient is the heterogeneity of skill in the group of students who take an the examination. The more heterogeneous in skill the group is, the wider will be the range of scores. Generally speaking the larger the spread of scores for a given test, the higher the reliability coefficient will be.

Intuitively you can see how this works. If scores are bunched up, a difference of only a few points between test and retest will significantly change a person's position in the score distribution. But if you can spread scores out farther, a small change in a student's score from test to retest will mean very little change in position among other test-takers along the score continuum. This is shown in Figure 4.5. Here in each distribution there is a person who, beginning at the lowest score, moves up two points. The effect of this two-point positive error is illustrated by position within the group. The change in status in distribution A is modest where the distribution of scores is wider. However, the change in position of a score two points above the lowest score moves the

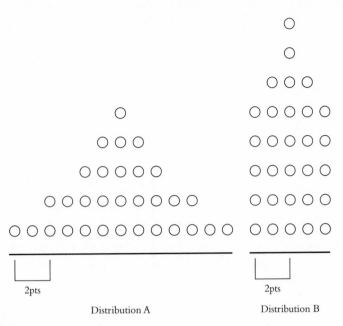

2pts

2pts

Distribution A

Distribution B

FIGURE 4.5

student in distribution B from lowest to average. In this case a two-point error makes a great difference for that person in the overall rankings of scores. Again, when you read the manual for a test note the heterogeneity of the group on which the reliability coefficient was computed. If it is based on a very wide range of scores, you can expect it to be higher than if it is based on a narrower range.

This brings up another point that should be noted by test-users; they must think about the homogeneity of the students with whom they will use the test. Will you use it to classify children within a rather narrow ability range? If so, the test's reliability for this group (having a small range of scores) may in fact be much lower than across the wide range reported in the test manual.

For example, suppose an achievement test reports the reliability coefficient across grades three, four, five, and six as .94. This looks very impressive. However, Mr. Drury is a fourth-grade teacher who is using the test's data in his class. The range of ability across grade four will be much less than it will be across grades three, four, five and six. Therefore, he should expect the reliability for the fourth-grade data to be lower than it would be across the range of several grade levels. This should make all of us a bit more cautious in using test data for placing children in a single grade using reliability calculated across several grades.

Level of Difficulty and Reliability

Another factor that affects reliability is the difficulty of the test items for the group who took the test. Difficult tests tend to produce narrower ranges of scores and skewed distribution with scores piling up in the lower ranges. Easy tests also tend to produce narrower distributions, with scores piling up near the top of the score range. We previously noted that a narrow spread of scores is related to lower reliability. Therefore, tests that are too hard or too easy tend to reduce the range of scores and hence reduce reliability.

In sum, length of the test, speededness, spread of scores, and test difficulty affect reliability of all tests. When making their own tests and other assessment procedures and in reading test manuals, teachers should note these factors and try to avoid these conditions that affect the size of the reliability coefficient. Generally, if you avoid short tests, give students time to try all (or nearly all) of the problems, and include a range of difficulty that will spread out the scores students achieve, you can expect better reliabilities for your tests.

✎ Problems

1. Mr. Jefferson, who teaches French, has a test on French verbs which was published by Bigtest Press. The content looks right but he has no further data on the test. Where can he look for information on the test's reliability and other characteristics?

2. Ms. McSorley has an arithmetic test for sixth-graders that is a good sample of the mathematics skills her students have worked on. The test-writer claims the test has a split-half reliability of .69. I want to find the class average for this set of skills. Is this test reliable enough to have confidence in the class average? Explain.

    I also want to know to which five students I should be giving extra opportunities. Can I have enough confidence in the scores of separate students to select these five students on the basis of the test scores? Explain.

3. The guidance counselor has a test of mechanical aptitude he would like to use in advising students who wish to take a mechanics program in high school. The test manual says it has a test-retest reliability of .91. However, the instructions say that students may have only 15 minutes to work the 50 problems on the test. What would you say about the reliability coefficient?

4. Ms. Bronte teaches fourth-grade students. She has made up a spelling test of 8 words to represent the 60 words the class has been studying this month. In what general range (low, medium, high) would you guess the reliability of Ms. Bronte's test is likely to be?

SUMMARY

1. Reliability refers to the consistency of an assessment. When two measurements of a given quality place the students in about the same order, the assessment is consistent, or reliable.

2. The degree of reliability varies from one test to another. Reliability is not an all-or-nothing quality of assessments, but is present in varying degrees.

3. The extent to which a test score for a student deviates from the student's "true" score is called measurement error. The most problematic errors are random errors. In assessing groups random errors average out, but when we are assessing a quality

of an individual we do not know what the impact of error is. Therefore, higher reliability coefficients are more desirable for tests used to assess individuals than for tests used in making decisions about groups.

4. In determining the reliability of scores from assessments, two scores from a common test are needed. These scores are correlated to determine the reliability coefficients for that assessment device. Correlation coefficients can range from −1.00 to +1.00, but for assessments we look for reliability coefficients above .80.

5. The test-retest method involves testing a group twice with the same test and correlating the two sets of scores.

6. In the alternate forms method testmakers obtain two scores by making two equivalent tests that both assess the same behavior domain. Alternate forms of a test are sometimes used to assess gains after a period of instruction.

7. Split-half procedures obtain two scores by sorting the items on a test into two subtests and correlating the scores from one subtest with scores from the other. The Spearman-Brown formula can be used to obtain a reliability coefficient for the entire test.

8. Internal consistency methods treat each item on a test as a separate measure and determine how well the scores from item to item correspond. Tests that assess a single, unitary trait should show high internal consistency.

9. When alternate forms of a test are taken close together and their scores correlated, the coefficient is referred to as a coefficient of equivalence. When there is a time lapse between the two assessments, the coefficient is referred to as a coefficient of stable equivalence.

10. Reliability data for commercial tests is found in the publisher's test manuals and in The Mental Measurements Yearbook.

11. Criterion referenced tests set a minimum passing score in order to divide test takers by "pass" or "fail" status. Their reliability is represented by indices of consistency of classification.

12. Factors that affect reliability include the length of the test, time pressure stemming from the speededness of the test, the heterogeneity of skill in the group taking the test, and the difficulty of the test.

PROBLEMS

1. I am writing a test of reading comprehension for my class of third-grade children. List four conditions of my test that will affect the reliability.

2. Millrite Publishers are creating a test to assess spelling ability of children in grades three, four, five, and six. They wish to have a test that assesses current spelling ability. (The test will not predict spelling in the future.) Describe three methods of finding the test's reliability.

3. Mrs. Pepper, a high school counselor, is looking over publishers literature on intelligence tests. The test scores will be in the student's file for teacher reference for three years before another test is given. In the manual for one of the tests it says "Spearman-Brown reliability based on 243 high school students was .88." What method

did the publisher use to get this figure? Is this approach to finding test reliability suitable for the use to which this test is to be put? Explain.

4. Mr. Quillen, who teaches third-graders, is building a test of the basic multiplication combinations. It will contain all 100 of the one-digit combinations. He believes if the children know these combinations they should be able to do them in eight minutes and that is his time limit for the test. How will this time restraint affect the reliability coefficient? Will it likely be low, medium, or high? Why?

KEY TERMS

reliability	KR 20
measurement error	alpha
random errors	stability
reliability coefficient	coefficient of equivalence
test-retest	coefficient of stable equivalence
alternate forms	kappa and P_O
split-half	speededness
internal consistency	index of consistency of classification

ADDITIONAL READING

American Psychological Association, American Educational Research Association and National Council on Measurement in Education. Standards for Educational and Psychological Testing. Washington, D. C. : APA, 1974. (Although there is a later edition of this book, the 1974 edition deals more directly with reliability.)

Anastasi, A. Psychological Testing, 6th ed. New York: Macmillan, 1988, Chapter 5.

Livingston, S. A. (1988). Reliability of test results. In J. P. Keeves (ed.) Educational Research Methodology and Measurement: An International Handbook. Oxford, United Kingdom: Pergamon Press, pp. 386–392.

Traub, R. E. (1991). NCME instructional module: Understanding reliability, Educational Measurement: Issues and Practices, 10 (1), 37–45.

CHAPTER 5

Errors of Measurement

How to Work with Them

Suppose I want to measure the length of a tabletop. I ask Gena, one of my seventh-grade students, to repeatedly measure the table with a 10-centimeter plastic ruler until she has 20 measurements. The first measurement is 200.1 centimeters, the second 199.3, the third 200.3, and so on. Gena's 20 measures of the length of the table (arranged in ascending order) are in the left column of the table below. In the right-hand column I recorded the number of times Gena's measurement rounded to each of these points.

Centimeters	Number of measures
204	1
203	1
202	4
201	9
200	4
199	0
198	1

Gena does not get the same result on each measurement because there is some inconsistency, or unreliability, in the measuring procedure. These variations are due to **errors of measurement.** This does not refer to mistakes in the typical sense—the measurement device may have pretty good validity, and Gena may be using it according to the best procedure, but for several reasons she did not come out with exactly the same number of centimeters every time she measured.

Now I will guess how much error is likely to be in any given measurement of the tabletop. I will begin at the point where the number of measurements are clustered in the middle of the above listing. I want to find the range within which most of the measurements are likely to be. If I include the measures from 200 through 202 centimeters it appears that this would include most of the measurements. Yes, there are measurements beyond these, but because I am interested in the most probable ones I selected the range within which the greatest number of measurements fell. Somewhere within the range of 200 through 202 centimeters is a good guess as to where the real (or "true") length of the table lies, and most of the measurements fell in the vicinity of that "true" length, though some imprecision is evident. This is due to errors of measurement.

Assessments of human behavior are like the measurement of the tabletop. They all have problems with these imprecisions we call error. Procedures of all kinds—observational plans, commercial achievement tests, personality and aptitude tests, and tests and other appraisal procedures that teachers make themselves—have problems with measurement error. As teachers you and I can best work around error if we understand where it comes from and how to manage it in the interpretation of assessment outcomes. That is the subject of this chapter.

What This Chapter Will Include.   In this chapter you will learn about:

1. The concept of measurement error
2. Basic test theory that will help in understanding the concept of error
3. Determining the most likely range of error in a test
4. Error and test reliability
5. Interpreting scores in the context of error—applying a "yardstick" to error

Errors of Measurement—The Basic Concept

The tabletop measurement data given above are like errors of measurement in education. These errors are sufficiently important that teachers should spend some time looking at them to see how they occur and how to deal with scores that contain error.

Here is an example. On a given test there are 50 items of which John gets 35 correct. If I could give John a second test that assesses the same arithmetic concepts (not the same questions, but from the same domain of mathematics) would John get 35 correct? Maybe, but probably not. I would guess his score would be close to the first one. But how close? At this point I cannot say, though knowing that all tests contain errors of measurement, I would bet the two scores would not be exactly the same. Why not? Errors of measurement are involved which make most assessments near, but just a bit (and sometimes quite a bit) off the mark.

Classical errors of measurement are evidenced in the difference between a student's actual (or "true") ability and the score received on a test of that ability. These errors exist in all kinds of assessment that educators use—both formal and informal.

Basic Test Theory

Chapter 4 noted that random errors of measurement lead to unreliability of test scores. The more random errors are present, the more they affect student scores, and the less likely we are of getting two scores on a student that are alike. If scores are infected with random error they cannot be expected to be consistent, i.e., reliable. Therefore, the nearer the reliability coefficient is to zero, the more the scores are made up of random errors of measurement. With this thought in mind, classical assessment theorists have conceptualized scores as having two components: one that is the **"true" score** portion, and one that is the error. Some part of any given score reflects the real amount of the trait the test-taker has, while the remainder of the score is made up of the inaccuracies of testing that psychometrists call random errors. This relationship can be written as follows:

Test score = ability (+ or −) error of measurement

In this formula errors are thought of as random; sometimes these add to a true score, sometimes they subtract from it. For any given student on any given test, you and I cannot predict which direction error will push the score. However, we believe that the chances are good that the score that identifies actual ability will be within a **score band** of a few points above and below the **obtained score** (the score actually found on the test paper) (Ferguson & Takane, 1989).

An example may help. My arithmetic test score was 23 correct out of 30 items. I admit it, I guessed at some items and got a few of these right. I may have made some foolish errors on other items in the test, too—misread the problem, reversed 23 for 32, or misinterpreted what the problem asked me to find. These tend to balance out my lucky guesses. So 23 may well be close to my ability. But, depending on the impact of my good guesses and my foolish errors, the score also could either under- or overestimate my arithmetic ability. There is no way of knowing.

Jeff, who sat next to me, felt depressed during the test. His motivation was very low. His score of 18 may have been an underestimate of his true ability—that is, errors of measurement could have made his score less than his real ability in arithmetic.

No matter which way errors move my obtained score chances are that the score on my paper, as well as the one on Jeff's, is most likely within a few points above or below the score that would show our real (true) abilities. Error could change anyone's scores quite a bit, but in well-managed assessments chances are good that it will not. Therefore, my math score, and Jeff's, may not reflect our true ability, but will not be far off it. The higher the test reliability, the more likely this statement is to be true.

Let's go back to the classical concept of scores for a moment. I have asserted that scores from any assessment—the aptitude test used by the school psychologist, the critical essay you wrote for your history class yesterday, the achievement tests just about everyone takes in grade school—contain some error. Controlling the sources of error in the construction and application of assessments will help test-users make more accurate decisions based on test results. However, teachers must always be wary of the fact that a part of the student's score is likely to be error of measurement.

Errors of Measurement and Test Reliability

The last chapter discussed the concept of reliability. You and I will now apply reliability to assessing measurement error. Reliability tells us about the consistency of measurement. If I do a test-retest procedure to determine reliability, a high reliability indicates that the students' scores on the first test look very much like their scores on the retest, that is, the test scores are consistent between the two testings. But if scores contain a lot of random error the first scores for individual students will not look like the scores on the retest, that is, the scores students make will not be consistent across the two tests. The test, therefore, is not very reliable.

The amount to which any assessment outcome contains random error of measurement is reflected in its reliability. If an assessment contains a lot of error, few scores on the first testing are expected to be similar to those on the second. In fact, it can be shown that reliability decreases to the extent that the error portion of test scores increases.

Here is an example. I have just given a test in earth science. If random error accounts for 5 percent of the score for students (on average) and true ability for 95 percent, the score I got on Form A of the test would probably be much like my score on Form B (as in alternate forms reliability.) The test would have pretty high reliability. However, if the random error portion of students' scores on the test was 65 percent and the true ability was 35 percent, my score on Form A will very likely not match my score on Form B, and the reliability would be much lower than in the previous example.

You can see how very important reliability is—it reflects the amount of error of measurement there is in a set of test scores or other assessment outcomes. Error makes it difficult to interpret scores for any given student because I do not know if that person's score is inflated by error or reduced by it. For example, suppose Perry has an academic aptitude score of 122 on the *Lorge-Thorndike* academic aptitude test. Perry's school has a cutoff of 125 for students moving into the accelerated curriculum. I know there is likely to be error in all tests, so I wonder—is it likely that the score of 122 is an underestimation of Perry's ability? If it is, he may have the ability for the accelerated program. However, from the score alone I cannot tell if I am underestimating, overestimating, or have hit the mark exactly.

An error in either direction can have unfortunate consequences, so educators want to make as little error as possible. How do we find out if scores on a test are apt to have a lot of error of measurement in them?

The answer to this question is found by looking at the reliability before I select a test. This is especially true for a test in which the stakes in the outcome are high, such as the student being put into a special class, having to take summer school to meet state standards on an achievement test, or meeting graduation requirements.

High reliability coefficients, say .80 or higher, mean that the scores marked on the test sheet are made up of large portions of the true score component, an indication that we are measuring quite accurately. However, the lower coefficients (i.e., .50 or lower) tell us that the scores on a test have a lot of error in them. The size of the reliability coefficient is our first clue to how much error there is in the test scores. We have less confidence in the accuracy of scores as reliability gets lower.

Ms. Waxworthy, a ninth-grade Science teacher, is looking at the results of the statewide test recently administered in her school. As she looks at her students' scores she wonders how she could use them in supplementing her grading data. She knows that if these scores have a large error component in them, they will not be usable as an aid to grading her class. How does Ms. Waxworthy find out how much error is in these scores? She looks for the reliability of the science tests. From the test manual she finds the reliability of the science subtest is .67, "Oh!" she ponders, "not a very reliable

TABLE 5.1

Range of scores*	Test reliabilities			
	.85	.75	.65	.45
50 points	4.8	6.3	7.4	9.3
40 points	3.9	5.0	5.9	7.4
30 points	2.0	3.8	4.4	5.6
20 points	1.0	2.5	2.9	3.7
10 points	.9	1.5	1.5	1.9

*The above data are based on 50 cases. The middle two-thirds of the group is expected to be clustered near the middle of the range and is found within the first and third fourths of the range of scores.

score—each child's score may have quite a bit of error. I'd better not put much reliance in these data for grading my class."

Students in Ms. Waxworthy's school who score low on the test may be asked to take summer session to avoid repeating a grade in school. She scans the statewide test score report looking for lower scoring students. She wonders which ones missed the cutoff for summer school because of random errors of measurement. "That reliability of .67 looks pretty important to interpreting this test," she thinks to herself. "I really wish it would be .85 instead of .67!"

Interpreting Error Ranges

How do we assess the amount of error in a set of scores on a test? Table 5.1 presents some figures that show the relationship of reliability and error for tests with different score ranges. In Table 5.1 "Range of Scores" means the difference between the highest and the lowest scores in a class. For example, if Jeraldine got 36 correct answers on her test, and this was the highest score in class, and Jo got 7 and this was the lowest, the range of scores would be 30 points.*

The numbers in the body of the table are score points above and below the actual score written on the student's paper. This is the range within which we expect the student's true ability score to fall.

Now look at the $+/-$ error ranges shown in the column under .85, the highest reliability in the table. Compare these with those in the column under the .45 heading, the lowest reliability in the table. The table shows that in all cases the lower the reliability, the greater the range within which the student's true score will likely be.

For example, a group of students in Central High School have just taken the Mathematics Achievers Test to be eligible for an accelerated mathematics program. The manual says that the test's split-half reliability is .85. The highest score was 54 items correct; the lowest was 25. The range of scores will then be (54 minus 25 plus 1) or 30 score

*The range from 7 to 36 is 30 points when we include the person with 7 points. (To verify this, count 7, 8, 9...36.)

points. Locate 30 on the third line of the table. I move across that line to the column headed by .85 (the test's reliability). The amount of error expected in the test is given there as 2.0 score points. We now have the amount of error expected in any student's score from that class. (Please note that unless your data fit the table data you have only an *estimate* of the error, albeit a useful one.)

Here are the steps to follow in finding the range within which the true score will fall.

1. Find the difference between the highest and lowest score for the class, plus one.
2. On the left-hand column of the table find the row (horizontal) that is nearest that difference.
3. Move across the row to find the column (vertical) on the table that comes closest to the test's reliability (from the test's manual.)
4. Where the row and column meet you will find the expected error in score points.
5. Add this amount to the student's score; and subtract this amount from the student's score. These two results will give you the range within which the student's true ability score is most likely to fall.

You and I will now apply this procedure to one person's score to see what it tells us. Amanda had a score of 48 correct on the same achievement test (range of 30 points; reliability of .85). The table says that this test will have an error of 2.9. The range within which Amanda's true score is likely to fall will be 48 (her score) minus 2.9 (the amount of error from the table) and 48 plus 2.9. Her true score on the test is most likely in the range of 45 to 51 (rounded to the nearest whole numbers.)

To grasp the impact of low reliability imagine the above test had a reliability of .45 instead of .85. For a total range of scores of 30 points the range within which Amanda's true score would fall would be 48 minus 5.6 (from the table) or 42 (rounded down), and 48 plus 5.6 or 54 (rounded up). You can expect that her true ability score lies between 42 and 54. The range of error within which Amanda's true score is expected to fall is somewhat larger in this case, where the test reliability was .45, than it was in the previous example where the reliability was .85.

If the reliability of the test is .45, looking at Amanda's score on her paper will hardly tell me what she can do in the subject matter of the test. Between 42 and 55 is a large range of scores; any one of the scores in this range could represent her true ability. Since I am confident that her true score was not below 42 nor above 55,* the test gives me information that is better than a guess about her skill. However, it is very imprecise information and not particularly useful in selecting students for a special class. We educators need assessments with higher reliabilities to help us make important decisions.

What we conclude from all this is that the lower the test's reliability, the greater is the range within which we expect true scores to fall. If reliabilities are high (say .80 or higher) the amount of error of measurement will be a relatively small part of the score; but if the reliabilities are low (say .50 or lower) the amount of error becomes a relatively large part of the score.

---

*There is a small probability her score could be beyond the 42 to 55 range, but largest probability is that it is not.

All this discussion brings out a very important principle to remember. Are you going to use an assessment of any kind to make decisions about individual children? If so, accurate placement of the student is essential. The range within which the true ability of the student will fall is inversely related to reliability. As reliability goes down, the range within which the true score falls gets larger and the accuracy of the score written on the assessment paper decreases. This means the assessment will be less useful in making decisions about individual children.

A Yardstick for Interpreting Scores

Unless a substantial portion of an observed score (the score on the student's paper) is based on the true score component, I cannot be sure that the score on a student's paper does indeed identify that student's true ability with any accuracy. Therefore, when I select a test I look in test manuals for large reliability coefficients. As illustrated in Table 5.1, only tests with large reliability coefficients will provide scores fairly close to the student's real ability. (Please recall that for making decisions about group status, more random error can be tolerated. Why?)

The Standard Error of Measurement (SE_m).   To make the concept of error really useful I need a device that assesses the magnitude of error—a kind of yardstick of errors. With this yardstick I could lay out a band of scores above and below the student's obtained score on a test. Somewhere within this range the true score for the test-taker will most likely be found.

Here is how I get the yardstick for assessing the range within which the student's true ability lies. Errors are random, and I cannot even tell if errors have fortuitously increased or decreased a given person's test score. Test publishers, however, calculate a figure to help us with score interpretation. This figure is called the **standard error of measurement.** It is illustrated in Table 5.2 which shows an example of what can be found in the instructor's manual of an achievement test for elementary school children.

The standard error of measurement is the same figure you found in the body of Table 5.1 and it is used the same way. For children who took the science test, the SE_m in Table 5.2 is 2.9 score points for Form S. Their true ability probably lies between one standard error above and one standard error below the actual obtained score. For John whose obtained score on Science (Form S) was 30, his true score lies between 27 and 33. (If you consult a statistician you will be told that about two-thirds of the students in large groups will find their real (true) ability between these limits.) As a rule for test interpretation, you may think of a given student's skill to be in a range of one standard error below and one above the score written on the answer sheet.

Here is another example of how to use Table 5.2. It is very similar to what you did with the data in Table 5.1, but this time you will be using data from an actual test manual. Renee has a score of 34 on the Social Studies test, Form T. Table 5.2 tells us the standard error of measurement for Social Studies is 2.9. Now add 2.9 to Renee's score; and subtract 2.9 from her score. This gives her a band of scores from 31 to 37 (rounded). These figures come from Renee's score of 34 plus 2.9 and 34 minus 2.9,

TABLE 5.2 Kuder-Richardson Formula #21 Reliability Coefficient (r), Standard Errors of Measurement (SE$_m$), and Related Data for the Intermediate 2 Spring Standardization Sample (raw score data)

Grade 6

Intermediate 2	Form S					Form T				
Test/Cluster	Number of Items	Mean	S.D.	SE$_m$	r	Number of Items	Mean	S.D.	SE$_m$	r
Science	40	25.7	5.8	2.9	.75	40	26.9	6.8	2.8	.83
Life Science	15	9.5	2.8	1.8	.61	15	9.9	2.8	1.7	.61
Earth Science	12	7.7	2.4	1.6	.57	12	8.3	2.3	1.5	.56
Physical Science	13	7.8	2.4	1.7	.49	13	8.7	2.7	1.6	.64
Science Process Skills	31	19.8	5.3	2.5	.77	31	21.0	5.4	2.5	.79
Knowledge	4	2.2	1.1	.9	.28	4	2.8	1.0	.9	.15
Understanding	10	6.7	1.9	1.4	.42	10	6.3	2.1	1.4	.54
Thinking Skills	26	16.2	4.5	2.4	.73	26	17.7	4.6	2.2	.76
Research Skills	10	6.4	2.0	1.5	.47	10	6.8	2.0	1.4	.48
Social Studies	40	25.0	6.6	2.9	.80	40	25.4	7.0	2.9	.83
Geography	8	4.3	1.8	1.3	.43	8	4.8	1.7	1.3	.36
History	8	4.4	1.6	1.4	2.9	8	4.5	1.7	1.3	.36
Political Science	9	5.5	2.1	1.4	.56	9	5.8	1.9	1.4	.46
Economics	8	5.6	1.8	1.2	.57	8	5.8	1.7	1.2	.53
Culture	7	4.6	1.6	1.2	.44	7	4.5	1.7	1.2	.50
Knowledge	5	3.5	1.2	1.0	.40	5	3.1	1.1	1.1	.10
Understanding	13	6.6	2.4	1.7	.48	13	9.0	2.7	1.5	.67
Thinking Skills	22	14.3	4.2	2.1	.76	22	13.4	4.0	2.2	.70
Research Skills	11	6.8	2.2	1.5	.50	11	7.5	2.2	1.5	.58

rounded to whole numbers. That seems like a fairly narrow range. If it is, the relatively high reliability (.83) accounts for this level of precision.

Here is a situation in which you must make a decision. The Science (Form T) test in Table 5.2 has a standard error of 2.9. Carlton has a score of 25. You can think of his true score as being somewhere in a range of 22 to 28. You are putting students into the accelerated science group based partly on their science test scores. Your cutoff is 27. Does Carlton, whose observed score is 25, qualify for the accelerated group? He may; the band within which his true score lies includes the cutoff score of 27, but certainly you would want information outside the test to support this conclusion.

Here is an example based on a different test and showing a different application of the standard error. Joel has a reading comprehension score of 42, while Maria has a 45. It looks like Maria is the better comprehender, but for verification let's apply the standard error and compare the range of scores. The standard error for this test is 2.4. For Joel, plus and minus one standard error would give him a score range of 40 to 44; for Maria the range would be 43 to 47. These score ranges are illustrated below.

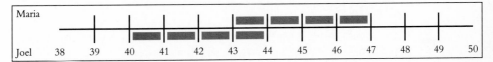

There is a definite overlap of the areas within which you and I expect the true comprehension scores to fall. Joel's true score could be as high as 44, while Maria's could be as low as 43. Based on these findings it is difficult to come to a confident conclusion of how the two students rank on reading comprehension, even if Maria had the highest score on her paper. If errors of measurement have subtracted from Joel's score, he could actually be a better comprehender than is indicated by his obtained score of 42. On the other hand, if we have overestimated Maria's score due to measurement errors, her true score could actually be equal to (or below) Joel's.

Standard errors help test-users avoid making definite conclusions that are not entirely accurate. If I had said with confidence that Maria was a better comprehender than Joel, I could have been right. I may also have been entirely wrong.

The conclusion about Joel and Maria is probably true, that is, Joel and Maria could be equal at reading comprehension. However, there is always a small chance that our test had more error than plus and minus one standard error of measurement. In arriving at our conclusion you and I have gone with the greatest odds, which say the range of error is plus and minus one standard error of measurement. This range includes, as noted above, 68 percent, or roughly two-thirds, of the students. This leaves about one-third of the cases to fall outside this range. So even though you use one standard error of measurement because it cuts off the range in which student's true scores are most likely to be, a very few students' true scores will fall even farther outside the range we have identified.

In evaluating test results I must account for the fact that a score on an answer sheet may well be affected by error of measurement. Most published tests will provide the standard error of measurement which I add to, and subtract from, the obtained score on the test paper. The odds are that the student's true score is within this range of scores cutoff by the results of plus and minus one standard error. I should use this idea of a range of scores in interpreting any score I see on a test.

Here are the steps for applying the standard error to help us interpret scores.

▼

Applying the Standard Error of Measurement

1. In the test manual (or the technical manual) find the table that lists the standard error of measurement. (It is usually in or near the report on reliability.)
2. Write down the values of the standard error of measurement for each test with which you are working.
3. Add the value to and subtract it from the score on the test paper. This will give you the score range within which the student's true ability is most likely to fall.

▲

The Standard Error and Non-test Assessment Data.   For the most part we have discussed using the standard error with test data. However, the concept of standard error is also applicable to all educational assessments. The conclusion about the adequacy of any product produced by any child is subject to error, and the child's true performance level is likely to fall somewhere in a range near the level assigned by the teacher. This applies to essays, to proficiency in group work, to portfolios, and to trumpet solos in a music contest. The standard error, in varying amounts, is always present in all types of assessments and all educators should be aware of the possibility of imprecision in our judgments.

✎ Problems

1. You are on a committee to find a reading readiness test for grouping first-graders who will start in the fall term. You write to several test publishers and get specimen (sample) sets of their tests. In the manual for the first test you find a table that says the reliability of the test is .88 and the standard error is 3.4. What does this tell you about a given child's score?
2. Marta has a score of 56 on the reading readiness test in Problem 1 and Luis has 52. Can you say with certainty that Marta is more ready than Luis for beginning reading? Explain.
3. The committee decides to set the score for the group of children who will get the most accelerated instruction in reading at 60, which is 10 points higher than average for a trial of 124 children reported in the test manual. Clark has a score of 56. Should we admit Clark to the accelerated group or not? (Look at his true score range, then decide.)

Sources of Errors of Measurement

Errors are those random influences that tend to make performance a bit inconsistent, or unreliable. They may impact performance considerably today but hardly at all tomorrow. Where do errors come from? The sources that are most suspect are:

Sources of Measurement Error

1. The test-taker
2. The test itself
3. The test administration
4. Scoring

Let's look at each of these source more closely.

Errors Due to the Test-taker

Everyone has fluctuations in mood, motivation, and vitality that influence alertness and intensity in performance tasks. When taking an exam students are sometimes distracted by what is happening in their personal lives and this can reduce or increase their ability to work at their optimum. One's physical condition—feeling rested or tired, ill or especially well—affects ability and motivation. Chance events such as just before class having looked at notes that revealed something crucial, or having just solved the right (or wrong) example in the assignment, having guessed above (or below) chance level, or having seen another student's right (or wrong) answer all influence scores in ways that do not reflect our true ability. Each of these conditions helps create errors of measurement, either positively or negatively.

Errors Due to the Test Itself

On some tests there are items that are not clear and are sometimes interpreted incorrectly. Or there may be items in which the reading level is too difficult for some to manage with full comprehension or the testmaker may have otherwise not followed good test-writing practices. Occasionally, test-writers inadvertently provide clues to the correct answer and testwise students capitalize on this. All of these lead students to erratic behavior that fails to reveal their true abilities.

Test errors are also caused by test items that do not accurately sample the performances that characterize the trait we wish to assess. For example, if I have three topics in my history unit and my test samples knowledge of one topic and all but ignores the other two, the test gives an advantage to students who know the sampled topic but may have less knowledge of the total three-topic unit.

Errors Due to Test Administration

Beyond the test-taker and the test itself, the administration of the test can be a source of errors of measurement. Administrators may inadvertently convey inaccuracies in the instructions for taking the test, fail to give complete instructions, or give confusing signals. They may also give too much help, not enough help, or may provide intriguing hints that can distract (or focus) students. All of these events lead to measurement errors.

Also, environmental conditions can sometimes have an impact on students. Was the testing room relatively quiet? Were the lighting and air temperature appropriate? Was there enough work space? Though these factors do not affect each student equally, deviations from standard conditions will be a source of test error. However, there is some evidence that environmental conditions do not generally have as broad an affect on students as once supposed. For example, students who take a test with periodic noise outside the room do not seem to perform (as a group) any worse than those who take the test without the noise. This fact should not deter test administrators from attempting to control distractions; individual students may be sensitive to features of the environment that are ignored by others.

Errors Due to Scoring

There are many ways in which error can creep in during the scoring process. Some students make very light marks on answer sheets, which are not "seen" by optical mark readers in computerized scoring, or make poor erasures which the machine "sees" as double answers. Or perhaps the answer key is incorrect. In hand scoring teachers sometimes miss a right (or a wrong) answer. Readers, while assessing the comments of the essay writer, may be positively influenced by the beautiful penmanship or negatively influenced by a grammatical error (when the topic of the test is not grammar.) When assessing the contents of a portfolio it is very hard for the reader to maintain a common standard of performance from one child to another. All of these are examples of errors of measurement that can slip into assessment at the point of scoring.

As you can see, there are many ways error can appear in test scores. Educators can control a portion of these errors through careful planning and construction of materials and through professional test administration and scoring. However, not all error can be controlled. Therefore, test-users should be especially careful to think about the standard error of measurement when interpreting test scores.

It is important to recognize that this knowledge about errors does *not* allow us to look at Kate's score and say, "I think she is a much better student than she shows on this test, and I should be especially lenient in scoring her this time." You and I must accept the obtained score because of its relative "objectivity." Before we are swayed from the obtained score, there must be convincing evidence that errors have influenced Kate's score in one direction or the other. Without substantial evidence to the contrary, teachers should consider the obtained score to be valid.

The following narrative describes some teachers considering the standard error of measurement when dealing with a borderline case.

A REAL CASE NARRATIVE

Ms. Rojas and Ms. Beck, kindergarten teachers, had just joined Mr. Adams and Ms. Bales, first-grade teachers, to discuss the placement of last year's kindergartners into reading groups to begin the first-grade. At the outset there would be two groups in the first grade: beginning readers and a continued readiness group. The children had all taken the All Schools Reading Readiness Tests. Last year's class was placed on the basis of a minimum score of 45 (of a possible 100), and this seemed to work well. (Other data were also used.)

The pupils whose scores were clearly above or below 45 were first discussed and placed. Then those near the score of 45 were considered. As the teachers began discussing these children, Ms. Adkins, the curriculum supervisor, joined the group. Mariana, one of last year's kindergartners was the first to be discussed.

Ms. Beck, who had worked with Mariana last year, looked intently at the scores list. "I really think Mariana's score of 43 may be an underestimate for her," she began. "She has done some poor work in her alphabet, but she does seem to be getting the letter sounds quite well." She shuffled through some folders and brought out some of Mariana's well done work. "I think we should give her a chance to go into the reading group," she concluded.

Ms. Rojas furrowed her brow for a moment. "I think if we admit one child whose score is below the criterion, we have to admit them all. How do you decide if you start second guessing the test?" she asked. Mr. Adams concurred that once a criterion is set, selectively ignoring it isn't a good idea. Ms. Beck nodded positively.

At this point Ms. Adkins, who had been paging through the test manual, broke in. "I see that this test has a standard error of measurement of 3.2 points." She looked at four incredulous faces focused on her. "If this is so, Mariana's real, true ability here is in the range of, oh, about 42 to 48. That means that if her real ability is in the upper end of that range, she is in the reading group; if she is in the lower end, she isn't. Lets look at her portfolio to see which conclusion the stuff in there tends to support!" she concluded.

The teachers looked at each other around the table. "Uh, will you elaborate on that standard error a bit, Mary?" Ms. Beck inquired.

What is your reaction to the discussion by these teachers? Should they go with a strict criterion, or is it permissible to follow Ms. Adkins' suggestion? Why do you say that?

SUMMARY

1. Errors of measurement are random influences on performance that divert scores from being precise indicators of the designated characteristic we intend to assess.
2. Test-users should think of a score as having two parts: one is based on the student's actual ability, while the other is the result of errors of measurement.
3. The higher the reliability coefficient, the less error we have in our measurement. Error is indicated by a value called the standard error of measurement. The higher the reliability, the smaller the standard error of measurement.
4. The score on a student's paper (the obtained score) may not be an indicator of actual (true) ability. However, the actual ability score is probably within a range of one standard error above and one standard error below the obtained score.

5. The most prominent source of error in assessments are conditions internal to the test-taker, influences in the tests themselves, the procedure for administration of the test, and inaccuracies in scoring. If test-users are aware of these sources of error they may reduce the influence of error in making judgments about children.

6. All assessments are subject to error of measurement. Conclusions based on assessments of any kind (tests, observations, essays, etc.) should be tempered by the recognition of errors of measurement.

Problems

1. In your own words describe errors of measurement and the standard error of measurement.

2. Make a list of six common sources of measurement error, such as "feeling of depression while taking the test." Be sure to cover the four source categories and include positive as well as negative influences.

3. I am looking at the test manual for the Triquie Letter Test of Reading Comprehension. It says that for the Word Recognition subtest the split-half reliability is .78 and the standard error of measurement is 4.5 points. Kent's score on this test is 32; the cutoff score for regular class work at the fourth-grade level is 35. Within reasonable probability limits, could Kent's "true" score on this test be as high as 35? Explain.

4. Marcine has a score of 36 on the same Word Recognition subtest. Is Marcine clearly better at word recognition than Kent? Explain.

5. I have two tests in freshman algebra that were each taken by 250 students. (Assume that the range of scores from the lowest scoring student to the highest is the same for each group.) The split-half reliability for the first test is .54, and for the second one .87. The standard error of measurement for the first test is 6.7 score points. Do you suppose the standard error of measurement for the second test is larger than 6.7, smaller, or about the same? Explain.

Key Terms

"true" score   standard error of measurement
"true" score band   measurement error
obtained score

Additional Reading

Anastasi, A. *Psychological Testing,* 6th ed. New York: Macmillan Publishing Co., 1988, Chapter 5.

Doppelt, J. E. *How Accurate Is a Test Score?* Test Service Bulletin, No. 50. New York: The Psychological Corporation, 1956.

SECTION II

PROCEDURES THAT TEACHERS CREATE FOR ASSESSMENT

TAILORING THE TEST TO THE PURPOSE
WRITING OBJECTIVE TESTS: MULTIPLE CHOICE
WRITING OBJECTIVE TESTS: TRUE-FALSE; MATCHING; COMPLETION
ITEM ANALYSIS: FINDING THE TEST ITEMS THAT WORK
ESSAYS AND TERM REPORTS: HIGHER ORDER PROCESSES
DELIVERING CONVENTIONAL TESTS: PACKAGING, ADMINISTERING, DEBRIEFING
ASSESSING STUDENT PERFORMANCE
COMPUTER APPLICATIONS IN ASSESSMENT AND GRADING

Teachers spend a large portion of their time in assessment of one kind or another. Most of this time is spent on utilizing assessment procedures they have created themselves—tests, observational techniques, reading reports, and so on. Section II is about creating and applying these techniques.

In this book I propose that multiple approaches to assessment provide the basis for better judgments than does any single approach alone, and that some procedures are more appropriate for a given objective than are others. Therefore, this section begins by discussing the selection of an assessment procedure that fits the instructional objectives.

Next, the section looks at the techniques themselves. I begin with objective tests because students are likely to be more familiar with these than with some others. I then show you how to identify the good items among those you have written and used.

Many student performances are assessed by having students write about how to do something, or to show the reasoning behind an event, or otherwise replicate a mental process by writing it down. Therefore, the next chapter deals with essays, term projects, and similar procedures. Many important assessments can be made using writing as the vehicle, but scoring must be done by closely following guidelines.

Next, I discuss the assessment of performances. This is the longest chapter in the book because there are so many applications, and many directions in which performance assessment is being applied. Teachers have long used performance assessment, but only in recent times have the procedures become somewhat formalized. Following these procedures may well lead to the assessment of very important outcomes of education. Not only must students know about a number of things, but also must perform the skills associated with them. This means performance assessment. This means observing a child actually do the task, recording the observation so it becomes a transportable record, and comparing records as indicators of improvement in performance.

Lastly, there is a chapter on computer applications to assessment. It deals with classroom assessment, but also discusses the many standard applications in the administration of widely published tests, such as the Scholastic Aptitude Tests and the Graduate Record Examination. It also deals with creation of classroom tests, teacher test banks, keeping of classroom records, administration of classroom tests, and writing to parents. Therefore, I have placed this chapter here with classroom applications, knowing that the reader will recall it at the appropriate time in the next section.

CHAPTER 6

TAILORING THE TEST TO THE PURPOSE

M s. Erdstein, a fourth-grade teacher, is in the middle of teaching a unit on the continents. She has begun with the general configurations of the continents and their hemispheric locations. Early into this activity she gave students a half-hour project: sketch the outline of the continents. Looking over the resulting outline maps drawn by the children she thinks to herself, "These are really pretty inaccurate! I can't even recognize some of them."

The legends printed at the bottom of each map show 12 of the 21 students have listed Asia as located in the southern hemisphere, 3 have the equator crossing the Mediterranean Sea, and 7 have listed Australia in the northern hemisphere. She frowns as she reads her notes on the number of errors made by the children. "Wow! These kids really haven't done well here at all!" she ponders. "Good thing I did an assessment at this point in the unit. By the end of the unit they really would have been lost! I'll have to do some reteaching and quick."

Ms. Erdstein's assessment supports her instruction; she used it to catch problems while the teaching was in progress. This is an effective technique for all teaching and at all stages of topic development and levels of instruction. It advises teachers and their students about student progress and tells teachers and students how well they have accomplished the tasks listed in their objectives.

The performances called for by assessments are typically indicated by the objectives. Therefore, the first consideration in creating an assessment procedure is to think about objectives. Not until an instructor has an objective in mind can the behaviors that define the objective be devised. These behaviors may be called out by a test of some type or by a performance problem which I will observe, e.g., a five-minute speech, starting the car in driver's education, or writing a paragraph. Objectives come first, spelled out in behaviors teachers (and students) can see. Then the exercises that require the behaviors can be created.

What This Chapter Will Include. Within the steps of the cycle of objectives, instruction, and assessment teachers must make decisions: What experiences will best develop the behaviors cited by the objectives? What behaviors can be observed as evidence that the student is appropriately making progress? What behaviors will show that the student has reached the objective? In this chapter you will look at the decisions a teacher must make before implementing an assessment procedure. In this chapter you will learn about:

1. The purpose of various assessments
2. Using a table of specifications to select the content and cognitive level of assessments
3. Selecting an assessment procedure that best serves the teacher's purpose
4. Selecting a sample of content
5. How many data points a good assessment must include
6. Reviewing the assessment procedure for insinuation of social, racial, gender, or disadvantaged group commentary or bias

The Purpose of Assessment

A teacher's first consideration is the purpose of assessing student performance at a given point in instruction. Typically, the purpose is served by three types of assessment:

1. **Pretests:** Are students ready to begin an instructional experience?
2. **Formative assessment:** Once a class is into instruction, how are the students progressing?
3. **Summative assessment:** Now that they have come to the end of the unit, how well did the students reach the objective?

Each of the three types of assessment provides a type of information that supports instructional plans. Whether teachers are using a conventional approach to teacher-led instruction or are involving students in a constructivist exercise, information on their progress is necessary to good teaching. These three types of assessment are essential tools for collecting this information.

Pretesting

The usual purpose in this phase of assessment is to determine readiness for the next step in a program, or to group children according to skill levels before instruction. The content of a **pretest** is a carefully selected sample of the skills needed to progress to the next level. They are often criterion referenced tests, i.e., the items reflect criterion skills, the skills needed to begin the next activities, and difficulty is aimed at minimally acceptable performance.

Pretests are used to identify topics to be reviewed and remediated before the teacher decides to take a given direction in instruction. They are typically shorter and more focused on minimum skills than are many other types of tests.

Assessments at this beginning stage of instruction may be informal, such as a teacher's question and answer session with the class, or having each child read a paragraph privately with the teacher. Alternatively, assessments may be more formal, such as a paper and pencil test that focuses on skills essential to the next step in a course of study—for example a test of the 100 one-digit multiplication combinations before going into multiple digit combinations.

When the purpose is to see if children have acquired the skills necessary to take up another unit of instruction, pretesting is the vehicle to use. These assessments advise teachers about the status of students but typically have no role in the grading process.

Formative Assessment

Formative assessments are procedures carried out as the instruction progresses. Their purpose is to verify that students are keeping pace with the concept and skills presented by instruction. They are a kind of "How are we doing?" exercise. If I find students are making many errors, I step back and review the topics involved. But if I find they are making few errors, I forge ahead. Formative assessments of all kinds inform both teacher and student by providing periodic feedback. They indicate if the class, or an individual student has missed a point (or points) in the focal concept. They advise instructors how to pace teaching and learning activities and indicate where difficulties may be occurring.

Formative assessments, like pretesting, are typically short, focused exercises. They are aimed at skill development at a given point in a specific unit of instruction. Sometimes teachers call them quizzes. Short and focused are the qualities that typically characterize formative assessment.

Summative Assessment

Summative assessments are used to determine the success of a section of instruction. Final tests for a grading period, assessments at the end of a unit (tests, term reports, summaries of portfolios), and end of the year assessments are all typical sources of summative data. They rely on a broad sampling of the relevant content; they focus more generally on all the objectives of the unit of instruction; and they are often a major part of the data collected for grading.

Summative assessments are usually norm referenced, where students are ranked based on the number of objectives in which they show proficiency. But depending on the approach to teaching, they may well be criterion referenced. For example, to certify students as having a minimum set of skills at the end of a period of instruction, criterion referencing would clearly be the choice. Suppose I have a list of skills involving the ability to identify specific phyla in biology. I would like to certify that each student can perform these skills at a specified level. Here again criterion referencing may be the best option.

Matching Assessment and Purpose: Two Examples

Teaching is driven by objectives. Teachers want to do an efficient job of helping students reach the instructional objectives, and assessment is an aid in this effort. Teaching and assessment can be compared to everyday events, for instance, a family outing to a state park. The family begins with an objective: Arrive safely at the park and have a picnic. From the objective they formulate a plan of events to be completed. They must collect and load supplies into the car. Each family member must be prepared for the trip, remembering such things as a teddy bear, a jacket, or some antihistamine. Is everyone ready to depart (the pretest)? The inventory is complete; everyone is ready.

But the driver does not begin driving in a random direction because the family has an objective for the trip and the driver wants to guide the family to the objective as efficiently as possible. Periodically, the driver checks a map to see if they are on course, checks the time and gas gauge, and inquires about everyone's comfort (formative assessments). Due to conflict it is agreed that the two children will change seats (adaptation as based on formative assessment), and the family progresses on its course.

Eventually they arrive at the park, unload the lunch supplies and the ball and bat. They have the picnic and then sit down and discuss how well this trip to the park had gone (summative assessment). In this example, three different types of assessment were demonstrated: pretesting, formative, and summative assessment. Each has its own purpose, and requires its own procedures. Each aims at unique decisions.

The assessment points and procedures described above are similar to those in teaching. Mr. Gronski is teaching a unit in chemistry. He begins with an objective—he knows where he wants the class to go. He assesses to see if the class is prepared to begin the unit of instruction that will lead to the objective (pretest). As he progresses with the learning experiences he will again assess to see if the class is moving well in the direction of the objective (formative assessment). If there are impediments to the progress of his class, he adapts to them (review, remediation, a slightly different approach), but keeps his eye on the objective. When the unit is finished by all students in the class, Mr. Gronski takes an inventory to see how well the class members have done (summative assessment).

In the examples above the assessments used for pretest, formative, and summative purposes are different in intent and content. Before making an assessment teachers must identify which of the three purposes their assessment will serve. The nature of the assessment procedure and the questions that will be answered with its results are different depending on where the class is in the cycle of instruction. Being aware of the purpose of assessing at various junctures in the unit will point to the technique, and will help the teacher aim the assessment at the appropriate instructional questions.

Therefore, *before creating an assessment activity, think about its purpose;* purpose determines what performances will be called for by the assessment. Teachers must look carefully at which function they want the assessment procedure to perform. When they have settled on the function, they will create the assessment procedure accordingly. So, among the questions you ask before devising an assessment procedure, the first will be: What is the purpose of this assessment I am about to make: is it pretest, formative, or summative?

✎ Problems

1. An English composition teacher is doing a unit on short story writing. He is concerned because as students begin writing they ask too many questions about paragraphing. He stops the short story exercise and asks the students to write three paragraphs on the events of the day. He reads these for clues as to what the problems

are in paragraphing. Of the three purposes of assessment discussed, which type is this? Explain.

2. In your own subject specialty choose a unit of work such as linear equations, insects, the past tense in French. Within that unit, describe the objective and give an example of the content of a pretest, a formative assessment, and a summative assessment.

3. Mr. Olmen, a physics teacher, has just given a multiple-choice test on electricity. It covered a wide range of topics including measuring currents, resistance, creating circuits, and more. What purpose is this test most likely to be serving? Why?

Specifying Content and Cognitive Level

Now that I have determined the purpose of this assessment activity, I am ready to think about content. What topics and/or processes go into this exercise? This takes me back to the table of specifications, which will direct me to a given objective. It describes the topics and tasks of each step to the objective, including their components and cognitive levels (see Chapter 2).

Teachers can use tables such as this in the following manner. If you decide to use a pretest, you look at the specification to determine what minimum skills students should have at the beginning of the unit on which they are about to set out. This will be the content source for the pretest. For example, if I introduce multiplication as successive addition, students must first be able to do addition. A pretest confirms or denies this.

If the class is already into the unit of instruction, and students and teacher need feedback on their progress, take another look at the specifications. Here I find the skills the class should have mastered to this point. The assessment procedure which I select can efficiently sample these skills once I sort them from the rest of the unit's topics. The table of specifications can help me do this. The decisions I must make about what content to sample in my assessment and its cognitive level are based on the topics in the table of specifications. Table 6.1 is a simplified example of how this can work.

Table 6.1 is a list of specifications for preparing students to write their first program in BASIC language. For the sake of illustration it has listed only Foundational Content and Application levels as the cognitive functions involved. Now suppose you have been teaching students how to start writing a simple computer program. Your instruction has covered topics one through four of the table. You prepare a simple test on the last two topics (drawing a flowchart and the requirements of a program line). This is a formative assessment to see how students are progressing toward the goal, writing a simple program that works on the personal computer. It is a progress report for both you and your students.

As teaching and learning progress, you and your class find yourselves at the end of the unit, the grading term, or the year. How well have students acquired the skills, knowledge, application, and concepts outlined in the objectives for the unit? This kind of assessment is unlike pretesting or formative work because your assessment procedure

TABLE 6.1   A Short Table of Specifications on Skills Needed Before Writing a First Computer Program in BASIC Language

Topic	Foundational content	Application	Items
1. Selects drive	Distinguishes drives	Performs on PC	2
2. Variable/constant	Defines, contrasts	Applies in program	3
3. Draws flowchart	Describes function, types of enclosures	Draws simple chart	4
4. Program line	Describes requirement	Writes lines	4

5. Performs basic commands:
    a) PRINT
    b) END
    c) RUN
    d) SAVE
    e) LOAD
    f) LIST
    g) DELETE
	Cites function, spells correctly	Applies correctly in program	7

6. Deletes lines	Describes function	Uses in program	2
Items	**15**	**7**	**22**

will cover all of the objectives of the course, or a major segment of it, and you are concerned about comprehensiveness. Once again you are directed by the table of specifications; it should be your primary guide for developing summative assessment work.

Here are some questions about which decisions should be made in generating summative data.

1. Do all the test items or other observational acts match the objectives?
2. Is this assessment controlled by the table of specifications? Are all the topics listed in the table represented in the assessment in the proportions and at the concept level specified by the table? Does the number of items on each topic and the cognitive level of each topic correspond with that shown in the table?
3. How many items (observational points) are needed to cover each topic sufficiently to allow the teacher to make important decisions reliably?

In sum, when teachers develop an assessment procedure the table of specifications will be their primary guide. In constructing the observational procedure, the decisions you make determine the selection of test content or identify the foci of your observations. The table of specifications will help you make these decisions so that topics and cognitive levels are neither neglected nor overemphasized.

Selecting an Assessment Procedure

In tailoring a test to its function, teachers must determine what kind of assessment device they should use to accomplish their purpose. They have several assessment procedures from which to choose at whatever point they wish to record their students' achievement. There are several types of objective tests (see Chapter 7), a few applications of essay work (see Chapter 8), and several observational procedures available (see Chapter 10). These procedures are usually divided into two categories: supply-type and select-type, depending on what the procedure requires the student to do.

Now suppose you and I are deciding on what type of procedure we will apply in the assessment. Some guidelines could help us make the necessary decisions, so here are some points of view to guide us in this task.

Supply-type Procedures

In some assessment procedures a problem is posed to students and they supply (write out, orally report, build a model of, or draw a diagram of) their solution. This is also how short-answer tests and essay tests work. Additionally, supply is evident in observing students' performances when they are working on a problem with equipment, with tools, or in group processes. The student sets out with a problem and the teacher assesses the quality of the responses they supply.

Supply-type assessments are not significantly influenced by guessing, although students do sometimes bluff. Nevertheless, an amount of uncertainty on the part of the students goes into selecting portions of the performance they submit for their records. Many real life activities are like supply-type performances; people are faced with many problems for which they have to devise their own answers. I wish to get to the mall ten blocks away. I have two through streets to cross and I want to get there as quickly as I can and with the least amount of physical expenditure. How shall I proceed and why choose that route? This is a supply-type assessment of a real world experience.

Select-type Procedures

In select-type assessments teachers provide problems, questions, requests for information. A set of options is then provided, one of which is better than the others by a given criterion of truth, economy, or some such measure. The students will select the option they believe fits the criterion.

Objective tests work this way. In a multiple-choice test a problem is posed: At the Wallgreen Drug Store soap is 4 bars for $2.79; at the K-Mart it is 6 bars for $3.89. At which store is the price per bar of soap the lowest? a) Wallgreens, b) same at both stores, c) K-Mart. Or a test item requests information such as: Which of the following are mollusks? This is followed by a list of five animals. Select-type assessments are efficient in collecting information at the Foundational Content level and can also be written at higher levels of cognitive demand. In addition, they also can touch upon many information points in a short period of time.

All objective tests are select-type assessments. There are many situations in life that are like select procedures in which several courses of action are given and we must decide which one is "better" than the others. You and I routinely face these situations and must select one answer based on a particular criterion. You go to the grocery store to buy a loaf of wheat bread. You want the most for your money. There are four different loaves (A, B, C, and D) on the shelf. The data you will need to make your decision is either on the shelf, or on the loaves. Which of the four loaves gives you the most ounces for the price?

And here is another example. You must reduce your intake of fat. You are at the lunch counter looking over the menu. You have three salad choices (A, B, and C). Which one will give you the least fat?

In school, as in real life, there are often a limited number of options available from which to choose the correct response according to a criterion. This is what students do in objective tests. Regardless of the cognitive level (Foundational Content, Application, Higher Order Processes) to be assessed, the two processes (supply and select) can both be useful. Knowledge of basic facts and steps in a process can be assessed by supply procedures, and abstract analysis can be assessed by select procedures. The difference is in whether the teacher wants students to create the answer or recognize it among other options.

Whether the teacher chooses supply or select procedures, the intent is always to tailor the assessment to the objectives of instruction. The decision will rest on which procedure best shows the achievement we have been moving toward and shows it most efficiently.

Comparing Supply-type and Select-type Assessments

Table 6.2 presents a comparison of supply and select assessments. In this table we see that each type has its advantages and its disadvantages. (It should be noted that the items

TABLE 6.2   A Comparison of Supply and Select Assessments

Supply	Select
• Requires students to devise and present the solution to problems	• Students select an answer from options provided
• Sample of topics is relatively few	• Samples topics broadly across total unit
• Relatively easy to construct; fairly difficult to score	• Difficult to create; easy to score
• Reliability of scores often not high	• Reliability of score typically in usable range
• Scores influenced by bluffing	• Scores influenced by guessing
• Scoring influenced by subjective elements in the context of the assessment	• Scoring is objective

in Table 6.2 do not apply to all forms of either type of assessment procedure—only to the most common ones.) The principal advantages of supply-type assessments lie in their dependence on the student's own problem-solving abilities, creativity, and imagination. The advantages of select-type are in their potential for wide coverage of material and ease and reliability of scoring.

The main difficulty of supply-type assessments is the few topics that can be sampled from all those covered by instruction. A second difficulty—subjectivity and unreliability of scoring—has been cited for many years (Ashburn, 1938; Diedrich, 1961). The principal disadvantages of select-type assessments are that they are difficult to construct well and are more susceptible to guessing.

Out of all the assessment procedures available, which ones will serve our purpose best? If you want to know if your third-graders know their one-digit multiplication combinations, an objective test is probably much more efficient than each child having a one-on-one session with the teacher. If you want to know if your class understands the difference between Newton's first and second laws of motion, you can provide real world events and see if students can select which are examples of the first law and which are examples of the second. These are a select-type procedures.

Similarly, if you want to know if Charles can apply the provisions of the first amendment to the Constitution of the United States to a disagreement between the editor of the school newspaper and the school principal, an essay response may serve the purpose best. This is a supply-type procedure.

Once more, the point is that teachers must decide what assessment procedure best brings out the behaviors called for in the instructional objectives. For a pretest, a question and answer session between students and teacher may suffice. A short criterion referenced test may also be appropriate. But for a summative assessment, these procedures are not so desirable. They do not sample the total content of the unit effectively, nor do they show the teacher and student what each child will do with a variety of situations (from the Foundational Content level to Higher Order Processing). A more expansive and often more complex system of assessment is required at this point.

Depending on how your grades are to be established at the end of any grading period, you are likely to want a very comprehensive assessment with a wide range of difficulty in tasks students perform. Because there is often a range of knowledge and skill in a class, the range of difficulty should spread from low to high the scores your students make. You want to do this if you use a norm referenced approach to grading. In Chapter 3 you learned that spreading out the range of scores increases the reliability of the scores from a measurement, a quality many test-users wish to obtain.

Guidelines for Selecting an Assessment Procedure

There are no simple answers as to which procedure—supply or select—is best. However, here are some things to keep in mind when deciding which type of procedure to select.

1. *What does my objective tell me to assess?* Is it recognition? Problem solving? Association? The course of action is determined by the instructional objectives. The procedure will be identified by your objective.

Here is an example involving a trigonometry class. Ms. Holcomb has been leading her class toward solving problems about triangles. Her objective at this point is: Students will show their understanding of the sine, cosine, tangent, and cotangent by identifying examples of each (Foundational Content level) and by applying each in solving problems with right triangles (Application level). Her purpose in assessment is formative, to find out how the class is progressing. Interviews with students could provide the information the teacher needs, but inefficiently. A class discussion of problems faced by builders of large buildings might illustrate examples of instances of applications, but chances are that not all students or all concepts would be involved. In this case, a short objective test relevant to her objectives would probably give the teacher the data she needs for her purpose.

2. How extensive is the job to be done? In part teachers choose an assessment technique based on whether it can be carried out in a relatively economical time frame. If a teacher has a very large group of students it is difficult to use observational methods or to read essays with any kind of reliability. In this case the teacher will probably try to develop an objective test that will fit the purpose. Even though objective tests are indirect assessments for some objectives, a good bit of the knowledge base that undergirds a performance can be assessed objectively.

Suppose a teacher has a project in which the class will design a playground for a section of the city park. In that section they will lay out several different playing areas (a tennis court, a softball field, a section for playground equipment). How many of these areas will fit into the allotted section? To solve this problem, the students may have to know how to figure the area of rectangles and circles. This knowledge can be assessed by a time-saving objective measure. Children who do poorly on this assessment will also have great difficulty laying out the play area. The correlation between performance on an objective test and a performance procedure is likely to be good in a number of situations. Therefore, to use assessment time economically some use of objective methods with supply-type items may be helpful.

3. How much time should I set aside for this assessment? Assessment is also helpful in developing a trail of evidence of a child's progress through a topic, which is useful not only to teacher and student, but also provides data for parent conferences. However, unless time is set aside for these assessments potential for benefit is lost. How much time should we set aside? No one answer fits all situations because the time needed depends on what type of information you are seeking. Do you need advice on where to start the instruction of a topic, to see how students are progressing, or to verify that they have achieved the objective? Time specifically planned and dedicated to assessment to achieve this instructional information is time well spent. However, because instructional time is always in short supply and is engaging, planning will be necessary to achieve dedicated time for assessment.

4. How difficult should the assessment be? Are you working on a problem where mastery is an objective? Or are you trying to spread student scores across a very large range, as in norm referenced grading, and provide a reliable ranking for some purpose? These questions deal with difficulty level of the tasks students are asked to complete in the assessment.

If you are looking at how many students can jump a minimum criterion hurdle, then the height of this hurdle will determine the difficulty level. The difficulty is reflected in the task. In contrast, if you wish to spread students' scores as much as possible you need a range of tasks at different levels of difficulty. (Actually, 50 percent difficulty, that is, where half of the class gets credit for any given task, is a good average.) What if you need to know how effectively your students are expanding their knowledge of American history? This could be a norm referenced question. In this case difficulty is a judgment call depending on what kind of behavior the teacher has described in the instructional objectives.

In looking back over the discussion above, one common feature of assessment emerges: the question is "What is the purpose?" In each case, the answer to this question will advise you on the appropriate length of the assessment procedure, the focus of topics, the type of assessment device, and the proper difficulty level.

✎ Problems

1. List three advantages of a supply-type assessment. Now list three advantages of a select-type assessment. In your subject area which of these advantages would you generally regard the most positive?
2. Identify each of the following as a supply or a select type assessment procedure.
   a. After discussing the role of line in an artwork, the fourth-grade children are painting with tempera as a procedure for seeing how well they understood the line concepts.
   b. In a history class the students are working on a matching test in which battles of World War II will be matched with their locations.
   c. Students in a senior literature class select one of five poems provided by the teacher. They are writing a critical analysis of the poem.

Determining Sample Size

Assessments of all types are samples of the knowledge, skills, and concepts that teachers hope to have fostered in a unit of work. These samples should be large enough to be a reliable representation of the relevant behaviors. Longer tests tend to be more reliable than shorter ones because the sample of content will be large enough to appropriately represent the unit of content.

However, you and I have agreed that formative assessment focuses more specifically on a narrower segment of the objectives than does summative assessment. We can do an adequate job on formative assessments with shorter procedures because the topic of concern is short and recently taught, and the information is primarily advisory for both teacher and student. Also, when we are doing a pretest for group placement shorter assessments will often suffice, because groups are typically formed on the basis of fairly broad characteristics of performance which are relatively easy to observe. For example, reading fluency is a characteristic often reported as the basis for assigning children to a reading group. We can observe this with a short assessment. In fact, the keen eye of a skilled teacher observing the class can sometimes do the job.

However, when doing a summative assessment we will need a larger collection of information about each student. Decisions that become school records should be based on summative assessments. To this end, summative assessments require attention to each of the variety of skills developed within the unit, that means a broader sampling of content.

How Many Data Points Do I Need?

How much assessment information do I need to make the decisions I want to make? The answer would be, ideally, "All you can get!" But assessments are only one of many teaching activities and must be integrated at appropriate points in a teaching unit. I cannot always predict when I might need information to guide my instruction. Therefore, setting dates for all assessments well in advance may not be pedagogically sound. The date may be too soon for the class to have completed all the experiences they should have, or they may have reached that point well before the set date.

Ms. Neu is teaching word attack skills to her first-grade readers. How are the students progressing with prefixes and suffixes? She needs a little formative information to guide her planning. It will not be a long and time consuming exercise, but enough to give her some data on how well the group is progressing. This formative assessment is not part of a long-range data collection plan, but is an important adjunct to teaching. It is scheduled in the short term because it should be collected near to the decision point, where data to support special decisions is needed.

Surely, we will want to have in our unit several specifically scheduled **data points.** Collections of data should be near points at which we will make major decisions about student progress. In my world history class, a mid-term and a final exam are data points on which to make important decisions about students. However, only two assessments put too much weight on each assessment. Variable errors play too large a part in the outcomes when teachers use so few data points. More regularly scheduled assessments should cancel out some random errors of measurement. But mid-terms and final tests are near decision points, and consequently well placed.

There is some evidence that older students (teenaged) prefer fairly frequent rather than infrequent assessments (Crooks, 1988). (However, if in the hallway you should ask them, they would probably say they want no tests at all.) Students feel that a course grade based on several data points is more fair than one base on only the so-called final exam, or on no formal assessments at all. Students who have had periodic examinations also tend to do better on the summative assessment than students who have not. Students seem to intuitively appreciate the concepts of reliability and validity.

The question about frequency of assessments must go without a definite answer. Only the keen eye of the teacher can see when formative assessments are necessary to inform instruction and learning. However, it is too easy to delay assessment activities and let time slip by. It is my experience that many teachers do this and often end up with too few samples of student behavior on which to make important decisions.

Effective instruction is informed instruction. Teachers need information on children and their progress. Short tests and focused observations (preferably recorded) provide this information. But those decisions about grades or promotion should be based on several performance records if they are to be reliable; collection of data from more than a few assessments is required.

Avoiding Bias in Assessment

The purpose of assessment is to provide information about children's progress in the skills, concept development, and other behaviors cited in the objectives. However, assessments sometimes project social, racial, and gender commentaries which are completely unrelated to the academic pursuits of instruction. For example, Tittle (1978) pointed out that tests often portray sex-role stereotypes, and that males are represented and referred to significantly more often than females.

A similar case could be made for various racial minorities in America (Williams, 1974). However, test publishers are now attempting to change these situations. Committees of both men and women, including racial minorities, are employed by testmakers to inspect published tests. Their job is to point out any unfair content or stereotypic references. But as teachers we must also be sensitive to these problems slipping into teacher-made assessment materials. For example, Mr. Cain, a mathematics teacher, included a problem like this: "Mrs. Wilson was doing the family laundry when it occurred to her that certain economies could be met . . ." This could be construed as gender stereotyping (women as housekeepers) even though the high rate of women in the labor force obviates that conclusion for many households.

As teachers plan their assessments they should think about the content and procedures of the assessment from the standpoint of possible stereotyping. Here are some things to help you accomplish this task.

1. Scan your tests and other assessment exercises specifically to eliminate race, gender, or other stereotypes.
2. Note inequalities in references to males and females in assignments and assessments, including gender reference pronouns such as "she" and "he." Equalize these references.
3. Ask yourself if the procedures in the assessment method are couched in a language or setting that favors one sex, one socioeconomic group, or one race over others.
4. Occasionally request a colleague whose gender and/or ethnicity differs from yours to review your assessment devices for aspects of stereotyping or disparity of referencing unnoticed by you.

Assessment procedures in any phase of their implementation should not allow educators to give favor, consciously or not, to one group of students. For example, in scoring an essay is the reader more likely to give the benefit of the doubt to females rather than males? Will the reader deal with the essays of minority students more (or less) critically than the essays of other students?

These events are not only unfair, but make a statement about the value of students who perceive themselves as being treated unfairly. We must always focus on the qualities of achievement of the instructional objectives. Projecting attitudes of worth to students in the context of assessment is to be avoided. In planning an assessment the consequences of our procedures should be as important a factor as the appropriateness of our behavior sample.

✎ Problems

1. A chemistry teacher's syllabus for the semester stated "There will be a mid-term examination on October 21, and a final examination on December 12. These will be three-fourths of your grade. The other one-fourth comes from my assessment of your laboratory notebooks." What do you think about this data collection plan?

2. Ms. Jeffers is about halfway through a unit on soil chemicals in her earth science class. She is about to get into soil analysis, but wonders if the students have sufficiently absorbed the section on chemicals. What type of test should she give at this point? Should it be long or short, involve many topics of content, or focus on fewer topics? What are the reasons for your choices?

3. Mr. Wilson, who teaches beginning Spanish to sophomores, said, "I never bother with tests—I know what these students can do from their class responses." How would you respond to this in reference to number of data points, and creating data at decision points?

4. Describe a situation in your subject area where a feature of a test conveys a message of worth to a subclass of students (such as males.)

A Real Case Narrative

You might ask, "How does all this work fit into real life teaching?" Consider the following Real Case Narrative in which there is a conversation between two actual teachers. Think about what advice you would give these people. How would you fit this into situations in your teaching area to see if you can make pretests, formative, and summative work more practical for you?

Ms. Gomer and Ms. Franks are carpooling toward Unionville Elementary School where they teach. "I am having a problem getting set for the parent conferences coming up next week," said Ms. Gomer with a frown. "I think I know quite a bit about my children, but how do I show this to parents?"

"How can you feel you know about your children if you don't have some evidence that you refer to and can show parents?" asked Ms. Franks.

"Well, I see them working and I visit with different students to see how the work is going, but this is all pretty subjective stuff. How can you show that to parents?" Ms. Gomer replied.

"I use a short test now and then to see if the class is ready for the next step in a unit. When we are in the unit I have several skills check lists I fill out on children as I observe them, as a guide to their progress. All this stuff, along with work samples, I keep in a file folder for each child," Ms. Franks suggested. "Well, I haven't done anything like that and it's too late for it now," Ms. Gomer replied.

"When you are in a unit, how do you decide you're ready for the next step if you don't do an assessment?" queried Ms. Franks. "Well, on Fridays we have an oral exercise, and if my slow Jennifer gets several questions, I figure the rest of the class can handle the topic," Ms. Gomer said with a sly smile. "Well," Ms. Franks began, "Notes on these exercises could be of some use to parents, as well as a guide to adapting your work to the kids," Ms. Franks noted.

"That's just it," Ms. Gomer replied. "I really depend on my personal judgment on these things, which really isn't too bad, but it doesn't give me anything concrete to show to parents, or to use as evidence if someone asks me to prove the kids are ready for compound sentences, or whatever. And as for parents, and at report card time, I really feel uneasy. I always hope no parents ask me to explain why their kid didn't get a superior mark!"

"Well," said Ms. Franks, "Give the kids a writing chore today—parents always like to see that, if nothing else."

Some Guidelines to Follow in Developing Your Assessments

1. In planning and executing an assessment procedure be sure the topics sampled match those in the table of specifications. In order to claim validity for your procedure it must match the content as defined in the table. Topics and cognitive levels must be sampled and behaviors observed in accordance with the table.

2. Plan assessments well before you will want to use them, especially in the case of summative assessment. This gives you a chance to review them, to fit them more closely to the instructional objectives, and to see that topics are appropriately sampled.

3. Compose instructions to students so that everyone understands the task at hand. No one should get a poor assessment report because the instructions were not well understood.

4. The plan for evaluating the product (scoring key, or checklist for reading a report or appraising a project) must be one that other professionals would agree is accurate and fair. Two separate evaluators using your plan should come to very similar conclusions about the student's work.

SUMMARY

1. There are a number of aspects of assessment that must be considered before the first test item or performance exercise is considered.
2. The choice of an assessment procedure and its content should be guided by the purpose of the assessment: pretesting, formative assessment, or summative assessment.
3. A table of specifications should be used to select the content and cognitive level of an assessment.
4. There are two basic types of assessment procedures: supply procedures, in which a problem is posed and the student constructs a response, and select procedures, in which the student is given a set of options and asked to select one of them.
5. Supply procedures reflect the student's higher level processing abilities; but the amount of material that can be covered through such assessments is limited and scoring may be subjective and unreliable.
6. Select procedures offer the potential for wider coverage of material and ease and reliability of scoring, but are difficult to construct and susceptible to guessing.
7. The choice of an assessment procedure is determined by the teacher's objectives, the extent of the job to be done, the amount of time available, and the desired level of difficulty.
8. The sample of content covered by an assessment should be large enough to be a reliable representation of the relevant behaviors.
9. Assessments should be done frequently enough to guide instruction, to provide objective evidence for parents, and to provide a sufficient number of data points on which to base a valid grade. Assessments should be done near to points where decisions are to be made.
10. It is important to avoid unfair and inequitable references to racial, ethnic, or gender groups in the construction of assessment procedures.

PROBLEMS

1. Contrast the purposes of pretests, formative, and summative assessments.
2. How is the use of a table of specifications different in formative and summative assessment?
3. You are about to do a summative assessment for a unit in your specialty. Would you use a supply- or select-type procedure? Why? What are the problems and advantages of using this technique?
4. In a syllabus from a beginning German language class the comment about assessment said, "We will have a mid-quarter examination on October 2, and a final on November 1. These two tests will be the basis for your grade for the quarter." Comment on this assessment procedure. How would you do it differently?
5. A problem in a drafting class dealt with planning a small office building including work space and adjoining rest rooms. In regard to the latter, the problem began, "Since the secretarial pool will be made up of women, and the executive suite will be predominantly men, the adjustments in restroom space. . ." Comment on this problem.

KEY TERMS

pretest
formative assessment
summative assessment

supply procedures
select procedures
data points

ADDITIONAL READING

Ebel, R. L. (1971). Evaluation and educational objectives. *Journal of Educational Measurement,* 10, 273–279.

Millman, J. and Greene, J. The specification and development of tests of achievement and ability. In R.L. Linn, ed., *Educational Measurement,* 3d. ed. New York: Macmillan, 1989, Chapter 8.

Schutz, R. E. The role of measurement in education: Servant, soulmate, stoolpidgeon, statesman, scapegoat, all of the above and/or none of the above. *Journal of Educational Measurement,* 8, 141–146.

Spector, S. J. (1981). Theory misapplied: Teaching by objectives and cognitive learning. *Journal of Experimental Education,* 4, 35–37.

CHAPTER 7

WRITING OBJECTIVE TESTS:

Multiple Choice

"Let's see, how shall I assess what my class has achieved so far?" Ms. Stahl, a beginning History teacher is about to give her first test. "Professor Jones, my history teacher in college, used essays; I guess I should, too. But people say multiple choice is good for testing facts. I've got a lot of facts I want the class to know, and Professor Wilkins used a lot of multiple-choice tests in her classes. Hmm! This begins to get complicated!"

Indeed, many teachers use the assessment procedures that were used on them when they were students and often with no more skill than their teachers demonstrated. But you don't have to copy your former teachers; you should use the procedures that best fit *your* objectives.

This chapter, and the next, deal with **objective tests** including multiple-choice, true-false, and matching test items. Tests of this type are called objective because they are scored objectively. That means all items have one right answer established before the test is administered to the students. No judgment-calls are involved in scoring these tests, although judgments are used in selecting test content.

Completion or short-answer test items are also included in this section. They have some of the qualities of supply-type assessment, but because subjectivity plays a relatively small part in completion tests they are discussed with true-false and matching tests in the next chapter.

This chapter outlines those procedures involved in writing multiple-choice tests. With skillful writing of this test type you will be able to assess most of the outcomes, at all levels of your taxonomy of objectives, to which objective tests can be applied.

What This Chapter Will Include. From Chapters 3 and 4 you realize the importance of reliability and validity. How you and I construct our assessment procedures will have a lot to do with how valid and reliable our procedures are. To this end, this chapter looks at multiple-choice testing techniques in an attempt to illustrate a) how to write good test items that will assess the attainment of the topics in your objectives, and b) how teachers can apply multiple-choice tests to a variety of subject-matter areas at all levels of cognitive demand. In this chapter you will learn about:

1. The anatomy of a good multiple-choice item including the function of each part of the test item

2. Some fundamental rules for writing good multiple choice items
3. How to write multiple-choice items at the higher order level of cognitive processing
4. Advantages and limitations to multiple-choice tests
5. How multiple-choice tests can be applied to many subject areas and sample items from several content areas

This chapter is designed to help you do a really expert job of test writing. Teachers have many objectives and therefore should be versatile in developing each of several assessment procedures. To help you become versatile in developing multiple choice items, a portion of the chapter is devoted to illustrating the flexibility of these items in assessing objectives in different subject areas and covering a range of cognitive demand.

Writing Multiple-Choice Tests

Multiple choice, true-false and matching are often referred to as selection-type tests. The student's job is to select the correct response from options provided. The most popular selection type item is the **multiple choice.** This popularity is due to the fact that it is very versatile. It can be applied to the measurement of all levels of the taxonomy (as discussed in Chapter 2), and is suitable for use in assessing outcomes in almost all subject matter areas (Osterlind, 1989).

Components of Multiple-Choice Items

A multiple-choice test item has two parts: the stem and a set of response options, of which one correctly responds to the proposition in the stem. The **stem** defines the problem; the **options** are the possible responses to the problem. Here is an example of the format.

stem   → In regard to size, Great Danes are

┌→ a) among the largest of dogs   ← **answer**

options ├→ b) considered to be a mid size dog ← **distractor**

└→ c) among the smallest of dogs   ← **distractor**

The options are of two types. The correct answer is the essential option. The other options are the **distractors,** or incorrect responses. The success of the multiple-choice test depends on how well each part of the item is written.

The Stem.   The primary quality of a good stem is that it gives students the problem before they consider the optional responses. The stem must clearly point to the subject of the test item. It must use clear and simple language in order to focus on the desired aspect of the topic being tested. What happens when this criteria is not met? Consider the following example.

Poor: The Battle of Hastings

a) was fought in 1066

b) was between the French and the Germans

c) began the first Crusade

The stem in this example gives a topic but does not pose a problem. Students do not know what information area the problem is covering. A better stem would contain a verb to provide a direction and might look like this:

Better: Which statement describes an outcome of the Battle of Hastings?

a) the French annexed Austria from Germany

b) it opened England to Norman conquest

c) it began the first Crusade

In the second example the student knows at the outset what the task will be; the item is focused on a single piece of information and can be quickly answered. This stem directs the student to the featured topic of the test item.

The Distractor.   Writing the distractors is probably the most difficult part of making a multiple-choice test. To help you become a writer of good distractors test specialists have devised some guidelines. Here are the most important of these.

All distractors should be plausible. If a distractor is not plausible it will be eliminated by the students and consequently performs no function in the test. This point is important because if one option can be eliminated it increases the probability that the correct option can be guessed from those remaining.

Erik is taking a test on popular animal stories the class has been reading. He encounters this item:

Which of the following is a German shepherd?

a) Lassie

b) Old Yeller

c) Rin Tin Tin

d) Black Beauty

Erik knows that a German shepherd is a kind of dog. He also quickly notices that Black Beauty is a horse, so he eliminates that response. He does not recall the type of dog the others are so he guesses. His chances of guessing the right answer are one in three. If he could not have eliminated the implausible alternative (Black Beauty), his guessing chances would have been one in four.

All distractors should be equally plausible to avoid this testwise technique of eliminating implausible answers and guessing among the remainder.

Distractors should not require an inordinate amount of reading. The test is not a reading comprehension exercise. Long distractors, however, involve a fair amount of reading to be intertwined with the subject matter for which the test is designed. Suppose I am a history teacher. My test should sort out students who have the best knowledge of history from those who have less knowledge. If the distractors require a considerable amount of reading it also increases the portion of the test that is a verbal skills exercise and not a test in history. Scores will be adulterated with the verbal skills factor, even though I am grading on knowledge of history. To avoid this we should keep the reading task as simple as possible.

All distractors should be about the same length in terms of number of words. Relatively long or relatively short distractors appear to catch the reader's eye, and are therefore more often selected than is expected in a random selection process (Chase, 1964). One reason we find long distractors is that test-writers may have to qualify an answer to make it correct. For example, suppose students have been studying the Pythagorean Theorem. One feature of the theorem deals with right triangles whose sides have a ratio of 3 to 4 to 5. Here is a case in which a distractor must be qualified to make it right.

> I have a triangle, one side of which is 3 feet long, and one side is 4 feet. What is the length of the hypotenuse?
> a) 5 feet, but only in cases where the triangle has one 90 degree angle
> b) 5 feet in isosceles triangles
> c) 7 feet in right triangles

The 3, 4, 5 aspect of the theorem works only if the triangle is a right triangle. This makes option a) the correct answer. I had to elaborate, hence lengthen, the first answer to make it correct. Testwise students look over these distractors very carefully to pick out situations like this. It will not always give them the correct choice, but it is a good guess if the answer is not known.

Avoid indefinite terms, or terms that state an absolute condition. Options should not begin with **indefinite terms** such as "usually" or "generally." These terms suggest that the testwriter knew there were exceptions to the answer given, and that to make the option a correct answer an opening for the exception had to be included. Here is an example.

> Drivers get the best gas mileage in an automobile
> a) usually when they drive at a moderate speed
> b) at a constant speed above 55 miles per hour
> c) at below 25 miles per hour in second gear

The correct answer is a), but with exceptions. Use of the indefinite word "usually" provides a clue for selecting a). (This option also has another indefinite term "moderate" which confounds the meaning of the option.)

Testwise students also look for **absolute terms.** Words such as "never," and "always" are clues that the option may be wrong because in very few instances does something always occur, or never occur.

The rule then is that options should be constructed so as to make either indefinite terms or terms reflecting absolute conditions unnecessary. They are clues that clever test-takers use to help them gain scores without necessarily reflecting knowledge of the content. (The use of indefinite and absolute terms will occur again when we examine other types of test items in Chapter 8.)

The stem and options should be consistent in grammatical construction. Each option, if appended to the stem, should present a clear and grammatically correct statement. If this is not the case the offending option will not be an effective distractor—students will tend to avoid it. Here is an example.

An "expatriate" is

a) people who were once soldiers in their homeland

b) a person whose citizenship was revoked in his homeland

c) one who has moved away from her/his native land

The first option does not agree with the stem in number; it is plural while the stem is singular. The same condition sometimes occurs in the tense of the verb; for example, the stem may be past tense, while the option is in the present tense. These grammatical inconsistencies distract test-takers and should be avoided.

Another rule is to avoid using the options "all of the above" and "none of the above." Suppose we have the following test item:

Trees that are classified as angiosperms are characterized as

a) including broad leaf trees

b) producing no sap

c) having needles and cones

d) all of the above

Now suppose I am not up on my tree information and do not know if angiosperms are the ones with needles or leaves. I do know that these are two different classes of trees. Knowing this, I also know that option d) must be wrong. Both a) and c) could not be correct, so "all of the above" has to be wrong. I eliminate it and sort out the rest. Now, if I must guess my odds of getting a correct answer are one in three, not one in four as would be the case if I could not eliminate answer d).

Use of "all of the above" and "none of the above" often allows test-takers to eliminate the option stated in that manner, and deal with the remaining ones. Instead of using "all of the above," this item could be made more useful by adding another plausible distractor, asking the student to make one more discrimination, as in the following example.

Trees that are classified as angiosperms are characterized as

a) having broad leaves

b) producing no sap

c) having needles and cones

d) reproducing from bulbs

Here the student must sort out four comments about trees, not just three.

To vary the difficulty of a multiple-choice item increase (or decrease) the homogeneity of the options. The best way to make a test "harder" is not by looking for obscure content around which to build items. Instead, if the options for an item all focus on a single point and are different in rather small ways, the student must make very fine discriminations, requiring more knowledge about the topic of the item to sort out the correct option. This is how we make items "hard"; we make the options more homogeneous. Here is an example which deals with an important conference among allied leaders at the close of World War II.

Which of the following topics was dealt with at the Yalta Conference?

a) the rate of monetary exchange among Allied nations
b) fishing rights in the North Sea
c) the USSR's control of the Kurile Islands after the war
d) the establishment of Israel as an independent state

This item could be answered only if one knows that the conference dealt mostly with the sorting out of geographic areas of control by each of the World War II Allies after the end of hostilities. This item could be made even more difficult by requiring more detailed knowledge of the Yalta Conference, specifically with its attention to Japanese possessions. It might look like this:

Which of the following topics was dealt with at the Yalta Conference?

a) joint Allied bombing of Japan to end the war
b) implementation of naval blockades of Japanese ports
c) USSR's control of the Japanese Kurile Islands after the end of hostilities
d) allied strategy for invading and holding the island of Formosa

Here the student must know much more about the topics of the Yalta Conference than was true of the example above. In this last item the options all deal with issues in the Far East. The options are more homogeneous in their focus and require finer discriminations to find the correct answer. The item is harder than the one above which did not present this amount of homogeneity of content.

These are the main points to note in writing distractors. If you follow all these guidelines you will have good multiple-choice test items.

Independence of Test Items

Another important characteristic of good multiple-choice test writing is that all items should be independent of each other. Information in one item should not be required in answering another. If the student misses the first item in a two item set, the other item in the set will also be missed even though the student may know what the second item requires. Here is an example. I begin with an item that requires the student to calculate the diameter of a circle, then follow with the calculation of the circumference. The items look like this:

1. Charles stands at the center of a circle. He measures the distance to the edge of the circle. It is 4 feet. What is the length of the *diameter* of the circle?
   a) 4 feet
   b) 8 feet
   c) over 12 feet

The correct answer is b). Now look at the dependent question.

2. What is the circumference of the circle in which Charles is standing?
   a) exactly 8 feet
   b) between 12 and 13 feet
   c) a fraction more than 25 feet

Now suppose in item 1 the student mixed up the concept of diameter (distance across a circle through the center) and radius (distance from the center to the edge of the circle) and chose 4 feet as the correct answer for the diameter. But suppose the student knows that the circumference of a circle (the distance around) is 3.14 (or pi) times the diameter. But having chosen the diameter to be 4 feet in item 1, this student multiplies ($3.14 \times 4 = 12.56$). Therefore, in item 2 option b), which is wrong, will be chosen.

The student appears to know how to calculate the circumference, but erred on the first item . Because of that error in item 1, a point is lost on each item. This does not reflect the student's actual knowledge on the topic of circles. If the items were written with completely separate data, the student could have missed item 1 but got item 2 correct.

This example may seem like a long way to go to emphasize the point that items should be written independent of each other, but the point is an important one.

Multiple-Choice Tests at the Higher Order Process Level

In the taxonomy of learning outcomes as discussed in Chapter 2, three levels of cognitive production are listed: Foundational Content, Application, and Higher Order Processes. A common criticism of multiple-choice and other objective tests is that they assess only at the lower level of knowledge. Certainly many classroom tests are pitched at the Foundational Content level, a condition that has existed for many years (Marso & Pigge, 1992). These are the easy tests to write and the safe ones to defend. If students question the answer you key as correct, proof of your choice can be found in the textbook or a class reference.

But what about assessing at the other levels of the taxonomy? In this section we will illustrate some techniques for writing items at higher levels than Foundational Content. You will want to try these techniques in your own area of teaching. A little practice will produce skill in developing test items at each of the levels of the taxonomy of outcomes around which you have built your instructional plans and procedures (Roid & Haladyna, 1982). Let's take a close look at some prototype procedures and examples that illustrate them.

Analyzing Written Materials

One way we write multiple-choice tests at the higher cognitive demand levels is to provide a piece of prose and ask the student to interpret, analyze, or generalize from it. We can provide a paragraph from a novel, a short story, a stanza from a poem, a paragraph from a political speech, a segment from a computer program, a mathematical proof, or anything that is relevant to the class work and objectives. Next we write one or more test items about the meaning or intent of the author. This procedure is often referred to as the "interpretive exercise." Here is an example.

Shakespeare says in *Julius Caesar*
"There is a tide in the affairs of men,
Which, taken at the flood, leads on to fortune;
Omitted, all the voyage of their life
Is bound in shallows and in miseries."
Here Shakespeare's point is that
a) Seamen must go with the ebb and flow of the ocean
b) Opportunity must be seized at the right time
c) If at first you don't succeed, keep on trying
d) Some people are doomed to failure no matter what

In this problem the student must take the elements and put them together into a conclusion. This entails more cognitive effort than does mere recall of a situation.

The interpretive exercise has applications in a variety of disciplines and not just in literature. Think for a moment how this might be applied in political science (interpreting a paragraph from a presidential address), in chemistry (a description of situation A is interpreted in terms of B), or in sociology (a situation is described for one locality, and out of it a conclusion is to be made).

Generalizing Across Instances

Some principles or conclusions fit several situations. Does the student recognize the generalizability of a given principal? This generalizing across settings involves higher order cognitive processing. Here is an example of this kind of application of multiple-choice items at a higher cognitive processing level.

How are lithium, helium, and beryllium alike?
a) they have atomic numbers less than 10
b) they are all liquids at 32 degrees F.
c) they are all flammable above 10 degrees C.

This item, which follows a study of elements in the periodic table, requires students to think about each of the listed elements and see how they compare. The comparison is made either on specific characteristics or against a given criterion. Items such as this require students to go beyond basic knowledge and to do some work at the higher cognitive processing level. We can apply this technique to several disciplines. We can contrast characters in a novel, compare events in history, compare natural resources (forest products, grain, etc.) across countries, and many other similar situations.

Interpreting Data

In this application a body of data is provided. Then, students are asked in the test items to make a conclusion, an analysis, or to combine bits of data to create a new aspect of the information given. Two possible ways to present data are the use of a graph or table. Here is an example of this procedure.

The following items are based on the data given in the table. (Data are populations, given in millions.)

	1990	**1995**	**Increase**	**Rate of increase**
Africa	645	753	108	16.7%
Latin America	453	501	48	10.6%
Europe	500	507	7	1.4%

In 1995 the population of Africa was about 1.5 times the population of Europe. If populations continue to grow at the present rate (1990 to 1995), how many times larger than Europe will the population of Africa be in the year 2000?

a) 1.7

b) 2.0

c) 2.4

In items such as this, several questions can be posed in reference to the same set of data. However, one must not load the entire test too heavily with one content area. Rather, item content must match the table of specifications (see Chapter 3).

Using Diagrams, Maps, and Pictures

Another way to assess at a higher cognitive level is to present a situation in pictorial form and ask the student to make an analysis, evaluation of a course of action, or to combine aspects of the pictured situation to lead to a new conclusion.

Many real life situations require this type of assessment. We see in the newspaper a graph of interest rates and three different propositions under which the bank will lend money. We interpret a graph to find the best option for a mortgage. We see a topographical map of Missouri and decide how likely it is that flooding will take place in a given area; or we look at a table that shows what percent of lawn grubs are within three inches of the surface at different average temperatures, and decide when to apply grub bait.

All of these examples require us to use data from the image presented and make a judgment about a given outcome. This is an application of multiple-choice assessment at the Higher Order Processes level. Figure 7.1 shows another example of this prototype situation in an elementary science class.

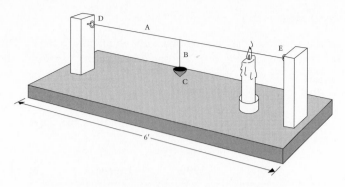

I heat the wire (A). What happens to the pointer (C)?
a) it slowly rises above the table
b) it does not change
c) it slowly drops toward the table

FIGURE 7.1

In this item the student is required to think about what happens to a metal object when it is heated and what the consequences of this would be in the pictured situation. Items such as this call for reasoning, in this case reasoning based on basic principles.

Recognizing Assumptions

In the newspapers and popular magazines students often encounter articles that report conditions and then make conclusions based upon assumptions derived from the relationships of the conditions. Here is an example.

> Dr. Johan Pierce has reported that in his study, educational differences were found between 240 young adults arrested and charged with a felony, and a second sample who had never been arrested. Of those who were arrested 98 percent had not taken chemistry, physics, or biology in high school. Of the group who had not been arrested, only 5% had not taken one or more of these sciences. He concluded that if students were required to take more science there would be less crime.
>
> The conclusion in this article implies that
>
> a) a lack of education leads young people to involvement in crime
> b) knowledge in general deters students from crime
> c) relationships such as noted in the article imply causation

In sum, the preceding examples illustrate the fact that multiple-choice items can be used to assess mental processes at higher levels than required by the mere recall of facts. Multiple-choice tests are very flexible in their application, and this is one of their great advantages. Teachers can effectively use multiple-choice tests at all levels of the taxonomy by following just a few guidelines (Talmir, 1991).

Strengths and Limitations of Multiple-Choice Tests

Multiple-choice items are favored by many teachers as well as commercial test publishers. This is because of their many strengths; the most important of which are listed below. However, they also have some limitations as we will soon see.

Strengths of Multiple-Choice Tests

Here is a list of the strengths of multiple-choice items.

Strengths of Multiple-Choice Tests

1. Multiple-choice tests can be written at all levels of the taxonomy.
2. Multiple-choice tests can be used in assessing outcomes in almost all subject matter taught in schools.
3. Multiple-choice tests sample a large number of information points in a test period.
4. Multiple-choice items provide information that helps diagnose learning errors.
5. Multiple-choice items reduce guessing.
6. Multiple-choice tests are easy to score.

In the next few paragraphs you and I will take a brief look at each of them.

Multiple-choice tests can be written at all levels of the taxonomy. Multiple-choice tests are often avoided because some users see them as assessing only at the factual level of learning. This, of course, is a criticism of the testwriter, not of the test procedure. You have just seen some examples of multiple-choice tests being used to assess outcomes involving higher order processes. Indeed, we can use multiple-choice tests to measure knowledge of factual material, but as we've demonstrated they have the capability of assessing outcomes at other levels of the taxonomy of educational outcomes as well.

Multiple-choice tests can be used for assessing outcomes in virtually all subject matter taught in school. It is sometimes claimed that multiple-choice tests are poorly suited to some subject matter areas. However, every subject matter area has some factual information, some application information, some analysis, synthesis, and evaluation in the list of objectives. Multiple-choice test items therefore have a role in assessing the attainment of objectives in virtually all subject matter areas.

Here are some examples. In art we might need to know the primary colors, what colors combine to make brown, what temperature is needed in a kiln, the steps in soldering, how artist A is like artist B in use of line, and how to use the vanishing point. In science there are a plethora of applications, analyses, syntheses, evaluations, and ways to regulate outcomes of events that are relevant to all fields of scientific inquiry. Some of these deal with scientific method, set-up and use of equipment, reaction under given environmental conditions, predictions, and control of events in all sciences. In music, there are historical periods with their identifying music, there is the meaning of symbols and vocabulary, rearranging of notation to achieve a different style, how to change a scale from the dominant to a minor key, recognizing themes from a famous work, plots of operas, all of which can be assessed using multiple-choice items.

Another advantage of multiple choice tests is that *they sample a large number of information points in a short time.* Assessments are only a sample of the total information teachers present in an instructional unit. That sample should be as wide as possible. In this context, teachers need an assessment procedure that will sample widely among the behaviors we hoped to develop. Multiple-choice tests fit that requirement.

Along with a wide sample of information, *multiple choice items can help diagnose learning errors* within that sample of content. By noting frequently missed items, teachers know that there are points in the unit of instruction that students did not understand. Also, by noting too frequently chosen distractors, teachers see misconceptions that students have about the topics in the test. Both of these features are diagnostic. By using the multiple-choice test, teachers can see where review work is needed and can straighten out misconceptions.

Multiple-choice items reduce guessing. Can students guess while taking multiple-choice tests? Of course they can. When there are four options to an item, students have a 25 percent chance of guessing an item correctly. But this is better than in a true/false test where the chance of guessing correctly is 50 percent. Some guessing will occur in multiple-choice tests, but the typical student will guess on a relatively few items, and the impact of guessing will be modest in most tests.

Still another advantage is that *multiple-choice tests are easy to score* compared to many other types of tests. Teachers often can utilize a machine-scored answer sheet (shown below). The tests are then read by an electronic optical scanner which provides a score for each student quickly and effortlessly. Even if the tests are hand scored, scoring is relatively easy. Scorers can use a blank sheet like those used for electronic scoring and punch out a key to overlay the answer sheet. The scorer then counts the blank holes— the wrong items—and subtracts these from the total number of items on the test. This is the score for that test.

Even without an optically scannable sheet or a punch-out key, multiple-choice tests can be scored rather quickly. When you type your test, type in a one-half-inch line to the left of the item number. Instruct the students to select the option they believe is correct and write the letter of that option on the line.

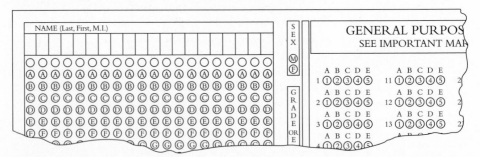

A typical machine scored answer sheet. NCS General Purpose Answer Sheet. National Computer Systems, Inc.

Now cut a two-inch-wide strip of paper and hold it along the side of the typed test. On this two-inch-wide strip write the item numbers matched up with the test-item numbers. On your answer strip write the correct option letter for each item.

For example, for item 1, whose correct answer is, say, c), write 1. c) on your strip next to where item 1 will be on your actual test. For item 2, whose correct answer is, say, a), write on your strip 2. a). Figure 7.2 illustrates what the key strip will look like.

Now the teacher has collected the marked tests, and alone at her desk at 4:00 P.M. she is ready to score them. She lays the key strip along the side of the first child's test, and looking across from the key to the child's mark for item 1, she can quickly mark it correct or incorrect. She does the same for item 2, item 3, and so forth. This is a quick way to score the multiple-choice test without machine assistance. In addition, the teacher can run the marking pencil horizontally across the edge of the key and onto the students paper each time a wrong answer is marked. These markings on the key will indicate the items most frequently missed. This is a quick way to locate topics on which students did not do well.

Limitations of Multiple-Choice Tests

Now let's turn to the limitations of multiple choice tests. Here are a few of the common ones.

Limitations of Multiple-Choice Tests

1. It is difficult to write multiple-choice items at the higher order processes level.
2. Distractors are not equally plausible.
3. The reading demand of multiple-choice items is often high.
4. Guessing does have some influence on scores.

Let's elaborate on each of these limitations of multiple-choice items.

It is difficult to write multiple-choice items at the Higher Order Process level. No good test is easy to write, but it is especially difficult to write good multiple-choice test items at the Higher Order Process level of our taxonomy of learning outcomes. How do we get at analysis, synthesis, and evaluation in a multiple-choice item? Take another look at the

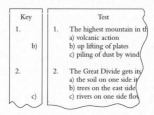

FIGURE 7.2

examples discussed earlier in the chapter. As noted, some practice in applying the structure of items given above—using situations in your subject matter area—will be helpful. Soon you will find writing items at this level much easier. But teachers do find that writing items at the Foundational Content level is easiest, and the path of least resistance often wins out. Resist this!

As discussed earlier, it is a problem when *distractors are not equally plausible* in a given item. If the test is made up of four-option items, there must be three plausible distractors in each item. If it seems especially hard to find three good distractors to accompany your correct option, you may wish to write three-option multiple-choice items for your entire test. There is some evidence that three-option items sort out the achieving students from those who are achieving less well almost as clearly as do four-option items. Sorting out achievers from nonachievers is what teachers want a test to do. If it is too difficult to write a plausible fourth option, go ahead and use three good options until you develop some skill. It will not materially erode the efficiency of your test to sort out the children who are reaching objectives from those who are not. However, having the same number of options for each item equalizes the guessing factor across items.

The reading demand of multiple choice items is often high. When dealing with complex concepts teachers have a tendency to write quite long stems and options for the test items. This makes the test increasingly a reading speed and comprehension test. When you are assessing how much sociology a student knows, your tests should be focused on sociology, and differences in reading skill should be a minor factor. When you are assessing knowledge of biology, differences among children in reading speed and comprehension should not materially affect scores. Hence, in writing all subject-matter tests, write at a low level of reading speed and comprehension. Use as simple language as possible, and keep your sentences short.

Finally, you noted earlier that multiple-choice tests tend to reduce guessing but that *guessing does have some influence on scores*. If I write good test items, with quality distractors, I will make guessing less productive. We know that all distractors must be plausible because if the student can eliminate one distractor as not plausible, guessing among the others is much more inviting. However, guessing cannot be totally eliminated.

✎ Problems

1. Here are some multiple-choice items that violate a guideline for writing good items. For each item find the guideline that is violated.
   A. To be an "insect" the creature must have
      1) not more than four legs
      2) a body limited to a head and abdomen
      3) no wings
      4) a body that includes three distinct parts: a head, thorax, and a functional abdomen
   B. The one that is a vegetable is
      1) beans
      2) an apple
      3) rhubarb
      4) thyme

    C. Trees
       1) are classified as hardwood and pithwood
       2) are gymnosperms or angiosperms
       3) create carbon monoxide
       4) grow only in temperate zones
    D. The health of an economy is hard to discern, but one indicator of the health of an economy that is often used by economists and many writers of financial columns in the newspaper and by stock market analysts is the rate of employment in a state or locality. This rate of employment is
       1) calculated by the number of jobs divided by the number of persons who do not have a job
       2) determined by the demand for labor at the available wage
       3) based on the number of members in all unions divided by those who are not unionized

2. Which is not true about multiple-choice tests? They
   a. are applicable to all subject-matter areas in schools
   b. tap a large number of points of information in a unit
   c. eliminate guessing among the set of options
   d. can be written only at the Foundational Content level.

3. Which of the following statements describes a problem with multiple-choice items?
   a. not all distractors are equally plausible
   b. the demand of reading is usually too low
   c. there are too many higher order items

SUMMARY

1. A multiple-choice item has two parts: the stem, which presents the problem, and a set of options, which include the correct response and a set of distractors.

2. Distractors should be plausible, not require extensive reading, be about the same length, avoid indefinite and absolute terms, be consistent in grammatical construction, and avoid "all" or "none of the above."

3. The difficulty of a multiple-choice item can be varied by increasing or decreasing the homogeneity of the content of the options.

4. It is important for test items to be independent of each other so that an incorrect response to one item does not automatically produce an incorrect response to another.

5. Multiple-choice items can be used to assess Higher Order Processes by using formats such as analyzing written material; generalizing across instances; interpreting data from tables; interpreting diagrams, maps, and pictures; and recognizing assumptions.

6. Multiple-choice items have several advantages: They can be written at all levels of the learning taxonomy; can be used in virtually all subject-matter areas; sample a large number of points of information; can be used to diagnose learning errors; they reduce guessing; and are easy to score.

7. The disadvantages of multiple-choice items include the following: It is difficult to write items at the higher order process levels; distractors sometimes are not equally plausible; items may demand high levels of reading skills; and guessing sometimes influences scores.

A REAL CASE NARRATIVE

Here is a narrative involving a conversation between a student teacher and his supervisor. It is depiction of an actual event.

Mr. Ross, a student teacher in biology, is discussing his first test with his supervisor, Mr. Alten. "I've gone through my textbook and have copied statements from the essential points. Each one is on my objectives list. I've made these into test items. I've decided to use a multiple-choice test to assess how well the students have got these points. I have 12 vocabulary items, and the rest deal with characteristics of the phylum we have just studied," Ross explained.

Mr. Alten rubbed his chin. "You have selected topics to fit your class objectives, but isn't your list of objectives broader than these items?" he queried. "Aren't there some applications listed among your objectives?"

Mr. Ross glanced over his course objectives. "Well, if I stick to the textbook, I am sure the answer to each question is right. I don't think I'm ready to hassle a student over a question's answer," he said.

"Well," Mr. Alten, frowning, began, "Aren't those applications of ideas pretty important?"

"I figure if the students know these basic facts they can apply them. I'd really like to stick with this," replied Mr. Ross.

Mr. Alten paused a moment and scanned the unit objectives. He noted the concepts and applications on the list. "Which is most important here, fitting your test to the class objectives or presenting students with a test that gets only facts?" he asked.

"Aren't those application-concept type things really hard to write?" asked Mr. Ross. What would you do if you were the supervisor for this student?

PROBLEMS

1. Pair up with another student who has a similar teaching specialty. Write an instructional objective in the field with which you are most familiar. Be sure this is written in terms of behaviors that can be seen and counted (for example, "Solves problems by applying the Pythagorean theorem"). Now write a multiple-choice test item that could be used to observe a student's progress in achieving this objective. Write three multiple-choice items based on this objective. Exchange papers with your associate and discuss the extent to which you see each other's work as being done well.

2. Now look at the items you have written. Choose any one of these items that is not on the higher order processing level of the taxonomy and rewrite it so that it assesses attainment of the objective involving analysis, synthesis, or evaluation.

3. Below are a set of test items. Critique each of them using the guidelines provided in this chapter.

    A. Which of the following is an example of a crustacean?
        1) a shark
        2) a crab
        3) a clam
        4) a rusty car

    B. Horses
        1) are found on almost all continents around the world
        2) weigh a maximum of 2000 lbs.
        3) run at speeds of 50 miles/hr.

    C. In Illinois the temperature all week has reached 85 degrees Fahrenheit. It is likely that people in
        1) Argentina are warm and the fields are green
        2) South Africa are wearing coats and heavy sweaters
        3) There is 11 inches of snow this morning in Quebec

    D. The largest single expenditure by the federal government goes for
        1) maintaining the military establishment
        2) services to citizens (e.g., social security)
        3) gifts to underdeveloped foreign nations
        4) all of the above

KEY TERMS

objective tests	distractor
multiple choice	indefinite terms
stem	absolute terms
options	

ADDITIONAL READING

Gronlund, N. E. *How to Construct Achievement Tests.* 4th ed. Englewood Cliffs, NJ: Prentice-Hall, 1988, Chapter 3.

Miller, H. G., Williams, R. G., and Haladyna, T. M. *Beyond Facts: Objective Ways to Measure Thinking.* Englewood Cliffs, NJ: Educational Technology Publications, 1978.

Osterlind, S. J. *Constructing Test Items.* Boston: Kluwer Academic, 1989.

Roid, G. H., and Haladyna, T. M. *A Technology for Test Item Writing.* New York: Academic Press, 1982.

CHAPTER 8

WRITING OBJECTIVE TESTS

True-False; Matching; Completion

Mr. Tandy, a Social Studies teacher, was looking over a recent multiple-choice examination. Frowning, he thought to himself, "My tests are so uninteresting, so inflexible, so lacking in variety; I really need some new techniques for getting at some additional objectives!"

Although multiple-choice examinations are suited to many kinds of assessment questions teachers wish to answer, there are several other types of objective test items that have some advantages, too. This chapter will discuss true-false items, matching exercises, and completion or short-answer items. These item types add some versatility and variety to tests and can expand our skills to assessing an even wider range of educational outcomes.

What This Chapter Will Include. Here are the topics about which you will have learned by the end of this chapter:

1. The structure of true-false, matching, and completion items.
2. Guidelines for constructing each of the three test-types.
3. Advantages and limitations of each of these test-types.
4. Application of each test-type to assessing higher order outcomes.
5. Scoring aids for each of the test-types.

True-False Test Items

A **true-false test item** is a declarative statement; sometimes it is correct (true), and sometimes it is incorrect (false). The test-taker's job is to decide which statements are correct and which are not. Here are some examples.

Spiders are mollusks.

The symbol for gold is "Gd."

Montana ranks 4th in land mass among the 50 states.

In "Crossing the Bar" Tennyson was talking about an athletic event.

These are declarative statements. Is each true or is it false? To decide you must have a certain amount of knowledge about the subject of the sentence. The more items a student gets right, the more information I hypothesize to be in his or her grasp.

Guidelines for Writing True-False Items

True-false items are difficult to write because plausible statements often give clues to the test-taker. Teachers can avoid this to a considerable extent by following a few guidelines. None is an absolute rule, but following the guidelines as closely as possible will make your true-false test a more valid and reliable assessment procedure.

The first guideline is to avoid specific determiners. Avoid what? Specific determiners are words such as "all," "none," or "no"—words that indicate situations that are without exceptions. They provide clues that an item is probably false. There is almost no situation that includes "all" instances of something; there are few circumstances in which "none" do a given thing. Sure there are exceptions, but we do not bet on exceptions.

Here are some examples containing specific determiners:

Mercury is always in a liquid state.

All broad-leafed plants are deciduous.

All of Shakespeare's published works are plays.

A second type of specific determiners are the "uncertainty" terms. Here you find "usually," "sometimes," "typically," and others words that denote "maybe so, but surely not without exception." When these terms appear in a true-false item, they point to "true" as the most likely correct answer. They say, "I know there are exceptions so I'll slant the item toward the most common outcome, but I'll leave an opening for those exceptions." Here are some examples.

Rembrandt typically painted portraits.

Red is usually considered to be a "warm" color.

Some birds fly over 100 miles in a day during migration.

These items could be considered true, even though I recognize that they do not fit all cases involving the subject. That is why I bet on them being true—I have the escape clause that says, "Yes, I know that there are exceptions, but I can show you a pile of cases where this really happened."

The above items could be better written as

More than 85 percent of Rembrandt's paintings were portraits

Your textbook identifies red as a warm color.

At least 220 species of birds fly an average of 100 miles a day during migration.

A well written true-false item of this type will state the item with definite proportions, or as verified by authority, or state specific numbers. This will give the student the unambiguous data to make a clear choice.

True-false test items should also avoid using terms that denote an indefinite degree or amount. Words such as "large," "a long time ago," and "often" are slippery. People do not agree on what they mean. To my archeologist friend a long time ago is measured in hundreds of thousands of years; to me it is in decades; to my elementary school-aged son it is in years. To some students having a date every weekend is "often," but to others, "often" is three or more times a week.

These indefinite terms tend to lower validity of a test. A student may have a good idea of the point in history at which the Bastille was attacked—the date, what else was happening in France at that time, and what was going on in the rest of the western world. But was it a "long time ago"? How this student, who clearly knows the relevant history, interprets a "long time ago" could cause the student to fall down this slippery slope of indefinite terms.

Here are some examples using indefinite terms in true-false items.

Not so good:	In his study of crime, Dr. Wye found a high negative correlation between age of one's mother and age of the child's first arrest.
Better:	In his study of crime, Dr. Wye found a correlation greater than $-.75$ between . . .
Not so good:	At room temperatures of 70 degrees F, exposure to air for a short while often makes phosphorus ignite.
Better:	At a room temperature of 70°, exposure to air for less than one minute will result in ignition of phosphorus in more than 50 percent of laboratory tests.
Not so good:	The Pilgrims landed at Plymouth a long time before the Revolutionary War.
Better:	The Pilgrims landed at Plymouth more than 100 years before the . . .

In the first item no one knows how to interpret the word "high," so the item is ambiguous. In the "Better" item there is a definition of sorts of what "high" means. In the second item, there are two indefinite terms, "short while" and "often." Is a short while 5 seconds? An hour? And how many times in 100 must exposure to air for 1 minute bring about ignition before we all agree, "Hey, that's often!" The "Better" item has given the reader definitions. And in the third item, the slippery word is "long." Indeed the Pilgrims were in America over 150 years before the revolution, but is this a long time? The "Better" item gives an actual time value. In the revisions, interpreting words such as "long" is unnecessary, because the actual definitions (percent, time) are given, our decisions are based on criteria given in the items.

The third guideline is to avoid testing knowledge of trivial information. Sometimes teachers think that if they include items on information or skills that are central to the instruction in the unit everyone will get them correct, and there will be no discrimination between good and not-so-good students. To create some differences in scores among their students some teachers feel they should include trivial, nonfocal bits of data among their test items. This is not accurate. True-false items should follow the instructional plan just like all other assessment types should. There are objectives for teaching a unit, and the assessment device should reflect the centrality and commitment of time and effort of topics just as our instructional procedures did. This is the road to content validity.

True-false items should be positively stated declarative sentences, constructed as simply as possible. As teachers we are not trying to confuse students with complex linguistic formulations. We want to know who has the information and who does not. Putting students through linguistic mazes introduces a test feature which is not part of our table of specifications. Consider these items.

Not so good: According to the State Department of Health, no epidemics of influenza have been associated with situations where inoculation campaigns have not been carried out.

Better: According to the State Department of Health, epidemics of influenza are associated with failure to carry out inoculation campaigns.

The second statement is more directly to the point and less confusing to the reader. The use of double negatives is one technique used to confuse students in deciphering the linguistic structure of a statement. Double negatives should be avoided in writing true-false items.

A final guideline is that roughly half of the test items should be keyed true and half false. If this is the case students cannot say, "I know Miss Tuff writes more true items than false, so I'll guess true on this item." Equalizing the number of true-false items discourages guessing one option (true, false) disproportionately.

Scoring True-False Tests

To facilitate marking and scoring, true-false tests should be accompanied with instructions that clearly designate how marking should be done. Shall items be marked with a plus for true, a zero for false? Shall students write out "true" or "false"? Certainly the use of a minus should be avoided because it can too easily be changed to a plus after the tests are returned to students, and additional points requested by a student.

If the test is to be hand scored, the test sheet should have a T and F typed to the left of each item number. If the student thinks the item is true, the T is circled; if false, the F is circled. However, many teachers have devised their own general answer sheets that can be photocopied for student use. An example is given in Figure 8.1.

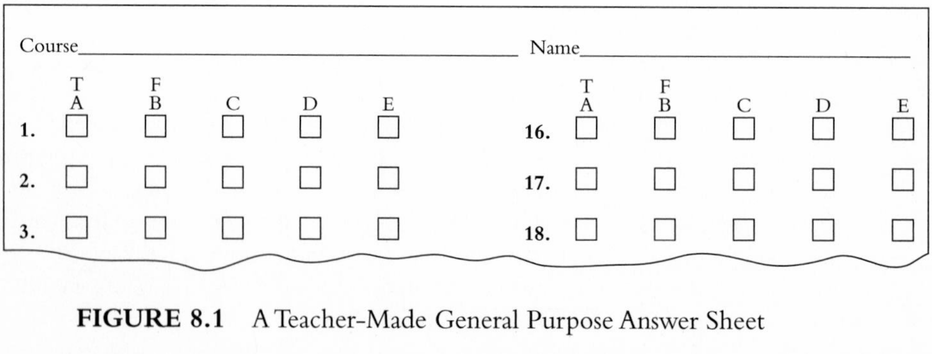

FIGURE 8.1   A Teacher-Made General Purpose Answer Sheet

The best system is an optically scannable answer sheet and machine scoring. This system provides rapid scoring and computer analysis, with an alphabetic list of the class with scores for each student. (Example is shown in Chapter 7, page 124.)

Using True-False Tests for Assessing Higher Order Processing

True-false tests have been criticized for focusing on the fact based, Foundational Content in a unit of instruction. Indeed many people do write such tests. They can be written quickly while paging through a chapter, and they are easy to defend when students challenge an answer. One need only look up the fact in the textbook. However, true-false tests, like multiple choice, need not be written only at the Foundational Content level. Here are some examples of how to write true-false tests at a higher level than that of basic facts.

Mr. Pavelle has just done a unit on the Constitution of the United States in his government class. Here are some test items he has written that require the use of complex skills.

Which of the following are true and which are false in regard to the Constitutional limitations on state powers?

T   F   a) The State of California can make an agreement with Mexico regarding the number of immigrants that will legally be admitted to the state.

T   F   b) The State of Arizona for its 100th anniversary of statehood in 2012 may coin an Arizona dollar which will be used in Arizona for legal tender during that year.

T   F   c) If the State of Michigan passes a regulation for inspection of all lumber imported from Canada, it may impose a fee on the importer to cover the inspection costs.

These items require the student to recall the limitations imposed on states by the Constitution and to analyze the content of the statement to see if one of the limitations applies to the situation cited. This is more than a simple recall of fact; it is a higher order cognitive production activity requiring analysis, perhaps synthesis, and evaluation.

Here is another example.

Rose deposited $300 in the Nation's Local Bank and Trust Company on January 1. She now wishes to know how much interest she has accumulated. What does she need to know to find this out?

T   F   a) Rose must know if interest is simple or compound.

T   F   b) She must know how many types of interest-bearing accounts the bank carries.

T   F   c) She must know the interest rate that applies to her account.

Again, these items require breaking down the subject of savings accounts into its many components and seeing which ones should be used together to solve Rose's problem. As before, this is more than a simple recall of facts; it is a reasoning question involving analysis and synthesis. We might even include a statement as to whether Rose has the most productive account (out of several types of possible accounts which we would describe.) This will add an evaluation aspect to the solution. Each of these is Higher Order Processing.

Here are more examples from different disciplines.

T	F	In "To a Mountain Daisy," Burns' point is that all life is beautiful.
T	F	Circle A has a radius of 4″ and circle B has a radius of 6″; Both circles can have the same circumference.
T	F	A pendulum hangs on a 25-foot steel wire; the pendulum will hang closer to the floor at 1 A.M. than at noon.

In each of these examples the students must interpret the situations in terms of what they know about the principles involved before judging the adequacy of the statement. This is higher order processing.

Teachers should expect that some additional thought will be required when constructing true-false items at the Higher Order Processing level, but with practice in developing items at this level the job becomes easier.

Advantages of True-False Tests

There are some real advantages in using the true-false question in assessing instructional outcomes. The box below contains the most common of these.

Advantages of True-False Tests

1. Many points of information can be assessed in a short time.
2. There is less demand in reading than in multiple choice.
3. Scoring is easy, fast, and objective, and scoring is typically quite reliable.
4. All levels of the taxonomy, and of your table of specifications, can be assessed with true-false items.

Let's discuss each of these advantages in detail.

Many points of information can be assessed in a short time. Any test is a sample of the instructional content defined in a unit of teaching. The more items a test contains the more adequately the test can sample the total range of content presented. Students can typically do 25 or more true-false items in the time it takes to do about 10 multiple-choice items. This means at least twice as many points of information can be cited on a true-false test as on a multiple-choice test.

As discussed in Chapter 3 and 4, longer tests can provide wider sampling, and sampling is the basis for greater content validity, and Chapter 4 showed that longer tests tend to have higher reliability. True-false tests can be more valid and reliable because they allow teachers to present students with more items for a given testing period than do other types of tests.

Another advantage of true-false tests is that *there is less demand on reading than in multiple choice.* As noted earlier, if items require a lot of reading, the test score includes not only a component of the knowledge of the skill area on which it is focused (chemistry, government, etc.), but also is adulterated by a large verbal skill component. This means teachers are grading students on a skill (reading) in addition to the one on which the grade is to be based. True-false tests help reduce the effect of the verbal component on scores.

Scoring is easy, fast, objective, and typically quite reliable. Educators want to spend as little time as possible on clerical tasks. True-false tests are easily scored following one of the procedures discussed in Chapter 7. In addition, true-false scores are objective because there is only one correct answer. Two competent scores would arrive at a common score for any paper. This means that the scores are not only objective, but also tend to be quite reliable.

Lastly, *all levels of the taxonomy can be assessed with true-false items.* In good assessment we may well wish to involve several types of procedures, for example multiple choice and true-false. In all cases teachers want to tap skills at every level of the taxonomy they have listed in their table of specifications. As we saw demonstrated earlier, true-false tests are adaptable for use in accessing higher order as well as Foundational Content. With practice we will be able to write true-false items at all levels and with relative ease.

Limitations of True-False Tests

Along with their advantages there are some limitations to true-false items that gnaw away at their usefulness. The main limitations are listed in the box below.

Limitations of True-False Tests

1. Scores are influenced by guessing more than in other types of tests.
2. A wrong response provides little information that will help teachers decide why a student missed an item.
3. Testwriters have a tendency to stay with basic factual content in true-false items.

A closer look at some of these limitations will help us see just how much of a problem they can be.

Scores are influenced by guessing more than in other types of tests. Guessing, for at least some students, is a big factor in true-false testing. Theoretically, a student using a coin toss could get on *average* 50 percent of the items correct. Students probably won't guess that often. Nevertheless, we should be wary of guessing.

Some books suggest the use of **scoring formulas** to adjust for guessing. The most common formula is

$$\text{Corrected Score} = \text{Number Right} - \text{Number Wrong}$$

This formula focuses on the items that were marked wrong. It reasons that all wrong items were the result of a bad guess. It assumes that for every item students guessed at and missed, they also guessed at one and got lucky (following the 50 percent correct, 50 percent wrong theory of guessing).

Suppose that I am scoring Khalid's paper. He has 23 correct and 7 wrong. I reason that he guessed at 14 items, 7 of which were wrong, and 7 correct (following the 50 percent theory). This means that I have included 7 items into his correct score even though Khalid did not know the right answers for them. They were simply good guesses. Therefore, for every wrong item we should eliminate one item from the right score because it was a "guessed at and got lucky" item.

Although the scoring formula has a logical foundation, it has problems in implementation:

1. It assumes a student's response is strictly a random guess. This is rarely the case. Most students know something about a topic and make educated guesses even when they do not know the exact information they need. Their probability of a correct guess is often higher than .50 because of the smattering of information they use as a base for the guess.

2. It also assumes that students are equally bold guessers. This, of course, is not true. When scoring formulas are applied one should instruct students to leave blank those items for which they do not know the answer. (Blank items are not counted right or wrong.) Some people will do this, but bold guessers will take their chances. The formula does not acknowledge this difference in student personality.

Therefore, the best way to administer true-false tests is to advise all students to give every item their best response. Scoring formulas are not generally helpful. Students end up ranked about the same way with or without a scoring formula.

Another limitation of true-false tests is that *wrong responses provide little information that will help teachers decide why students missed an item.* If in multiple-choice tests you saw a distractor that drew an unusual number of responses, you knew the point of the misinformation that students were bringing to the test. However, in true-false tests if the correct answer is "False," and a student marks the item false, we may surmise that the student knew the statement was wrong, but may not know what the correct circumstances are. "I know this is not correct, but I can't really say what the correct situation is." True-false tests are not very helpful in providing diagnostic information.

A third limitation in the true-false test is the *tendency of testwriters to stay with basic factual, Foundational Content.* Teachers, who are always pressed for time, often find it easier to write true-false tests along the path of least resistance, namely, at the basic factual level. As with multiple-choice tests, teachers often rationalize their focus on facts by pointing out that if a student questions an answer, it can be found in the textbook or in class papers. This gives teachers some security during that nervous period when returning student papers.

Mr. Presser, a fifth-grade teacher, is at his word processor constructing a summative test for the earth science unit the class is about to finish. It is 4 P.M. and he must stop at the drugstore before going home. He takes out the textbook and begins to note facts that can be quickly converted into declarative statements that are either true or false.

When he gets to the end of the chapter he has 28 statements, decides he would like an even 30, and goes back and picks out two more items. He then hurries out of his classroom, knowing his test is ready for tomorrow's class and that all items can be traced directly to the content of the textbook.

Quickly written tests like this typically target the facts in the unit, avoiding the reasoning, analysis, evaluation, synthesis, and application features Mr. Presser surely wants his students to perform. The press of time simply did not allow him the opportunity to get to these features. However, we have seen that this need not be the case in using true-false tests. The limitation is not with the type of test, but with the testwriter.

Some Conclusions About True-False Tests

In order for true-false tests to have maximum validity they must be carefully constructed according to specified guidelines. If these items are well constructed, they not only allow teachers to put variety into their assessment procedures, they also allow them to include many more points of information in their tests. They are easy to score and focus more on content and less on verbal skill in determining a student's status.

Unfortunately, true-false tests have their limitations. They are not always easy to write at levels above basic knowledge, guessing plays a big role in some scores (and scoring formulas do not solve this problem), and they do not provide diagnostic results. On balance, something is to be gained by use of the true-false tests as alternative assessment techniques, if they are thoughtfully applied. However, no one assessment procedure is completely adequate by itself.

✎ Problems

1. For each of the following true-false test items identify the error in its construction.
   a. Ancient man did not have iron tools.
   b. Usually the temperature is higher in a city than in the surrounding countryside.
   c. The Druids lived a long time ago.
   d. No insects never have a body made of a head and abdomen only.
2. In your teaching area write two true-false items at the higher order level.
3. List three advantages and three limitations of true-false items.

Matching Exercises

"Matching exercises are for primary children," one high school teacher once said to me. Indeed, educators have long used matching tests in the primary grades, because the job of test-taking is simple. Young children can understand what is to be done, and little reading skill is involved. Though well suited to primary grades, there are also some important applications in the upper grades as well.

In the **matching test** the teacher has a column of terms on the left side of the work sheet. The terms in this column are called **stimuli.** There is also one column of terms on the right, called **responses.** For each stimulus term there is a response term that some how relates to that stimulus. Here is an example.

In the space at the left write the letter of the state in which the Civil War battle was fought.

_____	1. Andersonville	a)	Mississippi
_____	2. Antietam	b)	Maryland
_____	3. Bull Run	c)	Tennessee
_____	4. Perryville	d)	Georgia
_____	5. Shiloh	e)	Virginia
_____	6. Vicksburg	f)	Kentucky
		g)	Pennsylvania

The matching exercise is often used for assessing association-type learning, but can be applied to many types of outcomes, including that of Higher Order Processing. The matching exercise can cover a collection of content on a given topic in a relatively short time. For example, the exercise above quickly covers location of major battles, something that multiple choice could not do in the same amount of time.

Even though matching can be used to assess attainment of higher order outcomes of instruction, it is seldom used at that level. Because of its easy adaptability to factual, associative material matching tests are often used in conjunction with other types of assessments which do access the higher level outcomes of learning. For example, matching may be used as an exercise following a multiple-choice or true-false test. In such cases care should be taken to avoid duplicating a point on the matching test that has already been covered on the preceding assessment exercise.

Guidelines for Writing Matching Exercises

As in the use of other assessment procedures, there are rules for creating matching tests. Here are several of the most important ones.

Each matching exercise should contain only homogeneous material. For example, an exercise that contains historic sites, should not contain a name of a person who performed a significant historic act. Here is one such situation.

1. Boston	a) first capital city of the United States
2. Bunker Hill	b) where tea was dumped into the ocean
3. Charles Pinckney	c) where the Declaration of Independence was signed
4. New York City	
5. Philadelphia	d) town on the Mississippi River
	e) early battle in the Revolution
	f) signer of the Declaration of Independence

If Charles Pinckney's name appears among a list of cities or other geographical sites, the students will match response f) as correct for Pinckney, not because they know who

Charles Pinckney was, but because f) is the only response that deals with a person. If this exercise had dealt with only historic sites, the test would not have given away this item to testwise students.

The stimuli should be numbered and listed in a column on the left; the responses should be lettered and laid out in a column on the right. This not only makes an orderly format students can use to figure out their associations, but also reduces marking accidents that erode reliability.

Stimuli should be listed in alphabetical, chronological, or some such logical order; responses should be in random order. Teachers want to facilitate the job of test-taking, and the ordering of stimuli makes the job of hunting for responses a little easier.

There should be at least one more response than there are stimuli. Suppose you have found a response for every stimulus except one. Since there are the same number of stimuli as responses in your test, that one remaining stimulus must go with the one remaining response (even if you had no idea why). Of course, the test should not give away the last stimulus by having only one remaining response. If, at the end of the matching exercise, you had several (two is usually enough) responses that are not matched with any stimulus, you must still make a choice among several responses for the one remaining stimulus. Therefore, matching tests should have more responses than stimuli.

All items for a matching exercise should be on one page. Turning pages back and forth sometimes confuses students and leads them into making random errors that would not have been made had the test been printed on a single page. This erodes reliability.

The number of stimuli should be limited to six to ten in the lower grades, and 13 to 16 in the upper grades. If more items are to be included on a matching exercise, make two or more exercises rather than make longer stimuli lists. This not only encourages teachers to make stimuli more homogeneous on a single exercise (requiring closer discriminations by students), but also reduces the "hunt time" for the student in completing one test.

Each exercise should be introduced by instructions for taking the test. In the lower grades teachers often tell students to draw a line between the "word on the left and the word on the right that goes with it." In the upper elementary, middle, and high school levels teachers usually print a line to the left of each stimulus term. They then ask students to write the letter of the response term that best fits with the stimulus.

This format facilitates scoring. A key can be made to match the number locations. The key is laid beside the student responses and the right answers are marked quickly. Figure 8.2, on page 142, is an example of this type of test design and the key that goes with it.

Higher Order Applications for Matching Tests

Matching exercises are often used on factual or basic content of a unit, but can also be applied at higher levels of cognitive demand. One way we can apply matching to the higher order processes is to list a set of principles, rules, or generalizations in the stimulus column. For the responses we then list examples where the principle, rule, or gener-

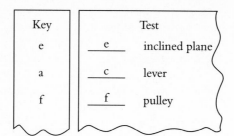

FIGURE 8.2   Key Strip for Scoring Matching Tests

alization applies. Figure 8.3 shows an example of this. In the example shown in the figure the student must determine what the operation requires and then find the machine that performs that operation. This procedure has a number of applications for science, mathematics, writing (parts of speech, etc.), languages (e.g., verb case), and several other content areas. It can be quite useful because it assesses the achievement of a number of understandings in a relatively short exercise.

Figure 8.4 shows an example of another type of problem, where getting the correct answer requires analysis by the student. Exercises like these employ the matching test in assessing at the higher order process level. In this case it does its job with a relatively short test and appears to be an efficient tool for assessing at higher levels of cognitive demand.

Select the machine that is illustrated by the example.

	Machine	*Example*
_____	1. inclined plane	a) operating a pump handle
_____	2. lever	b) cutting with an ax
_____	3. pulley	c) lifting cargo on a ship with a block and tackle
_____	4. screw	d) rolling a hoop along a street
_____	5. wedge	e) sliding a box down the tail gate of a truck
		f) drilling a hole with a bit or auger

FIGURE 8.3   An Application of a Matching Test to Assessing Higher Order Processing in Science

Match the most likely part with the functional problem.

	Problem	*Part*
_____	1. There is a marked loss of power on one cylinder only.	a) battery
_____	2. Car starts well, but as it warms up runs unevenly and then stops.	b) choke
_____	3. No electrical power is reaching the spark plugs, but starter cranks.	c) distributor
_____	4. There is gasoline in the tank but little is reaching the carburetor.	d) fuel pump
_____	5. The starter will not crank the motor.	e) valve
		f) water pump

FIGURE 8.4 Apply a Matching Test to Assessing Higher Order Processing in Auto Mechanics

Advantages of Matching Exercises

Like all assessment procedures, matching exercises has some strong points and some limitations. The advantages are listed below.

Advantages of Matching Exercises

1. Matching exercises offer a concise procedure for assessing learning of a set of related ideas, facts, or applications.
2. Matching calls for a minimum of reading.
3. Matching items are relatively easy to construct.
4. Scoring is easy and reliable.

A closer look at these statements will more clearly illustrate the advantages.

Matching exercises offer a concise procedure for assessing learning of a set of related ideas, facts, and similar content. This type of test is made up of single words (or short phrases) in one column which are to be matched with single words (or short phrases) in a second column. What could be simpler? Yet, we do not classify this procedure for use at the Foundational Content level only; it can easily do more.

Matching calls for a minimum of reading. With matching tests you can get at a set of related facts (or concepts) quickly and while requiring little reading on the student's part. Often a single match is based on only two words. This is one reason we use matching in lower grade levels. Reading requirements are minimal.

Matching exercises are relatively easy to construct. Once the list of related concepts with which the exercise is to be made is on hand, the test-writing time is short. It takes a fraction of the time that goes into a true-false or multiple choice test.

Scoring is easy and reliable. Scoring of matching tests is very quick and simple. This is especially true if students are asked to write the letter of the response on a line before the appropriate stimulus. Then, for rapid scoring a key may be compared with the column of letters students have written to the left of the stimuli. When marking the test, start your pencil mark on the key strip and move horizontally to the students paper. That way your key strip will show how many students missed each item—information that is helpful for reviewing and reteaching.

Matching tests are considered to be at least as reliable as multiple-choice tests (Shaha, 1984), assuming that the exercise is long enough and has been constructed well.

Limitations of Matching Exercises

Along with the advantages, there are a few limitations of matching exercises. The main ones are listed below.

Limitations of Matching Tests

1. Matching tests depend upon having a number of related stimuli for an exercise; something not found in every unit of study.
2. Matching tests are primarily suited to the Foundational Content level; items for objectives above this level are more difficult to construct.
3. Matching is not suited to wide sampling of a unit's content.

Now let's elaborate on these points.

Matching tests depend upon having a number of related stimuli for an exercise. This limitation is a result of the type of subject matter in which we are making an assessment and the skill of the testwriter and not of the procedure itself. Although most subject-matter areas have sets of related concepts that should be a part of our assessments, some do not. A careful review of our table of specifications for a unit of instruction will help us sort through content of instruction and decide if we have the related concepts that are suitable for matching exercises. This table is our first resource in laying out any type of test content.

Matching is primarily suited to the Foundational Content level; items above this level are more difficult to construct. As with all tests, it is easier and less time consuming to make matching exercises that are at the factual level than at higher order processing levels. However, it is not only possible to make matching exercises at the higher order levels, it is an efficient way to cover a set of concepts in a relatively short time.

Matching is not suited to wide sampling of a unit's content. A wide sampling of the unit of instruction will probably require use of multiple-choice or true-false formats. Matching tests will be used for assessing clusters of more specific, related content within the unit. Teaming with one of these other item types is usually necessary to do a nice job of assessment.

Some Conclusions About Matching Exercises

Educators often want to introduce variety into their assessment procedures. It increases student interest, and it increases the range of learning outcomes that are reflected in our total assessment of a student's achievement. Matching tests are one way to add another measuring device into that assessment.

Matching exercises require careful structuring to ensure their validity and reliability. Features in structuring should include: using only homogeneous material, arranging stimuli in a logical order, keeping all items on a single page, and limiting the number of items in an exercise to those that can be best handled by the age group for whom the test is created.

Matching tests have often been used to assess simple associative learning, but they can be used for assessing higher order learning outcomes, as well. More effort should be made toward this end, because matching tests are an efficient way to assess achievement of objectives at this higher level of learning outcomes.

✎ Problems

1. Following is a matching test. Identify its problems.

    Constitutional provisions are in column 2 with the amendment to the Constitution listed in column 1.

___ 1. II	a) search and seizure
___ 2. VI	b) trial by jury
___ 3. IV	c) freedom of speech
___ 4. I	d) speedy trial
___ 5. VII	e) father of the Bill of Rights
___ 6. VIII	f) excessive bail
___ 7. George Mason	g) right to bear arms

2. In your subject-matter area write a matching exercise at the higher order level of cognitive processing.

Completion Tests

Completion tests are a cousin to essay tests, but because they require very limited writing (a single word or phrase) they can also be scored somewhat objectively. Completion is a supply-type procedure, but because its scoring is much like that of objective tests, it has been included here with less complex tests.

There are two formats used in completion. One uses a statement from which one or more key terms have been dropped and a blank inserted to take their place. The student's job is to write the word (or phrase) in the blank that will make the statement correct. In the second format the completion item may be a question, the answer to which is a single word or phrase. The student will supply the word, or words, for the answer. Completion tests are supply-type tests because in both formats students are not given options; instead, they must furnish their own responses.

In the test types you and I have looked at—multiple choice, true-false, matching—the assessment involves recognition of the correct answer. Completion tests focus largely on assessing recall rather than recognition. For instance, in a multiple-choice test, the students need only recognize as correct one of three or four options. Completion tests give a few clues, but for the most part the student must depend on recall of the topic. This tends to make the completion test more difficult than a recognition test on the same topics.

But there are some topics in most school subjects that teachers want students to recall without prompting. Among these items are mathematical combinations (2 + 4, 4 × 6), translations of vocabulary, the sequence of historical events, traffic laws, materials dangerous to the environment, and many others. Tests of recall, such as completion, are valuable for assessing unprompted knowledge of these items.

The completion test, however, has its disadvantages. The most significant of these is that it is primarily adaptable to Foundational Content. Analysis, synthesis, and evaluation are less commonly touched by completion items. Nevertheless, teachers may wish to look at some ways to apply them to higher order operations. For example, a problem is given and the answer is to be written in the blank; a concept is given and a "real life" example is to be written in the blank; or the reverse, an example is given and a principle represented by the example is written as the answer. These examples indicate that completion has a fairly wide range of possible uses.

Completion tests are more difficult to score than any of the other tests discussed in this chapter. Machine scoring is not applicable to completion tests, and keys are difficult to make because several responses are often acceptable for an item. Nevertheless, because there is knowledge that children should have that depends on recall, completion tests have a role to play in the total assessment process.

Types of Completion Test Items

As discussed above, there are two formats for completing a statement. One is "fill-in-the-blank" and the other is the "short answer." In the first type, a single word (or possibly two) will complete a statement. Here is an example.

What is the name (first and last) of the current governor of the State of Indiana? _____.

The second type of completion item is the short answer question. It looks like this:

What is the last step in passing a bill into federal law? _____.

In this case the item is answered with a short phrase and not a single word. Fill-in-the-blank items are scored a bit more objectively than are short answer items. In the latter, some judgments are typically required to determine the correctness of the response, because students will record the response using a variety of terms and constructions.

Guidelines for Writing Completion Items

Following are several guidelines that will help teachers improve their skill in writing completion tests, avoid random errors, and improve the validity of test items. The guidelines fit both completion formats.

If at all possible, *completion items should be answerable with a single word*. Here is an example of a "not so good" item and a "better" one that illustrates this point.

Not so good: The purpose of the carburetor in a gasoline engine is to

_____.

Better: On a gasoline engine, what is the name of the part that vaporizes the gasoline? _____.

With a single word answer there is no judgment call required for scoring. In the first item, different students will use different phrasing, and the teacher must make a judgment for each student's response. You and I may not make the same judgment on every item, reducing the reliability of the test score.

Avoid lifting statements directly from the textbook. Lifting from the textbook encourages rote memory, an activity educators try to avoid. As in multiple choice and true-false, repeating the textbook does provide a measure of security for the teacher when accuracy of an item is questioned. However, this security does not warrant the encouragement of memorization of selected excerpts from the textbook. Memorization does not imply understanding.

Make the intent of the statement clear so that one, and only one answer will be correct. Look at this item:

Poor:

Abraham Lincoln was born in _____.

Several answers are true statements here. Possibly the writer of this item was looking for "Kentucky" as the answer, but surely other responses have validity. He was born in 1809, in a log cabin, in poverty. The student should get credit for several answers here, but you can bet that the teacher intended only one to be correct. Students who give other, often logical answers will say "I didn't know what you wanted there." Items like this will increase errors of measurement and reduce reliability.

We can improve the above item by rewriting it to read:

Better:

Abraham Lincoln was born in the year _____.

or

In what state of the Union was Abraham Lincoln born? _____

The blanks in a completion item should preferably be placed at the end of the statement rather than at the beginning. If the blank is at the beginning of the statement it tends to leave the reader without immediate orientation. Here is an example.

Poor:

_____ is the name of the town where Dwight Eisenhower is buried.

At the outset no one knows the direction the question will take. If the eliminated term is at the end of the statement the subject and predicate of the sentence is given to the reader before the answer is called for. Here is an example.

Better:

What is the name of the town in which Dwight Eisenhower is buried?
_____.

Do not give clues by making some blanks longer or shorter than others. All blanks should be the same length. Even if you do not intend to give clues by the length of the blank, some students will interpret longer blanks as meaning that a longer answer is required. This misinterpretation adds random error to the score.

Scoring Aids With Completion Tests

Every teacher wants to spend as little time as possible on scoring tests. Accordingly, they should construct their tests to take as little time in scoring as possible. Following are some ways to accomplish this goal.

Number the blanks in the narrative part of the test. Then along the right side of the page make a column of numbered blanks. This is the student's response column, where the students will write their answers to correspond with the numbered blanks in the text. Here is an example.

Abraham Lincoln was born in the State of <u>1</u>,   1. _____
and practiced law in the State of <u>2</u>. He   2. _____
became President in the year <u>3</u>.   3. _____

In scoring this exercise I need only lay my key along the right side of the student's paper and compare responses with those on the key. This is simple and is quick to do.

Here is another suggestion for scoring. Count all correct responses as equal in weight, that is, do not give two points for some, one point for others, and so forth. A good rule is to give one point for each correct answer, just as on a multiple-choice test. It is difficult to justify why one answer deserves more points than another, and without this justification, you probably should avoid the practice.

Advantages of Completion/Short Answer Tests

In this section we will look briefly at some of the advantages of completion and short-answer test items.

A list of these advantages follows.

Advantages of Completion Tests

1. They are easy to write.
2. Guessing is less likely than in other types of tests.
3. They are adaptable to many types of subject matter.
4. Completion test scores are quite reliable.

Here is a look at these strengths in more detail.

A key advantage of completion tests is that they are easy to write. As you look over your objectives for a unit of instruction you find a number of items at the Foundational Content level that you hope students have committed to memory. These are items you believe students can recall, not just recognize. You can access many of these with the completion test, requiring only a word or short sentence for each item.

Guessing is less likely in completion tests than in other types of tests. There is only one correct answer for a well written completion item. The student is not given options among which to guess. Students hate to leave blanks on their tests, so the test-taker may write an answer of which he or she is not certain, but this is not the same as taking a chance on one of several given options.

Completion scores are adaptable to any type of subject matter. Almost every school subject has basic content which students should be able to recall. Here are a few examples. In music: vocabulary, chords, notation, plots in operettas; in history: names, dates, sequences of events, documents and their content; in sciences: vocabulary, steps in a sequence, reactions to an event; in English/literature/language: vocabulary, grammar, personalities, sequences, styles of writing. Try your hand at expanding this list; it should be easy to do within your own teaching area.

Completion scores are quite reliable. There is evidence that they may be more reliable than either matching or multiple-choice tests (Zimmerman, 1984). Of course to be reliable the items must be well constructed and the scoring done in a systematic manner.

Limitations of Completion Tests

There are also limitations to the use of completion/short answer tests. A few of the most common ones are listed in the following box.

Limitations of Completion Tests

1. It is difficult to apply completion items to assessing Higher Order Processes.
2. Scoring is tedious and adulterated by spelling errors and alternate wording.
3. Because answers are limited to a single word (or phrase) some topics must be left out of the test because they require longer responses.

And now let's elaborate on these problems.

It is difficult to apply completion tests to assessing Higher Order Processes. The limitation of answers to a single word (or a few words) makes it difficult, but not impossible, to use this item in analysis, synthesis, or evaluation. Higher Order Processes usually require some elaboration or explanation. In tests that require short answers this is hard to do. As noted above, some application of completion tests to these higher level processes can be done using a device such as giving an example and requiring the principle. However, assessing at the Higher Order level can be done better with other kinds of test items.

Scoring is tedious and adulterated by spelling errors and alternate wording. Not all writing is easy to read. Some students will put limitations on their answers, while others will elaborate. Judging the adequacy of the answer is not a simple process of asking "is the word there?" Judgments must be made as to the adequacy of many responses. And shall I give partial credit if the answer appears to be there but is misspelled? If so, how much credit shall I give? Shall I give more credit for small spelling flaws and less for really poor spelling? Shall I give partial credit for short answers that appear to be partly correct? What criteria shall I use to make these decisions? (Although partial credit is not recommended, if it is given the rules should be justified to the students before the tests.) All of this makes the scoring somewhat subjective and opens the door to errors of measurement and reliability problems. Because fewer judgments must be made that bring in inconsistencies, the use of the one-word completion approach rather than the short answer is encouraged.

Because answers are limited to a single word (or phrase) *some topics must be left out of the test because they require longer responses.* Topics that require more than a word or phrase are best tested using the essay format. Topics of a more expansive nature are not appropriate for the short-answer type of test.

Some Conclusions About Completion Tests

Because completion tests assess topics educators believe students should commit to memory, they are a useful type of test item that has a number of applications within the school curriculum. They are easy to construct and can tap a wide range of subject matter topics. However, because they do not access Higher Order Processes very easily, they should not be used alone.

Completion items are difficult to score, time consuming and require judgments about partial credit, the criteria for which are not always firm and stable. However, there are topics of content that we want students to reproduce (and not just recognize), as they must do with real life information. To this end completion tests have a role in our total assessment operation.

✎ Problems

Following is a set of completion items. Critique these items.

1. Henry Ford manufactured his first car in _____.
2. The outcome of the Battle of Gettysburg was _____.
3. _____ was born in Arkansas, and elected President in _____.
4. The first successful airplane flight in America was done in _____.
5. Your textbook says "Tyrannosaurus rex lived _____ years ago."

A Real Case Narrative

In the previous chapter you read a brief narrative depicting a student teacher constructing his first test. The test was multiple choice, and factual. The student has now revised the test and is now about to discuss it with the supervisor. After you read the discussion, take the role of the supervisor and decide how you would help this student teacher with his test writing.

Mr. Ross, a student teacher in biology, has done a revision on his first test. The original test—a multiple-choice—concentrated on factual material in the textbook. He now discusses the revision with Mr. Alten, his supervisor.

"I've gone through the test and eliminated a few of the multiple-choice items, and substituted ten true-false items and two matching exercises. I can see that these give the test some variety while covering the same basic facts as the multiple-choice items I had before," Mr. Ross began hopefully.

Mr. Alten scanned the test. "Yes, the test does look a bit more interesting, but how well have you matched these items to your objectives?" he asked.

"Well, I tried to eliminate multiple-choice items whose content could be assessed by the other types of test items. To this end the test assesses the same topics that the first draft did," Mr. Ross replied.

"Let's see," Mr. Alten mused, "what did we agree the problem was with the first draft?"

Mr. Ross thought just a minute. "Well, I stuck too closely to the text, and, uh, it concentrated too much on facts and not enough applications."

"Of course, we use an item type because it does a good job at the level of an objective—like matching tests for associational material," Mr. Alten continued. He paused. "How would you compare this test with the first draft in terms of applications?" he asked.

Mr. Ross glanced at the test, frowning. "Well, uh, uh, can you explain this applications thing a bit?"

SUMMARY

1. True-false, matching, and short answer tests are tools that provide variety in our assessments, are relatively easy to construct, and are applicable to assessing achievement of many objectives.

2. A true-false test item is a declarative statement that may be either correct or incorrect.

3. Guidelines for writing true-false items include avoiding specific determiners and indefinite terms and avoiding testing knowledge of trivial information; true-false items should be positively stated, declarative sentences.

4. It is possible to write true-false items that require analysis, synthesis, and evaluation as well as recall of basic facts.

5. Among the advantages of true-false items are assessment of many points of information in a short time, less demand in reading, and ease and reliability of scoring.

6. Limitations of true-false items include susceptibility to guessing, lack of information about why items are answered incorrectly, and a tendency to be limited to basic factual content.

7. In a matching exercise a column of terms on one side of the page, known as stimuli, must be matched with a set of terms on the other side, called responses.

8. Matching exercises should contain only homogeneous material, laid out in an orderly fashion, and listed in a logical order; there should be at least one more response than there are stimuli, and the test should be accompanied by instructions.

9. Matching tests can be applied to higher order processes by listing a set of principles, rules, or generalizations in the stimulus column and examples of their application in the response column.

10. Matching tests are easy to construct and score and offer a concise procedure for assessing learning of a set of related ideas with a minimum of reading demand.

11. Matching tests require a number of related stimuli and are best suited to foundational knowledge; they do not provide a wide sampling of a unit's content.

12. Completion tests require the test-taker to fill in a blank in a statement or to provide a short answer to a question.

13. Completion items should be answerable with one specific word (and no other) and should not be lifted directly from the textbook; the blank to be filled in should be at the end of the item, not the beginning. Short answer tests should be answerable by one word or a phrase in order to support objectivity of scoring.

14. Completion items are easy to write, minimally susceptible to guessing, adaptable to any type of subject matter, and quite reliable.

15. It is difficult to apply completion tests to higher order processes; scoring is slow; and they are limited by lack of opportunity for elaborating one's answer.

PROBLEMS

1. Write an instructional objective in the field with which you are most familiar. Be sure this is written in terms of behaviors that can be seen and counted (such as "writes examples of the past perfect tense correctly"). Now write three true-false test items that could be used to observe a student's progress in achieving this objective. Exchange papers with another member of your class and discuss the extent to which you see each other's work as done well.

2. Are all of your items at the Foundational Content level? Choose one item and rewrite it at the Higher Order Processes level of the taxonomy so that it assesses attainment of objectives at this level.

3. Below are a set of test items. Critique each of them using the guidelines provided in this chapter.

T	F	a)	All broad-leafed trees lose their leaves in winter.
T	F	b)	Usually states have a senate and a house of representatives.
T	F	c)	The Declaration of Independence was probably written with a steel-pointed pen.
T	F	d)	The Sears Tower in Chicago is a very tall building.
T	F	e)	If the Speaker of the House of Representatives is not present this is not a reason to deny a motion to adjourn the meeting of congressmen.

4. Evaluate this matching exercise.

Column A		Column B
_____ 1. Washington	a)	sixteenth president
_____ 2. Concord	b)	first president
_____ 3. Jefferson	c)	site of Revolutionary battle
_____ 4. J. Q. Adams	d)	wrote the Declaration of Independence
_____ 5. A. Lincoln	e)	his father was also president

5. Here are some completion items. Comment on the adequacy of construction of each.
   1. Henry Ford manufactured his first car in _____.
   2. The outcome of the Battle of Gettysburg was _____.
   3. _____ was born in Arkansas, and elected President in _____.
   4. The first successful airplane flight in America was done in _____.

KEY TERMS

true-false test item   stimuli
specific determiner   responses
scoring formula   completion tests
matching test

ADDITIONAL READING

Anderson, R. C. (1972). How to construct achievement tests to assess comprehension. *Review of Educational Research, 42*, 145–170.

Ebel, R. L. (1975). Can teachers write good true-false items? *Journal of Educational Measurement, 12*, 31–35.

Frisbie, D. A. and Becker, D. F. (1990). An analysis of textbook advice about true-false tests. *Applied Measurement in Education,* 4 (1), 67–83.

Gronlund, N. E. *How to Make Achievement Tests and Assessments,* 5th ed. Boston: Allyn & Bacon, 1993.

CHAPTER 9

ITEM ANALYSIS

Finding The Test Items That Work

It's 4:00 P.M. and Mr. Alverez is looking over the test he gave today in his Biology class. "These test results are really surprising," he thought. "The good students missed some items I was sure they would get, and the not-so-good students got those same items correct! Something is really wrong with the items or with how I taught this unit!"

An **item analysis** of tests can help teachers find answers to the problem Mr. Alverez is facing. After you have written a set of test items, following all the guidelines for writing good tests, you cannot be sure every item will work. Test items are intended to sort out the students who have reached the instructional objectives from those who have not. An item "works" if the most knowledgeable students tend to get it right, while the least knowledgeable students tend to miss it. The procedure for finding which items work is item analysis. Item analysis not only sorts out items that are not working, but also makes educators better test-writers and helps them do a better job of assessing student achievement. In addition, it can tell them how well their instruction is getting through to the students. These points are valuable information for teachers (Kalstad, 1984).

What This Chapter Will Include. In this chapter you will learn about:

1. The concept and function of item analysis
2. How a "by hand" procedure for item analysis works
3. What information you can get from applying item analysis
4. How to improve tests with item analysis
5. Creating a test item file with item analysis
6. What an electronic item analysis looks like (from your school's electronic scoring machine)

Functions of Item Analysis

One important objective of testing is to identify how well students are achieving the objectives of instruction. Indeed, as teachers lead students through a unit, their observations give the teacher some idea of who is achieving well and who is not. But teachers like to confirm these hunches. They do this by asking the students to go through a series of common, specific performances—test items or controlled observations—that provide a more objective appraisal of each student's achievement.

Assessment of achievement depends on using items that work. The first thing you and I look for in identifying working items is their difficulty level. By **difficulty** I mean the proportion of the students who got the item correct. If everybody got an item right, it is defined as a very easy item. If everybody got the item wrong, it is defined as a difficult one. Most items fall somewhere between these extremes.

After my test is scored I count through all papers and find that 14 out of the 28 in class got the first item right. Fifty percent of the class got the item correct; that is the difficulty level for the item.

Difficulty, as used here, is always relative to the audience for which the test was prepared. An algebra item that would be easy for students in a tenth-grade algebra class, would be impossibly difficult for a group of fourth-grade pupils. When an item analysis is done on your class, the difficulty figures pertain to your students only, but that is usually all a teacher wants to know.

Probably the most telling feature of an item analysis is **discrimination.** You and I wish to see how well the items in our test are sorting out the students who are reaching the objectives from those who are not.[*] These items are said to be discriminating. These are the items that provide the information we want: they sort students who know the subject from those who do not.

For example, as I look over my last examination I spread out the papers on my desk. I note that of the ten students who got the highest total scores on the test all got item 1 correct, but among the ten students whose total scores were the lowest only one got item 1 correct. Item 1 looks like it will sort students who know the subject matter (high total scores) from those who do not. This item is a discriminating one.

Item Analysis Procedures

In norm referenced tests (see Chapter 1) total test scores are used to rank students in order from highest to lowest. The child with the highest score is ranked as first, the next highest, second, and so on. Students who know the subject matter best are expected to be among the high scorers, and those who know it less well are among the low scorers.

Since item analysis shows us how well each item sorts out the students who know the subject matter quite well from those who know it less well, I will first collect the highest scorers on the total test. Then I will collect the lowest scorers on the total test. This gives me two piles of papers—those of students who did well on the test (high scoring group) and those who did not do so well (low scoring group).

Once I have these two groups, I will complete two procedures.

---

[*]The discussion here pertains to norm referenced tests only. If you wish to do an item analysis on a criterion referenced test, see N. E. Gronlund and R. L. Linn, *Measurement and Evaluation in Teaching,* 6th ed. New York, N.Y.: Macmillan Publishing Co., 1990, 255–258.

1. First, I will find the item difficulty for item 1. If the number of students who pass item 1 in the high group added to the number who pass it in the low group turns out to be nearly all of the students, the item is easy. Alternatively, if the number in the high group added to the number in the low group who pass the item is relatively small, the item is difficult. (Details for the actual computations follow.)

2. Next, I go to item 1 to see how well it sorts out the students in the highest scoring group from those in the lowest scoring group. This will indicate item discrimination. If the number of students in the high scoring group who get the item right is somewhat larger than the number in the low group who get it right, the item sorts out the students who know the content from those who do not. Now suppose you find the students in the high scoring group who got the item correct is about the same as the number in the low scoring group. Item 1 is not sorting out students who know the content from those who do not.

I repeat these two procedures for each item on my test. They give me the two figures I need to assess the items: the **index of difficulty,** and the **index of discrimination.** As we shall soon see, item analysis also provides some diagnostic information that reflects on the instruction. But first you and I will go to the details of finding difficulty and discrimination.

The Item Difficulty Index[*]

Calculating item difficulty will give us the percentage of the high and low scoring students who got the item correct. The procedure below works for class sizes of 20 to 40 pupils. You may wish to make a work sheet like that illustrated in Figure 9.1 to follow in recording the data and figuring the difficulty of each item and its discrimination value.

1. After you have scored your test, sort out the 10 highest scorers on the total test. Then sort out the ten lowest scorers. Put aside the rest of the papers.

Item	$Right_{hi}$	$Right_{lo}$	$R_{hi} + R_{lo}$	$(R_{hi} + R_{lo})$/total	$R_{hi} - R_{lo}$	$(R_{hi} - R_{lo})$/.5 total
1.						
2.						
3.						
4.						
5.						

Continue to include all items in the test.

FIGURE 9.1   A Work Sheet for Recording Item Analysis Data

[*]The procedure described here is an adaptation of A. P. Johnson, Notes on a suggested index of item validity: The U–L indices. *Journal of Educational Psychology,* 62, 499–504, 1951. This procedure was further expanded in R. L. Brennon, A general U–L item discrimination index. *Education and Psychological Measurement,* 32, 289–303, 1972.

2. Now go to item 1 on the "high" papers. Tabulate the number of people who got the item correct. Then go to the "lows" and look at item 1. Tabulate all the "lows" who got the item correct.

3. Now compute the item difficulty index for item 1. You do this by adding together the number right from the "highs" and the number right from the "lows." Then divide this sum by the total number of pupils in the two groups (10 + 10 or 20 pupils). This produces a proportion ranging, typically, from 0.00 to 1.00. As a formula (in shorthand) it looks like this:

$$\text{Difficulty} = \frac{\text{Rights}_{hi} + \text{Rights}_{lo}}{\text{Total number of pupils in high plus low groups}}$$

After you have done this for the first item, go on to the second item and repeat the process with the data for that item. Then go to the third, and so on.

An Example.   Ms. Overgaard has 27 students in her seventh-grade mathematics class. She has just given a multiple-choice test on positive and negative numbers. She has scored all the tests and circled the total score for each student in the upper right-hand corner of the front page of the test. Now she puts the papers in order of total scores, picks out the ten highest scored papers and the ten lowest scored papers. She sets aside the remaining seven papers.

Next she looks at the first item on her test and counts the number of students in the two groups who got it correct. There were 9 in the high group and 5 in the low group who marked it correctly. She puts into her formula

$$\text{Difficulty} = \frac{9+5}{10+10} = .70$$

The difficulty level for this item is .70. This says that 70 percent of the students got the item correct. Next on a legal-sized pad she begins to develop a table. The data for item 1 are now recorded and look like this:

Item	Right$_{hi}$	Right$_{lo}$	sum	sum/20
1.	9	5	14	.70

Next Ms. Overgaard turned to the second item on her test and counted the number who got this item correct, in this case 5 students. She tabulated the number on her legal-sized pad. Then she turned to the low scorers and counted the number who got the second item right, in this case 3, and tabulated it. She then followed through the remaining calculations to expand her table to look like this:

Item	Right$_{hi}$	Right$_{lo}$	Sum	Sum/20
1.	9	5	14	.70
2.	5	3	8	.40

Ms. Overgaard now turns to the two stacks of papers to count the "rights" for the third item, then the fourth item, and so on through the entire test.

How large should an item difficulty index be? If you go to a psychometric specialist and ask what an ideal difficulty level is for an item in a norm referenced test you will hear values of about .50, or a little above. This .50 means that half of the group got the item correct, and half missed it. At this value the test gives you the greatest spread of scores from high to low. Spreading out scores helps you rank students on the entire score range, because fewer people share the same score.

Here is an example. A class of 20 pupils took a test of 25 items. On the test 6 students got a score of 14, 8 students got 15, and 6 students got 16. It would be very difficult to say which are the best students because they are all bunched up together. These data are in Table 9.1.

In Table 9.1, column B has 1 student at a score of 8, 1 at 9, 1 at 10, 2 at 11, and so forth. In column B it is much easier to identify the achieving students from those that are achieving less well. If items have difficulty levels near .50 (or a tiny bit more), the distributions tend to be more spread out. This helps us make more accurate decisions about who is reaching the class objectives.

If our norm referenced test has an item on it that is too easy, say a difficulty index of .90, it will not sort the capable students from the less capable very well because almost everyone in both groups got the item right. The capable and the less capable all score on that item the same way, so there is no discrimination. Try to avoid items that are either too easy (a difficulty level of .85 and up) or too hard (.20 or down). These items are not likely to be good discriminators.

TABLE 9.1   Frequency Distribution of Total Test Scores Showing Two Different Spreads of Scores

Student score	Group A	Group B
20		1
19		1
18		1
17		1
16	6	2
15	8	2
14	6	3
13		2
12		2
11		2
10		1
9		1
8		1

On a criterion referenced test, where you have set a minimum score for passing, you could use an item on which everyone did well. It would say that all students reached the criterion of success on the skill assessed by that item. But on a norm referenced test, where you are trying to spread students out across a continuum, an item that most everyone got right will not discriminate between high achievers and low achievers.

It should be noted that if you must do an item analysis by hand, you may not choose to do one on every test used in a course. However, even periodic item analysis gives you valuable information about how well your tests are written, and how well they are doing their job.

The Item Discrimination Index

The item discrimination index indicates how well the item separates the high scoring group from the low scoring group. Because teachers use tests to tell them who is reaching class objectives and who is not, they want their test items to sort the achievers from the other students. The larger the item discrimination index, the better the item is sorting achievers from nonachievers. As before, this analysis is for a class size of 20 to 40 and uses the ten papers with the highest scores and the ten with lowest scores.

There are only two steps to find a discrimination index:

1. Begin with item 1, and as you did with the difficulty index, count the number right for the high scorers, and again for the low scorers.

2. Next subtract the $Right_{lo}$ from the $Right_{hi}$. Then divide this by one-half the total group, that is, half of 20 or 10.

The shorthand of the procedure looks like this:

$$\text{Discrimination} = \frac{Right_{hi} - Right_{lo}}{\text{one-half of total students in high plus low}}$$

An Example of an Item Discrimination Index. When Ms. Overgaard finishes calculating her item difficulties, she already has on hand the data for her item discrimination indices. The data are in a table format similar to that shown in Figure 9.1. She now looks at her legal-sized pad and begins to calculate the index for the first item.

$$\text{Discrimination (item 1)} = \frac{9-5}{.5\ (20)} = .40$$

The discrimination index for item 1 is .40. Ms. Overgaard adds a column to her table for item discrimination indices, and records .40 for the first item. She then goes to the second item's data to calculate the index for the second item, and so on. For the first item her data look like this:

Item	$Right_{hi}$	$Right_{lo}$	Sum $R_h + R_l$	Difficulty Sum/20 $(R_h + R_l)/\text{total}$	Discrimination $(Hi - lo)/10$ $(R_h - R_l)/.5\ \text{total}$
1.	9	5	14	.70	.40

Item discrimination indices can run from -1.0 to $+1.0$, but most will run between .10 and .60. For a typical classroom test (where there are 20 to 40 students) item discrimination indices are often assessed as follows:

.50 and up   very good item, definitely use it

.40 to .49   good item, very usable

.30 to .39   fair, usable item

.20 to .29   poor, marginally usable

below .20   poor, use only with great caution, revise or abandon

Indices are good to the extent that on a given item good students (the high scorers on the total test) outscore the less capable students. The greater the difference between the number correct in the high group compared to that of the low group, the higher the index and the better the item discriminates between the two groups.

From the data in the table above we conclude that Ms. Overgaard's item 1 has a good level of difficulty (.70) and that the index of discrimination (.40) is quite acceptable.

A Simplified Approach

The procedure for doing an item analysis for a classroom test can be simplified just a bit. This simplified approach follows.

1. I subtract the "Rights" in the low scoring group from the "Rights" in the high scoring group. I do this for each item.

2. Next, I multiply one-half of the total students by .20, the lowest discrimination I will accept. From the previous example, that is $\frac{1}{2} \times 20$ (or 10 students) multiplied by .20 or 2 students. I do this only once for the entire test.

3. Any item that has a difference (from step 1) that is greater than the result of step 2 is acceptable.

In the case of Ms. Overgaard's item, as discussed previously, the simplified system can be applied as follows. In her first item the number of "Rights" in the high group was 9, and in the low group 5. The difference is 4. Following step 2 we multiply one-half the total number of students by .20. This becomes $10 \times .20 = 2$. If the difference in step 1 is greater than 2 students, the item is probably discriminating at least minimally well. Now that I have calculated step 2, I can apply this difference (2 students) to any of the items in Ms. Overgaard's test. Any of her items that produce a $Right_{hi} - Right_{lo}$ difference of 2 or greater is a usable item. However, you will want most of your items to produce differences greater than 2, so if you find many differences near 2 you may wish to take a look at the construction of those items to see why they are not discriminating better.[*]

[*]This simplified procedure assumes that any item that has a discrimination index of .20 or larger is acceptable. Putting this value into the formula for discrimination and doing a very little algebra results in the simplified procedure.

✎ Problems

1. Mr. Lemuel has just given a test on earth science in his fifth-grade class. The test had 30 items on it, but you were only able to get five items of his data as shown below. There were 28 pupils in his class. Find the item difficulty for each item and calculate the item discrimination index.

Item	Rights$_{hi}$	Rights$_{lo}$	$(R_{hi} + R_{lo})/20$	$(R_{hi} - R_{lo})/(.5 \times 20)$
1.	5	3		
2.	9	2		
3.	6	5		
4.	5	7		
5.	7	3		

2. Mr. Lemuel's test item 12 (which is not shown above) had a difficulty of .85, while item 22 had a difficulty of .47. Which of these items is the most difficult? Make a generalization about the magnitude of the difficulty index and the difficulty of the test item.

3. Item 16 on the test had a discrimination index of .26. How well is this item discriminating between the students who knew the material well and those who knew it less well? Is it a very good item to use? Explain.

4. Item 14 on Mr. Lemuel's test had a discrimination index of .32 and item 21 had a discrimination index of .45. Which item is the most usable in terms of sorting out students who know the content from those who do not? Explain.

Improving Tests Through Item Analysis

Item analysis can tell you how well your items are working, and they can tell you if the distractors are really catching anyone's eye. You hope the distractors will catch some of the low scoring students, but not the high scorers. In improving your tests you should look at not only how well the right answers are working, but also at how well the distractors are doing their job. Therefore, in improving your tests a good place to start is with distractors.

In this regard, item analysis can provide two kinds of information: It can tell us how well each of the distractors is working, and it can provide diagnostic information on the topics in the test.

Are Distractors Working?

On item 24 of Mr. Lemuel's test in Earth Science, the data was as follows. (The numbers represent the number of persons who selected the option; the starred option is the correct answer.)

Score	Options			
group	a)	b)*	c)	d)
High	3	6	0	1
Low	3	4	0	2

You can see that 6 of the high group chose the correct answer, and 3 of them chose distractor a), just as the low group did. What is it about distractor a) that attracted high scorers? You will want to look at the total item to see if there is a clue about option a). You may detect something about the item—an ambiguity, a misleading tip, or a misunderstanding—that may have made the item different than it appeared when you first wrote it. Without a tabulation of the options, you would not have received this tip about the item.

Now look at distractor c). This one did not attract a single student. It provided no distraction for the students at all. Clearly it is a nonfunctioning option. If Mr. Lemuel is to use this item again next year, a more attractive alternative must be written in place of distractor c).

Looking over the item analysis on distractors allows you to become sensitive to certain writing techniques that do not seem to work. With these techniques eliminated, you become a better testwriter. To this end, item analyses are instructional for the teacher who wants to become a better testwriter. For example, suppose one of Mr. Fields' items in his History test looked like this:

The nation of Sierra Leone formerly was a colony of the

a) British
b) Spanish
c) Dutch
d) was always independent, never a colony.

The data on the results are below. The starred option is the correct answer.

Score	Options			
group	a)	b)*	c)	d)
High	6	0	0	4
Low	3	2	1	4

In a class of 32 students the 10 high scorers and 10 low scorers have responded as indicated above. Distractor d) has been a bit confusing for both high and low scorers. When Mr. Fields took a look at these item analysis data, he decided that distractors like d) were not good sorting devices to include in a test. Beside breaking the rules of having options of similar length and disagreeing in syntax with the stem, it disagrees with the proposition in the stem. If d) is correct, the stem is incorrect. This kind of confusion is inappropriate for test construction. (How could you have written the item to include options such as d)?)

Teachers learn about item construction from looking at item analysis. Which distractors should catch the eye of some of the low scorers? What should distractors include that seduce the high scorers away from the correct answer? Teachers who study item analysis will pick up clues to answer questions such as these.

Diagnostic Information From Item Analysis

Item analysis also gives you some clues as to which concepts students understand and which ones they do not. In addition, it points to erroneous ideas students may have about certain topics. Here is an example of an item from a test in mathematics.

Cassy wants to find the circumference of a circle. The diameter of the circle is 5 inches. What is the circumference?

a) pi times 10

b) pi time 5^2

c) pi time 10^2

d) pi times 5

The item analysis data are below. The figures represent the number of students who chose a given answer, for example, 5 high scorers on the total test who chose the correct answer, a). In the following table you see that among both the high and low scoring students in the class, a fair number selected b), which is the procedure for finding the area of the circle and not the circumference. (The starred option in the table is the correct answer.)

Score group	Options			
	a)*	b)	c)	d)
High	5	4	0	1
Low	4	4	1	1

These item analysis data suggest that a lot of students have some misinformation about the difference in procedures for finding the circumference and the area of a circle. Therefore, you should review this concept before going on to other topics. This is the type of useful information item analysis provides that cannot come from the test score alone.

Applying Information From Item Analysis

Another feature of item analysis data is that it points out features of my test writing that can be improved. Following is an item from a Spanish language introductory class.

"¿Como se llama usted?" means

a) what is your name?

b) where is your home?

c) when do you eat?

d) where is your llama?

Now consider the tabulation of responses for this item, made during an item analysis. Again, the starred item is the correct answer.

Score group	a)*	b)	c)	d)
High	5	1	0	4
Low	3	4	0	3

The item analysis shows that on this item quite a few of the high scorers selected the correct answer, a), while fewer of the low scorers did so. This is how you want the responses to fall—high scorers on the total test getting the item correct, and low scorers missing it.

However, another group of high scorers selected answer d), a wrong answer. What is it about answer d) that attracted the high scorers? At this point you will investigate the item's construction. You will look for clues in the option that distracted some better students away from the correct answer. Here it may be the term "llama," which comes from the verb "to call," or the "llama" which is a South American animal. This term which is common to the stem and distractor d) may have seduced some good students. Ambiguities and imprecisions are often exposed in the item analysis.

The item analysis also points out that no one selected option c). How could you have constructed option c) to make it more attractive for students who did not know the answer? With c) nonfunctioning, you effectively have a three-option item, with a 33 percent chance of guessing the correct answer (or 1 in 3). You should revise option c) to make it more attractive, to make it seem more plausible as an answer.

When you have looked over features such as those exposed by the item analysis, you will find clues as to how to improve your test writing. You will avoid writing options such as c) because they do not attract any students. You have reasoned why option d) looked attractive to some high scoring students, and will want to avoid this problem in subsequent item writing.

Item analysis actually produces two categories of information. The first is about the item itself: Does the item sort out the high scorers on the total test from the low scorers; and does every distractor seem plausible to some of the class and are there incorrect options that attract too many high scorers?

The second category of information in an item analysis gives you clues as to how to become a better item writer. Features in the item analysis point to procedures that fail to make an option work the way we had intended it to. You and I hope not to repeat these mistakes on subsequent tests, thereby becoming better testwriters.

Item Banks

"I hate writing tests all the time," remarked Ms. Carlton, a junior high school Social Studies teacher. "It seems like I'm always throwing away one test just to write another."

Test writing can be a chore, but building an **item bank** can reduce the difficulty of that chore. Good items can be used again in successive semesters. However, teachers must be sensitive to the possibility of the item being passed along to students through the "pipeline." If possible a given item should not be used more often than once a year, and in each test a number of new items should be included. Items in the file for over a year are often seen as safe items to be used, assuming the topic still fits the table of specifications for the class.

Items in the file must, like all items, fit the current objectives of your instruction. They must also match the cognitive levels you intend to address in your test. You and I must let our table of specifications control the use of any item, including those in our test files.

Test-item files are most commonly of three types: on-test data files, 3 × 5 card files, and computer files. Each has its unique advantages.

On-Test Data Files

When I have given a test and analyzed each item on it, I simply write the discrimination index and difficulty level on a copy of the test. I write these data in the margin of the page and adjacent to the item. I also check distractors that do not work so I can revise them on subsequent use of the item. Here is an example of an on-test record.

Difficulty = .76   In which of the following ways are horses and cattle
Discrimination = .33   alike?

April '98

                      a)   they are both ruminants

                      b)   they both have cloven hooves

                      c)   they are both mammals

0 selected →   d)   both have been known to have horns

This is a part of a third-grade science test on which an item analysis was done. The teacher now has written the data for the item in the margin of one copy of the test and checked distractor d) which attracted no one. The next time this teacher writes a test on this unit of instruction, a look at this item, which worked well except for one distractor, may suggest it can be repaired and reused. Some of the other items may be abandoned altogether. All teachers have some of these nonfunctional items.

After each successive test, teachers will complete one copy of the examination with the item analysis data and keep it in a special folder of past tests. They can now refer to the previously used tests to select items that will fit their current objectives, use them again in the next year's tests, and save themselves writing new tests altogether.

The 3 × 5 Card File

A second way to keep a test file is to write each item that worked well on a 3 × 5 index card. These cards can be filed by unit titles and by subtopics within the units. Then the teacher can select items out of the file as they correspond to the instructional objectives. A convenient way to do this is to list the unit of instruction and topic at the head of the card and then write the test item in the center of that card. At the bottom or on the back of the card item analysis data can be recorded. An example of an item on electricity from a fifth-grade science class is shown below.

Sci 2, Electricity; Foundational Knowledge level
John has a meter on an electrical circuit. The meter says 100 ohms. He is reading an indicator of
a) speed of electrical current
b) amount of resistance
c) power of electrical force
d) leakage of electricity into the system
Diff. = .54 Discrim. = .41 a), d) 0 select Fall 1997

Items should be filed under the unit number and objective within the unit. This makes retrieval more expeditious. Once you have accumulated a number of items in your files you can draw on them as the items fit your objectives. This will significantly reduce the job of test writing. From the test file you can extract a set of cards and arrange them in the order you wish them to appear on your test. No doubt you will have to rewrite some distractors and create additional items to cover objectives not covered by items in your file. Also, new items are needed for continued growth of the file and for the replacement of items that do not produce appropriate difficulty and discrimination statistics.

The file must be kept secure to avoid having it explored by students who will be the recipients of the examinations. As with on-test files it should be noted that no item should be used too frequently in a program. Once a year is as often as an item should be used, and as our test file grows, we may not wish to use it that often.

Computerized Test Item Banks

The last way in which you may keep a test file is on a computer disk. You will use a disk because you cannot protect a file stored in computer memory as well as you can a disk. The test items will be typed in the file. They will be labeled by code letters that identify the unit, the topic heading, and level (Foundational Content, Application, Higher Order Processing) at which the item is written. You can follow this with item analysis data and dates when the test was used.

For example, I am building a test on Unit 4 (Constructing angles) in Geometry 101. I insert the disk that has my store of items for Geometry 101, and select that unit to find a collection of test items that focus on the content of the unit on which I am building a test. Furthermore, each item is coded for an objective and level of complexity according to the table of specifications for the unit. Items can be downloaded to a file, the order rearranged, and printed. All in all this is a very handy method for storing data.

There are a number of procedures teachers can use to record files like these. "Homemade" systems work for some people. There are also commercially available programs for item collections, and some spreadsheets may be adaptable for item files. Although the initiation of a test-item file may seem time consuming, it will save much time in the long run.

To create a computerized test item file, a teacher needs ready access to a computer and a good quality printer. Otherwise it becomes more trouble and time consuming than one of the nonelectronic methods.

Electronic Item Analysis

Some schools will have electronic test-scoring equipment and computerized analysis available. Your students will record their answers on a machine-readable answer sheet (the fill-in-the-bubble-with-a-number-2-pencil type). These systems typically provide a number of statistics both on the tests as a whole and the individual items in the test. The program will print out the average score for the class, the standard error of measurement, the test's reliability, and an alphabetical roster of your class with a score for each student.

Computerized scoring will also do a detailed item analysis for you. When it does the analysis it uses the entire class, not just the 10 high-scoring and 10 low-scoring students. Also, it uses correlation procedures to calculate the discrimination index. (The *point biserial correlation* is most often used.) These correlations look like the indices that we have calculated by hand and they are judged by essentially the same criteria cited previously for hand-calculated indices.

An index of difficulty is also provided for each item by the computer. It tells you essentially the same thing as the hand-calculated difficulty index, except here it is based on all the students, not the high and low scorers alone.

It should be noted that different computer programs for item analysis produce different formats for the data. These programs will have much of the same data in their printouts, though they may be arranged differently, and each will have some characteristics that are unique to that program.

Following is an example of what the results from one computerized item analysis might look like. (The star indicates the correct answer.)

Item		Options			
		a)	b)	c)	d)
1.	r	.05	.45*	−.10	.05
	%	19	50	15	16
2.	r	.38*	.22	.00	.11
	%	60	32	00	08

It includes the essential features of all systems of analysis: Item difficulty, the discrimination index, and the proportion of people who chose each option. In this computer analysis the *r* values represent the correlation of the item with the total score on the test. The computer correlates the item score (pass/fail) with the total score on the test to see to what extent getting the item correct is associated with getting high scores, and missing the item is associated with getting low scores on the test.

We want a computer analysis of our test to show not only how the keyed answer correlates with the total test score, but also how the distractor correlates with the answer. If a distractor correlates too highly with the total score, say .45 or so, it tells us that some of the better students are selecting that distractor, something we wish to avoid. We want distractors to correlate poorly (even negatively) with the total score on the test. This tells us that the distractor is sorting out the good students from the not-so-good ones—that is, the distractor is doing its job. In the table above both items correlate moderately with the total test score (.45 and .38). Difficulty (.50 and .60) also is satisfactory. However, distractor b) for item 2 is too attractive for good students, and distractor c) attracted no one—that is was nonfunctioning.

✎ Problems

1. Below is the item analysis done by hand for 2 items from a test of 30 items on the topic of art history. The starred option is the correct answer. There were 27 students in the class.

Score groups	Options a)	b)	c)*	d)
High	2	1	7	0
Low	2	4	4	0

   a. Calculate the difficulty index for this item. Calculate the index of discrimination.
   b. Evaluate the two indices you have just calculated. Is the discrimination index satisfactory? How does this look in terms of difficulty?
   c. From the data, what can you say about how well the distractors are working?

2. Here is another example based on a computer item analysis. These data are from item 1 of a test in reading comprehension for fifth-graders. The starred option is the correct answer.

Item	Options a)	b)	c)	d)*
1.	a)	b)	c)	d)*
r	−.12	.41	.08	.57
%	17	9	8	66

3. What is the item difficulty for this item? What is the discrimination index?

4. How are the distractors working in this item? (Note *r* as well as percent values.)

A Real Case Narrative

Some teachers who have trouble with assessment find that experience makes them more skilled in assessing how well students have achieved the desired outcomes, while other teachers find it easier to avoid any use of formal assessment. This narrative overheard in a teachers' lounge expresses some early frustration with a lack of skill in using tests. How would you respond to this teacher's dilemma? In your opinion is she likely to avoid the use of formal assessment, or will she develop the skill she needs to capitalize on testing?

In the teachers' lounge at Hopedale School two teachers and the school psychologist are chatting. Today, Ms. Young, a first year seventh-grade Social Studies teacher, returned tests to her class in a unit on state government.

"The kids found all kinds of things wrong with the test—they argued that some items had more than one right answer, they claimed several items were ambiguous. You name it, they didn't like it!" she fussed. "I'm ready to pitch it all and use my judgment for grading!"

Dr. Wechsler, the school psychologist, was reflective. "I hear you saying that you are unhappy with how the test came out."

"Of course I am. Nobody likes to wade through that kind of hassling," Ms. Young responded impatiently.

"Do you see yourself as basically prepared in the construction of assessments?" asked Ms. Terlite, a long-time sixth-grade teacher.

Ms. Young thought a minute, and frowned. "No, I really don't see myself that way at all. They taught me to teach, but never how to test. I do what I have seen around me, but I have no idea if it is good or not."

"You don't know if your tests are good?" Dr. Wechsler asked. "Have you ever done an item analysis to see how the items are working? Sometimes you can pick up some clues for improving your test-writing there. If nothing else, you can see if your pupils' complaints are likely to be true," she advised.

"I haven't a clue as to what item analysis is, leave alone having done one! You think that might be the way to start?" Ms. Young asked hesitantly.

Dr. Wechsler brushed back her hair, "Well, it's one way to see how well items work. I'll send you a pamphlet from my files. The appendix has an easy item analysis procedure. The chapters on test writing may also be helpful."

Three days later the pamphlet arrived in school mail. Mr. Young thumbed through it quickly. "Looks like a lot of work now when I'm busy with term reports . . ."

SUMMARY

1. Item analysis of norm referenced tests is the process whereby we determine the difficulty of an item, and find its ability to discriminate between good students and the not-so-good ones.

2. Discrimination refers to how well an item in a test sorts out the students who are meeting the instructional objectives from those who are not.

3. Difficulty refers to the proportion of test-takers who answer an item correctly.

4. In a classroom of 20 to 40 students, a difficulty index is calculated by sorting out the ten highest and ten lowest scorers on the total test, tabulating the number of people in each group who answered an item correctly, adding these two numbers, and dividing that number by 20.

5. For a typical classroom, a discrimination index is calculated by sorting out the ten highest and ten lowest scorers on the total test, tabulating the number of people in each group who answered an item correctly, subtracting the number of low scorers who answered it correctly from the number of high scorers who answered it correctly, and dividing that number by 10.

6. An item analysis reveals which distractors are not functioning well and also identifies misinformation students may have.

7. Test items can be stored in an item bank on a copy of the test, on 3×5 index cards, or on a computer file. Item banks must be secure.

8. Electronic item analysis is available in many schools and requires considerably less effort than by-hand procedures.

KEY TERMS

item analysis	index of difficulty
difficulty	index of discrimination
discrimination	item bank

ADDITIONAL READING

Aiken, L. R. (1989). Some simple item analysis statistics and significance tests. *Journal of Research and Development in Education, 22*, 42–48.

Baker, F. B. (1982). Item analysis. In H. E. Mitzel, (Ed.) *Encyclopedia of Educational Research: Vol 3,* pp.959–967. New York: Free Press.

Gronlund, N. E. and Linn, R. L. *Measurement and Evaluation in Teaching,* New York: Macmillan Publishing Co., 1990, pp. 244–260.

Trafton, P. (1987). Assessing for learning: Tests—a tool for improving instruction. *Arithmetic Teacher, 35*, 17–18.

CHAPTER 10

ESSAYS AND TERM REPORTS

Higher Order Processes

"As a philosophy teacher, I use essay tests altogether," said Ms. Oaks. "Philosophy is about thinking, and to get at students' mental processes you have to have them record those processes. That means writing!" she said with intensity. "But the quality of students' writing these days—they can't spell, or write a sentence without making a grammatical error," she continued. "I expect them to do better than that, and even on otherwise good papers I never award a high grade if I find mistakes in basic writing."

In most teaching, instructors hope that students not only acquire new ideas, but also that they be able to communicate these ideas. We expect students to expand their knowledge and pass it on to their colleagues, defend their own positions on controversial issues, and pose new alternatives to these positions. This often means writing down these ideas so they can be preserved, analyzed, and transported.

A considerable amount of education deals with ideas—what is a predicate, multiplication, an hypotenuse, anthropomorphism, existentialism, mercantilism, and thousands of others concepts. Teachers want to know what is in a child's mind when one of these ideas is presented. To many teachers this means they must have the child write to reveal the cognitive responses that are taking place. These teachers are acting on the belief that writing reproduces mental processes.

What This Chapter Will Include. In this chapter you will learn:

1. What an essay test is
2. Some major advantages and problems in using essay tests
3. How to construct the essay item
4. How to make essay scores more reliable and valid
5. How to help students write better essays
6. How essays compare with term papers; and how to use the same methods to evaluate and review both essays and term papers
7. The differences between open-ended format and multiple choice

Essay Tests

An **essay test** is one in which students are given problems or project situations—called **prompts**—for which they must compose the answer in writing, rather than by selecting it from several given. The answers may be as short as a few sentences or as long as several pages. Answers may require a rather focused response, or may ask the student to formulate a unique stance on an issue. For some items, there may be so many different approaches to the "correct" answers that only a very skilled reader can assess the extent to which the student has reached the objective.

The aspect that attracts many educators to select essay tests is that these tests require the students to construct their own responses. In many life situations everyone must indeed do this. In solving many daily problems there are no clearly presented alternatives among which to choose. Everyone must construct his/her own as best as he/she can. Not only must we often evaluate positions and choose one to defend, but also must explain this process to other people. This is what essay tests frequently ask the writer to do, a feature that attracts many educators to use them to assess higher order objectives in instructional units. To the extent that essay tests present realistic problems to students to solve, they approach authenticity, that is, they emulate the reasoning processes of solving life problems.

Essay tests, like other kinds of tests, are tied to objectives for the instructional unit. Within that unit essay tests are best used to organize, to analyze, to integrate and evaluate information, to be innovative in solving problems. If a test item asks students to recall and report what is presented in the textbook, it does not use the potential of an essay test. The table of specifications lists our objectives, some of which are at the complex cognitive level. The utility of essay tests is in assessing these complex operations in the solution of problems that emerge from the unit of instruction. These are the topics to which essay tests are best applied.

Advantages of Essay Tests

Like other assessment formats, essay tests have some advantages and some limitations. Following are some advantages on which teachers may capitalize.

▼

Advantages of Essay Tests

1. Essay tests are best used to assess complex learning outcomes.
2. Essay tests are relatively easy to construct.
3. Essay tests emphasize communication skills.
4. Essays reduce guessing.
5. Essay tests expand learning outcomes.

▲

Let's take a closer look at these advantages.

Essay tests are best used to assess complex learning outcomes. Teachers are increasingly aware of the importance of presenting and assessing higher order cognitive processing. To this end we need an assessment device that leaves the student on his or her own to sort out information and issues, to integrate information and arrive at new ideas, to look at options and evaluate each, to come to a conclusion in favor of one view over the others.

These are the kinds of things essay tests do best. Because they are time consuming for students to take, essay tests are inefficient when assessing items at the Foundational Content level of the taxonomy and teachers save time and effort by using other test types for this information. But when you want students to dig into their own cognitive resources and solve a problem, analyze an idea, or create a response to a set of conditions, essays have the advantage.

Essay tests are relatively easy to construct. Because essay tests are usually made up of four to seven items, the job of constructing them is small relative to multiple-choice or true-false tests where thirty or more items will be constructed.

However, in the construction of essay tests the teacher should concentrate on points where Higher Order Processing is a major part of the instructional objectives. Then in test-writing the teacher's job will be to sample these processes proportionately so that the integration of central issues of instruction become the essential issues of testing. Consequently, good essay tests are not as easy to construct as they appear in the final format, but they are easier to construct than are most other types of tests.

Essay tests emphasize the importance of communication skills. Communication is an integral part of most bodies of knowledge, and the use of essay tests reinforces that position. However, if you want to assess communication skills, you must also give time to communication in your instruction. For example, each discipline has its own unique vocabulary and its own logical systems. These should be specifically taught in order to facilitate the student's use of them in developing discourse in the discipline. If essay tests are to appropriately emphasize the importance of learning and using communication skills, teaching these skills in the discipline is part of every teacher's responsibility.

Still another advantage of essay tests is that *guessing is much less a factor in essay test scores* than in scores on objective tests. Guessing comes into play when options are given, and students must choose among them. In essay testing no options are given; rather students must construct their own responses. Hence, guessing, as it is usually thought of in objective tests, is not a part of essay testing.

Finally, *students' reflection at the Higher Order Processing level expands their grasp of the concepts with which they are working.* For example, when I am asked to find a principle common to both event A and event B, I now see A and B in a different perspective than when I saw them as independent events, and if I see those commonalities I have an expanded concept of A and B. This is an experience that is not likely to happen with objective tests. However, if teachers expect their students to expand their views in this manner, they must indeed teach them to deal with topics involving analysis, synthesis, and evaluation.

Limitations of Essay Tests

The advantages of essay testing make them appear quite attractive. There are, however, some limitations to essay tests that affect their utility. These must be considered because they have an impact on the reliability and validity of the data collected from essays.

▼

Limitations of Essay Test

1. Essay tests are a very small sample of the content of an instructional unit.
2. Compositional features of students' writing affect scores.
3. Students may not guess, but they will bluff.
4. Essays are difficult and time consuming to score.

▲

We will now take a closer look at these limitations.

Essay tests are a very small sample of the content of an instructional unit. Response time per item is comparatively long for essays. Therefore, in a standard class period students respond to only a selected few items. With a multiple-choice test you may include 30 to 40 points of information or application in a typical testing period. Using an essay format, at best you may get at a dozen shorter response points, fewer if the items require more elaboration. Therefore, for total sampling of the objectives of a unit of instruction, the multiple-choice format is preferable. Because of this, teachers should restrict essay tests to the function they perform best—assessing higher order processing.

If essays sample relatively few items on the table of specifications, many important features of an instructional unit will be left out if essays alone are relied upon as the assessment procedure. Consider how well a multiple-choice test with 30 or so items on it samples the total experience involved in a unit; then consider sampling with essay tests where only six or eight topics are covered.

Although essay tests tend to be smaller samples of the total content of a unit of instruction, in fairness it must be noted that essay test items are broader or less focused than the typical multiple-choice test. Consequently, a direct comparison of the two items is hard to make. However, the number of information points called for in an essay test remains below that of multiple choice or true-false.

The extent to which the test samples the points of instruction is a major factor in content validity of the test. Tests must sample the entire table of specifications (see Chapter 3) if a claim for validity is to be made for the scores that come from them. If essay tests are focused on higher order processes, much of the total content of a unit is not assessed. In using essays alone, for most subject areas we must stretch them very hard to make them appear to have content validity for the entire unit.

When you and I looked at test reliability in Chapter 4, we also noted that the longer a test is, the higher reliability tends to be. Essay tests have relatively few items compared to other types of examinations. Because essays are small samples of the content of an instructional unit, they tend to put reliability, and content validity, in jeopardy. The reliability of essay exams is typically lower than that for multiple-choice tests (Block, 1985).

A second limitation of essay tests is that compositional *features of students' writing affect scores.* Spelling, quality of penmanship, length and complexity of sentences, and other aspects of writing tend to have an impact on scores assigned to essays (Chase, 1968; Marshall & Powers, 1969; Eames & Loewenthal, 1987). Essay readers lean towards discrediting products that contain features such as spelling mistakes and poor grammar.

"But," you might ask, "shouldn't teachers expect students to be able to write a sentence without misspellings and grammatical errors?" Of course, they should! But when I am teaching students colonial American history, the scores I assign to their essays should be based on evidence of knowledge of colonial history, nothing more. Routine grammar and spelling are not part of my instructional unit in history. Consequently, these features should not have a part in the assessment of the student's knowledge of colonial history. If a student gets a "C" on the paper, it should reflect mediocre knowledge of history, not history and writing errors—the latter is another class altogether.

But readers are indeed influenced by errors in a student's writing. Even when teachers are asked to grade only on content, they continue to assign higher scores to papers that are not marred by spelling and grammatical errors. This also is true for papers on which the discourse is written with complex, difficult to read sentences (Chase, 1983). It appears that anything in an essay that distracts the reader from the content—poor penmanship, spelling errors, grammatical glitches, difficult reading format—is a potential detriment to getting a high score on the essay.

The literature on classroom assessment has cited a number of elements, beside the subject content of an essay, that affect scores (Coffman, 1971; Tollifson & Tracey, 1980; Huot, 1990). These features influence the validity of the test score. If Paula, who knows a lot about the Constitution of the United States, gets a low score because she misspelled some common words and used some poor grammar in saying what she knows, the test is not placing Paula very well on the knowledge-of-the-Constitution scale. Her writing style took away from her score in history. If the test score does not classify students on what they know about the topic of the class it is not a valid yardstick for assessing knowledge of subject matter.

The above commentary suggests that teachers should be unusually attentive so as not to be distracted by non-content features in scoring essays. This is not to say that teachers should condone poor writing habits. However, unless the writing has been taught as part of the instructional plan, it should probably not be considered in the grading of a student paper. If you have taught specific vocabulary in your unit, it is subject to testing. If you have illustrated how to manage writing exercises in your discipline, that which has been specifically taught is fair game for including in your evaluation. But features that have not been taught should not enter into the evaluation of learning outcomes.

Another consideration is that *in essay tests students may not guess, but they will bluff.* Students will seldom leave an essay item blank. They will try to write something. After all, the loss of a single item out of five means a 20 percent reduction in score, so students must try to get something on each item. Students bluff to see if they can get at least partial credit.

Here are some common ways that students bluff. If you see them in a paper you are reading, you may wish to consider the possibility that you are looking at a bluff.

1. The student has restated the question as a declarative sentence, and then elaborated on that statement. For example if the items says:

Contrast the painting style of Seurat and Monet in terms of use of color and brush technique.

The bluffer may begin:

Seurat and Monet are different in their choice of color and use of the brush. Color is a distinctive feature in identifying any artist. Each of these artists had his own color preferences, as well as his own brushing stroke and style. They have definite differences and some similarities.

The response does not address the task of the item, but essentially restates and elaborates the content of the original statement of the item.

2. Students may stress the importance of the issue in the question, even though they are short of (or missing) facts to support their declaration. For example, in response to a question about plants and air quality the student may say:

Plants play a vital role in the quality of air. Air pollution is a major problem today. Plants and their growth have been found to take a definite and vital role in that problem. The importance of this role certainly cannot be overemphasized.

They may continue the response in this way for several more sentences without ever giving details or citing relationships.

3. Bluffers often cite names for authority without telling how they are related to the issue. For example, in response to an item on free trade the student says:

According to a speech by Senator Eks, this is an important national question. This is born out by comments by Congressman Wye on "Meet the Press." Both agree that . . .

This name dropping without details goes on, but it does not cite the why and wherefor for solving the problem at hand.

4. Another technique for bluffing is writing on a topic parallel to the focus of the question, but never relating it to the question. For example, in response to the Afghanistan war with the Soviet Union, the student begins by saying:

This war is something like the Vietnam involvement of the United States . . .

and goes on to talk about the Vietnam war without actually making the parallels and relating them to the question.

5. Bluffers also use some situations that cannot be negated, and then elaborate on these. For example, to an item asking students to take a position on a newspaper quotation, the student begins with this common truism:

One cannot take everything reported in the newspaper as true. Therefore, we must question several aspects of the report.

The student then continues in this line of response.

Although it is difficult to catch all bluffers in their attempts to embellish their scores, being sensitive to the techniques above may clue you to an attempted bluff. This sensitivity can make your evaluations of essays more valid.

A final disadvantage of essay tests is that they *are difficult and time consuming to score.* Anyone who has read through a set of essays knows what a time-absorbing chore this is. Many hours go into doing a careful job of reading essays in any year's evaluation of a single class' achievement.

Besides the time commitment required, it is very difficult to do a reliable and valid job of scoring essays. Studies show that two competent readers reading the same paper will often assign different scores. Further, the same reader who scores a given paper on two different occasions may assign a different score on each reading (Coffman, op. cit.). This means that scoring may not be as reliable as you wish it to be. But educators want their assessment procedures to be as reliable as possible, and there are several ways they can improve on the reliability of reading essays: by writing better essay test items and by using a prescribed method of scoring. But as demonstrated in schools across the country today, essay testing is among the least reliable procedures applied in assessment of learning outcomes.

✎ Problems

Here are some examples of procedures using essay tests. Critique these in terms of their appropriateness.

1. Item found on an eighth-grade science test: "List the conditions you should have for the soil for growing a bean plant."
2. Ms. Jeremiah is talking with her student teacher about testing. "I just thumb through the chapter in the textbook and write down things the kids should recall, and ask them to write the answer. Some of the questions are defining vocabulary, recalling names, knowing the parts of something—stuff like that."
3. The essay item said, "Contrast property taxes and income taxes as to their fairness as a source of public revenue." Here are two responses by tenth-grade social studies students. Which one do you think is bluffing and why?

   a. Property taxes and income taxes are quite different in their fairness to tax payers. These two forms of taxation are widely used in America because they bring in large amounts of revenue for the states. There is no way you can work out a taxation system that is fair, and there are fairness questions in both kinds of taxation. Some people prefer the kind of fairness that is in the property tax, while others would choose the income tax. Nobody likes taxes, so people try to show that a tax is unfair so that maybe the tax will be eliminated, or at least reduced.

   b. The fairness issue depends on getting money for government from people most capable of paying. Both taxes to some extent tax the wealthy more than the less wealthy. But property tax is not graduated based on ability to pay. The *rate* of tax is the same no matter if you own only a house or if you have a factory. However, the income tax rate is a graduated tax based on one's income. The more income you have the higher is the *rate* of taxation. This means that the more capable one is of paying, the higher is the tax.

Writing Essay Tests

As in any test, the items in an essay test control the quality of the assessment. Following are several guidelines that will help you create better essay tests.

Reserve essay items for assessing the achievement of complex learning outcomes. Other types of tests can get at most outcomes with broader samples of information points and can be scored with higher reliability. But only essay tests can ask children to construct their own response to a question, combine information from a variety of sources and come to a conclusion, and take a stand and defend it.

If we are going to limit essay tests to higher order processes, the place to begin in writing items is the table of specifications. What was taught in the unit that required children to apply evaluation, analysis, and synthesis? What were the topics on which children were led to look at several sides of an issue, to construct alternatives, to merge data to reach a conclusion, or to select alternatives according to a criterion of value? These higher order processes are the proper focus of essay tests.

To this end, items should not be initiated by words such as "who," "when," or "list." These terms point to the Foundational Content level of learning, not to Higher Order Processing. Instead, in constructing an essay prompt we should use terms such as "compare," "evaluate according to. . . ," "relate," "interpret," and "critique."

The table below lists some common objectives assessed by essay tests with some terms that call out the appropriate activity to be observed. The terms in the table will point you, as a test-writer, in the direction of requiring higher order processing in your essay tests. They are good terms with which to start an essay item.

Objective	Terms that call out the activity
Analyzing	Break down, diagram, differentiate, explain
Comparing	Compare, contrast, classify, distinguish between
Creating	Compose, devise, propose, design
Evaluating	Critique, choose and defend, evaluate, judge
Inferring	Extend, extrapolate, predict, conclude, project
Interpreting	Illustrate, translate, interpret, convert
Synthesizing	Combine, construct, rearrange, conclude, compose

Here are some examples of essay items that use the verbs in the table:

Contrast the caucus system of nominating political candidates with the popular primary.

Some news media have reported that trees contribute to air pollution. *Explain* and *critique* this position.

You have plenty of gasoline in your car, but it will not start. Select three parts of the car's motor and *explain* how each of these parts may be causing your car not to start.

Another guideline for writing essay tests is to *write items that clearly tell the students what they are to do.* Many essay items are broad and poorly focused, and students may not know what the point of the question is. Use of the table above will be a first step in clarifying the problem. A well written item will tell the student what the task is. Here is an example.

Not so good:
What does Newton's third law have to say about the bounce of a rubber ball?

Better:
Using Newton's third law, explain why a ball bounces higher when dropped from 10 feet, than when dropped from 5 feet.

The first item does not provide the writer with much direction. (In fact Newton does not mention a rubber ball in his third law.) The second question points to the operation the student is to address and tells the student what to do, that is, *explain* according to a principle. Students can relate this type of item directly to an objective outlined in the unit of instruction. Good assessment should do that.

Another useful guideline is that *limiting the breadth of an essay item allows the answer to be relatively brief and more specifically tied to a single objective,* which points the student more directly to the area of the appropriate answer. The answer also can be assessed more reliably, because the reader will have fewer criteria to keep in mind while reading the response.

An item such as:

What were the causes of the Civil War?

is nonspecific, and a long dissertation could be written in response to it. We would have a tough time holding one set of scoring criteria up to all students' answers. However, if the item is limited to something such as:

Contrast the role of agriculture in the North and the South as a factor in the out-break of the Civil War.

though still somewhat large, provides more direction to the student in preparing a response. Also, this item's response could reasonably be held up to a set of criteria in scoring, a feature that should increase the reliability of scoring.

There is a second advantage in writing more specific essay items. The time to answer is typically shorter, and consequently more items can be included in the test. Teachers can cover more points of information from their instructional unit if they use more specific items.

Require all students to write on the same items. Do not provide a set of items from which students may select, such as "You must write on items 1, 2, and 3; beyond this, select one item from among 4, 5, and 6." One of the ideas of testing as an assessment device is that scorers use the same set of criteria for all participants. Suppose that Gene writes on items 1, 2, and 3, and selects item 4 from the optional items. Jorge writes on 1, 2, and 3, and selects item 6. These students have not jumped the same hurdles, and therefore one set of scoring criteria will not fit them both. They cannot be compared as to their relative standing in achievement of unit objectives. Grading typically requires a common scale.

All students should be asked to respond to the same sample of items, so that the teacher can observe them operating under the same stimuli. Students can then be evaluated with a common set of criteria. Measurement procedures are designed to do this, but allowing optional items takes those procedures away.

One final guideline is to *make sure that the test is accompanied with a set of instructions.* Students need to know how much time is allowed for the test. The test should indicate the stature of each item by listing either the approximate amount of time students should take for the item, or list the maximum number of points the item will receive. This information will allow students to budget their time and helps them decide how extensive, or condensed, their responses should be.

Whatever the student may find useful as a guide in taking the overall test should be considered for inclusion in the test's instructions. This helps close the gap between the student's and the instructor's idea of what a well done paper should look like. Misunderstandings at this juncture often add to errors of measurement, reduce reliability and validity of the scores, and antagonize students. Good instructions for taking the test will go far in solving these problems.

Following the five guidelines discussed above will materially improve the application of the essay test by helping instructors write items that will be more focused on the instructional objectives. In addition, they will make the task more clear for the students and as a result, help them to write better answers.

✎ Problems

Below are some examples of essay test items. Cite the item-writing techniques that could be improved.

1. How is tea related to the American Revolutionary War?
2. List five examples of one-celled animals.
3. Instructions: You must write on items 1, 2, and 3. Then you may select either item 4 or 5 to write on.
4. Explain how commerce in China is related to commerce in the United States.
5. List the five largest companies in America as of December, 1997.

Scoring Essay Tests

"I always think it is a good idea to use essay tests," says Ms. Reed, a high school History teacher, "until I have to score them all. At that point, I sometimes wish I hadn't used them. Scoring is so very problematic for me!" Anyone who has scored a set of essay test papers can identify with Ms. Reed. Indeed, the time and effort that goes into scoring essay tests is extensive. If each student in a class of twenty-five writes four pages—the minimum for most tests—this means 100 pages to be read. If an experienced reader can read one page every three minutes, this test will be read in roughly five hours. This is a big chunk of attention that must be given to working through the linguistic mazes that students sometimes create.

The scoring of essay exams is problematic in ways other than just its time commitment. As noted earlier, readers tend to be a bit unreliable in their marking of papers. They are distracted by a variety of incidental variables such as quality of the handwriting, grammar, complexity of sentence structure, and expectations the teacher has for each student. Ideally readers should avoid all these influences in scoring an essay. This is not entirely possible, but let's look at some things readers can do to minimize the distractions in the scoring system.

Ways to Improve Essay Test Scoring

Following are some useful procedures in reading essay test papers that will make your scores more reliable and probably more valid.

Before reading any of the papers, conceal the students names. Through classroom interaction we develop an expectation for each student's achievement. We will carry this expectation to the reading of essays written by that student, and allow it to color our evaluation (Hughes, Keeling & Tuck, 1983). I believe that Geraldine is a poor student in my Chemistry class. When I read her paper, I expect to find that poor quality of performance reflected in her responses. However, this time she may, or may not, conform to my expectations. Obscuring names helps us avoid being influenced by our anticipation for achievement for various students.

Before scoring any paper, read through a few papers to get a grasp of how the students as a group may have seen the test. Did they understand what the test required? Did they follow directions? Scanning a few papers will give us an idea of what the "typical" performance for the class may be. This will provide a brief orientation as we begin scoring.

Read only one item across all papers before going on to the next item. Read item 1 on all papers before going to item 2; then read 2 on all papers before going on to 3, and so on. This is done because it is easier to keep in mind the criteria for a single item, than to try to recall the criteria for all items. As a result, the reader keeping the criteria in mind for the item, is more consistent from paper to paper. This should increase the reliability of the scoring.

After reading through the first item on the test, shuffle the papers before reading the next item. We do this for two reasons: a) the position of a paper in the stack influences its score, and b) the quality of a response of one paper influences the evaluation of the next paper (Hales & Tokar, 1975). If your paper is near the top of the stack, it will get a different score than if it is at the bottom. Readers' views of scoring criteria change as they read through a stack of papers.

And here is another curious feature of essay scoring. If Melody has done a very good job in writing a response to item 1, Del's paper, which follows right after Melody's, will get a lower score than if it followed a poorly written response to item 1. No matter what you write on an essay item, your score is partly the effect of the quality of the person's paper that precedes yours. We cannot avoid these problems altogether. However, shuffling the papers after reading through all responses to an item will decrease the chances that a given paper will be subject to the same influence on item 2 as it was on item 1.

A final guideline for improving scoring is to *use a prescribed reading procedure.* Two such procedures are commonly advocated: a) the key procedure, and b) ranking.

The Key Procedure.   In the **key procedure,** readers write out for each item a set of features that characterize a good response. Then they list the score points that will be awarded to each feature. Features may be processes, arguments supported by facts, or whatever the class objectives indicate you are assessing by the item. Then, as the paper is read you compare the key with the content of each student's response and assign points as you see the features listed on the key. One prominent aspect of the use of a key is that it encourages readers to bring to each student's paper a common set of criteria, prompting the scorer to use the same yardstick with each paper. (See page 223 for an example.)

Ranking.   The **ranking** style of grading essay tests requires the reader to provide roughly four stacking locations. As the reader reads through the first item on the papers the best papers are laid on the first stacking location; the next best papers on the second location; and so on. After all the papers are stacked for the first item, go back through those papers on which you were uncertain. When the papers are all in their appropriate stacks, the reader assigns the papers in the first stack the highest score (in this case 4 for four stacks), the ones in the next stack the second highest score, and so on.

In a variation of this plan, you may wish to identify a specific percentage of papers that should be placed in each stack to simulate the famous bell-shaped curve. The bell curve has fewer cases at the lower and upper ends, and more cases in the middle of the curve. In using the curve as a guide you place many papers on the middle stack and fewer in the low and high stacks. Here are examples of appropriate percentages of papers in the stacks using four-stack scoring and again with a five-stack scoring. Using four stacks place 15 percent of the papers in the first (or highest scoring) stack, 35 percent in the second stack, 35 percent in the third stack, and 15 percent in the last, adding up to 100 percent. If you had chosen the five-stack procedure, you would have placed 3 percent in the first stack, 15 percent in the second, 64 percent, 15 percent, and 3 percent in the successively lower-scoring stacks. This will give you something of a bell curve, but keep in mind that it is a rare class whose abilities exactly follow a bell curve.

In any case, a prescribed scoring procedure increases reader reliability and has a prospect for increasing test validity, two features educators want to incorporate into any classroom testing operation.

✎ Problems

Below are several examples of reading an essay test. For each of the situations, cite what is being done poorly, and describe how you would improve the operation.

1. Mr. Swift is reading essay tests in History. There are five items on the test. He has fifteen papers to read, and has read all five items on the first ten papers, and is now down to item 4 on the eleventh paper.

2. Ms. Dashiel is reading a set of essays in English literature. "Ah, here is Mary Good's paper; she always writes well! Let's see how nicely she did this exam!"

3. Mr. Mix had just read item 1 across all his essay test papers. "Now I'll go back to the top of the pile and start reading item 2. Oh, yes! The handwriting on this first paper was terrible when I read item 1. I had a lot of trouble decoding it. And here it is again on the top of the pile where I start once more."

4. "Let's see, how did I weight this argument when I saw it on that paper back here is the stack? I wish I could remember how I scored these different features a bit better—my scoring would be a little more consistent if I could remember these details."

Helping Students Write Better Essay Tests

In many schools there is no place where children are taught to write essay test responses. Yes, they all have had general composition, but writing in a given subject-matter area has its own unique processes. In each program area instructors should teach students how to attack general item types. This will optimize student's chances of conveying what they know about the course objectives. Here are some ways to help students improve their essay tests.

How to Help Students Write Better Essay Tests

1. Emphasize vocabulary and logic unique to the discipline.
2. Advise students to begin with a declarative statement.
3. Teach students to read all questions before writing on any one of them.
4. Emphasize importance of legible penmanship.
5. Note the relevance of good grammar and punctuation.
6. Provide practice in essay writing before the test.
7. Promote study habits appropriate for essay test writing.

Let's look at these guidelines in detail.

As the instructor moves through the subject matter in a unit, *emphasis should be given to the vocabulary that is unique to the discipline.* The words that cover the ideas, that label objects, procedures, and concepts of the discipline are vital to communication. These should be emphasized in instruction.

Students should be instructed to begin their essay responses with a declarative sentence. These sentences determine the direction of the writer's argument or treatise. A strong opening statement by pointing the reader's attention to the argument makes the instructor's job of reading the essay more valid, and increases the chances that the reader will look favorably on the rest of the student's response.

Readers typically do not favor essays that begin with an apology, such as "I'm not sure of the facts in this case, but . . ." Teach students to begin their essays with a positive, declarative statement.

Students should be encouraged to read all the questions on the test before writing on any of them. This provides the student with an overview of the test and illustrates the extent to which emphasis is given to the various topics of the instructional unit. As students read the items, they should underline the key verb—contrast, describe, evaluate, and so forth—so that the intention of the question can be addressed without casual oversight.

Next, students should be advised to quickly make a brief outline of the response for each item using single words that will serve as reminders in developing their response. Once the outlines are finished, the student can move through the writing much more systematically. As students progress in the writing for one item, a thought may arise that is useful for another item. If so, this thought can be quickly inserted into the outline for the appropriate item. This alone is a good reason students should do an overview of the entire test and make preliminary outlines.

Instructors should encourage students to write legibly. We have already seen that the quality of penmanship influences reader's scores. The safest thing students can do is write in the best possible penmanship. They must not overlook this feature in creating a response. As computers become more common in schools students may be able to write tests with a word processing program. However, this is not yet a possibility in many schools; in the meantime, students should write as legibly as possible.

All faculty should emphasize that grammar is designed to promote communication skills. Poor grammar may not only distract the reader from an important point, but may also convey a message negative to the student's image, which can be projected into the grade. Instructors should try to ignore grammar when scoring essays in subjects where achievement in grammar is not the main focus. However, all teachers should write notes to students to cite errors in their grammar and punctuation and encourage them to improve their skills in basic writing. If you do not comment, it suggests that you approve.

A few days before a test *instructors should provide practice exercises in class* to illustrate how to attack an essay item. The teacher and class can discuss how different features of a sample essay improve, or erode, the quality of the essay. You may also review with your class the features cited in the box on page 185.

Teachers should also help students develop the type of study habits that will help them perform on essay tests. This includes collecting facts, being sure they see what the facts relate to, making generalizations from facts, forming conclusions about the details provided in a unit. When they form a conclusion, they should list the facts that support (and fail to support) it. Reviewing material regularly is also helpful (Holt & Eson 1989).

Helping students improve their essay test responses will result in a set of more orderly and proficiently prepared papers to assess. Accordingly, the reader's job will be easier; you will be glad you invested the time in this project.

Comparing Essays and Multiple Choice

A storm of controversy has existed ever since multiple-choice tests came on the scene in the first quarter of the twentieth century: Are multiple choice tests better, worse, or about equal to essay tests in dealing with reasoning processes? The validity of any argument here depends first on the quality of test construction, and second on what decision the teacher is trying to make about students. Should we consider how inclusive each test can be? Should the decision be on factors one test appears to assess more appropriately than another? Then, too, the questions of reliability and validity must be answered.

One study (Bridgeman & Rock, 1993) looked at the factors assessed by multiple-choice and by essays. They used a complicated statistical procedure to identify factors in the two kinds of tests, and concluded that "the open-ended analytical reasoning items were not measuring anything beyond what is measured by the current multiple-choice version of these items." Further, the correlation between scores on the two types of tests was .93, a very high value indicating that the rank of a person on one test is almost identical to the rank of that person on the other. (Correlation is discussed in Chapter 3.)

Other investigators (Ackerman & Smith, 1988; Thissen, Wainer & Wang, 1994) have added information to sustain the Bridgeman and Rock findings. Their evidence indicates that there is a role for both types of test, but point out the importance of selecting a test type in accordance with the objective of instruction.

Nevertheless, not all research confirms these findings (Ward, Fredericksen, & Carlson, 1980), and tests using different content with students of varying levels of age and sophistication may well produce different results. With so many variables that could possibly confound data in studies such as these, it is difficult to make an absolute conclusion. However, users of both multiple-choice and open-ended questions can feel that their system is not without some good features, yet they should not ignore the other.

Extended Essays and Term Papers

Term papers have much in common with essay tests. However, they are less specific in that each student has the advantage of selecting the topic. This means that the criteria for scoring are a little less specific, too. However, just as in essays the same elements of student writing are imposed upon the reader. Readers try to avoid the differences in handwriting among students by requesting that all students type their papers. Now, with the availability of computers, this is not as big an issue as it once was.

But computers also allow students to decorate their papers, to use graphics attractively, and use various eye-catching fonts. Do these impact the reader? At this point no one knows, but chances are they do. Writing features may still be a factor in reading an essay, even when computers are used to produce the term paper.

Reading Extended Essays

There are many common features between essay tests and longer papers (Popkin, 1989) that allow the reader to utilize some of the same scoring procedures for both types of performance. Here are some suggestions for adapting these procedures to scoring extended papers.

First, make a "key." All term papers will not be on the same topic; rather they will be on many diverse topics. A key that deals with content will not be appropriate. However, you can look for adequacy of style in presenting the topic, clarity of the presentation, suitability of data and its use in supporting a position, logic of, and support for, the conclusion, and so forth. Yes, you and I want our key to include features such as these when we read term papers, because this key will help us look for appropriate elements across all papers. They help us judge papers on common features such as those cited above, and to mark papers in reference to the presence or absence of these features.

In short, preparing and using a key helps the reader to do a more reliable (and valid) job of assessing a collection of term papers. The key directs the reader to note appropriate characteristics of good papers. It also increases the likelihood that all papers are scored on many of the same criteria.

As with essay tests, it is important to obscure all student names before reading the first paper*. Readers continue to be influenced by expectations while reading term papers, just as in reading essay tests. My estimate of Eloise is that she is a very good student; her work is consistently top-notch. I am now about to read her paper, "Primitive Americans: What We Should Learn From Them." How carefully shall I read this paper? Well, I know she does good work, and I tell myself that a careful reading just isn't necessary. Negative expectations operate similarly but in the opposite direction. "Sherry always does sloppy work, far below her potential. I had better look over her paper very carefully because it probably won't be too good." Both positive and negative expectations can have a significant impact on scores.

Helping Students Write Better Term Papers

Students regularly need advice on doing research and writing extended papers. To begin with, the instructor can provide students with some basic training in what a term paper in her or his subject area should include. Discuss matters of style, order of presenting topics, use of data to support propositions, and what types of data are acceptable. Give students an outline showing characteristics of an acceptable paper. Provide examples of well done papers and contrast them with poorly done work. You will appreciate the time spent when you see the improvement in quality of papers you receive.

You should also encourage students to select focused topics on which to write, in contrast to broad, rather general topics. It is easier for the student to research and write about a more specific topic. (It is also easier to do a reliable job of reading papers that analyze and elaborate a single issue problem.) These few points should improve the skill of students to produce the term paper that will function more powerfully as an assessment device. Give them a try.

A Real Case Narrative

In this narrative teachers are discussing assessment techniques. What would you like to say to each of them that would improve their data collection methods?

Mr. Derio, an Economics teacher, has stopped in to see what Ms. Carl is doing about preparing students for the statewide test that is coming up in two weeks. "Well," began Ms.

---

*Using small note paper that has the adhesive strip on the back (such as a Post-It®, is one way to quickly obscure names. These papers can be easily removed when all papers are read.

Carl, I'm a math teacher and my students need to know a lot of facts—can't think in math without the basic facts, you know," she said with raised eyebrows. "I use multiple-choice tests quite a bit in here and I think my students are pretty much set for the state exam."

"But what about reasoning with numbers, and application of math to my econom-ics situations?" asked Mr. Derio. "I expect that kids should be able to take a principle and tell how it could solve a local business problem—that means an essay, not those fact-based multiple-choice."

"OK," Ms. Carl continued, "so you give an essay exam—what about grading it? It's a chore I do not want. I've spent a lot of hours on them and wind up wondering if I have done an even-handed job—I've got to have more confidence in the score I give my kids. The last time I gave an essay we spent the next period haggling over a point here or there—not worth it. With objective tests I can show with formulas that my key is correct," said Ms. Carl with a stern expression.

"But don't you have as an objective that the students will use math in solving real-life problems?" asked Mr. Derio. "How can you believe they can if you don't pose some problems for them to work on that require them to apply math?"

"Well," replied Ms. Carl, "I use the same technique you use to decide that your stu-dents know the basic facts of economics," she grinned.

SUMMARY

1. In an essay test students are given problems for which they must compose the answer in writing, rather than selecting it from among those given.
2. Because essay tests do their best work in assessing higher order processing they should be used primarily for assessments at this level.
3. Advantages for essay tests are that they are relatively easy to construct, emphasize communication skills, reduce guessing, and can expand students' grasp of concepts.
4. Limitations of essay tests include the following: they cover a relatively small sample of content; scores are affected by compositional features of students' writing; students may bluff; and scoring is difficult and time consuming.
5. Essay items should clearly tell students what they are to do; they should be lim-ited in scope, and all students should be required to write on the same items.
6. In scoring essay tests, students' names should be concealed, a single item should be read across all papers before going to the next item, and the order of the papers changed after each item has been read.
7. Scoring procedures include the key procedure, in which the content of a paper is compared with a list of features outlined in a key; and the ranking approach, in which papers are sorted into a limited number of categories based on the quality of the responses.
8. Teachers can help students write better essays by emphasizing unique vocabu-lary, instructing students to begin with a declarative sentence, encouraging them to read all the questions before answering any of them and to create a brief out-line for their response, by stressing the importance of legible writing and cor-rect grammar, by providing practice exercises, and by helping students develop appropriate study habits.

9. Research supports the idea that both essay and multiple-choice tests can adequately assess student achievement. Objectives play a role in selecting one type or the other.

10. In reading extended essays and term papers general procedures used for essay tests are also useful, such as making a key of desired characteristics to guide the reading, including qualities of the essay such as clarity of presentation and suitability of data.

11. To prevent the impact your expectations might have on scoring, it is important to cover the students' names before reading any papers.

PROBLEMS

1. Here are some essay items. Critique each of these.

    List five generals in the Union army during the Civil War, and five that were in the Confederate army.

    Describe why a steam engine runs.

    Place the following animals into their correct phylum: paramecium, flat worms, crabs, oysters.

2. Criticize each of the following procedures completed by a teacher.

    a. Ms. LeFever has just finished a unit on plants in her general science class. She is now preparing a test for the class. At her desk she takes out the basic science text used by the class, and begins to thumb through the chapter on plants. As she skims through the pages she jots down essay test items, such as, "List three classes of broad-leafed plants," "How does photosynthesis work?" and "What is a gymnosperm?" By the last page in the chapter she has 6 essay test items. She decides this may be one too many so she decides to ask all students to write on items 1, 3, 4, and 6, and select either 2 or 5 to answer. Comment on at least two features in this testmaking procedure.

    b. Mr. Marker is sitting down to score a set of essay tests his students completed this afternoon. He sharpens two red pencils, pours a cup of coffee and begins. The first paper is Mary Smart's. "Hmm, good student, Mary!" He begins to read her response, and gives it full credit. "Not bad! Did she do as well on the second question?" He begins reading her second response.

3. Write an essay question in your own teaching area. Now compose a key for that question, listing the aspects of the response you feel represent a good answer and how many points each aspect will receive in the scoring.

KEY TERMS

essay test

prompts

key procedure

ranking procedure

Additional Reading

Cashin, W. E. (1987). Improving essay tests, IDEA Paper No. 17, Center for Faculty Evaluation and Development, Kansas State University.

Coffman, W. E. (1971). Essay examinations. In R. L. Thorndike (Ed.), *Educational Measurement,* 2d ed., Washington, D.C.: American Council on Education, pp. 271–302. (Although this work is somewhat dated, subsequent research has not changed its basic conclusions.)

Coker, D. R. et al. (1988). Improving essay tests: Structuring the items and scoring responses. *Clearinghouse,* 61, 253–255.

Quellmalz, E. S. (1984). Designing writing assessments: Balancing fairness, utility, and cost. *Educational Evaluation and Policy Analysis,* 6, 63–72.

Zeidner, M. (1987). Essay versus multiple-choice type classroom exams: The student's perspective. *Journal of Educational Research,* 90, (6), 352–358.

CHAPTER 11

DELIVERING CONVENTIONAL TESTS

Packaging; Administering; Debriefing

" I really don't like testing," Mr. Tokar at Jefferson Middle School reported. "When I pass out the test the kids groan; they always find something wrong with it, or they don't know how to deal with a part of it. And scoring is not a favorite task either. And when I give the tests back, there is always some one who wants to argue about the scoring or grade distribution!"

These comments reflect a nearly universal experience among teachers at all levels of instruction. At least part of the problem lies in the packaging, administering, and debriefing that goes into the testing. There are some procedures teachers can follow at each of these junctures to reduce the problems and give both teachers and students more of a sense of competence in getting through the period of testing. This chapter deals with those procedures in some detail.

Chapter 5 noted that one source of measurement error was in the administration of the test. Errors contribute to lower reliability, and they affect the test's validity. Administration procedures are not a casual, arbitrary feature of the assessment operation.

In this chapter several methods are discussed that will make test administration easier for both teacher and students, and will actually increase the test's reliability and validity.

What This Chapter Will Include. Although many procedures arose out of test management, most of the administration activities noted here apply to all types of assessment. In this chapter you will learn:

1. How to announce to the class an upcoming test.
2. The problems of test anxiety and some administrative activities that can allay them
3. How to assemble the test
4. The administrative procedures for the examination, essential instructions for taking the test, and the test-taking environment
5. Advice to give students on test-taking
6. How to manage cheating
7. Scoring the test, and some insights teachers gain from scoring tests

8. How to return tests to students, give feedback to students, reinforce the right answers, and clear up errors

Announcing a Test: What and When

Students, even those in lower grades, should know when a test is coming up. They need to have a time period to prepare for the exam, along with some advice on how to prepare. Students should be given the date, told what subject matter is involved in the test, and advised of what type of test you will present to them.

Students' achievement is increased when they are given help in preparing for the examination. A review period is useful. Accompany this review with a printed study sheet that identifies the main topics in which test-takers should be prepared. A class discussion of the topics informs students as to how they will be asked to show their skills. Will the test be multiple choice, a combination of several types of items, essay, or a performance demonstration? Some review should center on tasks at the cognitive levels that will be reflected in the test. The study sheet also can be a take-home aid for students who wish to review topics in their spare time.

In addition, students need some review of how to deal with the kind of assessment that will be made. Tips on taking an essay test (provided in Chapter 10) are helpful; some testwise procedures for dealing with objective tests (noted in Chapters 7 and 8) maximize a student's chance of getting good scores. Students will also want to know what teachers look for in performance assessments when they are being evaluated by this method. In any case, students should be advised of what is being measured and how to best deal with it.

Another aspect of announcing a test requires that teachers tell students what equipment they should be prepared to utilize. For example, in a physics test will calculators be permissible? Should students have two pencils or will they be allowed to leave their seats to sharpen pencils during the test? Students should be told what resources they should provide so that they can be prepared.

Some students find it helpful to have a short pretest as an example of both the test items that will be given and how the different levels of the table of specifications will be represented. This is especially useful for the first test you give to your class. If you will be using an answer sheet with which students may not be familiar, practice with it will reduce random errors. In later tests they will have already experienced your testing style and can prepare accordingly. This short pretest should be given several days before the actual test, and when completed, discussed with the class.

The time length students need to prepare for a test depends to a considerable degree on the nature and expanse of the test. Typically, a test should be announced about a week before it is administered. Longer periods of time tend to create anxiety in some students, forgetfulness in others. With shorter formative tests, in which smaller amounts of information are covered, the announcement may be closer to the exam date, but never give the students less than two days to prepare.

Student motivation for doing well on examinations is related to their seeing the relevance of the exam (Flanagan, 1955). It is therefore important in announcing a test to point out how it fits into the total assessment of the course, and to note how the test fits into the completion of school records and reports to parents.

As this discussion suggests, "pop quizzes" should be avoided. Pop quizzes are a crowd-control procedure, not an assessment device. They may encourage students to be in class, and to keep up with their assignments. However, pop quizzes often do not rank students well compared to their level of skill at the end of the entire unit of instruction.

Dealing With Test Anxiety

Ms. Chalmers, a fourth-grade teacher, reported during a room visit by a college observer, "Poor Richie, whenever I pass out a test he breaks down and cries. You should see his hand shaking when he picks up his pencil! I really feel sorry for him!" Richie is not alone. Some students become extremely anxious when faced with a test. They break out in a sweat, and a few actually cry when a test is to be given. Some have been seen to vomit.

The instructions given to students have some effect on test anxiety. Instructions that are tension oriented, that admonish students to do their absolute best, tend to increase test anxiety. Students who are prone to become overanxious in testing settings tend to do less well on their examinations under such admonitions.

The best instruction for test-anxious students is neutral in its plea for effort (Martin & Meyers, 1974). These instructions work adequately for other students as well. A few students may need extra encouragement, but this can be done outside of class. The neutral tone in instructions appears to be appropriate for the largest number of students at all levels of motivation.

Test anxiety is treatable, but even the best educators usually achieve only a reduction of anxiety, not its elimination. This alone is worthwhile. Teachers should consult with school counselors to determine the best course of action for managing the work for students who display anxiety when confronted with tests.

In any case, teachers can reduce anxiety by being sure they announce tests early, by discussing the content of the test so that students know what to expect, by providing ample time to prepare, and by directing students in this preparation. Let students know that all exams are important, but do not overemphasize this feature. Review sessions help, and a short practice test to discuss (and to take home) may also be beneficial.

Assembling the Examination

Begin building the assessment procedure (test, observation schedule, etc.) days before it will be used. This will give you time to edit it before it is needed. If assessments are to have content validity, they must be developed in association with the teaching activities. This includes the table of specifications which reminds the teacher which objectives, at which cognitive level, were developed by the unit of teaching. It also identifies the number of assessment exercises that would be appropriate for each objective. However, as teachers proceed through the unit they may wish to alter some of these activities and reassess some of the outcomes. Although teachers will use the table as their guide to assembling the test, they should be creating the test as they progress through the instructional unit.

You and I will do the best job of ensuring content validity into the test when we build test items as we teach. Every few days we should write a few items that correspond with the teaching objectives with which we have dealt. If we regularly write items and save them on a computer disk, we can quickly retrieve them for arranging in the examination that will be given to the class. These items are more likely to fit the instructional plan than items written some time after instruction has ended.

With this collection of items on hand the test can be assembled ahead of the day scheduled for administration. As that day approaches the items are assembled into the final product that will be administered to the class. Following are some steps to use in assembling your tests.

1. *Read over the test items* to be sure they cover the content the way you have taught it; no topic should be overrepresented in the test, nor underrepresented. All objectives should be represented in the items. Also, this reading should assure you that the items have been written according to the guidelines for writing test items. Items should also be clear, free of ambiguities, and contain no errors of grammar or content.

2. *Arrange items by item types,* that is, multiple choice in one section, true-false in another, and so forth. This allows students to apply one mind-set to all items in a section, and makes test-taking easier for the class. Teachers are assessing achievement of course objectives, not mental flexibility.

3. Within the various item types, *items should be arranged to follow the development of the unit of teaching.* Items that cover initial topics in the unit come first, those that cover the next topics come second, and so on. It is often suggested that a test begin with a relatively easy item to get the student off on a positive note, but there is no evidence that students do better with this kind of start.

4. When the items are arranged as suggested above, *write out the instructions.* These should specifically say what type of responses should be used and where they should be placed. For example, "Put your answer on the line to the left of the item number ..." is not enough. The actual response, a, b, c, d, or + and 0, which are more exact and should be used. Instructions should also state where notes may be written, and provide instructions about guessing (if relevant to your scoring method). Also, instructions should include time limits, your policy on asking questions during the examination, what to do if the examination is finished ahead of time, and what should be turned in at the close of the examination.

If your instructions comment on guessing, being sure to note the penalty for guessing, if any. Such penalties are sometimes implemented through the use of scoring formulas, but these are generally discouraged (see Chapter 8). Students may also ask about the advisability of changing answers. This topic is discussed later in this chapter.

Clear and specific instructions should be on a cover sheet which can be referred to during the exam. Along with the instructions there should be a line on the cover sheet that says "Please write your name here now." Every teacher has had to deal with unidentified papers. Instructions, which point the student to the location for writing his or her name, should avoid the problem of nameless papers.

✎ Problems

1. Miss Tyman, a seventh-grade Social Studies teacher, has just finished a unit on city governments. She now wishes to see how well students have achieved the class objectives. She sits at her desk during her free period and begins to thumb through the textbook. As she does so she writes test items covering the topics on the various

pages. When she comes to the end of the chapter that deals with city governments, she has 24 test items. She decides this will be enough to take up the half-period she wishes to devote to test-based assessment. She takes the test to the duplicating room and reproduces it. Comment on Miss Tyman's procedures.

2. Here are the instructions provided at the top of a tenth-grade history examination. Comment on the adequacy of these instructions. "For each test question there is a line in front of the question number. Put your answer there."

3. On Thursday Mr. Harding is just ending his Geometry class. He closes by saying to the class, "Please give me your undivided attention! Tomorrow, Friday, we will have a test over the content of pages 134 to 147 in your textbook. I will not say what the test will be like because I want you to be broadly prepared. We will spend the entire class period on the test. Bring all the tools you need for drawing in case there is a drawing item, bring your calculator in case there are calculations, and whatever else you think you may need to respond to the content on pages 134 to 147 in your textbooks. This test is extremely important in this grading period, so BE PRE-PARED! Class is dismissed!" Comment on this announcement.

Administering the Examination

Administering the examination includes those things you do to regularize the conditions under which students take the examination. It includes starting the test, monitoring the test, and collecting the results. The goal of administering the examination is to provide and maintain conditions that will enable all students to demonstrate their very best work. A student should never have to believe that a grade was affected adversely by the way the test was administered. There are some features to manage incompetent test administration.

You and I will now look at these conditions in detail.

Conditions for Administration

1. Test in the classroom when possible.
2. The teacher should be the test administrator.
3. Be prepared to go to work promptly.
4. Have printed instructions that are detailed.
5. Attend to the sensory environment in the classroom.

The Testing Room

Tests should be given in the same classrooms in which students have learned the subject matter. There is some evidence that students do slightly less well on tests when they are given in rooms other than the one in which the regular class is held. The familiarity of the scene appears to have a positive effect on student work.

The Test Administrator

Test administrators should project an atmosphere of work as usual. For this reason it is preferable to have the test administered by the regular class instructor. Having the regular teacher in charge of the testing situation emphasizes the relevance of the examination and promotes continuity between instruction and performance. It also conveys purpose and authority and contributes to proper control in the test setting. In addition, students will ask questions from time to time and feel only the regular teacher can relate the questions to the actual learning context.

A number of studies have been done on the race of the examiner and its effect on student test-takers. Graziano, Varco, and Levy (1982) reviewed 29 studies available at that time, 15 of which they believed used defensible designs. They concluded that race of the examiner had no detectable effect on test result. Skilled examiners, black and white, got essentially the same performance from children of both races.

Be Prepared

Test administration should be a businesslike process. To this end preparation is important. Have the tests sorted into stacks equal to the number of students in a row. If answer sheets are used have them inserted in the test, or have them sorted in stacks as you did the tests. Some instructors prefer to hand out answer sheets first because students begin writing their names on the answer sheets and immediately settle down. Students become active when they have to wait for their materials.

In observing and assessing skills in problem solving and similar performances, it is especially important to be organized. Students do not wish to sit and wait for the teacher to get the materials together. The social interaction that takes place among students while the teacher assembles apparatus clearly does not promote motivation to perform on the assessment exercise. The solution—be prepared!

Instructions

When everyone has received the test materials, go over the instructions slowly and precisely. Be sure every student understands what is to be done. Ask if there are questions about how to take the exam, but do not allow questions about the subject matter. This is not a time for review. If you are giving a nationally published test or state-mandated test, be sure to read the instructions exactly as written. These instructions have been created so that all children get the same information about taking the test. Bear in mind that casual remarks before or during the test could alter the motivation of the test takers. Avoid them.

If an answer sheet is to be used be sure the instructions include how to mark the answer sheet. Even if students have used an answer sheet before, include advice in the instructions.

At this time provide your policy for asking questions during the examination, for getting up to sharpen a pencil, going to the washroom, and any other policy you may have for regularizing of the examination procedure. It is important to both provide rules that facilitate monitoring and to avoid activities that may distract other students. If you decide that there are circumstances that warrant students leaving their seats during an examination, a good rule is to have no more than one person up at any given time. This is least disturbing and is easier to monitor.

Working time is another important feature of exams. Students will have to pace themselves and will want to know if they have a half-hour, the whole period, or some other length of time. If there is not a clock in the room, write the time on the board periodically, but not more than three or four times in an hour because it can be distracting for some students and anxiety-producing for others. It is more important to indicate time in the last half of the testing period than in the first. It is in the last half of the testing period that students are sorting out how to best utilize the remaining time. When the "Stop" time arrives, all students should be asked to stop working. Someone will often ask for five minutes more, and if you grant one person five minutes more, to be fair the whole class should be given five minutes. However, stop should mean "Stop!"

The Sensory Environment

"I really freaked out on that test last period," said Angie, a high school sophomore. "When that group of kids passed through the hall, talking and shuffling their feet, I was, like, totally distracted." We have all heard that the optimum testing environment is one in which there are no noises, where the seating and work space are comfortable, and where the temperature and humidity are controlled at moderate levels. This environment is indeed ideal, however in the real-school situations it is hard to achieve. What are the effects of deviation from the ideal?

Distraction.   Most test-takers can tolerate a considerable amount of distraction and still do well on examinations (Super, Braash & Shay, 1947). Distractions such as periodic trumpet playing in the area of the classroom, loud conversations in the hall outside the room, subtle comments and movement in the testing room, are unlikely to have much effect on scores. However, this does not mean that the teacher should not try to control noise. Some students will be influenced more than others by distractions, and for the sake of those students disturbances of any kind should be kept in check. Especially for students who are test-anxious, teachers should control the testing environment.

The conclusion is, then, that you should do your best to maintain a controlled environment for test-taking. This includes giving students instruction about disturbances and placing a sign outside the door stating that quiet is requested because a test is in progress. However, if moderate noises beyond your control occur, they should not be allowed to invalidate the test. Typically, the everyday noises of the world do not seem to affect test scores in any general way.

Physical Qualities of the Test Environment.   The ideal testing room would have a good writing surface, and optimum lighting for easy reading. However, there is some evidence that the adaptable human being can manage variations in these conditions. Rooms with dim lighting appear to produce no detectable effects on students' scores, nor do lap boards when they are used instead of desks (Ingle & DeAmico, 1969).

Teachers, however, must focus on the capabilities of students. Most students will see the use of lap boards in a dimly lit setting as unfriendly. Students with visual limitations or modest manual dexterity may find these conditions oppressive, and would perform less well than if they had been given a normally lit room with a desktop on which to work. The conclusion must be that we should always try to arrange optimum conditions for test-taking.

One factor that seems to impact students in testing situations is the quality of the air. Are "stuffy" rooms a problem? Slightly elevated levels of carbon monoxide do not seem to impair work; however, elevated levels of humidity and temperature do (Kingsley, 1946). Our objective then should be to attempt to control these elements of air quality. In many circumstances this is not easily managed, and students will need extra reassurance of their ability to do good work in these settings.

Fatigue.   One factor that needs attention but is difficult for the teacher to control is student fatigue. Here a distinction must be made between physical effects and psychological effects. In most testing situations the psychological effects are greater than are the physical. Students have been shown to operate well under physical fatigue conditions (defined as having no sleep over a 24-hour period) provided the psychological conditions for motivation can be maintained (Edwards, 1941). The key is maintaining motivation.

✎ Problems

The following situations are considerations in administering a test. How would you deal with each of these situations?

1. Mr. Gaulf has prepared examinations for his classes on Friday. He then takes a personal business day off, and a substitute teacher administers the examinations for him.
2. Ms. Fuller arrived in the classroom just as the bell rang. She had two stacks of xeroxed test materials in her arms—page 1 contained test items 1 to 15, while page 2 contained items 16 to 30. She announced to the class, "You recall that this is a test day. You should review for a few minutes while I staple these pages together."
3. Mr. Kulik entered the room, told the class to clear their desks, and then passed out two pages of test items and the answer sheets. He then said, "Are there any questions?" He paused, then said, "Start working!"
4. Mr. Ergstein, a Physics teacher, had just finished a unit on energy. His class had just ended a period-long test. Jaquie was not ready to turn in the test when the time was up, and begged for a few more minutes. "All right," said Mr. Ergstein, "we'll talk about tomorrow's assignment while you work."
5. The class had finished a test and was leaving the classroom at the end of the period. Angie turned to Bill, "Did you hear those kids pass through the hall during the test? How do they expect you to do a good job with a distraction like that!"

Test-Taking Procedures

Students are not equally skilled at working through the procedures that help them get the best score possible. Teachers can help by providing basic instruction on taking examinations. This section presents some tips that may be useful to your students.

Skimming the Examination

Students should be told to first skim through the examination to get an idea of the content. Often when working one item the student thinks of an idea that applies to another. But to do this one must know what topics are on the test. Students should be directed to skim through the exam quickly (taking no more than 2 or 3 minutes), and as they do so make a few notes citing ideas relevant to answering the questions they encounter. Now the student is ready to start working the items in sequence.

Guess or Not to Guess

Many students wonder if they will fall into error if they guess on some items. The answer is that they probably will not. For many of the items in the test students know something about the topic. If they know something about the item on which they are stumped, and they can offer an "educated guess," then they should guess rather than skip the item. By knowing something about the item students increase their chances of getting it correct. Their "educated" choice of the answer is better than a random guess. Therefore, if students have a clue they should give the item their best shot. In doing so they will probably improve their total test score (Michael, 1963).

Changing the Answer

When your students complete their tests it is a good idea for them to go back over the test to see that they have not made some accidental errors. When doing this a student may sometimes find an item on which they were unsure at the time they marked it. Now, on rereading it, they decide that another answer has some real possibilities. Should they change the answer to the one they now think is correct? On review of a test, if a student finds an answer that no longer looks like the best answer, the student should probably change it to the one that is now thought to be correct. Although not overwhelming, there is some evidence that says that students do improve their total score by changing the answer (Casteel, 1991). This is especially true for easy or moderately difficult items. Students should remember to carefully consider the alternative responses before making the change. Then if the first choice appears to be less adequate than the alternative, they should change the answer (Hills, 1976).

Cheating on Assessments

Cheating reduces the validity of test scores. It also is dishonest and unfair to students not involved in it. Because of this teachers want to reduce cheating as much as possible; however its complete elimination may be extremely difficult.

Just how common is cheating? Various studies claim that 40 to 90 percent of students have cheated. As many as one out of five children began cheating as early as the first-grade (Bushway & Nash, 1977). This does not mean that any given child cheats all the time. Cheating is done by some students rarely if at all, but by others it is a regular activity. A large portion of the cheaters are somewhere between these extremes. In any case, cheating goes on more than once in a while, and educators should try their best to curtail it. Failure to do so is tacit approval for deception, and opens the door to an attack on test validity.

Reducing Cheating

There are several things to do to reduce cheating on examinations, papers, and reports. Much cheating comes from the student's perception of pressure for achievement. Some of the things teachers do to lessen the amount of cheating involve reducing that pressure. Following are some things to consider.

How to Reduce Cheating

1. Schedule a complete review before the test.
2. Schedule exams more often so one score does not heavily influence the term's work.
3. Be sure examinations are fair.
4. Be scrupulous about test security.
5. Write new tests rather than use old ones.
6. Arrange seating to reduce pupil contact.
7. Create alternate forms of the test.
8. Be a diligent proctor.

Now let's take a look at each of these.

Schedule review sessions before examinations. Students who are better prepared will be less likely to cheat. Be sure the review session defines the content of the unit of instruction and involves the students as much as possible. Their involvement will help them see how well they know various topics and identify those areas for which they should prepare further. The more prepared students feel, the less likely they are to cheat.

Schedule more examinations across the grading period. If there is only one big examination as the basis for grading, this creates a lot of pressure on students. "Blowing" this one exam is disastrous for the student! However, if there are several shorter examinations, the pressure from any one of these is not so great. One bad day will not ruin the term's work.

Be sure your examinations are fair. A student who faithfully covers the topics of the class activities, and then finds the test concentrates on one or two topics, feels unfairly dealt with. If students realize that the test has tricks in it and covers the subject matter unevenly, they feel less reticent to cheat. A lack of fairness in the test opens the door to another lack of fairness, namely, cheating.

Be scrupulous about test security. Do not leave tests on your desk where roving eyes can scan them. Do not casually discard master copies used with duplicating machines; destroy them completely. If you create tests on a computer, save your test to a disk that can be taken with you so that students who also use computers cannot retrieve the file containing your test. Are students employed in your duplicating service? If so, make some other arrangements for your tests to be copied. Do not invite students to be dishonest by making it easy for them to be!

Write new test items on a regular basis. This will reduce the likelihood that copies of old tests will be of any benefit to subsequent classes of students. Test item files, in which you have accumulated a large number of items on each objective of your course, will be helpful here. When you wish to create a test with a different set of items than those you used last term, simply go to the file. (We have talked about item banks in Chapter 9, and will talk more about them in Chapter 18.)

Arrange the testing room so that cheating is more difficult. When possible seat students in alternate desks. This does not eliminate the possibility of students seeing their friends' papers, but makes it more difficult. It also makes proctoring easier. You can see better what a student is doing when there are spaces between occupied desks.

Create alternate forms of the test. If adjacent students do not have the identical tests it is very difficult for one student to scrutinize the work of a classmate. You can make alternate forms of a test without writing new items. Arrange the items on one form in a different order than on the other. Some teachers simply reverse the items on one form of the test as compared to the other. Yes, it means two scoring keys, but this is a small price to pay for the reduction in cheating and the resulting increase in validity.

Proctor carefully and continuously during the test. Do not sit at a desk and read a book or grade papers or prepare lesson plans while "proctoring" an examination. Instead, be curious about any unusual activities or use of auxiliary items such as book bags and make-up kits. If scratch paper is needed, as in a mathematics test, you provide the paper—select a different color for each test so students cannot appear with a sheet of notes on white paper and exchange it for your scratch paper. Older children are very clever at disguising notes, so be wary.

Good proctoring is essential to reducing cheating.

Dealing With Cheaters

Ms. Harmon, a seventh-grade English teacher, stormed into the principal's office. "Anthony, I just saw Marsha Smith using crib notes during an examination. Can I give her an F for this test?" she blurted out. The principal quietly went to the file and shuffled through several folders. "Here you are, Emma, the school's policies on cheating. Look these over and we'll decide then what your options are."

In earlier times a teacher was essentially free to implement whatever policy seemed appropriate when cheating was observed. Teachers used their own judgment as to the quality of the evidence and the punishment that fit the violation. However, times have changed. Declaring a child as a cheater can be a serious event for that student, and teachers can no longer deliver punishment without "due process." Schools must have written policies on dishonesty of all kinds. These policies should describe the procedures for adjudicating charges of various offenses. They should also describe what evidence is needed to support the claims.

Each teacher should be aware of these actions and be prepared to respond to the requirements of due process. Teachers cannot take unilateral action in most cases, except as directed in the policies manual. However, teachers, in accordance with the school policies, may develop policies within their classrooms. These policies should be announced to the class at the outset so students know what to expect.

Due process usually requires that a hearing of some type be provided for the accused student before anything beyond a warning can be carried out. Hearings must provide time for students and teachers to prepare their presentations. Hearings require evidence. The testimony of a teacher who says that a student copied from another one is weak evidence by itself. Copies of "crib" notes confiscated during a test, witnesses who saw the copying, and the comparison of identical responses (including wrong answers) on answer sheets of two students are all evidence that cheating has taken place. You must be prepared with all the evidence you can collect to support your accusation.

With some teachers it is easier to ignore cheating than to go through due process. However, cheating is dishonest behavior that should not be reinforced. In fairness to other students, teachers are first obligated to proctor diligently to reduce the opportunity for casual cheating, and second, be willing to collect evidence and follow the process through to a conclusion.

Scoring the Test

In our previous discussions of writing test items, several methods for facilitating scoring were cited. One of these methods will probably suit your style of testing. If observational assessments are to be made, the method will lay out a summarization scheme. (Chapter 12 will discuss this further.)

There are, however, several general considerations about scoring that fit best in this discussion of administration of tests. Three considerations will be presented here: weighting of test items, use of formula scoring, and timing.

Weighting: Should All Test Items Count the Same?

Conventional scoring provides one point for each correct item on a test. However, many teachers believe that they should award more than one point to items that cover central themes in a unit.

There are three problems with this approach. The first is that it does not expand the number of topics sampled from the unit and consequently does not improve content validity. The items are the same sample of content, even the teacher awards them two points (or three) rather than the one point. To improve content validity teachers should write more items for the central themes of the unit, thus increasing the breadth of the sample of topics. Simply weighting items does not extend the sample.

The second problem with weighting test items is that the correlation between scores based on one point per item and those based on weighted scores is quite high. This means that weighted scoring tells teachers and students roughly the same thing as the unweighted in terms of the rank of a student's score in the class. If this is true, the extra fuss of weighting scores is not worth the trouble (Echternacht, 1976).

Another issue raised by weighting is that of justification. How do I explain why item number 4 is worth twice as much as item number 6? Can I argue that instead of giving item 4 two points, it should in fact have only one and a half points? How do I come up with that exact weight of two points? Weights are very difficult to justify and open the door to a great deal of discussion. If an item can be seen to cover two points in the table of specifications this could be used to justify differential weights. But expanding the sampling of the unit seems like a more defensible position than does giving more points to some items than others. If the topic of item 4 should get two points, write two items each representing a different aspect of that topic.

The recommendation, then, is to avoid weighting of items. Instead, increase the number and cognitive levels of items that fit into the central issues of a unit of teaching. This in effect weights the topic, not the items that sample it. As we've discussed, the selection of the number of items should match the table of specifications.

The above discussion pertains for the most part to objective tests. In essay tests and observational assessments we routinely weight items because the breadth of a single test question varies much more than in, for example, a multiple-choice item. Some essay items can be answered in three or four well thought out sentences, while others may require four or five paragraphs or more. We do weight these essay items to reflect the scope of content involved. This appears to be a legitimate procedure when done with deliberation and matching items with the content of the table of specifications.

Scoring Formulas

In the discussion of true-false tests (see Chapter 8) the conclusion was made that scoring formulas are not very useful and probably should not be employed. This is mainly because its assumptions were difficult to justify, and typically a student's rank in the class is not appreciably altered by using a scoring formula. This conclusion is true not only with true-false tests but also with multiple-choice tests. The formulas add extra steps in the scoring, but these extra steps do not improve our ability to sort out the students who know and can use the subject matter from those who are less well prepared (Cronbach, 1984).

Timing of Scoring

Rapid feedback is an essential ingredient of learning. Scoring should be done as soon as possible after tests are given because the impact of feedback is inversely related to time that elapses between testing and feedback. The less time that passes, the more effective is the feedback as a learning and retention reinforcement.

To facilitate feedback some teachers will post a correctly marked answer sheet at the door of the classroom. As students leave the room they can check items immediately upon handing in their work. This indeed facilitates feedback, but needs some adjustment to ease the potential traffic problems as student exit the room. Another location in the room, not in view of test-takers, would be preferable.

Some teachers give students shorter examinations so that the class can discuss the examination immediately after taking the test. Students are asked to mark answers on their answer sheets and on the test itself. Answer sheets are handed in and the teacher immediately reviews the test content with the class.

There are two problems here. First, shorter tests are less reliable than longer ones (see Chapter 4). Second, it means that in junior and senior high schools different tests will have to be made up for each section of the class you teach, but this is not a bad idea anyway. If alternate forms are made for successive classes, immediate feedback, a useful learning experience for students, is possible.

In conclusion, whether you hand score or have a machine scoring system, prompt scoring should be a top priority so that feedback is carried out in an expeditious manner; it is the best way to make a test be a teaching-learning aid.

✎ Problems

Comment on each of the following events associated with test-taking and scoring.

1. I am always anxious to start taking the test so as soon as I get the test I go to item 1 and start working on its answer!
2. I have finished my test and have ten minutes left. I am reviewing my marked items. On item 15 I marked option b); I now think c) looks a bit better. Should I change the answer or is the first mark always the best?
3. List four things teachers can do to reduce the incidence of cheating.
4. Mr. Green announced to his sixth-grade class, "On this mathematics concepts test there are 20 true-false questions. Questions 2, 5, 12, and 19 are worth 2 points each. Problem 10 is worth 3 points, and all the rest are worth only 1 point."
5. At the top of Ms. Deutch's test in German vocabulary was written, "This test will be scored with a formula that compensates for guessing. Items left blank will not be counted as right or wrong, so if you are not sure of an answer, leave it blank." What is your response to the use of a formula?

Returning the Papers to Students

Returning tests to students involves three important functions in the learning process: confirmation, correction, and review.

When a student sees that an item was given credit, it is an affirmation that the student in fact knows the material of which the item is a sample. The typical student, however, does not get all the answers correct and the posttest review is your opportunity to extend your teaching of the unit. Any misconceptions, errors, or lack of knowledge can be corrected at this time.

Students should not be allowed to leave a unit with false ideas about the information and application of the topic of that unit. Going over tests with the class allows them to make necessary corrections to their ideas. But, because there is no way of knowing what questions will be asked by students, the teacher should be ready to respond to the topic of each item in the test with a short elaboration.

As time goes by everyone begins to forget information that once was at hand. Periodic reviews build up that information bank and reduce the rate at which students forget. To this end reviews are productive in promoting retention—a good argument for posttest reviews and for comprehensive final tests.

When you return test papers is a good time to conduct a review of the content of the topics you sampled with your test. As you go through each item on the test, preface your comments about a given item with a generalization about the topic. For example, on an item concerned with Charles and Boyle's law about pressure of a gas, begin by stating the law. Then turn to the item. This will show the answer to the item in context of an idea, rather than an isolated fact.

Here is another example. In a sophomore American history class, a test contained an item that read:

The Boston tea party was carried out by

a) Indians who were trying to disrupt colonial business
b) Colonists who were objecting to the king's taxes
c) British sailors who were angry because they had not been paid

Ms. Longview, in her review of the test, provided the following preamble to this item. "We noticed that in the American colonies the people were not represented in the British parliament. But the Crown continued to impose heavy taxes on the colonies. The colonists objected—they were being taxed without the right to debate the taxes, or to have their representative vote on a tax. The Boston tea party was planned to show resistance to the taxation without representation policy."

At this point Ms. Longview turned to the item. In the context of her preamble, the item becomes meaningful. Her preamble also provided a review of one of the features that lead to the revolution—and to the writing of the item for this test. This example illustrates how returning tests to students can be a learning event as well as a feedback event.

Allotting Time for Review

Here is a key to allotting time in reviewing a test: in scoring, note which test items were missed most often. The context within which these missed items were developed will need the most attention, and in some cases considerable reteaching. When you have identified these items, think of how to present a quick review of them in their appropriate context. Then prepare the background material for presentation with these items. Machine scored tests will typically provide a printout showing the percent of the class that missed each item. This is a great help in preparing for a review of the test. The ability to obtain information about which items were most often missed, and the option that was most often selected for each of those items, is one reason that teachers should be involved in scoring. This information is lost when students exchange papers and score each other's tests.

Testing should not be the end of a unit of instruction. Teachers need to analyze test data to see what students have learned well, what they have not learned well, and what they have not learned at all. These conclusions come from a quick study of the test results. Then when teachers return the tests to the class, they can selectively review topics in terms of how well the class has scored on each of the various elements of the unit. This is an essential step in the cycle of instruction.

Dealing With Student Remonstrance

In the discussion of tests, some students will object to the scoring of a given item or items. Some of these students truly believe that their answer is a correct one, and vigorously try to defend their position. Some join the discussion to get more points on their test. The term "trick question" sometimes arises. Many students call any question in which they missed a central idea a trick question.

The first response by the teacher to any allegation about an item is to ask students to explain their answers. Listen to the explanation; appearing uninterested will only increase the student's antagonism. A response that begins, "You feel that . . ." which then essentially paraphrases the student's explanation is a good way to put the explanation back to students. They hear their own position and have a chance to rethink it. Now wait for their next response.

You may also wish to ask other students, who got the answer correct, to explain why they chose their answer. Then you can return to the concept on which you developed the test item and explain how the item was derived out of that concept.

In Chapter 9 you read about item analysis, a process that shows how the class responded to each option for a given item. If the item analysis shows that an overwhelming portion of the class got the right answer, your position is stronger; but if an item analysis spots evidence of ambiguity (good students missed the item, less capable students got it right) you may wish to eliminate the item from scoring, which should be done before handing the papers back to the class. Having item analysis data on hand will also aid in discussing items in the test.

In cases of student challenge, never appear intransigent, and never cave in at the outset. Always listen to the student's explanation carefully, and ask questions to get a further elaboration. Do not ask for a show of hands among students as to the right answer. Instead, concentrate on explaining the concept. If you have made the examination carefully, your answer will probably hold up. If the student continues to object, do not take class time to discuss the matter again. Make arrangements to see the student alone. Deferring the decision allows for a cooling-off period in intense situations.

A promise for arbitration is also possible in rare cases of strong remonstrance. If another teacher will agree to look over the item and hear your explanation and the arguments of the student, this should be acceptable to both sides.

In any case, discussion of a single test item should not be allowed to consume much of the class period. It takes up the time of the unconcerned students and delays the progress of the class toward more productive objectives. This is the value of seeing a student out of the regular class situation.

Even though some disagreements occur, review of the test with the class is important as a pedagogical aid. Students learn new content and correct misunderstandings. Teachers should not deprive them of this opportunity.

A REAL CASE NARRATIVE

The following describes a test administration in a local school. Comment on the procedure described.

Mr. Gomer, a high school Economics teacher is meeting with his student teacher, Mr. More. "Friday we will be giving the class a unit test. I have reserved the cafeteria for an hour so we can spread the class out. I want you to give the test," he advised Mr. More. "I'll have the tests made so you can pick them up before the class meets," he continued.

On Friday Mr. More showed up in the cafeteria with two stacks of paper, took some time to staple the two sheets together, then announced that the test was ready and students should put away all materials except a pencil. He then passed out the tests and announced that the test would be over at exactly 10:45 A.M.

During the test students passed noisily in the hall, and at one point a cafeteria worker dropped a large pot. Muffled conversation was occasionally heard in the nearby kitchen.

SUMMARY

1. The success of an assessment program relies heavily on its management; this chapter is about that management.
2. It is important to announce a test far enough in advance to allow students to adequately prepare for it.
3. Students benefit most when they are given help in preparing for a test through class discussion of topics and nature of the test, experience with pretests, and advice on test-taking procedures.
4. Test anxiety can be reduced by instructions that are not demanding of the student and do not admonish students to work hard.
5. In assembling the test the teacher should read over the items to be sure they cover the content appropriately according to the table of specifications, group items by item-type and in the order they were covered in the instruction, and write detailed instructions for taking the test.
6. A test is best administered in the students' regular classroom, where the teacher is the test administrator, and instructions are clear so that all students understand the task at hand.
7. Although their impact is not universal, some attention should be given to controlling the sensory environment in which a test is administered, especially in terms of

possible sources of distraction and physical comfort qualities such as work space, light, and ventilation.

8. Students should be advised that they will do their best job on tests if they skim through the entire test before beginning to respond to specific items, guess in the face of uncertainty, and upon rereading change items that appear to have been marked wrong the first time through the test.

9. Cheating can be reduced by providing review sessions before tests, scheduling more tests throughout the grading period, making sure tests are fair, being scrupulous about test security, writing new test items on a regular basis, arranging the room so that cheating is difficult, creating alternate forms of a test so that students sitting side-by-side will have different forms of the test, and proctoring the test carefully and continuously.

10. Schools should have written policies on cheating that describe the evidence required and the procedures for adjudicating the charges that cheating has occurred.

11. Instead of weighting test items it is preferable to write more items on focal topics in an instructional unit.

12. Scoring of tests should be done as soon as possible to ensure rapid feedback to students.

13. Returning tests to students serves several functions. It confirms in the student's mind the items answered correctly, provides a chance to correct errors of information, and provides opportunity for review.

14. In handling student protest to the scoring of an item, it is important to listen to student explanations and to review the concept carefully, agree to see the student privately, and to submit the answer for arbitration by another teacher.

PROBLEMS

1. List at least seven things a teacher can do to reduce cheating on tests. Select three of these as the most important and tell why you think these are important.

2. You have caught a student using a notepaper during your class test. What should you do?

3. Mr. Stonewall does not discuss his test after returning papers to students. He says it takes too much time from instruction. How would you respond to him?

4. Ms. Eks scores her multiple-choice tests with a scoring formula (right minus one-third wrong). She also gives 2 points for some questions and 1 for others. What advice would you give Ms. Eks?

5. Ms. Taylor noted that Dan occasionally looked at the palm of his hand during the history test. As the students passed out of the room she called Dan aside and looked at his hand. There were several dates and places written there, and several unit-relevant vocabulary words. Ms. Taylor remarked, "Dan you get a zero on this test, and I think you know why!" Comment on this scene.

ADDITIONAL READING

Chase, C. I. (1978). *Measurement for Educational Evaluation,* 2d ed., Reading, MA: Addison-Wesley Publishing Co., Chapter 13, "The test-taker in his environment."

Clemens, W. V. (1971). Test Administration. In R. L. Thorndike (Ed.), *Educational Measurement,* 2d ed., Washington, D.C.: American Council on Education. pp. 188–201.

CHAPTER 12

ASSESSING STUDENT PERFORMANCE

It's 4:30 on Friday afternoon and Mr. Gomez is heading for the parking lot. Exiting from the door of the school building just behind Mr. Gomez, Ms. White is searching through her purse for her grocery list.

"You're looking a little somber, Mary, everything OK?" asked Mr. Gomez.

"I just finished scoring a test in my class on child care. I'm really unhappy with it," Ms. White replied. "Multiple choice just doesn't tell me what these kids will do when they have a real child on their hands. I need to see them in action, decide how well they do it in a lifelike setting!"

"I know where you're coming from," Mr. Gomez acknowledged. "Last week I gave a test in my business math class. I felt just like you do. How well will these kids solve real business problems if they get a chance? I had to admit I wasn't sure."

Many teachers have shared the concern expressed by these two instructors. Yes, children can do what we ask them to do on a test, but what happens when they are put into a real-life situation where they have to generate alternatives and complete a solution? Can they handle it? This is the question that **performance assessment** tries to answer.

Performance assessment is not new, though recent refinements in procedure have made it more valid. Effective teachers have always watched their students for behaviors that indicate a child is "doing it right" or "is not doing it right." This is an informal type of performance assessment, but performance assessments are found in many levels of complexity. For example, performance assessments may run from an in-class essay, to figuring out how many low-cost houses can fit on a specific irregularly shaped lot that faces Elm Street, between 12th and 13th Avenues.

Performance assessment does not obviate the use of conventional paper and pencil tests such as multiple choice (Bridgeman, 1994). The acquisition of much information can be economically assessed by these tests. A child cannot deal with the solution of real-world problems involving a number of triangles unless the child can find the area of a triangle, know the relationship of sides to the hypotenuse, and so forth. Without this basic information the child would have difficulty solving the low-cost housing problem mentioned above. Conventional paper and pencil tests are a convenient method of finding out if indeed this pupil understands these basic concepts. Nevertheless, performance assessment has an enormous role in viewing the final outcomes of education. The task of the educator is to balance the role of objective tests and performance assessments so as to utilize the best of each methodology (Wood & Power, 1987). One proponent of performance assessment (Stiggins, 1993) concluded:

> . . . . performance assessment methodology . . . is just one tool capable of providing an effective and efficient means of assessing some—but not all—of the most highly valued outcomes of our educational process . . . it is critical that we keep this form of assessment in balance with other alternatives.

Although teachers constantly employ informal performance assessments, this chapter will focus on formal, planned performance assessments; assessments in which teachers have both an objective for their assessment and a prearranged plan for their observation and for making a record of their observations. Performance procedures have been used for years by shop teachers, home management teachers, judges at band contests and scorers at a diving meet. For decades judges have rated the performance of gymnasts, figure skaters, and boxers. All of these long-standing activities possess at least the rudiments of formal performance assessment.

In regular classrooms a teacher can only know how well a pupil does something when that something is seen being done. This requires performance assessment, not just in special areas, but in most if not all instructional settings. Ability to manage real problems is a desired outcome of learning. Do the students have this ability? To make this determination we must see them perform and then assess the performance.

In sum, performance assessment appears in many forms and at various degrees of complexity. It is not designed to assess achievement in all outcomes of instruction but weighs heavily in deciding how well children can deal with problems. Can the child do it in a real-world setting? This is a question that performance assessment answers.

What This Chapter Will Include.   The first part of this chapter deals with the development of performance assessment procedures. Later sections discuss recording methods and the portfolio as an assessment device. In this chapter you will learn about:

Section A. Developing and using performance assessments
1. What performance assessment is
2. Components of a performance assessment
3. Some areas of performance assessment in schools
4. Formative and summative purposes of performance assessment
5. How to carry out a performance assessment

Section B. Creating devices for recording and summarizing observations

   1. Anecdotal records—how to write them and analyze them
   2. Checklists and rating scales

Section C. The portfolio

   1. What the portfolio is
   2. Dealing with portfolio content
   3. Managing complications in portfolios

What Is a Performance Assessment?

In this section you will learn what to consider in developing performance assessments and the procedures used for applying performance assessments to increase their reliability and validity.

When a student demonstrates a skill, is involved in an activity, or produces a product, and the teacher assesses the quality of the demonstration, this is performance assessment. When students face a science question do they use the scientific method—information collection, posing a problem, and developing and testing hypotheses? In machine shop can Jan diagnose the cause for a malfunction in a motor? In my business class how effectively does Henry develop a plan to market a product? Does science student Zhang know how to wire a circuit board to accomplish a given result? To find the answer to these questions you must see the students in action or see the product of the action. Noting the appropriateness and quality of these actions and their outcomes is performance assessment.

Performance assessments must involve to some extent the professional, subjective judgment of the teacher. To avoid being unduly influenced by extraneous environmental factors in making judgments teachers must be skilled in the techniques of performance assessment. They must focus on the target of the exercise, develop criteria for their judgments, and devise a "scoring" scheme to assess the quality of the target performance. For example, when I am assessing the child's ability to locate a point on a map when given latitude and longitude, I must not be distracted by neatness of the work. If accuracy of the location is the focus of my observation, I must have criteria for accuracy and an a priori scoring plan that will acknowledge the different approaches students will use.

Performance assessment, like objective tests, is linked to the instructional objectives of the teacher. The teacher wishes to guide students to the performance of a given act, such as applying basic arithmetic in solving a problem, demonstrating skill in planning an expenditure of money, dissecting a laboratory insect, or analyzing a speech for propaganda purposes. In all of these examples the student must do something; and the teacher must see it done and evaluate the process, or see the product and assess its quality in terms of a set of criteria, or sometimes both of these. Only then can we conclude that a student has achieved an instructional objective.

Components of Performance Assessment

The structure of a performance assessment includes four distinct components which we shall look at in some detail in this section.

Components of a Performance Assessment

1. Identify the target skill for assessment.
2. Identify activities that display target skills.
3. Know what features to observe and record as evidence of skill acquisition: the rubric.
4. Compare with performance standards.

The Target Skill

The first component involves delineating the focal skill, or product, which is the subject of the assessment. This is my **target.** In this component of assessment I focus on the target, not the vehicle that demonstrates it. For example, Ms. Erikson is a Social Studies instructor and one of her objectives is relating climate to population migrations. After the class has studied information about this phenomenon, can the children communicate the relationship of climate and population movements? If so, they have the target skill Ms. Erikson wants to observe. Children may choose different ways to express their ability, and Ms. Erikson must not be distracted by the nature of their projects. A theme on population migration with a neatly designed, graphics embellished cover sheet, printed on a laser printer should not entice the teacher away from focusing on the target—relating climate to population migration. To help teachers concentrate on the characteristics of the target, a list of relevant qualities of the target should be constructed. This list will be the teacher's guide for observation—it is often referred to as the *rubric.*

Activities That Illustrate the Target

The next component of a performance assessment is to identify situations in which the target ability may be observed. This is the **context** of the problem, and refers to the specifications of the field in which the target manifests itself. For example, ability to use specific verb forms can be seen in a variety of communication situations—writing a theme, presenting a short speech, locating the verb forms in an article from the news paper. These are context settings. There are no doubt a large number of situations through which target skills can be observed. However, not all of these situations isolate the target performance equally well, nor will all the observed behaviors be appropriate samples of the domain or total field in which the target may be viewed. To be a valid sample of the field, and hence have content validity, the observed behaviors should allow the teacher to generalize to the total domain of settings (Linehan, 1976). In a performance assessment the teacher may select the context, though letting the student do it also has advantages.

Here is a rudimentary example. The target is the use of topic sentences in writing a paragraph. The teacher-assigned context is an essay. There are several context features that show the student's expertise in the domain of writing essays: spelling, grammar, sentence structure, paragraph structure, use of descriptive and illustrative language such as simile, and so on. In assessing how well a fourth-grade student has used the topic sentence, the target, the teacher must concentrate on the target—how well the student deals with topic sentences—and not let contextual features influence the judgment.

In instances of student choice of content the situations that demonstrate the target performance may be different from student to student in the class, but the target may be the same for all, or nearly all, students. For example, in the Social Studies situation above, some students will write an essay on the relation between climate and migration. Others may make weather maps and incorporate population migrations. Still others may select an annotated statistical report. All these are focussed on the same target, within the same domain. But the plan for assessment should accommodate this diversity of approach. The conclusion about migration should generalize across all projects.

Authenticity.   In some cases, the teacher presents a fairly structured exercise, such as providing a single prompt for an essay to be written in class. However, some advocates believe such requested activities fail to be entirely authentic. By **authentic,** they mean that the performance represents the student's response to a problem that involves or replicates a real-life event for the student, either in the academic setting or in the student's life in general. Authentic tasks are intended to apply academic work to the solution of problems that have meaning for the student. They derive their importance by approximating nonroutine, naturally occurring problems (Newman, 1991). For example, after a group discussion of the flat tax, a letter written by the pupil to a congressman is direct evidence that this student can produce a correctly composed (and purposeful) product and is based in a real-life problem.

Because authentic assessment focuses on events students encounter in real life, it is based on experiences students are having and the questions they are facing. The solution to the problem will be in the student's hands, and includes selecting, planning, analyzing, and synthesizing material and coming to a conclusion. All this promotes the idea of student ownership of the problem and its solution, a condition that promotes student motivation.

Although many problems arise out of an authentic situation, others are based on teacher-planned events that create a student problem consistent with course objectives. For example, the class has been looking at persuasive speech. The teacher plays a tape of an example of a persuasive speech and asks the students what they think of it. Many opinions are presented, with some disagreement. The teacher then asks the class to develop a set of criteria for evaluating persuasive speeches so that such speeches could be compared on quality. The criteria will then be applied to recordings of recent political speeches. Here students are faced with a real problem and it is up to them to devise the solution. The teacher's role is that of adviser. In this instance the teacher has an instructional objective (recognize the qualities of a persuasive speech), and the students are asked to perform the behavior that will show attainment of the objectives.

Number of Observations.   Along with deciding what the performance activities will be, the teacher must also decide how many of these performances will be enough to establish a stable, reliable conclusion about student achievement of the objective. If a second-grade student makes correct change for a purchase once, can the teacher reliably conclude that this child knows how to make change? Several observations of an activity will be needed possibly in different contexts.

Suppose the teacher concludes that the child cannot exchange money. Why has the child failed to accurately do so? What is the part of the skill that is causing error? To answer these questions the teacher lists the observations by category and checks each off as successfully done, or not. (In the case of making change an objective test of arithmetic may help.) Several observations may be needed to diagnose this student's case. Not only are single observations less reliable than multiple ones, but they may not carry enough specific data to diagnose the source of performance difficulties.

Visibility of Performances.   When preparing to assess a performance, the process or outcome product to be assessed must be observable. Performance assessment, like all assessments, must depend upon activities that observers can see happen, activities that show a grasp of the process and the attainment of a goal. Intangibles, such as appreciation, must be defined in terms of activities that correlate with it, and can be seen. For example, appreciation of literature could be defined as reading and reporting on the classics or writing material in the style of several classical writers. But conclusions here are based on inferences, not direct observations. They may show an understanding of literature, but to hypothesize appreciation requires a logical leap that may be difficult to support. Therefore, whenever possible teachers should use activities that are directly observable.

Performance Standards

After I have defined the performance, and identified the relevant exercises that portray it, I must specify the methods for managing the results. Performances to be assessed require standards of adequacy often referred to as **performance criteria.** In performing a science experiment there are agreed-upon procedures that must be followed; in performing a Bach fugue there are recognized qualities of accuracy and musicianship that pertain to the performance. The same standards of adequacy must be the basis for appraisal in each application of performance assessment. Standards cannot be varied from performer to performer. An observation schedule helps us apply a common standard.

In Mr. Ohmstead's science laboratory the class has just finished the study of electricity. One aspect of this study is the development of the concept of electricity operating within circuits. Mr. Ohmstead is now ready to assess the students' skill in constructing circuits.

He has prepared a collection of circuit diagrams, beginning with simple ones and increasing difficulty up to fairly complex circuits. He has collected the materials students will need to prepare circuits. He has developed the list of performances he will observe with each level of complexity of the diagram. These include completion of a working circuit, solid connections at all junctions, wires appropriately separated to avoid shorting the circuit, all objects—switches, resistors, etc.— firmly affixed to the circuit board. Now he will ask students to begin with a simple diagram, select the appropriate materials, and put together the circuit described in the diagram. When this is done, the students will go to the next more difficult circuit, and so on.

Afterward it is time to make some conclusions about each student's work. What are the standards Mr. Ohmstead applies to his observations? Who has performed well enough to go to the next step in his instructional objectives? Before student work Mr. Ohmstead must set performance criteria on which to make his decisions. These aspects of criterion performance should be listed on his rubric—his assessment guide for judging quality of performance.

Application of Performance Assessment

At a recent Parent–Teachers Association meeting the guest speaker discussed performance assessment. At the intermission a teacher was heard to say, "In some classes, such as science and music, I think performance assessment has its place. But I'm a social studies teacher. It's hard to fit performances into a study of the Civil War."

Actually, performance assessment can fit into all studies. Sure, it fits more obviously into some classes, such as science where steps in problem solving are taught, and teachers require students to solve problems about the physical world by applying those steps. But if your teaching involves the creation of a product, the simulation of a procedure or structure, the solution of a real problem, demonstration of a skill, or the reenactment of an event, then observational techniques for assessment are not only appropriate, they may well be necessary. Only by asking children to do something can teachers conclude they can do it.

Indeed, performances are intertwined into almost every classroom instructional situation. "Knowing" is only a part of the objectives; "showing it being done" is also essential. Teachers want their students to demonstrate that they can apply knowledge in solving problems, in producing products, and in creating alternatives to routine behaviors. This may require teaching with an aim toward application, which means that performance will be an essential outcome of almost all good instruction.

Though not limited to these subjects, performances are often seen and judged in the sciences, arts, music, and physical development classes. Following are some examples of performances in areas that are central to our school programs, but in which performances are often less evident.

Social Studies.   A committee writes an ordinance dealing with control of air pollution; the class acts as the city council and debates the proposed ordinance and the final product (the proposed ordinance) is forwarded to the president of the city council. Students plan and create the terrain of the Battle of Gettysburg, and with small blocks illustrate the movement of soldiers on each of the days of that war. Students write an analysis of selected current events in terms of Constitutional provisions. Students structure their city's government, and each department (made up of students) reports on its function and current issues before it. The class identifies three of the most pressing local issues with which government can deal, develops a proposal and determines the steps the proposal would have to go through to become a city ordinance.

Language Arts.   Written products are performances to which a set of standards can be applied. The evaluation of the product in terms of the standards is performance assessment. Noting quality of changes from a first draft to the second is performance assessment. Deciding on the quality of a written analysis of the content of a poem or novel is performance assessment, as is judging the adequacy of a student's comparing and contrasting of several literary works of their own selection. Any written product—a short story, an expository essay, a poem—is a performance.

In addition to written products, speeches given by students to their classes and appraised by the instructor's observation are also performance assessment. So are appraisal of student discussion groups, debates, and plays composed and acted by student groups. In all cases behavior is held up to performance criteria.

Mathematics.   A business mathematics class takes one local small business and does its ledgers for a month. A sixth-grade mathematics class defines the areas and dimensions of a recreational complex for a proposed city park, while a seventh-grade general mathematics class figures out the expenses involved in keeping a single 18-wheeler on the road for a month. A trigonometry class figures out the height of several nearby mountains (or multi-story buildings). In these examples the students will have to decide what information is necessary and what to do with it to reach the conclusion. In the write-up of the project, teachers can observe not only the selection of the information, but also the use of the data and the validity of the conclusion.

General Behavior.   The area of personal development—emotional growth and ethical maturation—is important to school achievement, but is probably only peripherally part of the objectives of any one class. It is a function of many in-school experiences as well as a multitude of out-of-school events. Nevertheless, on report cards teachers mark items such as "pays attention," "turns in assignments on time," and "gets along with classmates."

If teachers are to mark such items on the report card, speak to parents, plan a learning exercise for a child, or discuss a pupil with other teachers, they should have some evidence that their comments are well founded. This requires specific observational data, such as anecdotal records or checklists. These data are transportable and can serve as a record of the events. They will be the basis for a generalization about a child's ability to perform a task. Whatever the source of data, this is a performance evaluation and should be managed as such. General impressions here are no more reasonable than in any other performance area.

Formative and Summative Performance Assessment

In Chapter 1 two of the several functions for assessment were described. These are formative (midstream in our progress toward an objective to see how students, and teacher are doing), and summative (at the close of a unit of instruction to see how well the objectives were achieved). Performance assessments fit well into both formative and summative work.

Teachers across the decades have used informal performance assessment to see how well students are progressing in a unit. While students are working at their desks or reciting, teachers have noted features of each student's performance and drawn conclusions about how well the students are progressing. Diagnosis is the main feature of these observations. Where is the child succeeding in the target area? Where is he or she not succeeding? What seems to be the impediment to progress? What instruction seems appropriate at this point? Where is a review needed? Viewing the target in several contexts is helpful.

The main criterion here is to improve the production in terms of the target. The teacher is working from a sense of the tasks children are performing and a knowledge of how to track the objective. Observations such as these characterize formative work.

Here is an example. Mr. Jefferson is an algebra teacher in middle school. The class is in the middle of a unit on the order of operations in an equation. He has developed some exercises around school situations which require students to multiply and divide before adding and subtracting. The students have turned in their problem sets and Mr. Jefferson is going over them. His target interest is in seeing if students have the correct order of operations, but he also notes errors in addition, subtraction, and in use of parentheses to sort out operations. He is first interested in the target, but also in improving student work in the overall context.

Mr. Jefferson has structured a situation which calls for the target skill to be demonstrated. At this mid-unit point the information he gets from this is not only aimed toward helping students acquire the focal skill, but also advises him on how to proceed with the instruction.

At the end of the unit of instruction, teachers determine how well each student has achieved the objective. This is summative evaluation. Can Jessie, a first grader, at the end of the first grading period read the words on the sight vocabulary list? At the close of a sixth-grade unit on multiplication, can Chondra solve community problems using multiple-digit computation? After studying how science generates information, does Cameron, a biology student, use the steps in the scientific method to expand information about a phenomenon? These questions all point to summative evaluation.

Performance assessment accompanies good teaching at all stages of developing a unit of instruction. As a unit progresses, it provides diagnostic information for both students and teachers. It also informs teachers as to how instruction should proceed; this is formative work. By the end of the unit, teachers hope that student experiences have altered their behavior in observable ways. They want students to demonstrate that they can really utilize these changes in skill level, idea development, and understanding. This means that students must perform something and teachers must observe and evaluate this performance; this is summative work.

✎ Problems

1. Think of a unit of instruction in your teaching area. List five outcomes of the instruction that require a performance as evidence of having acquired the objectives.
2. Many teachers rely on objective tests to assess their students. Does this affect their mode of instruction? Compare and contrast the instructional procedures of two teachers, one of whom uses objective tests entirely, and one who relies exclusively on performance assessment. What outcomes is each most likely to focus on?

3. Which of the following are formative and which are summative applications of performance assessment?

a. Ms. Harriad is developing a unit on the use of resource material in her fourth-grade class. She will include the dictionary, the thesaurus, the encyclopedia, and the *Reader's Guide to Periodical Literature.* When each of these sources are familiar to students she will introduce the computer as a resource for providing much of the same information. So far the class has looked at the dictionary and the thesaurus. They have posed ten questions about word meanings and are now working with the necessary resources. Ms. Harriad has decided to check the skills of several pupils and moves around the room to see if these skills are indeed being applied.

b. Mr. VanAllen, an Art instructor, has been working with his students on the use of line and color in acrylic painting. For three weeks each student has been working on one product. Mr. VanAllen now has the products and is assessing the use of line and color in each.

c. Ms. Voight teaches Social Studies to eighth-graders. For the last month they have been studying the ten amendments of the Constitution called the Bill of Rights. Next, each student has taken an issue found in the local news in the last week and has written an "opinion" paper about the issue, based on provisions of the Bill of Rights. Ms. Voight is now assessing the papers.

d. Mr. Rojas teaches a high school class in expository writing. He has talked about arguments in writing and has asked students to write a paper on topics they select themselves. To see how well students are grasping the ideas, he has assigned a first draft of a paper due half-way through the unit.

Carrying Out a Performance Assessment

Classrooms are busy places. There are so many instructional activities that must be attended to that teachers often save little time for assessment of any kind. But formal performance assessment is especially time consuming; each child must be seen in action, through either the physical solving of a problem or through a product such as a paper describing the solution. All this takes up large chunks of instructional time.

The need for careful planning is clear. Following are the steps that will help you put efficiency into assessing performances of your students.

Steps in Performance Assessment

1. Describe the purpose of assessment and show how it relates to instructional objectives.
2. Identify the settings in which the performance can reasonably take place.
3. Prepare a rubric to follow in observing skill acquisition.
4. Observe and record the results of the observation.

You and I will now examine these steps in more detail.

1. *Describe the purpose of the assessment.* All assessment procedures are carried out for a purpose typically found in the objectives of instruction. In Chapters 2 and 3 you learned that objectives should be stated in terms of observable behaviors, that is, performances, and that both students and teachers should have the objective in mind at the outset of instruction. The performance assessment, at the appropriate time, is done to answer the question, "How well have the members of this class (ability group, interest group) demonstrated the behavior described in the objectives?" Teachers have to see the student perform an overt act, before saying, "Yes, that child can do it!"

Suppose that our objective is for students to perform a five minute expository speech. Students could write an essay on how to do this. They could respond to test items on good and not-so-good practices in giving a short speech. From these sources a teacher may infer that students can actually stand before a group and present an expository speech. However, if you see the students perform, you no longer have to make an inference. You have seen them in action and made your decision based on controlled observations of that action. A first-grade teacher may have a child read aloud to identify aspects of reading in which the child is having difficulty. Elsewhere, a biology teacher may use a performance assessment to assess how capable a student is in using a microscope before moving to the next unit which deals with microscopic animals and where this skill is essential.

In all of these cases, performance assessment requires that teachers have delineated the objective (the target) toward which the child should be progressing. This objective is the guide for making observations. As observers who appreciate the need for reliability and validity in all assessment procedures, teachers must stay focused on the target of the observations they are making. Otherwise, they may be lured away by attractive, or unattractive, aspects of the context in which they are making their observation, and allow their decision to be influenced by these ancillary features. Concerns for reliability haunt the performance assessment movement, where reliability has sometimes been identified as below par for good appraisal of student work (Haertel, 1990).

2. *Provide a setting in which the performance can reasonably take place.* Many performances that teachers wish to observe occur regularly as a part of classroom routine. If this is the case, we do not need to arrange a special situation for making observations. For example, to see how well students in a French class can use the proper gender of nouns, a normal classroom conversation may suffice as formative evaluation. If the instructor wants to see if students can calculate the area of various enclosed figures (circles, squares, parallelograms, trapezoids) this can be managed in the course of regular classroom work.

However, there are some observations for which teachers must make special arrangements. Booting up a computer and initiating a word processing program may not be events that occur daily in your instruction, so you may wish to arrange a special occasion for observing such an event. In Mr. Ohmstead's science class, where the students were wiring circuits, special exercises and materials had to be assembled. To apply geometry and other mathematics to sorting out space for different activities (horseshoe pitching, tennis, volleyball) in a limited area of a new city park, a visit from a parks department employee and the collection of references that describe spacing for different sports may be required before students can attack the problem to be observed. This is providing the setting in which the performance can take place.

In all assessment, useful conclusions based on observations must be reliable. You learned that with objective tests short tests were less reliable than longer ones. The same is true with observations. A single observation is less reliable than several. This may mean that teachers have to arrange a number of settings for observing a performance for each child.

3. *Identify the features of the performance that will be observed.* Teachers have objectives in a performance assessment. But what are the activities that show the achievement of an objective? Teachers should begin by identifying the essential parts of a performance, and from this make up a guide to the appraisal of the performance. This guide is sometimes called a **rubric.** As the performance is observed, teachers can note a student's progress toward the objective by looking at achievement in the parts that make up the performance. An example of a rubric for assessing an essay is given in Figure 12.1.

Ms. Dickens has taught students to keep a focus on the purpose of writing and to try to confine a paragraph to one idea, to use a logical sequence of events in essays, and to vary their sentence patterns and adjust their language to fit the tone of the situation described. Now she has several students who have chosen a topic for a theme and have prepared a first draft. Because Ms. Dickens has a rubric (such as that shown in Figure 12.1) she knows what features to look for at the outset.

It is at this point that content validity comes into performance assessment. You recall that content validity is determined by how well the test samples the total domain described in the objectives. In a performance assessment the teacher observes relatively few parts of the performance domain. Because of this there is a risk that the sample does not represent the domain of behavior the teacher is hoping to observe (Crocker, 1995). Each aspect of the performance weighs heavily in the validity of the observation. A well-developed rubric, by being representative of the field, helps the teacher to focus on validity of the performance assessment.

What is observed depends on whether teachers are assessing a process or product. Am I observing a pupil to see if the scientific method is guiding the solution of a problem? This is a process. A given sequence of behaviors will reveal that the pupil is, or is not, following appropriate steps. But what if I am assessing a paper maché model of the solar system? This is a product. In either case, I will have a list of components (the rubric) to guide me through the performance assessment. A good procedure in determining the components of a performance is to break down the task into its major parts, steps, and features. Then try it out with a few observations. You will probably see that a few revisions could be made to improve the precision of the observations. However, do not break the performance into too many features. If you do this, observations can become so complex that your attention to detail distracts you from the goal of the performance. Also, students faced with too many details to follow may well lose the point of the exercise. Concentrate instead on the essentials.

The benefit of breaking down observations into essential components is that teachers want the results of the assessment to be diagnostic. With only essential components to tend to, you can easily list those things students do well and those they do not. This will provide information in directing instruction for that student.

Teachers using performance assessment for the first time may wish to look in the literature for lists of the components of a performance in their subject areas. Some school textbook writers are including performance components in the teacher's manual, but these may not match exactly how you have taught the necessary skills. To be

FIGURE 12.1 Analytic Writing Development Rubric Grades 6–8 (Draft—January 1996)

	Ideas and Content	Organization	Style	Voice
	Writer:	Writer:	Writer:	Writer:
6	- stays focused on task/topic - includes thorough and complete ideas and information	- organizes ideas logically	- commands dynamic vocabulary - demonstrates writing technique - uses varied sentence patterns	- effectively adjusts language and tone to task and reader - shows active interest in topic
5	- stays mostly focused on task/topic - includes many important ideas and information	- organizes ideas logically	- uses dynamic vocabulary - demonstrates writing technique - uses some varied sentence patterns	- effectively adjusts language and tone to task and reader - shows active interest in topic
4	- stays partially focused on task/topic - includes some important ideas and information	- organizes ideas logically	- uses ordinary vocabulary - attempts varied sentence patterns	- attempts to adjust language and tone to task and reader - shows some interest in topic
3	- strays from focus on task/topic - includes some ideas and information	- attempts to organize ideas logically	- uses ordinary vocabulary - relies mostly on simple sentences	- attempts to adjust language and tone to task and reader - shows some interest in topic
2	- misunderstands task/topic - includes very few ideas or little information	- does not organize ideas logically	- uses limited vocabulary - relies mostly on simple sentences	- may use language and tone inappropriate to task and reader - shows little interest in topic
1	- has no focus on task/topic - includes almost no ideas or information	- does not organize ideas logically	- struggles with limited vocabulary - has problems with sentence construction	- may use language and tone inappropriate to task and reader - shows no interest in topic

valid an assessment guide must fit your instruction. Feel free to change the components in the manual to match you instructional goals.

In addition, some states have included performance assessment as part of their state curriculum guides. If this is true in your state, ask for the components of the performance used to assess students across the state. These could be a guide for development of your own performance components.

Figure 12.2 shows an example of a set of performance criteria for preprimary mathematics taken from a state study guide by one teacher. This example utilizes observable behavior in the statements and can be used to identify tasks the child can perform and those that still need work.

Another utility of listing components of the performance is that these help students become better self-evaluators. If students know the components of a performance and can be shown specific elements of their performance that are done well, and those that are not, they can do a better job of assessing the quality of their own performance.

4. *Summarizing the observation.* Now that we have focused on an objective for our observation, listed the essential features of the performance for assessment, put together a setting for the observation, and have seen it happen, how shall we handle the results? Several alternatives are available. I must first decide if I want a **holistic** or an **analytic** evaluation. In the former, I complete the observation with a generalization about the overall quality of the performance. In the latter my conclusion is a summation of the components of the performance.

Holistic summaries are usually preferred when errors in some components can be tolerated if the overall performance comes out well. For example, Juanita, a fifth-grader and a certified birdwatcher, is writing a report on the building of bird nests. Her report has several misspellings and a grammatical error in agreement of subject and verb, and several run-on sentences. However, her overall report stated the problem well, followed with her data collection, and made a conclusion consistent with her findings. A holistic analysis would view the project in its entirety, rather than detail, and make an appraisal based on the broad structure of the report.

Task	Yes	No
1. Counts to 20 without error	_____	_____
2. Counts to 20 by 2s without error	_____	_____
3. Writes numbers 1 to 10 correctly	_____	_____
4. Points to drawings of a square, circle and triangle	_____	_____
5. Groups objects into sets up to 5 items	_____	_____
6. Compares objects to show bigger, smaller	_____	_____
7. Points to penny, nickel, dime, quarter when asked	_____	_____

FIGURE 12.2   A Sample Checklist of Performance Criteria for Preprimary Mathematics

Holistic evaluations are most often made when teachers are making general decisions about the learner. If I am deciding what reading group a child will go into, I may settle for an overall assessment based on several oral reading passages. In deciding if Betty is moving along with the class in English composition the teacher may quickly scan a one page essay Betty has put together during the class. Decisions based on holistic evaluations are typically intended to identify the general level of progress of the student. An overall score is typically given in the range of, say 1 to 7, defined as to total theme quality. Each score level is carefully defined.

But suppose that the teacher is doing a diagnostic assessment of Juanita's performance in writing. Here spelling, grammar, paragraph structure, organization of ideas, and so on are each viewed as separate parts of the performance to be assessed. The work is summarized by merging the ratings of the parts. The conclusion of the assessment is a diagnostic account of the things the student did well, in addition to the difficulties seen in the components listed for observation. This information will help the teacher in devising instructional experiences for the student, as well as providing one element for grading. It also guides the student in evaluating her or his own skills.

It is not necessary to conclude a performance assessment with a score. However, in some cases scores are actually written on the observation sheet. In this case, we list our components for observation. Then, for each component, descriptions of about four levels of proficiency are provided. Each level awards points based on increasing qualities of performance. For example, in a diagnostic assessment of an essay, the teacher may have listed spelling as one component of the observation. The scoring sheet might look like this:

Spelling Component

No errors – (4)

1 to 2 errors – (3)

3 to 4 errors – (2)

More than 4 errors – (1)

Different score values (e.g., 4, 3, 2, 1) are awarded for each level of accuracy.

When performance assessments are used as a diagnostic aid, scoring may not be especially useful. I am trying to sort out from the various components of the task the ones in which the child does well and the ones not done well. In this case, an overall score may well obscure this sorting of skills. However, I may use a procedure, like the spelling example above, to decide what "done well" means. In addition, some type of rating scale or checklist would be very useful.

✎ Problems

1. Mr. Volmer is a physics teacher who is in the middle of teaching a unit on electricity. Students, working in pairs at lab tables, are now constructing simple electric motors, utilizing their knowledge of magnetism. Mr. Volmer walks among the lab tables and notes what students are doing, stopping to comment on neatness of some setups, how to use tools with others, and so on. He then goes back to his desk and writes notes on the skill of each of the pairs of students. Comment on the procedure used by Mr. Volmer.

2. Think of a unit of instruction in your teaching area. Now think about a performance you would like to see done by students to illustrate their skill, knowledge, and/or understanding of the content of the unit.
   a. List your procedures in carrying off this performance assessment.
   b. Sketch out a rubric for the assessment.

Creating Devices for Recording Observations

Records are important because memories can fade and drift toward generalizations that do not always fit a given child. Records are "hard copy" that can be transported and can be used to recreate a situation. This section describes a few ways to generate these records.

Rating Scales

In formal performance assessment teachers may wish to convert their observations to a continuum of numbers representing the skill they are rating. If so, they will construct a **rating scale.** These scales begin with a statement that identifies the component of behavior to be observed. Then, at regular points on a line, increasing amounts of the skill are described. As teachers observe the listed component, they look for the description that best characterizes the behavior of the child being observed. They mark this description with an X, and proceed to the next component of the overall performance. This procedure is known as the rating scale method.

Rating scales allow the observer to judge each component of performance along a continuum from completely inadequate to very adequate. Typically, scale writers begin by stating each step in a given performance. Then for the first step a line is drawn horizontally below the statement. At intervals along the line, descriptive words (or phrases) are given, depicting increasing proficiency, or increasing evidence of a skill, or whatever is being rated. These defining words or phrases are called **descriptors.** In rating the skill shown in the first step in a performance, the observer selects the descriptor that most accurately characterizes the student's performance and checks this on the line. Here is an example.

Accuracy of Math used in study

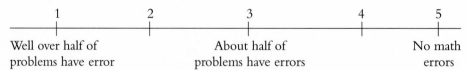

In some rating scales, the descriptors are given at each numerical point, but some (as above) allow the rater to infer what the intermediate point represents. Defining the extremes and the midpoint is often all that is needed.

Guidelines for Making Rating Scales.   It is our intent to make scales that are reliable and valid refections of the child's performance. Following are some guidelines that will help you maintain these essentials of measurement.

▼

Guidelines for Creating Rating Scales

1. Include only those behaviors you intend to develop in instruction.
2. Descriptors must depict observable behavior.
3. Should contain both positive and negative features of behavior.
4. Limit each item to a single dimension of behavior.
5. Avoid judgmental terms as descriptors.
6. Include only pivotal elements of a performance.

▲

Here is a closer look at these guidelines.

Rating scales should only be applied to the assessment of behaviors which instruction is designed to develop. Rating scales, like other assessments, should aim clearly at an instructional objective. Mr. Tempes who teaches history will not make a scale to assess neatness of work, because it is not one of his objectives in teaching history. If a category of behavior seems desirable, but educators make no effort to develop it, then they should not assess the behavior.

Instead, teachers will have definite instructional objectives in mind when, for instance, they observe a child working on a science project. How well is the child grasping the scientific method as evidenced by the reports of problem solving this child is turning in? Understanding the scientific method is a skill that teachers hope their students will acquire, and a rating scale would be a good method of recording a teacher's observation of that skill.

Descriptors in rating statements must depict observable behaviors. The items that I will rate must be differentiable parts of the total behavior that reflect an objective of instruction. Each scale item must focus on an act that can be observed. It is "usable knowledge" the teacher is interested in. For example, Ms. Ilpeut, who teaches French, may say:

"In conversation, uses appropriate gender article with nouns."

and build a rating scale to go with it (like the one above). Now, in a period of conversation in French class she can actually identify the proportion of occasions in which the correct gender article was used. The rating scale could be graded in proportion of occasions, approximate percentages, or another such indicator. It provides a permanent record of the child's progress as of the date of the observation, and can be used when doing summative evaluations, when talking with parents, or when dealing with the student on a one-on-one instructional activity.

Rating scales should contain both positive and negative statements. Some raters are believed to have a "set" for marking at one end (left or right) of the rating line. The scale should be constructed so that occasionally a statement is negative, reversing the end of the response line that expresses the positive regard. This encourages the rater to concentrate more on the feature being rated than when all statements are positive and negative descriptors always begin on the left.

The steps across a rating line should represent changes in quality (or quantity) of a single dimension only. The rater is assessing the appearance of a specific component of behavior, and all descriptors should represent an amount or degree of that component. Following is an example of an item that lists descriptors that do not represent a single dimension of behavior. It was used during a group project in which committees built a paper maché sphinx.

Shares materials with other children

Shares materials with other children

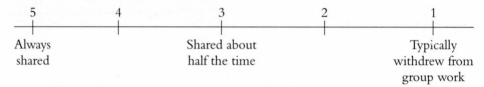

The last descriptor does not deal with sharing behavior. It is also a poor rating scale descriptor because it does not point to specific observable behavior. (What do I see the child doing that tells me this child is "withdrawing"?) In any case, withdrawing is probably not a part of the dimension called "sharing." This item could be improved by using a different descriptor at number 5 on the scale, possibly, "Almost never shared."

Descriptors should be stated in objective terms. The rater can see a child sharing; this is relatively objective. But the rater cannot as easily see a child "withdrawing," except that the rater sees a set of behaviors, collectively leading to the inference that the child is withdrawing. Descriptors should point at something raters can directly observe, not to something they must infer. Here are some examples of other descriptors that are either observable or inferred.

Observable	Inferred
Pushes children aside to . . .	Wants to be first
Makes multiple poor erasures	Is a messy writer
Breaks materials accidentally	Is awkward
Drops "t" and "d" sound in speech	Enunciates poorly
Does not use steps in scientific method	Is a poor problem solver

Although you may want to make an inference about a child's behavior after summarizing a rating scale, you should not embed inferences in the rating scale. You are reporting observations, behavior that you and I could agree did happen. If inferences are in the scale, your inference may not agree with mine. In an overall performance assessment you may wish to make these inferences, but if you do, you must have the observations of objective (seeable) features that support the inference.

In addition, descriptors should provide definite observable points along the continuum. In the above rating scale of sharing you could have identified the middle of the scale as "Shared regularly." However, this is not a definite benchmark because it means something different to each observer. However, if you say "Shared about half of the occasions" you have a more stable concept that has a similar interpretation from rater to rater. Whenever possible, use terms that represent a quantification of the feature being observed.

Rating scales should include only the pivotal elements of a task. Performance assessments are time consuming. Teachers want to invest a minimum amount of time in them. Therefore you should include only the essential features of a task on the rating scale. These will provide a basis for making the generalization you want to make.

Checklists

"Look!" said Mr. Cain, "In my chemistry class I have this list of safety precautions. All I want to know is does the student observe them, or not. I just want to check off the precautions I see being taken." Like Mr. Cain's list, some records of observations do not require the careful gradation of judgments that apply to rating scales. Instead, a simple notation of presence or absence of components of a task is adequate to assess the student's ability to carry it off. This is called a **checklist.** (See Figure 12.3.)

Teachers present students with a number of skills that, like Mr. Cain's list of safety precautions, are made up of a set of components that must be included in a given operation. Sometimes the components are steps in a process that must be in a given order; sometimes they are qualities of a product. A successfully completed process or project contains all the features listed on the checklist. This then becomes the yardstick for deciding if the student has reached the objective of instruction, and provides a paper trail of a student's development as well as the basis for the teacher's judgment about the student's skills.

Here is a brief example of a checklist. The teacher has arranged a set of events that characterize the skills and procedures required in writing a paragraph. The student writes a paragraph on an individually selected topic. The observer reads the paragraph and checks whether the various behaviors are present. This is the checklist system of recording data in a performance assessment. In most checklists what is "present" need only be listed; in some situations, however, evidence that you noted an item missing is also helpful.

Item	Present	Absent
Outline of paragraph	_____	_____
Topic sentence	_____	_____
Paragraph single topic	_____	_____
Content in logical order	_____	_____
Conclusion supported	_____	_____

FIGURE 12.3   A Simple Checklist

Checklists are useful not only in providing a record of an observation of a performance, but also in assessing social and psychomotor skills, provided you have actually taught them. For example, you may wish to see how children interact in a committee problem-solving situation. You begin with a list of behaviors you wish to observe, such as "begins work promptly," "volunteers information or ideas," "reacts supportively to ideas from others," and so forth. If the behaviors are there, you check them off on your list. A similar list could be made for students performing a motor task, such as jumping a hurdle (leads with the correct foot, takes the correct number of steps between hurdles, and so on). You can also use a check list to record activities in playing a musical instrument, in operating a computer, in using reference materials, for following steps in a process, and for many more activities teachers intend for students to learn.

As with other recording devices, following a few guidelines for constructing them should improve their reliability and validity. Following are the main guidelines for creating a checklist.

Guidelines for Creating a Checklist

1. Identify the objective of the assessment.
2. Construct a list of observable components that make up the behavior being assessed.
3. Arrange components in the order they are likely to appear.
4. Devise a simple "present /absent" marking system.

You and I will now take a closer look at these guidelines.

Identify, and focus on, the objective to be evaluated. The observation is intended to lead you to a conclusion about how well children perform a target skill. You must begin at the outset to look at features that support that skill. This means looking carefully at your instructional objectives. Your checklist must relate to and reflect only the focal objectives. You must not allow yourselves to be distracted by features of the performing context that are not relevant to the target being assessed.

Here is an example. Joel sits at the computer, turns it on, checks all peripheral equipment to see if it is functioning, inserts the data disk in the appropriate drive, and calls up the program. If Joel's hands do not appear to have been washed for a week, they should not be allowed to distract us from the target—his skill in booting up the computer.

Construct a list of clearly observable behaviors that will be evidence of having achieved the objective. To check off an item as present, you must be able to see it, not infer it. If you are assessing the acquisition of a process, the steps in the process will be listed. If you are assessing a product, the essential features of the product will be listed.

Lists of components of the behavior should include those on which students most commonly make mistakes or fail to complete. Your attempt here is to make the checklist diagnostic by including at least the most often missed hurdle on the track. What steps in the procedure need reteaching? What behaviors were counterproductive? Your checklist will provide a record of these by absence of a check, but it can do so only if you find the topics on the list.

Arrange the components on the list in the order in which they are likely to be observed. You want to make the checklist as easy as possible to use. This means that the observer should not have to scan the entire list to find the item to check when it appears. Behaviors do not always have to appear in a given order, but to the extent that many behaviors tend to appear in order, you should arrange them accordingly. This will facilitate use of the list.

Provide a simple marking system. Usually a checklist will have a short line after each component of behavior to be observed. Here you simply put a check mark to indicate the behavior appeared. Some more complex shorthand procedures have been devised to indicate qualities of the behavior observed, or some manner or sequence problem, but these are typically individualistic and often not focal to the evaluation. Try to stay with a simple check mark for the observed behaviors.

How do teachers summarize a checklist? Checklists can be simply added up for a total number of components the child performed. If your objective requires that all items on the list be evident, the total score will indicate this. However, raters typically wish to make instructional decisions based on the assessment. To this end, a narrative summary will be most useful. A short sentence that says what the student has yet to learn will suffice. A summary about all students as a group may also be useful in that if a number of them have not managed a given component skill some reteaching of that element may be indicated.

Checklists (and rating scales) have two very important features to support their use. They "dissect" an objective into its parts, and become a dated record of the appearance of the parts. Informal observations do not do this. Also, informal observations may attend to some features, but lose sight of others—you have no guide for your observations. For example, you may observe components 1, 3, and 5 for one student, and 2, 3, 4 for another. When you are making a conclusion about the total performance each component should be observed. Checklists and rating scales provide a guide that leads observers to each component of the skill they are assessing.

Second, checklists (as noted with rating scales) create a transportable record of what you observed at a given point in time. Time erodes the accuracy of recall of a given event. With a physical record of what you observed you can go back and to some extent reconstruct the activities and assessment of them at that time. This greatly improves your objectivity, reliability, and probably the validity of your conclusions based on observations.

Transportability also provides you with data to use in case studies, in discussions of a child with supervisors, and in parent conferences. Parents and others are interested in the general achievement of a child. However, you introduce a degree of specificity into the discussion if you can document diagnostic information for them and illustrate changes over time.

✎ Problems

1. How would you change this check list assessing the quality of a science project report?

   The conclusion is supported by the data   _____

   The use of equipment is poor   _____

   Followed the steps in the scientific method _____

   Statement of the problem is unclear   _____

   The outcomes of the study are inconsistent _____

2. Choose a performance in your area of teaching. Construct a rating scale item that could be used to assess the performance during an observation. Ask a friend to evaluate it for you.

Anecdotal Records: Narrative Notes About Behavior

Good teachers have forever used note taking as a reminder of behaviors they have observed and what to do about them. Bryan was noted as having trouble with deciphering some words in oral reading, and his teacher wanted to remember to help him with some word attack skills. She wrote: "Bryan—oral rdg. wrd. attack sk." This is a very rudimentary form of an **anecdotal record.**

Although teachers wish to keep the work of creating records as simple and time sensitive as possible, they may need a bit more information than was reported about Bryan. This information should be in hard copy so that it can be referenced and can become transportable. Now and then there are special problems or children with special needs for which a more formal record would be useful. One way teachers can do this is to write periodic anecdotal records. A set of these records can be summarized to assess progress (or lack of it) over a period of time. Anecdotal records are usually kept only on special children on whom case conferences will be held or with whom the school psychologist is working. Such records allow other members of the conference, or the psychologist, to get closer to behavior of a given child and see the problem more directly.

How to Write Anecdotal Records. Like any assessment procedure, anecdotal records are designed to record a sample of behaviors in as objective a manner as possible. Like any assessment procedure, these records should be reliable and valid if they are to be useful in making decisions. Here are some guidelines that will help us increase the reliability and validity of anecdotal records.

Guidelines for Writing Anecdotal Records

1. Set the objective before observations begin.
2. Record only objective events; avoid recording your opinion.
3. Record an event soon after it occurs.
4. Limit the record to a single event.
5. Record both positive and negative events.

Now let's expand on the guidelines a bit.

As in other assessments, *the objective for the records must be established before beginning to collect them.* Many records are done to assess progress of social skills of a given child.

Others are done to assess personal traits—like concentration, or persistence—of a specific child. You must keep these objectives in mind so you will not be distracted by features that are not central to the goal.

For example, if you are interested in describing Jeremy's social behavior, you will not profit from recording his high quality of work in making a map for his geography project. This is not social behavior. The observer must have the focal trait in mind (the target) and know what its characteristics are before beginning the observation.

Anecdotes should be limited to descriptions of actual (objective) events. Begin with a short description of the context in which the event occurred, followed by the event. Avoid recording your opinion. The observer should strive to make the record as objective as possible. To do this follow three steps: a) note the setting and include the date and time of occurrence, b) list what behaviors occurred, and c) report how it came out. If you really feel your interpretations and feelings are necessary, reserve them to a final note under a heading such as "Interpretation" or "Opinion." This identifies the next comment as your impression about what happened but may not represent the feelings of the person you have been observing. Here is an example:

> Ten minutes into math class, 1:20 P.M., 2/12—Darin looking at book, wrote some number combinations on paper, looked back in book, erased numbers so hard the paper tore, read again in book < 1 min., crumpled paper in palm and crushed it by pounding with fist, closed book with force, put head down on desk.
>
> *Opinion.* Darin handles frustration very poorly, prefers to act out through hostility instead of working through problems.

This anecdote is brief but tells us in objective terms what happened. It could have begun, "Darin was angry in math class!" But this is an opinion and as such gives one person's interpretation as to what Darin was feeling. Teachers want only the evidence. Conclusions about Darin should be reserved until a number of anecdotes have been accumulated and the themes that thread through them identified.

Useful anecdotes do not contain generalized descriptions, such as ". . . always acts this way when . . ."; do not include evaluative comments such as "good," or "unacceptable"; and do not interpret behavior ("She does this because . . ."). This last example is an hypothesis, which we will discuss later in this chapter.

Record events soon after they occur. As time passes people's minds alter events making some features more conspicuous, and some less so. Human beings try to make events fit together in a logical whole. If I record an event shortly after it happens, it is most likely to be on file the way it happened, not the way I recall it after time has eroded (or elaborated) it.

Limit each anecdote to one specific event. The anecdote, like a test, is a sample of a student's behavior, and therefore should be a unitary element in the life of that child. We want the anecdote to speak to one segment of behavior. For example, our target is to get information about Harold's sharing behavior. Our anecdotes will focus on this aspect of behavior and will not be complicated by his tendency to give up when faced with problems, or his tattling to the teacher on every miscue other students make. The anecdote should focus on instances where he is in sharing situations.

Record both positive and negative incidents of behavior relevant to the stated objective. In an assessment teachers are interested in all aspects of behavior that are relevant to their objective. To adequately describe a child in relation to a given objective more than a single sample of behavior must be taken over days and perhaps weeks. These samples should reflect the child's full repertoire of responses. Some may show progress toward the objective; some may not. In any case the full range of a child's behavior in regard to the target will be needed.

Here is an example of an anecdotal record that was recorded by a teacher in the third grade.

> Objective: Christy's attention management. 1:00 P.M., 3/24, 30-minute free reading period after lunch.
>
> Christy sat at her table manipulating a compass making circles on a tablet for less than 5 minutes. She dropped the compass on her table and went to the book collection at the back of the room, picked up a book, thumbed through it, and sat down on a stool to read. She appeared to read for < 10 minutes, then put the book on the floor and began looking at the book collection again. She selected another book, skimming through it and appeared to read an occasional page. She returned to her table where she began reading one of her own books, but soon picked up the compass and began making circles again. She looked out the window, pointing the compass pencil at items outside. I asked Christy to come to my desk, opened a book, and asked her to read to me. She read 6 pages with two miscues.

In this anecdote, note that the objective, time, and setting are given the activities are described in actual behaviors that can be seen; and the report is confined to the description of a single unitary event—Christy's acts in the free reading period. The teacher has avoided use of conclusions or opinions. You and I probably see Christy's short attention span, but the anecdote not only leads us to that conclusion, but also helps us see the nature of her behavior.

The time schedule for recording an anecdote cannot be prescribed because the appropriate settings are different from child to child and objective to objective. However, for a given child whose behavior is of concern to the teacher several anecdotes per week seems reasonable. Anecdotes should be collected only long enough to make an analysis reasonable, and should always be kept in a secure, labeled file.

Analyzing Anecdotal Records: Looking for Themes.   Once you have a number of records on hand some analysis may begin. Observers are hoping to make a statement about typical behavior of a child and therefore more than a few observations are necessary. When the teacher has accumulated a dozen or more anecdotes over several weeks, it may be time to begin analyzing them. There are two steps in doing this: looking for recurring themes, and posing hypotheses and testing them against the observations and other data sources.

Begin by arranging the records by date. Then look at the first record to identify one behavior mode, sometimes more, that pervades that anecdote. This is called a **theme.** A typical theme might be "destroying materials," or "withdrawing to work alone," or "belittling other children for mistakes." Themes must be stated in terms of observable behavior, not opinion.

Themes that are found are then recorded and those that are repeated are tabulated. As the reader goes through the remaining anecdotes new themes are added as they appear and are tabulated as they arise in subsequent anecdotes.

At the end of the reading of anecdotes, the reader has a set of themes with tabulations that show the frequency of occurrence for each. This tabulation identifies **recurring patterns** of behavior for the child. The next step is to explain the most common behavior seen in the themes. You approach this by testing hypotheses about the child's behavior. First, pose a reasonable hypothesis to explain the recurrence of a given theme; then look for reasons to explain it.

Here is an example. Ms. Neu has collected a set of anecdotes on Sean. She has gone through the anecdotes and has come up with one theme which recurred 10 times: "looked out the window (for 6 minutes or more) while other children were doing seat work." Ms. Neu proposed the hypothesis that the work was too difficult and Sean was retreating from it. To test this hypothesis, she went to the tabulation of themes and found that Sean had sometimes actually proceeded with his work and finished it. She went to her folder on Sean and found several writing reports that were very well done, and a few that were not. She also found problem sets that were for the most part done well. In conclusion, the assignments did not seem too difficult, so Ms. Neu rejected that hypothesis.

Hypotheses continue to be tested until the observer has one or more that can be supported with corroborating data. These are then pursued by outside advisors (such as the school psychologist or social worker). Parents are also good sources of data with which to test hypotheses, but in this case the data must be handled with care so that the parent does not become defensive.

Collecting and analyzing anecdotal records impose a time demand on the teacher. Because of this anecdotes will typically be reserved for special students who appear to be working through personal difficulties.

✎ Problems

1. Here is an anecdotal record written by a biology teacher who was assisting in a case conference on a student. Evaluate the record.

   Anne is not a very cooperative student. She destroys lab materials. She either attacks other students' viewpoints or ignores them entirely. Today in class, she made a sarcastic remark about another student's honest remarks. She broke two slides containing paramecium specimens, became angry, and took her work to a remote corner of the room away from other students.

2. Observe another student in one of your classes. Following the guidelines write an anecdotal record about this student.

3. Here is an anecdotal record written by a teacher. Identify a theme in it.

English comp., 2p, 3/5/97. Jason sat at his table, apparently reading in the *Canterbury Tales* for ten minutes. At this time I opened a discussion of the story. Jason continued to read. I asked for a response to a question, he asked for the question to be repeated, then said he didn't know the answer and returned to focus on the story, periodically turning pages.

Portfolios: Collections of Work Samples

One of the problems of assessing a student's progress in solving so-called real problems is that teachers often have little evidence accumulated over a period of time. Essay papers are returned to the students and are gone. A set of problems a student solved was returned to the student for review and reworking, and it too is gone. Teachers need a system for accumulating records of student performances so that they can review them, identify recurring difficulties, and document progress. **Portfolios** can serve this function. Portfolios have long been used by artists, writers, thespians, contractors, and others to demonstrate their expertise. Educators can benefit from their use as well.

Purpose and Content of Portfolios

Although procedures vary greatly from place to place, portfolios used in educational settings have a large common core of design and intent. A portfolio is a purposeful collection of records of successive productions that define the student's achievement at points in time, and progress over extended time. Its contents are work samples and their appraisals that expand the quantity and quality of information used to assess growth in learning. It also communicates to teachers and to students the idea that assessment, like learning, is a team effort—something in which students, teachers, and parents all participate.

There is no one answer to the question of what goes into a portfolio. Content varies considerably depending on who is making the decision of what to include. In some situations teachers determine what goes into the portfolio, and examples of typical performance at a given point in time are selected. In others classes students and teachers together select contributions. In a few instances, students "own" their portfolios, and they alone choose the documents that will go into the record.

In some cases, students include evaluative commentary on pieces of work, noting what they like about it, what they could improve, and how they would redo a record. On subsequent products students may comment on how their work is different (and better by a stated criterion) than the previous work. In other cases, teachers annotate the student records, citing the setting in which the product was made and its relevance, pointing to good features of the product, and to aspects where improvement could be made. Summary evaluations by teachers are also included in the portfolio from time to time. To this end, the portfolio is an instructional vehicle as well as an assessment tool.

Advantages of Portfolios

Advocates of portfolios cite a number of advantages in their use. Some of these are listed below.

▼

Advantages of Portfolios

1. Portfolios are potentially authentic involving problems from real life.
2. They show growth in skills.
3. Portfolios may empower students to manage their own work.
4. They foster communication between student and teacher.

▲

We will now look at each of these in some detail.

Students may work on problems that they face in real life, as long as it relates to a course objective. For example, in an English composition class a student who will soon be applying to colleges may research and write about college admissions. A student in Spanish who will travel in Argentina next summer may collect, and analyze in Spanish, items from Spanish newspapers about American students traveling in South America. An art student who is preparing a collection for an application for art school may place a design in the portfolio, critique it, and tell how it will be changed for the next entry. In each case the context is a personal one for the student. It is authentic. However, the objectives of the class are being met through the exercises, and their evaluation is improving the product.

The important items to include in a portfolio are those that represent a student's work at a point in development. To this end, *the portfolio illustrates growth in skill as time passes.* Only a few of these samples from a given point in time are probably sufficient to show growth in skill. Beyond this, appraisal of added products will only increase the time taken to review the file.

When teachers have before them several successive products that a student has added to the portfolio over a year's time, changes in skill across the time period can be seen. This is one of the features of a portfolio—concrete evidence of change in the ability of the student.

To some extent *use of portfolios in assessment of performance empowers students by allowing them to participate in their own evaluations and in planning their own course of action.* This involvement increases the responsibility of students in directing their own activities. For example, Dolores is dealing with the involvement of the Constitution in daily affairs. She has been clipping items from the newspaper and writing a synthesis of the Constitutional positions reflected in each. Last week she submitted this paper for her portfolio. Today she withdrew it, noted the instructor's comments, and attached a list of ways she could revise it to make her argument stronger. She then returned the item to the portfolio and began the revision. Dolores is in control of the activity that creates and refines the product.

The use of portfolios increases the opportunity for communication between student and teacher. They may discuss the current item in the file to arrive at improvements, or the teacher may comment on the student's paper how the product could be improved, and the student may respond by citing changes that will be made in the revision. All of this instruction-oriented interchange keeps the teacher better informed on the student's skill level, and increases the personal interaction between the student and teacher.

Limitations of Portfolios

Portfolios, like all assessments, have psychometric and practical limitations. The very aspects of portfolios that make them attractive (authenticity, growth oriented, empowering, problem centered, fostering communication) are the ones that make them complicated and ambiguous.

Limitations of Portfolios

1. Classroom assessments have multiple uses in education some of which are not well served by portfolios
2. Assessing the content of portfolios consumes large amounts of time
3. There are some psychometric problems with portfolios

And here we will look at some elaborations of these points.

The first problem with the use of portfolios is that *classroom assessments have multiple uses in education, some of which are not well served by portfolios.* While teachers applying portfolios effectively as an aid in instruction and in the promotion of individual student learning, teachers face problems of accountability and communication with school officials and with parents. These operations are important, but have quantitative requirements different from portfolios. If portfolios are used to accompany other types of assessment for summative purposes, a more effective way must be found to summarize, or "score," them. Various efforts have been made to form descriptive categories and to sort each of the portfolio's content into one of these categories. This is a difficult and time consuming operation.

Because the products deposited in the portfolio often represent individualistic interests of different students, no common base for comparison across students is developed, nor is it needed for instruction. But for administrative purposes schools require some common criteria of performance. Administrators, and the public, want to know what percent of students rank with the national, state, or district average for a skill. Money and jobs may be dependent on these figures. This kind of information cannot come from a portfolio assessment.

Another disadvantage of portfolios is that *assessing their contents consumes large amounts of time.* There is no shortcut in carrying out this task. If a teacher has two sections of literature, and 25 students in each section, at least half of these will have papers in the file each week that must be read and comments made for student revision. This eats up exhaustingly large chunks of teacher time. Over the school term teachers put in much time with the portfolios, and at the end of the term summarizing them consumes even more time.

There are also psychometric problems with portfolios. Portfolio assessment is nagged by problems of meeting psychometric standards. Opinions of several competent readers as to the status of the content in a portfolio lacks the level of agreement that pychometricians normally wish to find. This means that reliability is not as high as they would like to see for summative information (Koretz, Stecher, Klein & McCaffrey, 1994; Moss et al., 1992).

Another issue arises in connection with validation. Normally educators will validate their assessment by matching them with the table of specifications that reflects a concept of instruction (see Chapter 3). Since the content of portfolios is aimed at higher order cognitive processes, and because student activities may well pursue different objectives, portfolios may not be a close representation to many teachers' specifications. This is a question of validity. In addition, educators may have other concerns.

How sensitive is portfolio content to instruction? Are the qualities of good entries to a portfolio the kinds of things that are taught and learned? Are the assessments of portfolios fair to students of all backgrounds? Do they minimize the effects of aspects of the context that may be irrelevant to the focus of the assessment? These are all validity related questions the answers to which are not entirely clear at this point. This means that educators must wonder about the validity of assessments until further data on these questions are available (Baker, O'Neil & Linn, 1993).

Comparing With School Standards.   What standards will teachers use to assess portfolio content? It is one thing to use portfolios as a teaching device and motivate improvement in performance. But educators are called upon to compare the student's performance to a standard for passing from grade to grade, to graduate, or to meet a level of public expectation. How are portfolios used then?

For example, teachers may wish to report that Merle, a fourth-grader, is good at application of mathematics skills. At what grade level of mathematics complexity is this statement being made? Does he perform this way at the third-grade level, the fifth-grade level, or is he actually using intuitive algebraic processes in his solutions? Schools have objectives for each grade level, and certify that students who pass through the years have met the standard for each of these objectives. Traditional testing has, at the present time, an advantage over portfolios in dealing with standards. These tests may not cite specific improvements in each child's performance, but they can show that Merle is performing above, or below, the "typical" fourth-grade student on whom the test was originally tried out; and if criterion referenced tests are used educators can tell what skills have been mastered. With portfolios this is more difficult.

Complicating this issue is the fact that there is a great variability in the kinds of records found in portfolios. They are collected in different situations (in class activity, laboratory work, or self-devised projects carried out at home). The variety of circumstances in which records are created results in much variability in their content. In cases where students deposit their "best," "worst," and "typical" papers in their files, the content from student to student will be varied. No two students have the same interests or produce for their portfolios the same type of evidence of achievement. How can educators stretch one yardstick—the public standard—to cover this diversity?

Diversity of Content.   How can teachers manage the diversity among students using portfolios as the assessment tool? Among students there is a wide range of modes of expression that are learned as a result of the social context of their lives. Marjorie is very verbal, writes well, has a good vocabulary, and knows how to use the spell-checker and thesaurus on her computer. Mikiko immigrated from Japan two years ago, and continues to have some trouble with English. On a unit on the Civil War, Marjorie wrote an analysis of the strategy of generals at the Battle of Gettysburg. She also typed up a letter she would like to have sent to President Lincoln after the first Battle of Bull Run, and one she would like to have written to General Sherman as he pillaged and burned his way to the Atlantic shore. She also developed a report on the changes in the economies of the North and South during the war, including personal vignettes she researched and related to data from the lives of the residents of Altanta and Boston (where Marjorie lives).

Mikiko, felt her verbal communication was weak but her graphics skill was strong. Nevertheless, she wrote a detailed summary of the strategy of General Grant in attacking the Confederate army. As a support for her written work, she chose to draw a map of the United States showing location of what her encyclopedia said were the ten most significant battles of the Civil War. She cited terrain and demographic features on the map as evidence for or against selected strategies. Lastly, she composed several computer graphics showing economic changes during the war.

The approaches of both students provided written records for the portfolio. But the mode of response is quite different. If the teacher is assessing writing skills, Marjorie has a different background of developing skill than does Mikiko. She used a much more verbal approach to presenting the events. If the historical features are assessed, the teacher will have a difficult time assessing the two students; their records are not in the common response domain. To generalize, conclusions about students' capabilities in any subject area (such as history, mathematics, literature) based primarily on student-selected records can vary with the preferred presentation mode of the teacher who evaluates them.

The most common type of record deposited in portfolios is written. A common criticism of evaluation of written work is that other factors beside content (grammar, readability, etc.) influence scores (see Chapter 10). If so, with portfolios educators may be encountering a criticism commonly cast upon other types of assessment.

Problems of Management

Assessment by portfolio is demanding to manage. The collection of records, the counseling of individual students on their progress, the "scoring" of portfolios, the sheer effort of maintaining the filing system, are very time consuming. Moss, et al. (1992) found that a portfolio with as few as six to seven entries took experienced readers about a half-hour to assess. This means a teacher with three sections of composition averaging 25 students per section would invest over 37 hours of work in reviewing portfolios once during the term. This is almost equivalent to one week's normal work time. This time, of course, must be taken from the normal teaching day which often does not provide enough instructional hours at best.

Some advocates of portfolios will argue that the reduced instructional time is more than compensated for by increased individualization. Indeed, this has a potential for some compensation, but the extent to which it makes up for the time taken from the regular instructional period is at this point unknown.

The above discussion suggests that there are still problems that must be worked out before portfolios will be easy to work with. Nevertheless, they should first be considered from the point of view of their effect on learning, motivation, and individual reflection. All systems have problems. The salient question is whether the problems overwhelm the advantages.

✎ Problems

1. Think of how you would employ portfolios in the subject area in which you teach. Do you see portfolios as a favorable means of assessment? List the advantages and the disadvantages.
2. A teacher who works in your building comes to you asking for help in setting up a portfolio system. Describe how you would direct this teacher to proceed.

SUMMARY

1. Most teaching is designed to help students gain a skill in applying knowledge to the solving of real problems. The overt behavior that goes into the solution is a performance. Performance assessment deals with identifying the quality of this performance in terms of the problem solution.
2. Consistent with all classroom assessment, performance assessment is linked to instructional objectives. Assessment of a performance includes the target skill, an activity that elicits the performance, and criteria of success.
3. Problems should arise out of the student's real life, and if they do are referred to as authentic.
4. Stable, reliable conclusions depend on having several observations of a performance.
5. Historically performance assessment has been utilized in science, art, music, and physical development, but it is also vital to assessing many aspects of social studies, language arts, foreign language, mathematics, and general behavior.
6. Performance assessment can be applied in formative assessment to locate a student's problems in acquiring a skill and assist the teachers in planning instruction; and in summative assessment to making conclusions about how well the student has acquired the skills identified by the course objectives.
7. The steps in carrying out a performance assessment are: describing the purpose of the assessment, providing a context in which the performance can take place, identifying the features to be observed, and observing and recording the success of the performance.

8. Summaries of observations may either be holistic (assessment of the overall quality) or diagnostic (focusing on components of the performance).

9. To record observations three techniques are often used: rating scales, checklists, and anecdotal records. Rating scales present a range of quality for each characteristic rated, while checklists note presence or absence of each of a list of essential behaviors. Anecdotal records are short vignettes of a school incident.

10. A rating scale should be linked to an instructional objective, depict observable (not inferred) behavior, include negative as well as positive statements of behaviors, be limited to a single dimension of behavior, and include only essential elements of a performance.

11. In checklists the teacher should identify the target performance, list the observable events that will complete the performance, arrange these in a logical order, and check whether or not the event was carried off.

12. Anecdotal records should report only objective events (not opinions), be recorded soon after their occurrence, be limited to a single event, and record both positive and negative events.

13. A portfolio is a purposeful collection of successive student productions that define that student's achievement at points in time, continuing over extended periods of the student's schooling.

14. Advantages of portfolios are: they encourage a problem centered, authentic approach; they show growth of the student's skill; they empower the student by allowing for student planning and input into the assessment of work; and they foster communication.

15. Problems with portfolios are: they do not provide data for the multiple purposes for which schools collect evidence; the reliability of their assessments may be lower than desirable; the diversity of content in portfolios makes it difficult to apply common standards to them; and they are time consuming to manage.

PROBLEMS

1. In this chapter we have looked at the assessment of performances as evidence that students can solve "real" problems. Focusing on your area of teaching, identify one unit of instruction. Outline a plan for assessing achievement of students in terms of things you observe them doing, citing what procedures you would use, why you chose them, and how you would implement these procedures.

KEY TERMS

performance assessment   rating scale
target   descriptors
context   checklist
authenticity   anecdotal record
performance criteria   theme
rubric   recurring patterns
holistic summary   portfolio
diagnostic summary

Additional Reading

Baker, E. L., O'Neil, H. F., and Linn, R. L. (1993). Policy and validity prospects for performance-based assessment. *American Psychologist,* 48, 1210–1218.

Cizek, G. J. (1991). Innovation or enervation? Performance assessment in perspective. *Phi Delta Kappan,* 72, 695–699.

Finch, F. L. (Ed.), *Educational Performance Assessment,* Chicago: The Riverside Publishing Co., (1991), especially Chapters 1, 3, and 5.

Frechtling, J. A. (1991). Performance assessment: Moonstruck or the real thing?. *Educational Measurement: Issues and Practice,* 10 (4), 23–25.

Koretz, D., Stecher, B., Klein, S. and McCaffrey, D. (1994). The Vermont portfolio assessment program: Findings and implications. *Educational Measurement: Issues and Practices,* 13 (3), 5–16.

Merhens, W. A. (1992). Using performance assessment for accountability purposes. *Educational Measurement: Issues and Practices,* 11 (1), 3–9; 20.

CHAPTER 13

COMPUTER APPLICATIONS IN TESTING AND GRADING

"Hardware, software, peripherals, megs, CD ROM, RAM, bits and bytes! The language warp is too much for me, leave alone learn the systems!" exclaimed Mr. Gurri, a twelve-year ninth-grade Social Studies teacher. "And now computer applications for testing? Come on, I have enough trouble with assessment already. I haven't got time to figure this one out!"

Not only has the emergence of computer technology expanded vocabularies of educators in new and unique ways, it also has had a very large impact on what teachers do in schools. Teachers teach with it, "talk" to other teachers around the world, call up encyclopedias on it, and use it for research; students research and write papers with it, and create their own "home pages" with it. There are many other uses for computers in classrooms limited only by our imaginations. No tool since the book has had an impact on school practices like the computer. And in spite of Mr. Gurri's perception, the computer has become a time saver.

Among its many applications, the computer has had a growing impact on assessment practices. Teachers put together tests with computers, administer tests, score them, convert the raw scores to T-scores, and write out the grade distribution with them. Performance exercises written on word processing equipment by students are much easier to revise, and more revision can be expected by the teacher in a given time period.

What This Chapter Will Include. This chapter is divided into three parts. The first section provides a review of some computer terms to activate relevant vocabulary. The remaining two sections present computer applications in classroom assessment, and describe sample programs that will aid teachers in their assessment work. Here are the specific topics on which this chapter reports.

1. A glossary of terms to review the computer
2. How to apply computers to assessment tasks
   a. Developing objectives and tables of specifications
   b. Writing items and compiling tests
   c. Test analysis in your classroom
   d. Administering tests by computer

    e. Using the computer for writing up performance assessments

    f. Observational data by computer

    g. Letting the computer do the grading

3. Some programs to assist you with assessment

Reviewing the Computer: A Glossary of Terms

Because computers are common in almost all schools in the nation, this section is limited to a review. The Glossary below lists the main component features you will find in computer literature and used throughout this chapter. If you are familiar with these terms move on to the next section.

A Glossary of Computer Terms

Bit	The memory unit—a single digit of information, for example, a letter, a number such as 1, or a comma.
Byte	A group of bits, usually 8 to 16.
CD ROM	Much like a music disk, this device can hold a very large amount of data, pictures, and graphics (that can be rotated and moved), but requires a CD ROM reader to operate.
CPU	The central processing unit, the "brain" of the computer that manages the executive functions, such as calling up a program from a disk or interpreting a program.
Hard drive	Operator for a hard disk—repository for very large amounts of data, where a number of data files and large programs may be stored.
Hardware	The physical equipment that makes up the computer, for example, the keyboard, central processing unit, and monitor.
Input	Entering data into the computer; usually done with the keyboard, or by use of a floppy disk or scanner.
K	An abbreviation for Kilobyte, a thousand bytes of memory.
Meg	An abbreviation for Megabyte, one million bytes of memory.
Memory	The ability of the computer to store information; part of memory holds data only when the computer is running, another continues to hold data even when the computer is not running. (See also RAM and ROM.)
Output	What computers send to the user after having completed designated processes; typically done by printers creating "hard copy," by creating a message on the monitor, or by recording information on a disk.
Peripherals	Additional equipment appended to the basic computer to extend its functions.
RAM	Random Access Memory stores data until the computer is turned off.

ROM   Read Only Memory contains permanently stored information; it carries routine systems that operate the computer, such as the disk operating system (DOS).

Software   The programs written for the computer that tell it how to respond to the data we are about to input.

There are two types of desktop computers, each with a unique operating system. The first is the Apple Macintosh, which is widely used in schools. The second is the IBM or IBM compatible (such as Dell and Compaq) which are favorites of many computer users. A program written for an Apple Macintosh machine will not necessarily run on an IBM, and vice versa. This is an important feature to note when buying hardware and in looking over assessment software to use with your equipment.

✎ Problems

1. Define the following: a) hardware; b) software; c) CPU; d) input; e) output; f) kilobytes; g) megabytes; h) program; i) peripherals; j) memory; k) hard disk
2. How many bits in a byte? How many bytes in a kilobyte? How many bytes in a megabyte? How many bytes in 640 K? How many bytes in 8 megs?
3. You have a data set of 148 numbers. You want to compute the average of these data. Cite the parts or features of the computer in order that would be involved in calculating these statistics, and what each device would probably do. Begin with entering the data into the computer. (No actual program language required here.)

Applying Computers to Assessment Work

Administering tests by computer is becoming increasingly popular, so teachers should expect to be administering at least some tests by this medium. Computer programs for grading and keeping of grade books are now available, as are programs for test analysis. Many of these programs allow you to perform these jobs on your own desktop computer, though some depend on the help of the computing service of your school. These procedures can be great time and effort savers for teachers.

Developing Objectives and Tables of Specifications

The first step in teaching and in assessment is to know at what objectives instruction is aimed. Writing of objectives, course outlines, and lesson plans are done on the computer with considerable ease. Word processing programs allow teachers to move sentences around, to quickly erase and rewrite. They even have spelling checkers and a thesaurus. With these tools the writer can concentrate more on the objectives, themselves.

Computers make it easier for educators to create a table of specifications, too. Quick tabulation settings, easily changed statements, reordering of topics, and so on make the computer a handy tool for making your tables of specification for each unit.

In addition, these tables can be easily altered as teaching progresses in new directions and topical content changes. Computers can also help in preparing next year's work in a given course. With the course objectives stored in a computer file, teachers can open the file containing the list, retain the ones that are most appropriate for the next time they teach this same course, and write new ones. Computers are very handy for selecting and sorting elements like objectives in our table of specification and items in our test bank.

Writing Test Items and Compiling Tests

Mr. Neiss, an Earth Science teacher, is writing a test for his class. He taps the eraser end of his pencil against his chin as he thinks. "Let's see, the objective deals with identifying rocks. An item that goes like this might do: "Which one of the following is an example of igneous. . . No, that isn't quite what I want." He picks up an eraser and begins to erase the whole statement. The paper slips and tears. Mr. Neiss scowls. "Writing tests is a real pain!" he mutters to himself.

If Mr. Neiss had been using a word processor to write his test his experience would have been much more pleasant. He would not have to deal with the accidents that befall paper and pencil work, and the writing (and erasing) is faster. There are two ways computers are a big help in writing and compiling tests, and Mr. Neiss's example is the first of these ways. First, the computer is a very handy writing tool. Content is quickly entered and changed. Content can be moved around and topics reordered. Graphics are also available in most word processing programs, although it may take some extra effort to acquire the necessary skills to use them. Formulas can be written by most word processing systems. "Real" settings can be quickly depicted, either verbally, with graphics, or put into motion with a CD ROM.

After presenting situations such as graphic representations to the class, teachers may ask questions at both the Application and Higher Order Processes levels about the situation shown. The general form of such items looks like this: "Here is a situation from the real world (the graphic), but it contains this problem (statement of the problem). What is the solution?" When writing an item like this by hand teachers often see that their first draft is less than what they had hoped for, but erasing or crossing out and rewriting is inconvenient. Computers make it possible to change or eliminate script and insert phrases or whole sentences without any delay or extra fuss. Word processors are the easy way to write a test.

It should also be noted that there are computer programs for writing test items. These programs are based on prototype items and depend on the user to feed in items of content. Many users find the programs inflexible and their items stereotypical. However, such programs may fit your needs, and you may want to investigate them (Baker, 1989).

Compiling Tests With Computer Assistance

Now suppose that we have persuaded Mr. Neiss to use a computer in building his test. Furthermore, he has been saving test items in an item bank (see Chapter 9), coding them by objective, and including the difficulty index (percent who passed the item) and discrimination (distinguishing between high and low scoring students) with each item.

All this is stored on a floppy disk which he guards very carefully. Now Mr. Neiss is ready to write a test. He begins by identifying the first objective of instruction he wishes to represent on his tests. This objective has its own code number. His computer program then asks for a list of all test items from the bank that have the code number for the first objective.

He next reads through these items, and selects the ones that best fit the instruction he managed this term. The computer is asked to print out these items. He repeats this process with the second objective, the third, and so on. With these items Mr. Neiss has gleaned from the item bank in a matter of minutes, the test is about two-thirds done. Since he adds new topics each term, and deletes some old ones, alters the focus of some instruction, and so forth, not all of the stored items will be appropriate. He must write some new items that fit his most current instructional outline. But this is much more efficient than writing a whole new test.*

Here is another use of the item bank. Two students were ill on the day the tests were given. They wish to have a makeup test, but of course the tests just given will not do. The students, including those who were absent, will have hashed them over among themselves pretty well by now. Teachers really need a different test for the makeup, but one that assesses the attainment of the same objectives as the ones given to the rest of the class.

Mr. Neiss now goes to his computer and from his disk of test items pulls out another set for his makeup examination. He selects them according to objectives and difficulty level just like before, but for the most part these will be items not included on the tests taken by the rest of the class.

These two operations—composing the table of specifications and developing and using the test item bank—make the job of assessment much more convenient, less time consuming, and allow us easily to make appropriate changes in our work.

Test Analysis in Your Classroom

In Chapter 9 you learned how to calculate the difficulty for a test item and how to determine how well an item sorted the capable students from the less capable ones. This whole process was called item analysis. You probably guessed that these operations can be put onto the computer and the calculations done without any arithmetic on your part. Of course, this requires an item analysis program, but these are available commercially and are inexpensive. (Several of these programs are listed later in this chapter.) The knowledge of how the test items are working is very useful in deciding if the examination was successful. The figures you get from an analysis help you select the best items for the bank and also provide important records for each item in your item bank.

Item analyses are most efficiently done if your school has an electronic scoring service that scores your tests and provides an item analysis. If this service is not available,

---

*Some teachers manage much of this with a spreadsheet program, but most will want a commercial program for doing it. These programs are inexpensive and readily available as noted in the last section of this chapter.

there are avenues open that will allow you to do item analyses very quickly on your own desktop computer.

Administering Tests by Computer

Wouldn't it be nice if you could remove the task of administering tests from the daily routine of the classroom and assign it to the computer? Well, you can. The computer will not only administer the test, but will also score the test and put the scores into a list from low to high. It can calculate averages and show the spread of scores, and assign grades according to a plan you determine, beside doing an item analysis for you.

There are two ways to accomplish all this. The first is the administering of the test in the same form as a paper and pencil test, and the second is called **computer adaptive testing.** (Because the latter requires a large item bank, and its output is in statistics not regularly seen by educators, it will only be described briefly.)

Computer Testing in the Classroom.   Suppose you have written an objective test in the manner of a typical classroom examination. It was objectives based and contained 35 items. Normally, you would pass out the tests to students along with the instructions on how to take the examination. Students would finish the test and turn in their papers.

Now let's do that job on the computer. The test items are put into the memory of the computer. The student sits at the computer, logs in with a personal identification number, and a second number to identify the class and test. Then the computer writes instructions on the screen. When the student is ready to proceed the return key is pressed and the computer presents the first test item.

Suppose this is a multiple-choice test. The student reads the first question, selects an answer and presses a key on the keyboard that represents the answer chosen. For example, if the student thinks the answer is a), the "a" key is depressed. The return key is then struck, and the next item is brought up on the screen. This routine goes on until the entire test is completed.

When the test is completed the computer scores it and immediately reports the score to the student. The score is also tabulated in the class distribution of scores and recorded on the grade book. When all of the students have finished the test the teacher may instruct the computer to do an item analysis on the test.

This seems like a very efficient way to handle the administration of a test. Teachers get a lot of information out of the process, and with very little effort. However, this process requires a bank of computer stations connected to a central "server" where your test and the programs for running the system are accessed. Each student will have to have a keyboard and a monitor. If your school has a computer laboratory you may be able to schedule it for testing. For shorter tests, a set of computers in the classroom where students may work in 15 to 20 minute periods each may suffice, assuming the machines are connected to a common server to run your program and accumulate your students' data. In many schools making hardware available is a problem.

Adaptive Testing.   A second form of computer testing is called computer adaptive testing, or CAT. This system involves some complex psychometric work which the commercial vendors of the necessary programs will have provided for you. Also, you will have to develop a substantial bank of test items for each unit of work for which you wish to use the system.

To take the test using CAT the student sits at the computer, logs in with a code number identifying the test-taker, the course, and the test. The computer will randomly draw an item from your pool of test items. This item will appear on the monitor. The student responds, as before, by pressing the key that corresponds to the answer chosen. For example, if the chosen answer is c), the "c" key on the keyboard is pressed. If the student gets the correct answer, the next item selected by the computer will be a bit harder than the last one.

If the student misses the first item, the next item the computer presents would be a bit easier. The procedure continues until the student's level of proficiency is identified by a criterion set by the teacher. For example, the teacher may wish the process to continue until the student has selected the correct answer in 8 of the last 10 items, or until the degree of measurement error is reduced to a given limit. When the student has reached the criterion, the test is ended. This may come after only a dozen or so items for some students, while others may need many more items to reach the criterion. Typically students reach the criterion in somewhat less time than it takes to complete a paper and pencil test scores can be reported to the student almost immediately. The CAT process is shown in a flowchart in Figure 13.1.

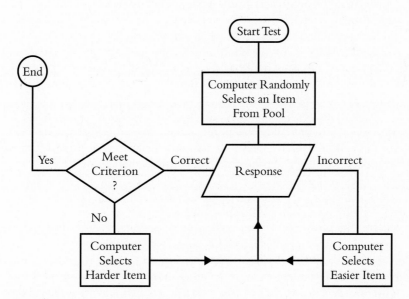

FIGURE 13.1   A Flowchart Showing How Computer Adaptive Testing Operates

It should be noted that in CAT the student's score is stated in terms of difficulty of material the student can manage, not in total number correct. This idea requires some rethinking on the part of teachers, who as students and teachers have always dealt with the number right as the summation of student performance.

An advantage of CAT is that no two students take the same test. Indeed some items may appear in more than one test, but because all students are different in their knowledge of the content, they will take items at different difficulty levels. The test taken by Roger, who is an average student, will likely be made up of items that are not the same as the one taken by Suzanne, who is a very capable student. The item set will be different for the two students because the difficulty levels will be different. Because this is the case you may wish to administer the test over several class meetings with perhaps a third of the class taking the test each day. This means that fewer computer consoles are needed to administer the test.

CAT has another advantage. Some teachers who use a performance standard for grading allow students to take the examination a second time, provided they show evidence they have prepared more thoroughly. CAT can be run again for such students with some confidence that the system will present the student with a set of items the second time that is different from the first.

By now you must be asking "how many items do I need for each testing?" This is a good question. The item bank must be large, several hundred items. This is a major problem in setting up the system. Not only must the item pool be large, but all items in the pool must be tried out so that their difficulty levels can be established by item analyses. This means a lot of work has to be done before CAT can be implemented, but once the system is established, the effort is rewarded.

It should be noted here that CAT is not a system that a single teacher is likely to set up without considerable knowledge of computers or without a dedicated bank of computers. Special programs are needed to run the system.

Despite the effort involved in implementing it, computer assisted testing is coming on line in a number schools, in state testing, and in commercial programs (e.g., the Scholastic Aptitude Tests and the Graduate Record Examination) and will be more widely used in schools as time goes on.

Like conventional testing done by computer, some editions of CAT will also recompute item difficulties each time an item is used. It will also do a class distribution for you and will assign scores to a class record sheet. This relieves the teacher of some necessary record keeping and saves some time, too (Carlson, 1994).

Student Reports and Papers

Perhaps the most obvious application of computers is for students to compose essays, term reports, analyses of experiments, and other writing projects with the aid of a word processing program (Hartley, 1993). This not only makes the written material easier to read, but also eliminates the differential in scoring due to handwriting quality (see Chapter 10). Further, students can revise their work with greater ease. With a word processor students can delete a word, a sentence, or a whole paragraph and replace it very quickly. Sentences or paragraphs can be lifted and moved to a different location on the page. Thesauri are available on many computer programs and spell-checkers can eliminate another source of distraction for the reader.

Teachers also feel freer to ask students to assess and rewrite their products if they feel they could do a better job. On long-term projects several revisions may be necessary, some initiated by the teacher and others at the student's own initiative. With a computer the job is reduced to one of dealing primarily with the concepts involved in the paper, not with the rewriting or retyping of whole pages.

By using the computer for developing reports on experiments, field trips, analysis of a newspaper article, and so forth students will save many hours of work and make their product easier to assess. However, to the teacher asking students to use the computer in creating documents I offer one word of caution. The availability of, and experience with, a computer may not be equal across the class. If this is the case, another form of discrimination could be introduced into the assessment of performance.

Recording Observational Data

Small, hand-held, and reasonably light portable devices are now available for teachers to use to record their observations and anecdotal material. They operate by "pencil" writing on a screen. Teachers can also call up previous comments, student records, checklists and rating scales, and immediately these will be put into the teachers file for the designated student.

At this writing the programs for managing these devices are not widely available, although they soon will be. Before long these devices and others will be on your desk allowing you to send and retrieve materials from your computer files.

The Computer and Grade Assignments

Mr. Meire has spent an hour accumulating student work for the grading term. He has only partially completed this tedious and exacting job. To complicate the matter, the battery has just gone out in his desk calculator. At this point a salesperson knocks on his door.

"Mr. Meire, I'm Joe Pedlman from Sunshine Programs, and my company has some classroom application programs I'd like to tell you about," Mr. Pedlman began. "I see you are working on a grade report so let's start with that grade book you are working on," he continued. "Suppose I told you that you will never have to keep another gradebook in your life, never have to record another observation on a student, never have to accumulate student performances across another semester, never have to make out grades for your classes again. What would you say?"

Mr. Meire looked skeptical, and ran his fingers through his hair. "Well, I'd be delighted!" he said as a smile began to replace his expression of skepticism.

What Mr. Pedlman said to Mr. Meire could very likely be true. There are several good software packages available today that will do just what Mr. Pedlman said his will do. They will keep your records over any designated time period, accumulating them with each observation you add. They can even convert your scores into one common score scale (Chapter 15), if you wish. At the end of the term, the program will assign grades. Typically the program will provide you several options for grading, and you select the one that best fits your idea of what grades should mean. Most will let you set the cut points between the grade marks—where the A's start, between what scores the B's fall, and so on. A time and labor saver? Indeed it is!

No grading system should be entirely mechanical. You, the teacher, must control the parameters. But the biggest chore of applying your plan to each student is done for you by the computer. You have the option, indeed the responsibility, to review the grade distribution to see that it does what you intended it to do.

✎ Problems

1. Describe five operations relating to assessment (such as writing items) in which computers can facilitate the work of the teacher.
2. Compare and contrast the standard administration of a test by computer and CAT. Especially note differences in what the final score tells us.
3. How is a test bank used in compiling a non-CAT test?
4. What in your estimation are the advantages of computerized grading? The disadvantages?

Some Available Software

There are dozens of commercially available programs that are designed to help you with your assessment records. Most will give you a class roster with grades and will accumulate data over a grading period. Others expand the utility by computing several types of score transformation (such as percentages, number grades, or letter grades) and will calculate averages for a single class or across several classes. Most commercial programs are inexpensive, running (at this writing) at less than $100, although some can run much higher. Also, some are written only for Apple Macintosh machines, and some for IBM-type machines, an important feature to note when you are considering a program. Also note the amount of RAM needed to run the programs.

To help you with your grade-book keeping, and with test-score management, here are some examples of the kind of programs you may wish to consider. This list includes telephone numbers where you may get additional materials, price quotations, and in some cases, sample materials. It is not intended to represent the "best" programs on the market. Only users can decide what is best for their situation. Also, this listing does not imply an endorsement of any product. (Keep in mind that some software companies are mobile, so you may not locate all of those listed at the addresses given.)

The Apple Grader.   This program presents a computerized grade book that will record grades either as letter marks or as numbers. It provides some statistics including averages and graphing for grade distributions based on single tests or on accumulations of scores over several tests. It claims to hold up to 70,000 grades on a single disk. The program is designed to be used with Apple-type computers. This program is quite affordable. Contact Adrian Vance, AV Systems, Inc., P.O. Box 60533, Santa Barbara, CA 93160. The telephone number for information from AV Systems is (805) 569-1618.

LXR-Test.   This program is a test-builder aid as well as a test-score manager. It provides for item banking, including classification of items on a number of characteristics. It will assist in creating tests by calling up items from the bank by objective and item type, maintaining item statistics and tracking them with each use of the item. It will scramble items to facilitate the creation of alternate forms with one item set. It can also be used with electronic scoring devices for immediate input of student data. Many additional features are available.

The manual is very helpful. Instructions are well done with illustrations of screens that appear with Windows commands. LXR-TEST is a bit more expensive than some programs, but provides many extra services some programs do not. When all this is considered the price is not high. The program is written for the IBM PC, but has some features that accommodate the Mackintosh computer group as well. Write to Logic eXtension Resources at 7168 Archibald Avenue, Suite 240, Rancho Cucamonga, CA, 91701–5061, or telephone (909) 980-8706.

The Microcat Testing System.   This is another fairly comprehensive system that includes an item banking module, the computer testing module, and an item and test analysis module. Each of these modules performs an expansive array of services for the test-user. Users can do item analyses, store items, create paper and pencil tests; the program also provides for computer assisted testing. The complete program is relatively expensive, but is a full-service test operation. The modules can also be bought separately. This system works on IBM equipment on DOS 3.3 or Windows 3.1 or higher, and on Macintosh equipment with a DOS emulation program or hardware and Super-Drive (high density) diskette drive. To get more information on this system, write Assessment Systems Corporation, 2233 University Ave., Suite 200, St. Paul, MN 55114, or telephone (612) 647-9220.

Micrograde.   Two different programs are available from this vendor, one for the elementary school level, and one for middle school up into the college level. It will handle over 400 students per class and 126 assignments per class. It will accommodate different grading systems, curve the class, drop a grade for a student, and add extra credit assignments. It is sold by Chariot Software, 123 Camino de la Reina, San Diego, CA, 92108, or telephone (619) 298-0202.

Electronic Gradebook.   Reports for this program can be identified by ID numbers or by student names, it can handle letter or number grades, it handles up to 39 students per class, and 100 grade entries per student. The system will also transfer records between classes. It is among the least expensive and provides all services most people want in an electronic grade book. For detailed information write Queue, Inc., 338 Commerce Drive, Fairfield, CT, 06430, or telephone (203) 333-7268.

The programs above are a small sample of those available, and their listing is not intended as an endorsement of any of these over others on the market. All programs require some input time on the part of the teacher, but so does writing tests and other assessment procedures. The advantage is that once the data (scores, observation summaries, test items) are in the computer memory, the computer will store these items as long as you find them useful, will manipulate them in helpful ways, and allow you to get into the files and reuse some material that has served you well in the past.

SUMMARY

1. Computers have made the teacher's work easier in documenting the table of specifications, writing tests, utilizing test item banks, scoring, recording observational data, and keeping student records.
2. Common terms applied to aspects of computer operations are: input, output, hardware, CPU, peripherals, software, memory, bit byte, K, Meg, RAM, ROM, CD ROM.
3. Two types of computerized testing are: standard (in which a typical test is administered by the computer, scored and recorded), and a Computer Adaptive Testing (CAT).
4. Computer adaptive testing (CAT) requires a large item bank for each class unit that is tested. The first item given a student is randomly selected from the pool; the next item selected is based on whether this student got the last item right, or missed it—if right, the next item selected will be harder. Final scores are based on level of difficulty at which the students can perform.
5. An advantage of CAT is that no two students will take identical tests, and it allows a student to retake the examination since the second test is likely to contain new items. However, this requires a large bank of items with difficulties for each item pretested.
6. Computers help students by allowing them to write and revise papers, reports, and similar projects with much more ease than with other writing devices.
7. Teachers can utilize the computer to keep grading records, and to do statistics on these records, such as class averages, and assigning grades according to a preset distribution of marks.
8. There are a number of programs on the market that are designed to assist teachers with classroom management of assessment. Some of these are relatively economical and will provide a variety of services. Examples are Apple Grader, LXR-Test, the Microcat Testing System, Micrograde, and the Electronic Grade Book
9. Before buying software be sure to note whether it runs on your type of computer.

PROBLEMS

1. A teacher comes to you and says "This program will require 1,000 K of memory. What does that mean?" How would you describe 1,000 K?
2. The PTA has allotted funds for a computer to be assigned to the teacher who can come up with the best plan for using it in assessment. Describe the uses you

would put into a response to this offer. You should know at least five or six different uses.

3. The principal has just sent a memo around to the teachers saying that modest funds were available for "software" that will run on 4 megs of RAM, and asked for suggestions. The teacher in the next room to yours has cited this memo, and asked, "What on earth is software and what is 4 megs of RAM?" Give an answer that would help your neighbor.

4. Why is it difficult for many classroom teachers to implement computer adaptive testing in their teaching? What are the advantages of doing computer adaptive testing?

5. I've read in a magazine about a test administration program, but it said it was based on the Apple Macintosh operating systems. I have an IBM machine. How useful will this program be for me?

KEY TERMS

computer adaptive testing	K
bit	meg
byte	memory
CD ROM	output
CPU	peripherals
hard drive	RAM
hardware	ROM
input	software

Additional Reading

Baker, F. A. Computer technology in test construction and processing. In R. L. Linn (Ed.), *Educational Measurement,* 3d ed., New York: Macmillan, 1989, Chapter 10.

Kingsbury, G. G. and Houser, R. L. (1993). Assessing the utility of item response models: Computerized adaptive testing. *Educational Measurement: Issues and Practices,* 12 (1), 21–27.

Picciano, A. G. *Computers in the Schools: A Guide to Planning and Administration.* New York: Merrill, an imprint of Macmillan Publishing Company, 1993. A useful survey of computer applications in the schools.

Roid, G. H. Computer technology in testing. In B.S. Plake and J.C. Witt (Eds.), *The Future of Testing,* Hillsdale: Lawrence Erlbaum Associates, 1986.

Wetzel, K. and Best, A. (Eds.), *Computers and the Writing Process. Teacher's Guide to Organizing and Evaluating Student Writing.* Eugene, OR: International Society for Technology in Education, 1992, Chapter 3.

SECTION III

UNDERSTANDING AND INTERPRETING PUBLISHED TESTS

STATISTICAL PROCESSES APPLIED TO TEST SCORES
STANDARDIZED TESTS
ACHIEVEMENT TESTS: SURVEYS OF ACADEMIC SKILLS
ASSESSING GENERAL ACADEMIC AND SPECIAL APTITUDES
LEGAL AND ETHICAL CONSIDERATIONS IN TESTING

A very large industry has arisen out of the school demands for published tests. These are the achievement tests virtually every public school child has taken, usually in the spring, and the aptitude tests that many schools use to estimate the ability level of the children. Published achievement and aptitude tests provide some unique information that teachers do not get from their locally constructed assessments.

This section emphasizes what these tests can tell educators and the meaning of various scores that come from them. To help you work with scores a little statistical information is discussed at the outset. For the most part this is at the conceptual level, and computation is at a minimum. Its purpose is to help you interpret the scores that come from achievement and aptitude tests and to deal more effectively with scores from your teacher-made tests.

With this information well in hand we move into a discussion of the tests themselves. First, I discuss what it means for a test to be standardized and what the significance of this is. Then you and I look at achievement tests—those tests that assess the skills of children in the "three Rs" and other curriculum areas.

This is followed by a chapter on academic aptitude, the tests that purport to assess the propensity children have for achieving in school-type work.

The discussion of tests is followed by a chapter on legal ramifications and subsequent guidelines for testing. Here I cite several court opinions that have put structure into the use of tests of all kinds. These opinions have had an impact not only on how tests are constructed, but also on how tests are applied. Although this has complicated the activities of some publishers as well as test-users, the end result has been an attempt to protect children.

Overall, the tests in this section have important uses in most schools. However, they must be used wisely and interpreted appropriately. The topics in this section are intended to help you do just that.

CHAPTER 14

STATISTICAL PROCESSES APPLIED TO TEST SCORES

When educators give a test or use some types of performance assessment one of the outcomes is a score. Although some types of assessment are not reported in numbers, many are. What should be done with the numbers to get the most meaning out of them?

LaShonna has 28 correct on her test of 40 one-digit multiplication combinations. She stopped at Mr. Wall's desk as recess began. "I don't think I know what 28 right means," she said. "Is it good?"

"Well, let's see what you did here," Mr. Walls replied quietly as he scanned her paper. "Looks like you had trouble with zeros; 0×7 doesn't equal 7, it equals 0. If you have no sevens, you have 0. And here is 0×5 also missed."

"I see that," LaShonna said a bit impatiently, "but is the score of 28 good or just fair, or not good at all?"

"Why don't you run on out to recess, and we'll work out a time to talk about this," replied Mr. Wall.

What would you tell LaShonna? Right now it is hard to say if 28 is a good score, but what if I told you the criterion of success was 90 percent? Now is her score good? What if I told you 70 percent of the class did worse than she did? Now does 28 look good? How can we bring meaning into these numbers we get from tests? You have already dealt with one of the more complex data analysis procedures; in Chapter 3 and again in Chapter 4 you looked at the interpretation of correlation coefficients. Now a little more arithmetic will help in the interpretation of scores.

Although the figures you will calculate in this chapter are very important to managing assessment results, the calculations are not complex. In some procedures a description alone will allow us to apply the idea. There are several concepts in data analysis that will give teachers a better understanding of the numbers produced from tests. Few educators will actually calculate some of these statistics, but they must regularly interpret most of them. The interpretation is the focus of this chapter, but some simple calculations will be a fundamental adjunct to this.

What This Chapter Will Include.   Scores that teachers get from student tests and other assessments are not very meaningful by themselves. Some calculations are necessary to help users interpret them. This chapter is about a few of the simple procedures statisticians use to make sense out of collections of numbers. Many of these will be most useful if we can actually apply them to our own test data. In this chapter you will learn about:

1. Putting scores in order
2. Finding the "typical" score for a group
3. Understanding indicators of the spread of scores
4. The normal (bell) curve
5. Percentile ranks—an indicator of position in a group
6. Standard scores—z, T, stanines, and normal curve equivalents

Putting Scores in Order

When you score a set of tests you end up with a variety of numbers written on the answer sheets. Educators want to know some things about the scoring outcomes right away. What is the highest score that any student got; what is the lowest score? What is the most common score, the typical score? Are the scores really spread out from fairly low to fairly high, or are they compressed near some central score? What percent of the students scored below a score of 15? Above 36? The answers to these are found by putting the scores in order. To do this the common starting point is to rank the scores in order from low to high. The result of this procedure is called a **frequency distribution.**

Begin by making a list of the scores beginning with the lowest and going up to the highest. Then go to the answer sheets. For the first student's score record a tally mark (/) on the list of scores you just made. Make this mark immediately beside the listed score that equals the student's score. For example, LaRoye got 19 correct on her vocabulary test. On the listing go up the scale and find 19. Beside it record a tally mark. When you have tabulated all student scores count up the number of students at each score level and write that number to the right of the tally marks. Table 14.1 shows the result of the entire class on the vocabulary test.

In Table 14.1, I find the answers to the above questions. I can see that the lowest score was 13, the highest was 25. The greatest accumulation of scores was between 17 and 18, with 33 percent of the students obtaining those scores. I also note that there are four students who scored somewhat higher than anyone else. These students scored 23 (one person), 24 (two people) and 25 (one person).

A quick overview of the frequency distribution gives educators a picture of the performance of the class on the vocabulary test. Frequency distributions are a first step in describing class performance before planning the next move for instruction. They are also useful in determining a grading scheme (to be discussed in Chapter 19). For example, suppose I am using a criterion referenced approach with the vocabulary list. The criterion is 92 percent accuracy on the 30–word list. The criterion will be 28 items cor-

TABLE 14.1   A Frequency Distribution Based on 24 Students Who Took a 30-item Vocabulary Test

Score	Tally	Number of pupils
25	/	1
24	//	2
23	/	1
22		0
21		0
20	//	2
19	//	2
18	////	4
17	////	4
16	///	3
15	//	2
14	//	2
13	/	1
		24 pupils

rect on the test. The frequency distribution shows me immediately that most of the class still has a way to go to reach the criterion. I can plan my instruction accordingly.

Typical Scores: The Mean, Median, and the Mode

When I look at a set of scores, I often wonder what is typical performance for the group. This is usually defined by locating a central point in the frequency distribution, a point around which scores tend to pile up. "Typical" is often defined as meaning most common. In Table 14.1, a third of the pupils' scores fell between 17 and 18. Somewhere in this range is the point I would call typical performance. The most common indicators of typical performance are the **mean** and the **median**. The other indicator, the **mode**, is not as widely used.

Indicators of Typical Performance

1. Mean—the arithmetic average.
2. Median—the middle score that separates the lowest scoring half from the highest scoring half.
3. Mode—the most frequently appearing score.

The Mean

The **mean,** designated by the symbol $\overline{X}$, is the arithmetic average for a set of scores. To find the average of a set of scores, add them up and divide by the number of scores you have. If you want the average amount of money three girls have—Milly has $2, Ilona has $3, and Maria has $4—you would add up their separate amounts (2 + 3 + 4 = 9) and divide by the number of persons who showed their money, that is, three girls. Then $9 ÷ 3 = $3. Here $3 is the average. It is also the mean amount of money for these girls.

In the distribution in Table 14.1, when I add, 25, 24, 24, 23, 20, 20, and the rest of the scores, I get 433, the sum of the scores made by the 24 pupils in that distribution. To get the mean (average) I calculate 433 ÷ 24 = 18.04, which I can round to 18. The mean for this set of scores is 18 test items correct. Typical performance as shown by the mean is a score of 18.

The Median

A second indicator of the typical performance is the median. The **median** is that middle score that separates the lowest scoring half of the students from the highest scoring half of the students.

Although there are precise ways of calculating the median, for most school work it is quite suitable to divide the number of students in half (N ÷ 2) and then count up to find the score that equals that number. In Table 14.1, half of the students (24 ÷ 2) is 12. I begin at the bottom and count up until I find 12 students. From Table 14.1, I need all the students up to, and including, the score of 17 to find the twelfth student. The median is roughly a score of 17. (Actually it is 17 and a bit more, but it rounds down to 17, and that is accurate enough to serve my purposes.)

The median and the mean may be different values, but are usually very similar. Look at the cluster of scores in the middle of the distribution in Table 14.1. You can see that scores stretch out more on the upper end than on the lower end of the distribution. This lack of symmetry in the distribution is called skewness. If distributions are really very skewed, the mean and median will be quite different. But most distributions are not badly skewed, so the mean and median, although not the same, do not differ much.

The Mode

The mode is the one score that more students achieved than any other. In a frequency distribution it is quick to spot because it has more tally marks than any other score. Sometimes two scores will have the same number of tallies, such as seen for scores 17 and 18 in Table 14.1. In this case, the midpoint between the two scores may be taken as the mode. If there are two scores, each with the largest number of tallies, and they are clearly separated from each other, the distribution is **bimodal.** The main advantage of the mode is that it is quick to identify in frequency distributions. It is a rough estimate of typical behavior but is not widely seen in the literature on testing.

Which Indicator of Typical Performance Shall I Use?

Both the mean and the median are indicators of typical performance on a test or other set of scores, but they will often be a little different in value. In that case which shall I use?

The answer to this depends on several factors. First, the mean is often favored by statisticians because across samples of children of a given age it tends to be most stable, that is, the mean on one sample is likely to be much like the means of the other samples.

But some distributions, like that in Figure 14.1, have a few scores that "tail out" to one end. These distributions are skewed because the data on one side of the central pile up of scores string out somewhat farther than they do on the other side of the it.

What does skewness have to do with selecting the mean or the median? Well, those widely deviating scores in that tail that string out pull the mean in their direction. In fact if the scores spread far enough in one direction, the mean is pulled away from the bulk of the scores and may not represent that central accumulation of data anymore. If this is true, the mean may not be a good choice for an indicator of typical performance.

The median, however, is not influenced by widely deviating scores. It only looks for the point that divides the group into two equal segments, one 50 percent segment in the upper half, one in the lower half. The median is unaffected by skewness in the distribution. For this reason, if the distribution of scores is markedly skewed I may wish to use the median as my indicator of typical performance.

Here is an example of selecting the mean or the median in a set of data. Look again at the left-hand distribution of scores in Figure 14.1. The data depicted are scores on a reading comprehension test given to three combined classes of fourth-grade students in St. Carmine's Elementary School. The data are skewed to the right, toward the higher scores. The mean of the set is reported to be about 25, while the median is about 23. The mean is pulled in the direction of the skewed scores to the extent that it is not representative of the large cluster of scores between 21 and 24. The median, however, is right in the midst of that cluster. Here I may wish to use the median as most representative of the children in the fourth-grade.

The saying goes that "Figures don't lie, but liars can figure." Here is one of those opportunities for figuring by selecting the mean or median, whichever best fits your objective. The principal at St. Carmine's School found in the test manual that the "national average" for fourth-grade reading was 23. She announced to the local news-

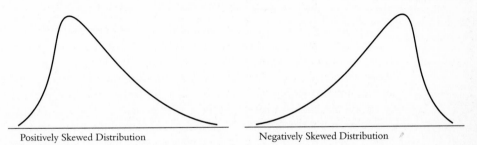

Positively Skewed Distribution   Negatively Skewed Distribution

FIGURE 14.1   Skewed Distributions

paper that St. Carmine's fourth-graders had averaged 25 (the mean) and consequently were above the national average. At the next school-board meeting a group of concerned parents of children in St. Carmine's claimed that the typical score was only 23 (the median) and appealed to the board to correct the error in the news paper.

The board took a short recess, gathered in a corner heads together, talking in low voices and scanning the test results. The board members begin nodding affirmatively to each other. The meeting was called to order and the chairperson announced that the parents had identified the wrong figure (the median). The meeting was then quickly adjourned.

Statisticians will look for the figure that best represents the data. Politicians may wish to look for data that best fit their interests. In the situation above the parent group probably chose the score that represented the bulk of the students, while the board chose the one that made their administration of the school look best. In your professional career be on the lookout for situations like this.

✎ Problems

1. Martin Luther King, Jr. Elementary School has just given the Ready Reading Skills test to first-graders at the end of the year. In all classes there were 36 children. Here are their scores. (Each number represents the score for a different child.)

   17, 9, 13, 10, 13, 11, 15, 10, 16, 11, 14, 11, 10, 11, 10, 12, 16, 14

   a. Put the data into a frequency distribution.
   b. Calculate the mean (round to one decimal place), and find the median. Are the mean and the median the same? Explain.
   c. Which indicator of central tendency (mean or median) do you think best represents the "typical" child in the class? Why?
   d. If you were arguing (based on the data above) that achievement was low in the class, would you use the mean or the median to support your argument? Explain.

Illustrating the Spread of Scores

Describing the performance of a group of students requires more than just a typical performance. It is also important to know the spread of ability shown by the scores. Is the class fairly homogeneous, or is it very heterogeneous? The spread of scores will answer this question. If the lowest score is, say, 5 points from the highest score, the class is showing very homogeneous skill. Or, the test may not be discriminating between the students who know the subject matter and those who do not. If the test does not spread out the scores a bit, it is difficult to see who has a good grasp of the topic and who does not. But if the test spreads out the scores over a wide range, it may be very discriminating. Therefore, teachers need an indicator of spread of scores to see how the test performed.

There are several indicators of spread of scores: the range, the semi-interquartile range (SIR), and the standard deviation, abbreviated by the Greek sigma (σ). The most important of these is the standard deviation.

▼

Indicators of Spread of Scores

1. Range—highest score minus lowest, plus 1
2. Semi-interquartile range—Quartile 3 minus Quartile 1, divided by 2
3. Standard deviation—an indicator of spread of scores that in the bell curve cuts off 34% of scores above the mean and 34% below it

▲

The Range

The **range** is simply the difference between the highest score and the lowest score, plus 1. That extra point is added to make the range inclusive, that is, so that it includes all the scores. The range is easy to calculate, and indicates how broad the distribution stretches out, but it depends on only two scores—the lowest and the highest. This makes it a bit unreliable as an indicator of spread. For example, a single child's score at the high end of a distribution can be 1 point, 2 points, or 10 points larger than the next score below it. This can make a big difference in the size of the range.

The Semi-Interquartile Range (SIR)

The second indicator of spread of scores is the **semi-interquartile range** (sometimes called a quartile deviation). A quartile is a point that cuts off a group of 25 percent of the students in a distribution. The semi-interquartile range is found by first locating the score that cuts off the lowest scoring quarter of the group of students. This is called the first quartile (Q_1). Next find the score that cuts off the highest quarter (Q_3). The semi-interquartile range is the average distance from the median to the two quartile points. This means you subtract (median $- Q_1$), and ($Q_3 -$ median), then add these two values and divide the sum by 2. This formula is presented as a summary of the procedure, not as a guide to calculation. You probably will not wish to calculate a semi-interquartile range (although its title sounds impressive in conversation). However, you will see it cited in test manuals and in the periodical literature. For that reason it is presented here to help you be a better reader of these materials.

If in a symmetrical distribution (in which one-half of the distribution is a mirror image of the other half) the semi-interquartile range is added to the median, you will have found the score that cuts off the 25 percent of the students just above the median. Now if one semi-interquartile range is subtracted from the median you will have found the score that cuts off the 25 percent just below the median. The median plus and minus one semi-interquartile range has identified the middle 50 percent of the students in the group. The wider the spread of scores, the farther apart the scores that identify the lower and upper limits of the middle 50 percent will be. To this end the semi-interquartile range is an indicator of spread of scores.

The Standard Deviation

The most widely used indicator of spread of scores is the **standard deviation** (σ). It is the only one of the three cited here that utilizes all of the scores in its calculation.

When looking for an indicator of spread of scores it would be nice if we could determine, on the average, how far scores deviate from the mean. [Here deviations are the score (X) minus the mean $(\overline{X})$, i.e., $(X - \overline{X})$]. In a distribution in which scores cluster near the mean, the average deviation of scores above and below the mean would be relatively small. But in distributions in which scores deviated quite far from the mean, the average deviation would be relatively large.

This line of reasoning appears valid, but it is not. Because half of the deviations will be above the mean (positive) and half will be below the mean (negative), the average deviation will always be zero. This is not a useful indicator of spread of scores. The standard deviation avoids this by squaring the deviations so that they are all positive values, that is, $(X - \overline{X})^2$ will always be positive. Now find the average of these squared deviations and then "unsquare" them. This will give you an indicator of spread of scores, called the standard deviation (σ).

Here is a simple example. The X is any student score, the $\overline{X}$ is the mean for the group.

Student score	$(X - \overline{X})$		$(X - \overline{X})^2$	
18	$18 - 15 =$	3	9	$\overline{X} = 75/5 = 15.0$
16	$16 - 15 =$	1	1	$\sigma = $ Sq. root of 20/5
15	$15 - 15 =$	0	0	$= 2.0$ score pts.
14	$14 - 15 = -1$		1	
12	$12 - 15 = -3$		9	
Sums 75		0	20	

In this example the distribution is thought of as centered at the mean with the indicator of spread, the σ, marking off blocks of scores above and below the mean. Here one standard deviation above the mean would be 15 (the mean) plus 2.0 i.e., (1 standard deviation), or 15 + 2.0, or a score point of 17.0. One standard deviation below the mean would be 15 - 2.0, or a score point of 13.0. That large cluster of scores that most distributions have in the middle usually would be between one standard deviation above the mean and one standard deviation below the mean. In the above data that range is from 13.0 to 17.0, a distance of 4.0 score points. (Of course, with only 5 cases the scores do not really cluster.)

For a moment let's go back to the range to make a conclusion about the standard deviation. In the above example the range of scores was (18 − 12) + 1, or 7 score-points. Here is a second example with the same mean but a wider range of scores: $(21 - 9) + 1$, or 13 score points.

Student scores	$(X - \overline{X})$	$(X - \overline{X})^2$	
21	$21 - 15 = \quad 6$	36	$\overline{X} = 75/5 = 15$
18	$18 - 15 = \quad 3$	9	$\sigma =$ Sq. root of $90/5 = 4.2$
15	$15 - 15 = \quad 0$	0	
12	$12 - 15 = -3$	9	
9	$9 - 15 = -6$	36	
75		0 \qquad 90	

Both distributions have a mean of 15. However, in the second case the spread of scores is much greater. In the previous example, the range is $(18 - 12) + 1 = 7$ score points; in the second case the range is $(21 - 9) + 1 = 13$ score points. The second distribution has the larger range of scores. The standard deviation in the first group is 2.0 score points, whereas in this second distribution the standard deviation is 4.2. You can see the spread of scores in the first distribution is smaller than in the second, and the standard deviations verify this observation. The conclusion is that the standard deviation gets larger when the spread of scores is broad, but is smaller when the spread of scores is narrower.

Is all this calculation for the standard deviation necessary? Why not just look at the score range? There are three good reasons. It is often awkward and time consuming to lay out a distribution if the number of scores is large. Second, only two persons (the ones at the high and low ends of the score range) determine the range of scores, putting too much weight on a single score in a group. Third, you shall soon see that the standard deviation is required to interpret certain kinds of scores. The range alone will not work there; you must use the standard deviation.

Shortcut Standard Deviation.   If you are in a hurry and a pretty good estimate of the standard deviation is adequate, you may wish to use a shortcut procedure for the calculation. It works well with 30 or so scores (the size of typical classrooms), but not so well for smaller groups of 20 to 25. The larger the group (up to about 40) the more accurate the shortcut method is. The procedure goes like this.

1. Find the range of the scores in the distribution by subtracting the lowest score from the highest, then add 1.
2. Divide this range by 4. This is the estimated standard deviation for the distribution (Hills, 1976).

Now that's easy, isn't it? Here is an example. Mr. Basch, a middle school mathematics teacher, has just given a test in dividing complex fractions. There were 38 items in the test. His class has 32 students in it. To find the standard deviation, he first finds the lowest score, which was 17. Then he locates the highest score, which was 37. He subtracts the 17 from 37, and finds it to be 20 score points, and then adds 1 (the procedure for finding the range). Next he divides the range (20 plus $1 = 21$ score points) by 4. The answer is 5.25 score points. This is the estimated standard deviation for Mr. Basch's set of data.

Do you find this procedure fairly easy? It is an estimate of the standard deviation, but accurate enough for most school situations. (If high stakes decisions are tied to score analyses the calculated, not the estimated, standard deviation should be used.)

The rationale behind the estimated standard deviation is that you usually find that with a typical group of 26 to 40 people or so, the lowest score will be about 2 actual standard deviations below the mean, and the highest one about two standard deviations above the mean, a total of four standard deviations. If you divide the total range of scores by 4, you will have a good estimate of the standard deviation. As the group size gets larger than about 40, the procedure loses accuracy.

Here is another example of the shortcut method in action. The scores are from 28 students who took a spelling test.

Student score	Number of persons	
20	1	Range of scores = $(20 - 12) + 1 = 9$
19	2	Estimated standard deviation = $9/4 = 2.25^*$ score points
18	1	
17	2	
16	4	
15	7	
14	5	
13	4	
12	2	
	28	

*If calculated using the deviation method described above the standard deviation for this group of scores would equal 2.0, very close to the estimated value.

✎ Problems

1. Here is a set of scores. Using the deviation method, find the standard deviation.

   10, 5, 7, 9, 8

2. With the following distribution estimate the standard deviation with the short-cut method.

   23, 34, 12, 14, 17, 10, 35, 25, 27, 23, 26, 25, 19, 27, 21, 14, 28, 13, 32, 38, 35, 23, 26, 14, 29, 25, 26, 26

The Bell Curve and Its Functions

Almost everyone has heard the term, the **bell curve.** Some teachers grade "on the curve." This is a reference to a system for distributing grades that is based on a frequency distribution that awards many average grades and fewer high and low grades;

the result looks somewhat like the familiar bell-shaped curve. But the bell-shaped curve is more useful to teachers in other areas than it is as a guide for grade distribution. It helps teachers make sense out of test scores, especially large bodies of test data—such as the once-a-year achievement tests.

When you and I make a frequency distribution we see that scores often cluster in the central area of the score range. If we graph that frequency distribution it would look like a vertical cross section of a bell. However, here we are going to explore a specific bell-shaped curve called the **normal curve.**

Not all bell curves are "normal." The normal curve is a bell-shaped curve derived by a specific algebraic formula. The normal curve has proven useful as a model for the distribution of many psychological traits. For example, suppose you had IQs on 1,000 eight-year-old children. You made a frequency distribution, and graphed this distribution. I expect that a plot of the scores in the distribution would follow the normal curve like the one in Figure 14.2. The importance of this fact comes in applying what is known about this curve, and that can be easily used, in interpreting scores such as IQ. This normal curve is called a mathematical model of children's traits because it can be generated by a mathematical formula, and it fits what sociometrists believe the distribution of many human traits look like.

One use of the normal curve is to help get a sense of how high, or low, a given score is in a distribution. Imagine that I lined the members of a football team along the sideline of the field. I bunched them up near the 50-yard-line, but put fewer and fewer along the sideline as I got farther away from the 50-yard-line. They would look like Figure 14.3.

Now you ask me, "What percent of the team was standing between Goal 1 and the first 40-yard-line?" I count up to see how many players were between Goal 1 and the 10-yard-line, how many between the 10- and 20-yard-line, between the 20 and 30, and the 30 and 40. When I add them up it equals 10 players. There are 30 players altogether, so 10 ÷ 30 = 33 percent that are between Goal 1 and the 40-yard-line. Using Figure 14.3 you can find how many were standing from Goal 1 to the 50-yard-line, to the second 30-yard-line, and so on.

Let's go back to the normal curve. When you make a frequency distribution of IQ scores, for example, you line your scores up along the baseline of a distribution (like the sideline on the football field). Along this line is a list, in order, of all the IQs (like yard-marks on the sideline). Now suppose you want to know how many children rank below a given IQ. With what we know about the normal curve, statisticians can quickly find out what percent of the people fall below that IQ point. That is very useful information when you are trying to make sense out of IQs or any other type of test data.

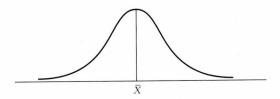

FIGURE 14.2   A Bell-Shaped Curve, $\overline{X}$ is the Mean

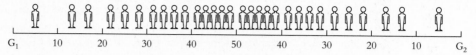

| G_1 | 10 | 20 | 30 | 40 | 50 | 40 | 30 | 20 | 10 | G_2 |

FIGURE 14.3   Distribution of Players on a Football Field

Although statisticians can divide up the normal curve in great detail, the divisions of the curve given in Figure 14.4 are often adequate to give teachers some idea of how many people fall below a given point on a scale. In this figure I have divided the baseline of the curve into standard deviation units. They are analogous to the 10-yard markers on the football field. First I need to know the mean and the standard deviation. Then I can get an estimate of how "low" (beginning at the mean, how far down the score scale) a given score is. This estimate is not precise but it will give you and me a good sense of how a score ranks among others in the distribution.

Here is an example of how this works. First I assume that my data when graphed look much like the normal curve. Now suppose I have IQ data on children's record cards. Korry has an IQ of 85. From the intelligence test manual I find the mean for the test is 100, and the standard deviation is 15. How "high" is Korry's score among his age mates? Korry's score is 15 score points below the mean. Korry's score is the mean minus one standard deviation, or $100 - 15 = 85$. I now go to Figure 14.4 and see where 1 standard deviation below the mean (-1) is on the baseline. I then add all the segments from the lowest end of the curve (-3) up to one standard deviation below the mean (the point where I found 85 to be.) This is

$$2\% + 14\% = 16\%$$

Korry's score is above 16 percent of his agemates. Just looking at a score of 85 does not give us this enlightening information.

But what do I do if a score is not so near a standard deviation unit mark? Statisticians have a system for working this out, but I get a general sense of the status of a score, not a precise indicator of status, when I can again turn to Figure 14.4.

Here is another example of applying Figure 14.4 in estimating a child's status in the group. Cuonzo, a ten-year-old, has a score of 35 on the "Home and School Vocabulary

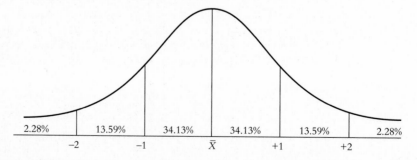

| 2.28% | 13.59% | 34.13% | 34.13% | 13.59% | 2.28% |
| | -2 | -1 | $\overline{X}$ | $+1$ | $+2$ |

FIGURE 14.4   A Normal Curve Divided into One Standard Deviation Units; $\overline{X}$ is the Mean

Test." The test's manual says that the mean of the test for ten-year-olds is 30, the standard deviation is 6 score points. This means Cuonzo's score of 35 is almost but not quite one standard deviation above the mean. His score is 5 points above the mean; the standard deviation is 6 score points.

The score of 35 is almost equal to the mean (30) plus one standard deviation (30 + 6 = 36) above the mean. Looking at Figure 14.4, I find that Cuonzo's score is above approximately 84 percent (2% + 14% + 34% + 34% = 84%); that is, there are 84 percent of the cases expected below a score of 36, and Cuonzo's score is near 36. His score of 35 is a bit less than above the 84 percent of the students who took the test. You and I have now estimated where Cuonzo ranks in the group. The information we get from the curve shows Cuonzo as clearly above average, and that is usually sufficient for what we want to know.

✎ Problems

1. I look in the test manual for the Standards for Achievement Test and find that for fifth-grade children the mean mathematics score is 25 correct. The standard deviation is 4 items correct. The distribution is believed to be bell-shaped, that is, normal. (Use Figure 14.4 with these problems.)
   a. Coral has a score of 30. About what percent of the fifth-graders who took this test does Coral rank above?
   b. Joel has a score of 20. About what percent of the group does Joel rank above?
2. What percent of the group is expected between Coral and Joel?
3. On the "Home and School Vocabulary Test" the manual says the distribution looks normal, the mean is 100, and the standard deviation is 15 score points.
   a. Aaron has a score of 116. About what percent of the group who took this test is expected to score below Aaron?
   b. What percent is expected to be above Aaron?

Standard Scores: What Are They; What Do I Do With Them?

Besides making it possible for educators to estimate where a given score is in a distribution, the standard deviation (σ) allows us to calculate standard scores. With **standard scores** users of test data convert scores to standard deviation units so that scores from two different measures (such as a spelling test and a reading comprehension test) can be compared. For example, suppose you want to compare your score on reading comprehension with your score on mathematics problem solving. But the reading test has 40 items on it. The mean is 26 items correct, and the standard deviation is 6 score points. The mathematics test has only 35 items on it. The mean is 21 correct, and the standard deviation is 4 points.

As you look at these data you see that a score at the mean of the reading test (26) is numerically unequal to the mean of the arithmetic test (21). It is more than one standard deviation (4 points) less than the arithmetic mean. You wonder how we can compare scores across the two scales. The problem is that the results of the two tests do not have the same range of scores. The mean of the reading test is five points higher than the mathematics test (26 − 21). The reading test also has more spread across its scores (6 point standard deviation compared to 4 points). Now let's put these two sets of data onto the baseline of the normal curve, both means at the mid-point of the curve, standard deviations at their points below and above the mean. Now in terms of standard deviation values we can compare from one test to the other.

This procedure provides us with a device for putting both tests on a common score scale. Then we could compare rank on one test with rank on the other. There are several types of standard scores, any one of which will do that for us.

Is there a call for this kind of thing in testing? Yes, there is! When you explore achievement testing (see Chapter 15) you will see that these tests have several subtests—one in reading comprehension, one in reading speed, another in mathematics computation, problem solving, science and social studies, and possibly more. All of these subtests have a different number of items from the other tests. Each has a mean that is different from the other tests, and a different standard deviation. But when you get the score report the subtests are all on one score range, so that you can compare one skill with another. The test companies do this with standard scores.

What Is a Standard Score?

Suppose you begin walking at Center Street in your town. You walk due east for 547 steps. I say to you, "Yes, 547 steps, but how many blocks is that?" You wrinkle your brow and look back down the street towards Center. "It takes 210 steps for each block, so I have gone 2.6 blocks!"

With standard scores the method is similar. I begin at the mean of a distribution and move up (or down) the score range. But instead of score points (like the steps in the example above) I use the standard deviation as my unit of measure (like the blocks above). With standard scores I identify a score point in terms of how many standard deviations it is from the mean. This particular type of standard score is called a **z-score.** A z-score is a test score converted into how far above, or below, the mean that score is, as measured by standard deviation units. These z-scores are the base of all other types of standard scores.

In standard scores I begin at the mean of a set of data. Then I locate the score that I will convert to a standard score. Each score is identified in terms of how many standard deviations (or fraction of a standard deviation) this score is above, or below the mean. A score one standard deviation above the mean gets a standard score of +1; a score one standard deviation below the mean gets a standard score of −1; a score one-and-a-half standard deviations above the mean gets a standard score of +1.5, and so forth. To figure out how many standard deviations the target score is above or below the mean, I subtract the mean from it. That tells me how many score points the score is from the mean. I then divide this difference by the standard deviation to show how many standard deviations this score is from the mean. (This is like the walking situation above, converting your steps into blocks.) Again, test scores converted to standard deviation units such as those above are called z-scores.

The conversion of scores to the z-score type of standard scores has been written into a handy formula. It starts by finding how many score points the score is from the mean, then finds out how many standard deviations this is. The formula looks like this.

$$\text{z-score} = \frac{\text{test score} - \text{mean}}{\text{standard deviation}}$$

or

$$z = \frac{X - \overline{X}}{\sigma}$$

To find out how far a test score is above, or below the mean (in units of the standard deviation) just subtract the mean from a test score (watch the positive and negative signs), and then divide that difference by the standard deviation. The result tells us in standard deviation units how far a score is above or below the mean. If the z-score is positive the score is above the mean, if negative below the mean. Here is an example.

On a test of 38 vocabulary items, the mean is 25, and the standard deviation is 5. Your score is 31 items correct. In the above formula you have

$$\text{z-score} = \frac{31 - 25}{5} = +1.2$$

The standard score is +1.2. The plus sign says the score is above the mean, and 1.2 says it is 1.2 standard deviations above the mean. (I could now take this to Figure 14.4 to see how this ranks among other scores, if I wish.)

Ansil's score on the same test was 20. When I put this into the above formula, I get −1.0. The minus says that the score is below the mean, and 1.0 says it is one standard deviation below.

Using Standard Scores to Compare Scores from Different Tests

It's May. You have just got back the results of the achievement tests your school recently administered to your children. You pull open the envelope and find a stack of 27 alphabetically arranged reports, one for each child in your class. Look at all those numbers!

On top of the stack is Atwood, Arnold B. "Let's see, now, yes, here is Arnold's reading test score. It's 54. And his mathematics score is 62."

You frown at these numbers for a moment, then turn to the cover sheet for the tests and read, ". . . all test scores are in standard score form. The test means are converted to 50 and the standard deviations of all tests are converted to 10 score points. Our intention in making these conversions is to allow you to compare a child's performance on one test with another."

"Oh! Now I get it! The average performance is 50 on all tests, and the middle 68 percent of students (-1σ up to $+1\sigma$) range from 40 to 60!" (That is one standard deviation below the mean, and one above, as shown in Figure 14.4.) "OK, now I can read these score reports."

Arnold's score of 54 in reading is a bit above average. His score of 62 in mathematics is just over one standard deviation above the mean. That means Arnold's mathematics score is above the scores of 84 percent of the kids in this grade level. (Again, this comes from Figure 14.4.) Arnold is doing a great deal better in mathematics (where he is over a standard deviation above the mean) than in reading (where he is just slightly above average).

The point here is that before I can compare scores across tests, I must put them onto a common score scale. In this case I have used a kind of standard score to do this. Without some type of standard scoring system, I could not compare performance across tests.

This generalization goes for tests across a semester. Miss Staphail, a tenth-grade French teacher, gives two vocabulary tests each term. At the end of the term she adds them up to arrive at the students' vocabulary performance for the grading period. This fall there were 36 items on the first test. On the second test there were 50 items. The data shown in the table below are the scores made by two of Ms. Staphail's students.

	Mean	S.D	Antoinette	Roger
Test 1.	25	4	29	25
Test 2.	32	8	32	40
Sum			61	65

Both of these students had one test on which they were just at the class mean, and one on which they were one standard deviation above the mean. Across the term, they appear to have performed about equally in terms of position in the group. But when you add up their scores Roger gets the advantage. Is this right? Maybe not. You are adding scores from two tests that have very different score ranges. Roger may have benefited by getting his high score on the test that has the broad score range, whereas Antoinette got her high score on the test with the shorter range. What we need here is a scale that would convert their test scores to the same score scale. Of course, standard scores would do just that.

If I had converted the above data into z-scores I would get, for Antoinette's first test:

$$z = \frac{29 - 25}{4} = 1.00$$

For her second score I would get a z-score of .00 (right at the mean).

Using this procedure for Roger I would get a z-score of .00 on the first test, and 1.00 on the second test. Their standard score data are in the next table.

	First test z-score	Second test z-score
Antoinette	1.00	.00
Roger	.00	1.00
Sum	1.00	1.00

The sum of the standard scores for Antoinette is 1.00, and for Roger it is also 1.00. When I put the test data onto a common scale—the standard score scale—I get the same total performance score for each of these two students for this term. That is what the sum of the z scores says. Putting the scores into standard scores simply puts the hurdles depicted by each test at the same height before I ask how high the students have jumped.

Since on the achievement test data teachers receive on their classes show all scores (reading comprehension, mathematics, and so on) on a common scale, how do you suppose the publishers get them that way? They use a kind of standard score. A knowledge of standard scores will help you make sense out of nationally published score reports. There are some classroom applications, also.

T-Scores: Another Standard Score

In the z-score system used above, the half of the distribution below the mean gets a negative z-score, while the z-scores above the mean will all be positive. Some people find it awkward to work with negative and positive scores together. For this reason a variation of the conversion used above has been created. This variation begins with the z-scores. The creators of the T-score system wanted the mean of the standard score scale to be 50, so they added 50 to the mean of the z-scores, that is, (50 + 0). Also they wanted the standard deviation of the T-score scale to be 10 points, so they multiplied 10 times the standard deviation of the z-score scale, or 10 × 1.0. The procedure looks like this.

$$T = 10z + 50$$

This may seem like a little mathematical magic, but it is completely legitimate. When students' scores are put into this formula, it converts all scores into a distribution with a mean of 50, and a standard deviation of 10. Scores in this distribution are called **T-scores.** They were used in the achievement test at the beginning of this section and are shown on line 4 of Figure 14.5.

Actually, once I know the mean and standard deviation of a set of scores (and the distribution is reasonably bell-shaped) I can convert any set of test scores into a distribution with any mean and standard deviation I wish to. For example, I could create a set of scores with a mean of 100 and a standard deviation of 15; or a mean of 500 and a standard deviation of 100 (somewhat like SAT scores). All these conversions are done in order to put scores of different tests on a common scale. Test publishers use these techniques all the time to put different subscales into a common score scale so educators

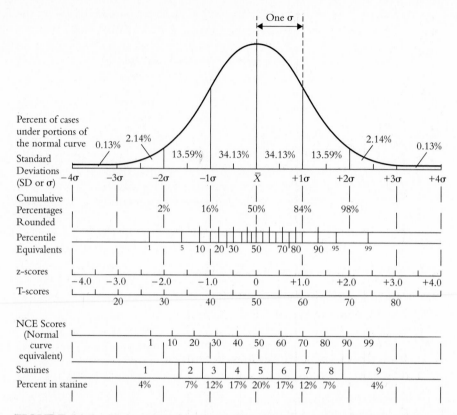

FIGURE 14.5   Various Standard Score Distributions Across the Normal Curve. This figure helps us decide what "low," "middle," and "high" may mean in reference to a given standard scoring method.

can compare a student's status on one subscale (such as total reading) with another (such as total mathematics), which we do indeed wish to do.

✎ Problems

1. On a 50-item final test in Spanish language, there were two parts. One part was on vocabulary, one on grammar. The mean in vocabulary was 34 items correct, and the standard deviation was 6 score points. The mean for grammar was 22 items correct and the standard deviation was 4 score points.
   a. Juwan had a score of 39 correct on the vocabulary test. What is his standard (z-) score? What does this score tell us?
   b. On a test in grammar Juwan had a score of 24 correct. Is he doing better in vocabulary or in grammar?
2. Jarred has taken the Allschool Algebra Test. His T-score was 45. Approximately how does Jarred rank among students who took this test? (Check Figure 14.5.)

3. On the Allschool Algebra Test Veronica had a T-score of 60. About what portion of the persons who took the test was she above?

4. Corine had a T-score of 40 on her Science Light Achievement Test. Above what percent of the national group on which the test was built does she rank? (Which Figure shows this?)

Some Indicators of Status

When I use norm referenced tests I rank students relative to other students in the class. To do this well I need an indicator of status in a group of students of similar age or grade level. The one most often used is the **percentile rank.**

Percentile Ranks

A percentile rank is a number that tells me what percent of the group fell below a given score. For example, the makers of Handy Achievement Tests may create score report tables for sixth-grade children who take the test in April. They will have a conversion table that shows percentile ranks for each score on the test. The conversion table for this test shows that on the spelling test a score of 36 converts to a percentile rank of 85, that is, there are 85 percent of the children below a score of 36 items correct.

Percentile ranks may range from 1 to 99. A percentile rank of 50 is at the median of the distribution. As I can see from the baseline of the curve in Figure 14.5, percentile ranks are not equal distances from each other at all points on the scale. They are much closer to each other near the middle of the distribution than at the ends. This is because it takes less distance on the baseline at the central part of the curve to add one percent of the people. This concept is illustrated in Figure 14.5. The numbers on the percentile-rank line tell teachers what percent of the group who took the test rank below any given score. Note how close the units of percentile ranks are in the center of the distribution compared to either the upper or lower end. To add two values at the center of the curve is putting together two very small units, whereas adding two values at the end of the curve is summing two very large units. When adding we assume that the units are all equal. The point here is that percentile ranks should not be used in arithmetical calculations such as averaging.

Stanine: A Band of Scores

An increasingly common type of standard score is known as the **stanine** (pronounced STAY-nine). This word comes from a contraction of two words—standard nine. The stanine system divides the distribution into nine segments one-half standard deviation in width. I begin at the mean and move .25 of a standard deviation above and below the mean. This creates the middle stanine, that is, stanine 5. From this central unit, three more units, each one-half standard deviation wide, are marked off along the upper end of the curve. These will be units 6, 7, and 8. Three units are also marked off along the lower end of the curve. These will be 4, 3, and 2. Stanines 1 and 9 are made up by the rest of the lower and upper tails of the curve, respectively. Students in stanine 1 are performing far below average, while those in 9 are performing well above average. Those in stanine 5 are about average in their performance. This arrangement is shown in Figure 14.5.

Now let's go back to percentile ranks to better understand stanines. Suppose that June has a percentile rank of 45 on a reading comprehension test and Jan has 48. You ask them to read a short story and then quiz them about the content. It is very unlikely that any one can see a difference in their reading comprehension. The score distinction (45 and 48 percentiles) is just too small for making decisions. However, stanines cluster a group of children under one score, all of whom are similar (but not identical) in talent. The difference between stanines 5 and 7 could be important. To many test users this 9-point stanine scale makes more sense in sorting children than a 100-point scale.

Normal Curve Equivalent (NCE) Scores

Some federally supported programs have required the use of **normal curve equivalent** scores, or NCEs, in their reports. To accommodate this requirement, some published achievement tests also report their scores in NCEs.

Like the T-scores discussed above, NCEs have a mean of 50. They have, however, a curious standard deviation: it is 21.06. This figure was chosen so that the range of NCEs is 1 to 99. Scores at the low end of the normal curve will begin with 1, and at the upper end they will terminate with 99. But do not make the mistake of assuming that because NCEs and percentile ranks, both running from 1 to 99, are equivalent. They are not. To illustrate this, here are some equivalent NCEs and percentile ranks.

As illustrated by the data below, NCEs are much more spread out at the extremes than are percentile ranks. They correspond with percentile ranks only at an NCE of 1, at 50, and at 99. At no other place on the scale are they equivalent.

Unlike percentile ranks, NCEs are in equal units along the base of the curve. (This is seen in Figure 14.5.) Unlike percentile ranks, all NCEs are based on standard deviation units. Therefore, you can compare NCEs across tests, such as reading and mathematics, and you can do arithmetic with them.

TABLE 14.2

	Equivalent Scores
NCE	**Percentile Rank**
99	99
90	97
75	88
50	50
25	12
10	3
1	1

✎ Problems

1. Mr. Hadley is looking over the statewide test results for his class and finds the scores are reported in percentile ranks and NCEs. He notes that the two scores do not match, so he goes to the principal to point out the differences. If you were the principal what how would you explain the differences?
2. Mr. Hadley next decided to get the average percentile rank for his class, so he added the percentile ranks across all children in the class, and divided this sum by the number of children in his class. What is your response to his procedure?
3. Mr. Hadley also decided to average the NCEs for his class. He added the NCEs across all the children, and divided this by the number of children in the class. Comment on this procedure.
4. In terms of position in the class, interpret the following children's percentile rank.
   a. Missy 47
   b. Atar 66
   c. Shunji 87
   d. Diego 32

A Real Case Narrative

If you wonder how these procedures relate to you, here is a conversation between two teachers about test scores. Comment on their preparation and point of view for dealing with test data.

Ms. Feurster, a third-grade teacher is at her desk at 4 P.M. when Ms. Eltentag stops in to visit. "You know what I hate about tests? asks Ms. Feurster. "It's numbers! You always get these numbers, and what do they mean?" she continues, wrinkling her forehead. She shuffles through *Midstates Achievement Tests* score reports. "Now here is Jeanie's test results—Reading 56, Mathematics 44, and on and on. What does all that mean, anyway?"

Ms. Eltentag looks sympathetic. "Making numbers meaningful for us is not an easy job. When a professor talked about numbers we figured it was something he liked to teach, but something we wouldn't need to know; now I wish I had listened more," said Ms. Eltentag wistfully.

"You've got that right," Ms. Feurster added.

"I've got an idea," said Ms. Eltentag. "I still have my textbook on assessment, why don't we do a little study session together and learn how to deal with these numbers. Each of us could take a section of the score report to dope out, then we could teach the other. I'd like to know what this all means not just for my students, but also I'd like to be able to explain some of this to parents at conference time."

"Sounds good, but what kind of time are we talking about here?" asked Ms. Feurster. " If we let this thing ride for a few weeks school will be out and I won't have to deal with the numbers again until next spring! I'm ready to give it up!"

"Well, I think I will at least get the manual and see if it has a quick review of how to interpret these scores." said Ms. Eltentag. "If so, I'll bet I dope out this report form myself."

SUMMARY

1. A test score has very little meaning by itself; it must be interpreted in terms of percent correct or the position of that score among others in the group of tests.
2. A first step in interpreting scores is to arrange the scores from low to high in a frequency distribution.
3. Indicators of typical performance include the mean (the arithmetic average), the median (the score that divides the students into half above that score and half below it), and the mode (the most frequently appearing score).
4. In choosing between the mean and the median it is important to consider the skewness of the distribution (the extent to which the distribution lacks symmetry) because in skewed distributions the mean is pulled away from the central cluster of scores.
5. Indicators of spread of scores include the range (highest score minus lowest score, plus 1), the semi-interquartile range (quartile 3 minus the median plus the median minus quartile 1, divided by 2), and the standard deviation (the square root of the average squared deviations of scores from the mean).
6. A quick estimate of the standard deviation is found by dividing the range by 4. This applies to classes of about 25 to 40 students.
7. The "normal "distribution provides a curve that is bell-shaped and can be used to determine a student's status in a group.
8. In a normally distributed group of scores one standard deviation unit from the mean cuts off 34 percent of the group, so a score one standard deviation below the mean and a score one standard deviation above the mean cut off the middle 68 percent of the group who took the test.
9. Standard scores, such as z-scores, put two sets of scores on a common scale so that we can make comparisons across tests that have different score ranges. Standard scores involve identifying a score in terms of how many standard deviations it is above, or below, the mean.
10. Because z-scores are negative if below the mean and positive if above the mean, it is sometimes awkward to use. The T-score scale is more convenient because it has a mean of 50 and a standard deviation of 10.
11. Score types that indicate status in the group include percentile ranks (which show what percent of the group fell below a given score), stanines (which divide a distribution into nine segments of one-half standard deviation in width), and normal curve equivalent scores—NCEs (which have a range of 100 equal-sized units with a mean of 50 and a standard deviation of 21.06).

KEY TERMS

frequency distribution	bell curve
mean	normal curve
median	standard scores
mode	z–score
bimodal distribution	T–score
range	stanines
semi–interquartile range	percentile rank
standard deviation	normal curve equivalent (NCE)

ADDITIONAL READING

Chase, C. I. *Elementary Statistics,* 3d ed., New York: McGraw-Hill Book Co., 1984. Chapters 2, 3, 4, 5, 6.

Diederich, P. *Short Cut Statistics for Teacher-Made Tests,* Princeton, NJ: Educational Testing Service, 1960.

Lyman, H. B. *Test Scores and What They Mean,* 5th ed., Englewood Cliffs, NJ: Prentice Hall, 1991.

Sprinthall, R. C. *Basic Statistical Analysis,* 4th ed., Boston: Allyn & Bacon, 1994. Chapters 2, 3, 4, 5.

CHAPTER 15

STANDARDIZED TESTS

It's the spring of the year. In North Dakota a sixth-grade teacher says, "Next week the *Iowa Tests of Basic Skills* begin. I've got a lot of work to do with my class, yet!" Mr. Adams, a fourth-grade teacher was heard to say to his class, "In two weeks we will have the *Metropolitan Achievement Tests,* so let's store our materials for the geology study of Monroe County, while we begin our review for the tests." Getting ready for achievement tests is a spring ritual in schools in virtually every state.

Standardized tests appeared in American schools in the 1920s, and have increased in use ever since. Today, millions of these tests are being administered across the nation. Just about anyone who has attended public schools has taken a standardized test. This chapter is about these tests—their construction, their uses, advantages and disadvantages.

What This Chapter Will Include. Standardized tests are so pervasive in school systems that every teacher is likely to be asked about their validity, scoring, and interpretation. Teachers are not alone in wanting to know more about these tests. Students and parents are interested too. To help you be better informed, in this chapter you will learn:

1. Why these tests are called "standardized"
2. What types of tests fit under the term "standardized"
3. The main uses of standardized tests
4. How standardized tests are constructed compared to the tests that teachers create
5. What educators should look for in choosing a standardized test
6. Whether performance assessment will obviate the need for standardized tests in schools
7. About state mandated tests
8. Where we can find information on standardized tests
9. If standardized tests can be interpreted as criterion referenced test

In this chapter, the focus will be on standardized achievement tests, because most people have had some exposure to them. However, the discussions apply to almost all commercially published tests. In Chapter 16 we will look at several achievement tests, but first we need to learn some fundamentals about standardization.

What Are Standardized Tests?

There are several meanings to the word "standard." In one sense it means the minimum acceptable performance, the criterion. In another it means regular, or following a common form or policy. It is the latter definition that we are concerned with here. Tests are **standardized** to the extent that their administration, content, scoring, and interpretation follow a common form in all situations where they are used.

When the *Iowa Tests of Basic Skills* is administered in Nevada, the same instructions are read to the children as are read in New Hampshire or Hawaii, Arizona or Alaska. The time limits for the tests are the same in all administrations. The test content is the same (or equivalent) at each school that uses the test. The scores mean the same thing in every school. It is these regularized, uniform features of test administration and interpretation that make a test standardized.

An example of the regularizing of instructions is shown in Figure 15.1. Here is a section of the instructions provided by the testmaker for a popular achievement test. I

SAMPLE 1: We will work the first two problems together. Look at row S1 at the top of the first column. David has two red and two blue marbles. How many red marbles and bluemarbles does he have? Again, David has two red and two blue marbles. How many red marbles and blue marbles does he have? Fill in the circle under your answer.

Pause while the students read the responses and fill in the circle.

SAY: You should have added two plus two, which equals four. You should have filled in the circle under the *four*.

Make sure all the students have filled in the correct circle. Then say:

SAMPLE 2: Now we will do the other sample problem. Look at row S2. Carol has three aunts and two uncles. How many more aunts does Carol have than uncles? Again, Carol has three aunts and two uncles. How many more aunts does Carol have than uncles? Fill in the circle under your answer.

Pause while the students read the responses and fill in the circle.

SAY: You should have subtracted. Three minus two is one. The correct answer is one, but *one* is not given as an answer choice. You should have filled in the circle under the *N*, which stands for *not given*.

Make sure all the students have filled in the correct circle.

FIGURE 15.1   An example of the directions provided by an achievement test, here level 8, Iowa Test of Basic Skills, Directions for administration Form K, Complete Battery, Page 25. *Reproduced by permission of Riverside Publishing, 425 Spring Lake Drive, Itasca, IL 60143-2079.*

quickly see that the instructions are specific and leave no latitude for "freelance" work by the administrator.

A great deal of effort goes into creating a test that has been standardized. As you shall soon see, the test will typically be carefully written, undergo a field trial on many students, and be revised based on that trial. A second field trial may be required. It is a long and expensive process.

Importance of Standardization

Suppose you and I are at a sports fair. Children are participating in all kinds of sporting events to show their skill and prowess. Officials are about to award a ribbon to the child who jumped ten hurdles in the shortest time. The ribbon goes to Charles Zorbicek, a ten-year-old who jumped the hurdles in 47 seconds.

But what's this? Antony Allman's father is contesting the decision. The average height of the hurdles Charles had jumped was 25 inches. Anthony's hurdles averaged 28 inches, and Anthony's time was 48 seconds. Besides the starter for Charles' race used a starter pistol, while Anthony's starter just shouted "If you're ready, GO!" Also Anthony's race was timed by a stopwatch, while Charles' race was timed with a sweep second-hand on a wristwatch.

The dispute here is based on the fact that the contests were not standardized. The administration was different from race to race, the content (hurdle height) was different, and the interpretation (timing) was different. If the hurdle race had been standardized, this dispute would not have happened.

These problems are the kind test publishers try to avoid in standardizing tests. They want to see what children can do on the so-called "level playing field." If the procedures for administering the test are the same for all children, if the content of the tests is the same (or equivalent), and the methods for interpretation are the same, the differences between one student and another must be in their skill in managing the subject matter. This is the proposition behind standardized testing.

Chapter 5 noted different sources of error in measurement. One of these sources was in test administration. Some procedures give students a different orientation to the test than others. A second source of error was in scoring. A standard, objective procedure tends to reduce scoring errors. The content of the test also is a source of measurement errors. It is the purpose of standardization to eliminate these sources of error by creating the same (standardized) circumstances for all children who take the test. Then these classic sources of error cannot differentially affect children's scores.

Following prescribed routines in testing is essential if educators are going to make comparative judgments with the results. These routines can either foster motivation and point the students in a productive direction, or promote confusion about procedures and the work period. Unless procedures are standard across all administrations, no two test administrations will be the same. This may influence test item difficulty and validity, and can mean that test scores will not be useful within the prescribed interpretation procedure.

The principal quality of standardized test administrations is that the instructions for taking the *Iowa Test of Basic Skills* in Washougal, Washington are the same as those given in Minnetonka, Minnesota, and in Floral City, Florida. The procedures and content across these sites for a given grade level are the same (or equivalent) and the interpretation of results is the same.

Types of Standardized Tests

By far the most common type of standardized test is the **achievement test.** This is the comprehensive test, given often in the spring, with which educators look at skills in reading, mathematics, spelling and composition, science, and social studies. Virtually all children in American schools have taken such a test at some time.

But achievement tests are not the only standardized tests used in schools. Many schools periodically administer **aptitude tests** for academic advising and vocational counseling. These tests are designed to illustrate the potential children have for schoolwork or for some specialized area, such as mechanics. Like achievement tests, aptitude tests must be administered to all children in a standard format, the content must be the same, and the data given for interpretation must be the same across all tests.

There are several other types of tests used in schools that are also standardized. First-grade teachers are interested in grouping their children based on their readiness to begin reading instruction. Several reading readiness tests are used to assist teachers in making decisions that lead to grouping children for reading instruction. These tests, like other achievement tests, are standardized.

Counselors are limited in time they can spend with any one student. Their efforts may be made more efficient if some data on skills and aptitudes of a given child are available for them to apply in talking with student clients. Typically these tests are specialized aptitude scales, illustrating a child's potential for work in clerical, mechanical, technical, and other areas of work. This gives the counselor a head start in discussing career and academic choices with the student. These tests too are standardized.

Counselors may also use personal adjustment and vocational interest inventories. These help make the counselor's work more efficient; the former rapidly identifies areas where personality problems may exist, and the latter is an aid in selection of a career area. These inventories are also standardized.

An important condition of standardization for tests is that the process allows us to have a sense of the average and the range of scores for a defined group of children (e.g., a large national sample of ninth-graders). If a child's score ranges well above the average of the national sample of children, this child is likely to be especially skilled. Or if the score is notably below average for the national sample, the child may well lack the skill in question. This kind of sorting would not be possible if tests were not standardized.

In the types of tests just discussed educators look at a child's score as a measure of success in the tasks presented. This usually means a score must be related to a standard—the average, or a minimum criterion score. To do this, educators must feel confident that influences such as administration, content, and score interpretation are constants across testing situations before they speculate about a child's status.

Functions of Standardized Tests

One of the purposes of using tests is to sort out students who are doing really well, from those who are doing adequately, from those who are doing very mediocre work. That is to say, one of the purposes of any type of assessment is to rank children in terms of their accomplishments in pursuit of a given objective.

If children are to be ranked, the score scale on which they are ranked must be based on the results of administering the test to many children. All of these tests must contain the same (or equivalent) content and the same instructions. Only then can publishers provide a common set of data on which interpretations can be made.

Standardized tests are used to rank students in a controlled situation because educators want to make some decisions about both students and programs. There are several questions that standardized tests help answer. Which are the most advanced students? Are there enough of these to support an advanced class? Are there students who are not grasping the ideas represented in a subject area? Should a special class be developed to remediate the deficiencies? Is there something about our program that needs changing? Shall the principal appoint a curriculum committee to investigate program options?

But standardized tests have possibilities aside from assessing general achievement. If teachers believe that a given skill, such as reading, is made up of several subskills, test-makers can build a set of items for each subskill. If this test is standardized, teachers can determine average performance for each subskill. Then they can compare a child's scores with this set of average scores to see in what skills this child is not doing well. Tests that are used in this way are called **diagnostic.** They are intended to look inside the operation of a given academic performance to see on which subskills the child has developed, or failed to develop, the operations that support performance in the overall skill. Diagnostic subtest structures are not only available in tests of academic skills, but also in some aptitude tests.

Diagnostic tests typically provide a **profile** of the subskill scores. A profile is a presentation of the separate subtest scores wherein the student's subtest scores are converted to the same score scale, such as percentile ranks or stanines.

Luckily, you now know about conversion systems. In Chapter 13 you saw conversions of scores into z- and T-scores, into percentile ranks, stanines, and normal curve equivalents. All of these are systems that put different sets of scores onto a distribution with the same mean and the same spread (standard deviation) of scores. Because subscales on diagnostic tests typically have different numbers of items from each other, profiles are produced in terms of standard scores, not raw scores.

Figure 15.2 is a profile of a child's performance on the *California Achievement Tests.* The scores on the left are given in several types of standard scores. On the right is the profile—the pattern of achievement—for this child. Unless scores on each test were converted to the same type of standard score, no profile could be made. But in standard scores, a stanine of 6 places the child at the same place in the group on one test as on any

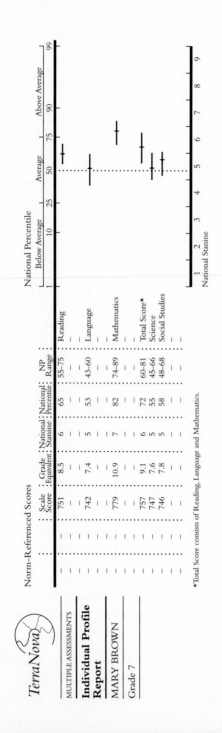

Norm–Referenced Scores

	Scale Score	Grade Equivalent	National Stanine	National Percentile	NP Range	
MULTIPLE ASSESSMENTS	—	—	—	—	—	Reading
Individual Profile Report	—	—	—	—	—	—
MARY BROWN	751	8.5	6	65	55-75	—
	—	—	—	—	—	Language
	742	7.4	5	53	43-60	—
	—	—	—	—	—	Mathematics
	779	10.9	7	82	74-89	—
Grade 7	—	—	—	—	—	Total Score★
	757	9.1	6	72	60-81	Science
	747	7.6	5	55	45-66	Social Studies
	746	7.8	5	58	48-68	—

★Total Score consists of Reading, Language and Mathematics.

FIGURE 15.2   An Example of an achievement test report produced by the Terra Nova System used by the California Test Bureau (CTB McGraw Hill), reprinted by permission of the McGraw Hill Companies, Inc.

other test in the set. Therefore teachers can compare performance across tests when identifying strengths and weaknesses in a child's achievement.

It should be noted that standardization of each of the subtests is necessary before the profile can be used with any confidence. To put a child's score among other children's scores all of them must have taken the test under the same conditions, content across all tests must be equal, and scoring must be the same. Only if these conditions were met can I put a subtest into a profile with other subtests. Each subtest must be standardized before going into the diagnostic profile.

Construction of Standardized Tests

As a teacher you will occasionally be involved in a discussion about the structure of commercial tests. Here are several points to consider in such discussions. The building of a standardized test is a detailed and complex process. First, the test is designed to assess a given quality or trait of an individual, for example, academic aptitude, achievement, or adjustment. Initially, the job is to specify the domain (analogous to building a table of specifications shown in Chapter 2). Specialists in the area of the designated trait, with the help of psychometric and technical assistants, will agree on the behaviors that most notably characterize the focal trait. For example, the specialists may agree that ability to deal with abstractions is one type of behavior that characterizes students with academic aptitude. The list of behaviors are used as a guide for constructing items that are intended to assess the focal trait and support the claim for the validity of the test.

The next job is to write the test items. The specialists and assistants will decide what kind of items will be used (e.g., multiple choice) to assess each of the topics in the domain. The trait specialists, with the advice of the psychometrics people, will write a large number of items, usually two to three times more than they expect to print in the final form of the test. These items are carefully edited so that they will call from the testtaker the behaviors that characterize the trait. This item construction is based on the definition of the trait, another effort to build in validity.

The test, including instructions for taking it, will be assembled. Several forms of the test are usually made because any one group of students cannot be expected to complete all the items that must be pretested. The forms are edited one final time, and then **field tested** in relevant populations such as schools which have agreed to cooperate in the building process.

After the field testing the items are analyzed by statistical processes much like those illustrated in Chapter 9. The items that meet minimum statistical requirements will be retained, and those that do not will be eliminated (or held for later revision). The items are then put into a final test form according to the specifications of the domain being assessed. If enough items can be retained on each of the topics listed in defining the content of the test, equivalent forms of the test will be constructed. Many test publishers have two or more equivalent forms of their test available to the consumer.

The test is now ready for its final field trial. School systems are selected that represent a cross section of American schools. The tests are administered in these schools and the results accumulated for analysis. This time the analysis will be in terms of final reliabilities, and for conversion of scores students made to standard scores, such as T-scores. This large data set will become the reference data against which future students will be compared. These data are often referred to as **norms.** The students on whom the test is tried out are often referred to as the **reference** or **norms group.**

The test is now ready to be marketed.

✎ Problems

1. Two mathematics teachers have built a test that they believe assesses the skills that are necessary to do passing work in the special advanced class in mathematics for high school seniors. They have used it for a year preliminary to selecting students for the advanced class, and have two semesters' data on the success of the tests. What do these teachers need to do to make this a standardized test?
2. Describe where norms come from and tell how they are important in standardized tests.

Standardized Tests and Performance Assessment

Teachers very much want to see children apply academic skills in solving real life problems. Performance procedures are designed to observe and assess this happening. These observations are typically planned so that the appraisers are prepared to look for and record specific categories of behavior. Some observer time must be spent with each student in making a record of how well each student solves the problem.

However, there are many academic skills that underpin performance in life problems that can be assessed with standardized tests in a fraction of the time required by observations. For example, a student will have difficulty in solving an authentic problem involving bookkeeping if that student knows nothing about entry systems. A child who has a solution to a problem will have difficulty composing a report if spelling skills are poor and the rules of grammar unknown. These deficiencies can be easily identified by standardized tests.

Standardized tests differ also in the extent to which they meet basic psychometric standards. Standardized tests continue to produce the highest reliabilities when compared with performance assessments. When high-stakes decisions are being made—promotion, graduation, selection for special programs—educators must be sure that a repeat observation of a student would give them results similar to the first observation. That is, the assessment must be reliable; the data on reliability seem to favor standardized tests.

You have seen that makers of standardized tests try out their tests on a large sample of children and develop a distribution of scores (typically converted to standard scores) against which teachers may compare the work of their students. This distribution lets them decide how their children are doing compared to a national sample of children.

There is no set of national norms to describe performance behavior of students. Some publishers are developing performance assessment systems with scoring procedures that do produce scores. However, users must follow a set routine when making their observations. If so, unique problems and unique features of a child's behavior may not be identified in the rigor of a standardized scoring rubric. When publishers formalize observations they take away from the teacher the permission to apply that diagnostic eye that characterizes the experienced educator. In addition, formalized observations reduce the reality often found in problems posed at the local level.

Still another area in which standardized test may be preferred to performance assessment is in satisfying the demands of accountability. To be accountable implies that educators have a standard against which they compare children. An average or other relevant statistic to illustrate gain or the numbers of children reaching a goal, is important. These demands are best met with the standardized test. They provide all these data and provide a reference group against which to compare local students' work. Some superintendents find this to be an advantage for standardized tests when they face the school board, or the regional accrediting association, and must have reference groups to point out strengths of the local program. In these large scale assessment situations performance exercises prove to be more problematic (Mehrens, 1992).

Nevertheless, teachers who use performance assessment with a set rubric can describe the criterion used to define success and can sort students who have reached that level of success from those who have not. Because performance records correlate with standardized tests teachers can sort students, but with standardized tests, no one has actually seen students perform the real world task. Some students whose test scores appear to be adequate may not be able to do the real thing. This is not true when performance is the thing being formally observed.

Choosing a Standardized Test

Surely there is a plethora of standardized tests on the market. In this context how does a school system find the one it wants to use? As you begin to look at test catalogs, there are several important features to note in selecting a test for your school system.

When teachers construct a test, they hope that it will fit the content of the course with the same emphasis with which the course was taught. This is not always the case with standardized tests. The makers of these tests look for defensible concepts on which to base their instruments, though these may not fit the local concept of the trait. Nevertheless, they will describe what the trait is in terms of the literature they have compiled. From this you may decide whether it fits the local concept.

Bases for Selecting a Test

1. The content fits the educator's concept of a trait.
2. Norms are based on a population that represents citizenry of the local area.
3. Tests and subtests are reliable.
4. Score reports are easy to read and provide score interpretation aids.
5. Turnaround time for receiving scores is short.

Here is an example. Local counselors have a concept of general academic aptitude they wish to apply in advising students. They will look for a test that reflects that concept. Similarly, mathematics instructors want a test that samples content the way they teach it.

And the assessing of achievement in American history must take many forms across the nation. Although there are common features in all programs, there are local and regional themes, too. Consider, for example, a comparison of the salient features of the westward movement as they might be presented in Malden, Massachusetts, Union, Utah, or Calaveras, California. Some topics will be the same, but there will be clear differences in regional interests. Other topics, such as the time and intensity with which teachers look into the colonial period will likely be different across these three locations. Standardized tests do not accommodate regional differences very well.

For these reasons, when selecting a standardized test, you must always compare its content with the local concept of the trait to be assessed. The test with the closest fit has the greatest content validity for your program (see Chapter 3). One device for managing this comparison is the table of specifications (see Chapter 2), in which the topics and the events that build them have been listed by the teacher based on their importance in local instruction. This table is an excellent guide to evaluating the content of the standardized test. Tables of specifications can guide the selection of commercial performance tests, too. Look for them when selecting these tests.

It is also important to ask whether the norms group on which the test was tried out includes skill levels that are characteristic of the local population. Educators will want to use the converted scores that are provided by standardized tests, but these scores are based on the children on whom the test was built. To use the norms with our own pupils, testmakers must have included in the norms data from children resembling those in our schools.

In addition, when selecting a standardized test you should check the manual to see that the norms group has demographic characteristics that closely match the population from which local students come. This does not mean that the norms group must come from the same region, but the mix of social classes, ethnicity, and other important population characteristics should closely resemble the local population.

The manuals that accompany tests should provide the information on how the test was developed and should describe the norms group. The manual will also report the test reliabilities, an important feature because it says how stable scores are for children (see Chapter 4). If you see a child classified well above average in mathematics, you want to believe that a parallel test would also classify that child well above average. If you do not have that confidence you cannot effectively use the scores at all. Reliability coefficients tell educators how stable scores are, so look for high coefficients, about .85 or higher would be desirable.

Another feature to consider is the ease of reading and interpreting the score report. A test publisher should create score reports from which consumers can easily get information. This means that the scores should be those most commonly used, such as T-scores, and are arranged in a logical manner. Score interpretation aids should be provided that will help consumers review the application of each score-type used. For example, if a score report form uses stanines the manual should give a brief summary of how this is derived in the reported data. If profiles are used, the bar-graph form is a good one. The continuous nature of line graphs implies a connection among adjacent skill scores which probably does not exist.

The manual should give a sample of a score report form, with scores included. You should be able to easily read the sample form. If you have trouble with it, this should send up a red flag of warning for this particular test. Local educators—teachers, administrators, counselors—must easily make sense of test results if the data are to be used.

Some test publishers will provide a narrative score report which interpret the numbers for a given child. Teachers who are not comfortable with the statistical methods of testing find these narrative reports especially helpful. The manual will tell you if such a report exists, and should provide a sample. Read it over and see if it is helpful in understanding scores.

You will need to know what the turnaround time is for receiving score reports. Most standardized tests are scored by the publishing company that sells them. If it takes several weeks for the test results to be returned to a school, this time lag may reduce the usefulness of the scores. If an achievement test is administered in the spring and the results do not arrive until summer when school is out, it may not be helpful for grouping students, for providing reteaching of topics, or for supporting grade reporting and curriculum changes.

In some cases local scoring may be provided. But keys for most standardized tests are copyrighted and come only with royalties to the company. For this reason local scoring is rarely done.

Sources of Information on Standardized Tests

There are a number of good sources of information on standardized tests, and if you know a few of these you'll find that they cover most of your needs. Here are some of the more popular ones.

The Mental Measurements Yearbook.   In Chapter 3, the **Mental Measurements Yearbook** was introduced as an important source of test information. A sample of one of its reviews is given on page 46. The *Yearbook* is currently compiled by the Buros Institute, University of Nebraska, in Lincoln, Nebraska. For most purposes, only the recent editions are useful in schools.

As shown in Chapter 3, the *Yearbook* provides a description of the test and its construction, usually followed by the commentary of a reviewer or two. The information in the reviews is very helpful in selecting a test to be used in your schools. Reading about tests in the widely used *Yearbook* is an efficient way to reduce the number of tests you need to look at in specimen sets. You can look for the *Yearbook* in the teachers' library, the school counselor's office, or the central office materials center. If you cannot locate one, it should be ordered. You may also find it in the library of a local or nearby college.

Specimen Sets.   Publishers have prepared packets for their tests called **specimen sets.** In these sets are copies of the test, a copy of the score report form, the test manual, and whatever else the publisher thinks will promote the test.* When selecting a test, a school committee can learn a great deal by reviewing the actual test and its supporting services. How well does the test content fit our program? This can be determined only by looking at the test items themselves. How was the test built, and what does the norms group look like? The test manual will describe this. Can you easily interpret the score report? One of these report forms will be included in the specimen set. How much does the test cost? Price lists and a publisher's catalog of other tests are often included.

Specimen sets will also include additional useful materials such as directions for administration, time limits for various ages, availability of machine-graded answer sheets, and the cost of the scoring service. Toll-free telephone numbers will allow you to ask any questions you may have about the tests. But remember, test companies are often large operations and you may not get the appropriate person for your question immediately. Be persistent; it's their telephone account, and you need the information.

Specimen sets involve some expense for the company to assemble, and therefore they want you to share in this expense. Specimen sets are rarely free, but they are sold at a reasonable price. Keep in mind that when ordering a specimen set you must do so on school letterhead; you may need endorsement from the principal or other school official.

Publishers' Catalogs.   Publishers print catalogs that include the various tests school professionals may wish to buy. These catalogs are often free to schools. They briefly describe development of the tests, tell how long each test and subtest takes to administer, how to obtain scoring services, and a number of other interesting things about the tests and the company. After looking over the section in the catalog that includes the type of test you are interested in, you may wish to look in detail at one or two. The catalog will include an order form for specimen sets, or you may wish to use the toll-free number provided.

Evaluating Standardized Tests

Each of the tests that interest you will not be equally suited to your purpose. If you hold each test up to the same criteria you will be better prepared to make a selection. Figure 15.3 shows a proposed rating scale to guide you in reviewing tests. It is a prototype and can be altered as needed to fit any situation. You may wish to make your own form to suit the special interests of your schools. In any case, some such form should be used so that you have common information on all tests being considered.

Standardized Tests and Criterion Referenced Testing

Mr. Downs, a fourth-grade teacher and Ms. Principia, the curriculum consultant, are looking over the results of the *Stanford Achievement Tests* for his class. "These results do

---

*A list of test publishers and their addresses is given in the appendix.

1. Test name _____ Date _____

    a) Subtestnames _____

2. Publisher _____

   Address _____

   Telephone _____ Toll-free _____

3. Grades/ages _____ Forms available _____

4. Administration   Directions

                  easy to use |---|---^---|---| hard to use

                                       Timing

              very appropriate |---|---^---|---| very inappropriate

5. Scoring

    a) Local scoring available? _____ Cost/pupil _____

    b) Company scoring available? _____ Cost/pupil _____

    c) Turn around local _____ company _____

6. Norms

    a) Sample size _____ Grade levels _____

    b) Appropriate for our population?   Yes _____ Moderately _____ No _____

    c) Type of scores available _____

7. Test manual available? _____   Useful?   Yes _____ Moderately _____ No _____

8. Psychometric qualities

    a) Validity—content: good local fit |---|---^---|---| poor local fit

    b) Reliability Type _____ Size(s) _____

    c) Score report: easy to use |---|---^---|---| difficult to use

9. Conclusions

    a) Strengths _____

    b) Weaknesses _____

FIGURE 15.3   A Guide to Evaluating Standardized Tests

not tell me which children can and cannot do long division," Mr. Downs complained. "It doesn't tell me which children can cite the theme of a reading passage. How do I make decisions based on this test?"

Ms. Principia looked grim. "This is not a criterion reference test, George," she replied.

Some users of standardized achievement tests, like Mr. Downs, want to apply the results as though the tests were criterion referenced. Although there are a few criterion referenced achievement tests, most standardized tests are norm referenced. Items are not grouped by objective, and are not focused on a given skill level. The decisions made from them are based on a student's status when compared with the norms group.

Under certain conditions these tests can be criterion referenced tests. Some publishers have grouped items around a specific skill. Some list objectives and identify the items that assess each objective. With this information in hand a teacher can measure a child's success in dealing with each objective. However, if this approach is used with standardized tests, there must be enough items for each objective to make decisions reasonably reliable. Objectives with less than ten items should probably not be used for criterion referencing. Many topics in achievement tests do not meet this ten-item requirement.

The conclusion is that norm referenced achievement tests cannot readily be adapted to criterion referenced use. If you wish to use them for criterion referenced applications, be sure you can identify the items in the test that refer to your objectives, and that there are adequate numbers of items for each objective to allow some degree of reliability.

SUMMARY

1. Tests are standardized to the extent that their administration, content, scoring and interpretation follow a common form in all situations in which they are used.

2. The most common type of standardized test in schools is the achievement test, which measures students' skills in a particular domain. Other types of tests, such as aptitude tests and interest inventories, are also standardized.

3. The construction of a standardized test begins with specifications of the domain, followed by creation of test items that fit into that domain, field testing, statistical analysis, and a second field trial.

4. Standardized tests are used to rank students on test scores achieved in a controlled situation, in order to support decisions about students and programs.

5. Diagnostic tests are used to determine subskills within a broader skill area that students possess and those they do not. The results are often presented in a profile.

6. Key features to look for in choosing standardized tests are how well the test content fits the local concept of the focal trait, whether the skills of the norms group are similar to those of the local population, how reliable the test is, ease of reading and interpreting score reports, and turnaround time for receiving score reports.

7. Sources of information about standardized tests include the *Mental Measurements Yearbook,* specimen sets provided by publishers, and the test publishers' catalogs.

PROBLEMS

1. For each of the following questions, select the most efficient resource from among the *Mental Measurements Yearbook,* a specimen set, or a publisher's catalog.
   a. I want to compare content of the test with our instructional program.
   b. I want an independent professional review of the test.
   c. I need two equivalent forms of the test, and I personally want to see these to compare content between the two forms.
   d. I want to know what achievement tests this publisher makes and how they are different.
2. You are about to select a standardized aptitude test for your elementary school. List five features you will look for in rating a test.
3. You are entering a debate—the argument: Performance assessments eliminate the need for standardized tests. Write a paragraph defending the position. Now write a paragraph against the position.
4. Do state mandated achievement tests fit the basic requirements of a standardized test? How so?
5. You want to devise a standardized test to assess aptitude for schoolwork in the second, third, and fourth grades. List the steps you would go through in building this test.
6. Fredie's number-correct score on an arithmetic test for grade seven is 36. This does not tell us much about Fredie's status in arithmetic among seventh-graders. The partial conversion table shows the correspondence between scores and percentile ranks.
   a. Find Fredie's score in the table below and decide if he has a high, low, or middle ranking. If you saw this procedure in a test manual, would you say it is an "easy" presentation for teachers to use in interpreting a score?
   b. How do you suppose this conversion table was devised?

Score	Percentile rank
42	84
41	81
40	79
39	77
38	76
37	75
36	75
35	74

KEY TERMS

standardized tests	field test
achievement tests	norms
aptitude tests	norms group
diagnostic tests	reference group
profile	*Mental Measurements Yearbook*
	specimen set

ADDITIONAL READING

Burrill, L. E. How a standardized achievement test is built. *Test Service Notebook, No. 125,* New York: The Psychological Corporation. (Not dated.)

Freeman, D. J., Kuhs, T. M., Porter, A. C., Floden, R. E., Schmidt, W. H., and Schwille, J. R. (1983). Do textbooks define a national curriculum in elementary school mathematics? *Elementary School Journal,* 83, 501–513.

Millman, J. and Greene, J. (1989). The specification and development of tests of achievement and ability. In R. L. Linn (Ed.), *Educational Measurement,* New York: American Council on Education/Macmillan, pp. 335–365.

Phillips, G. W. and Finn, C. E. (1988). The Lake Wobegone effect: A skeleton in the testing closet. *Educational Measurement: Issues and Practice,* 7 (2), 10–12.

CHAPTER 16

ACHIEVEMENT TESTS

Surveys of Academic Skills

Karl, a fourth-grader, is gulping down his breakfast. "Whoa, hold it!" his mother calls to him as she prepares for work. "Your breakfast will sit like a lump in your stomach if you eat so fast!"

"But, Mom, we start our Stanford tests today, and I want to be in school a little earlier. We've been pumping up for this for two weeks and I want to get to it," Karl explained.

Almost every child who has gone through grade school in America has taken one or more standardized achievement tests. Days were set aside in your school and devoted to achievement tests. Chances are you had a very good review of your work in reading, writing operations, mathematics, and science before the test date. You took the reading and language tests one day, the mathematics test the next, and the science and social studies test the last day. Then it was over. Teachers took awhile to get back to the routine, and so did the students.

Achievement tests have developed a stature that no other assessment technique has. Their results carry strong implications of finality. Do they really deserve this status? This chapter should help teachers decide for themselves.

What This Chapter Will Include. Achievement tests are very difficult to develop, do not tell us everything we want to know, and have an uneven utility across different school functions. This chapter sorts out what an achievement test does and what it does not do. In it you will learn:

1. How achievement tests are built
2. How they compare with teacher-made tests
3. On what skills achievement tests focus
4. What scores achievement tests report
5. How achievement tests are used in diagnostic work
6. The Teacher's responsibility in achievement testing
7. Applications of results of achievement tests
8. About statewide testing
9. About national testing—the NAEP

Construction of Achievement Tests

"I sometimes think these test publishers sit down on Monday mornings and slap-dash their tests together, package them in bright colors, and sell the schools a big publicity job!" said Ms. Blue, a third-grade teacher. "I know the tests miss more than a few things I teach and I'll bet the rest of you think the same thing," she continued, gesturing to the other teachers in the lunch room.

In the last chapter you and I looked at what goes into making a standardized test, and learned that achievement tests are one type of standardized test. Let's take Ms. Blue on a visit to a test publisher and find out what goes into constructing a test. Let's see if her critique is on target. Any company that endeavors to construct an achievement test is undertaking a difficult task. To start, think about constructing tests to cover skills at least at grades two through six, and in these grades, create tests to assess knowledge in at least a dozen different skills. Then add to this the building of at least three forms of each test. I doubt that any educator is ready to start this job tomorrow. The planning period alone is enormous.

In the last chapter we saw the plan for developing a standardized test. Achievement test-builders essentially follow this plan.

Content Review

We saw that the first step in developing a standardized test is to delineate the characteristics of the trait to be assessed. In achievement tests this is done by curriculum experts who go through textbooks, state curriculum guides, and the commentary of curriculum leaders to find common topics of content. This is done for each subject matter area and for each grade level.

Imagine yourself sitting behind a stack of textbooks in your field of specialty. Your job is to go through each book, tabulate the topics, note levels of complexity, and show examples. Then you turn to state curriculum guides, and do it all over again. Of course, a test publisher will employ many people to work on this operation, but you can see it is a very large task.

In spite of the size of this job, it must be done accurately. The results of this search will determine the content of your tests. If the content is inappropriate for the classes for which publishers are building their tests, it will not become commercially successful. Schools will label it as incongruent with their curricula, and the work is in vain. The content search is a vital part of building an achievement test.

Once you have tabulated the topics across all the reference material, the next job is to look for the most commonly cited ones. Achievement tests focus on content that appears in many curriculum sources. In their effort the testmakers target the topics that are most likely to appear in school programs across the country. They will avoid topics that are unique to a few programs that have local or regional interest.

Here is an example. George Washington's commanding of the revolutionary army probably appears in history books in all states, but George Rogers Clark's successes against the British in Indiana will be judged by state curriculum planners as important only to a few states in the Midwest. Similarly the westward trek of Lewis and Clark will be in most history books, but the work of Junipero Serra in the Southwest in the 1700s is likely to be more important to students in California than in Vermont or Virginia. These regionally important events are not likely to appear on achievement tests designed for a national market. This does not mean that topics of regional interest are unimportant, only that for a test to be used on a national scale these topics are not relevant to the broad population the test serves.

Item Construction

Now that the test publishers have selected the topical content that appears to be relatively common across all states, the next step is to write items. Here curriculum and psychometric specialists combine skills and assemble the items that will be used in the tests. How many items are needed? Remember that we are building tests for all elementary grades, and in some cases, for middle and high school, too. Also, the publishers will create at least two forms of the tests at each grade level. We all—including Ms. Blue— will want different test items in each form, although each form will sample performance in the same knowledge domain as the other.

Items must be reviewed for good item construction procedures (like those noted in Chapters 7 and 8), and for reading difficulty level appropriate to the grade level at which the test will be administered. This means publishers will have to create several times as many items as they think may be needed in the final tests. Some items will be dropped during initial editing, some will be removed from the pool after the item analysis following the field test, and some will be dropped later because they did not fit well on any form of the test.

The Field Test

Test publishers are likely to try out many thousands of items in their initial field trial of the test items. This is a tremendous logistical problem. The plan is for each item to be taken by at least 200 students or more. Imagine teams of test managers fanning out across the nation, each with tens of thousands of test items to be tried out. Then these managers go to schools, like the one in which Ms. Blue is a teacher, that have agreed to assist them in the trial run, administer some items (but certainly not all) in each school until each item has been taken by at least 200 children. This is a costly chore that requires months of planning and more months of execution.

When the test items have been taken by children in their schools, the tests are returned to the publisher for item analysis. Here the work is done by computers in a fashion something like that described in Chapter 9. Although they have been carefully constructed, not all items will make it past the item analysis. In fact, testmakers expect to drop as many as half of the items at this point. The remaining items are ready for sorting into the appropriate tests.

Professional Editing

Now, as Ms. Blue watches, company personnel sort the items into the tests, at the appropriate grade levels and with a balance among the topics and skills to be tested. They want items that assess all skills in the number that corresponds with their original test plan. Also, to make the test (more nearly) fair for all test-takers items are screened for various biases, such as ethnicity/race, gender, and rural/urban biases. Although such screening has gone a long way toward reducing bias in testing, there continues to be a feeling among some groups that tests are still biased. Chapter 17, where aptitude assessment is discussed, will cover the bias problem in more detail.

Outside Review and Norming

Up to this point the work has been done by the test publisher, and employees of a company naturally share certain ideas about the job's objective. Because of this, have workers been blind to some features they should have included in the tests? The next step in the construction process is designed to eliminate this problem. Teams of educators with diverse professional, ethnic, and regional backgrounds are assembled to review the final set of tests. When these teams are done, the tests will be put into final form.

The tests are now ready for norming. Once again the tests are taken to schools for administration. These schools are carefully selected to resemble schools across the nation. The data collected will be used to develop all the statistics, such as grade-level norms, NCSs, and percentile ranks that will be used to help educators interpret scores.

But there is really more work involved than you and Ms. Blue have seen. During the time test-writers have been working on items, instructions for administering the tests have to be written. Researchers have been sorting items to ensure comparability of test forms within a grade. The technical manual which covers such features as reliability and validity, describes the norming group, and explains how standard scores are found, is being written.

By now Ms. Blue will see that developing a general achievement test for school use is not only a very large task, but also a time consuming and expensive process to complete.

Comparing Achievement Tests with Teacher-Made Tests

The construction procedures for teacher-made and commercial tests are not markedly different in the phases of their development, but are very different in the sophistication of the steps in the process. Obviously, teacher-made tests are not written by test experts and do not go through field trials. Only occasionally do teachers do an item analysis or convert test data into standard scores for future reference. Reliabilities on teacher-made tests are rarely available.

Teacher-made tests deal directly with assessing class progress on objectives for one phase of instruction. The teacher writes test items to correspond with the work children have been doing—items that fit the objectives of instruction. Because of this, teacher made tests have the advantage of tailoring the content very closely to the local objectives. This is the truly great advantage teacher-made tests have over standardized tests. If teacher-made tests are done well the test assesses what the class has specifically studied. Standardized tests, on the other hand, include only those items that are common threads of content found in reviews of textbooks, state curriculum guides, and other materials. The content will cover many salient points but will not be a close fit for the instruction of any one class. Teacher-made tests, however, should be a very good fit.

The score on teacher-made tests is typically the number correct. Standardized tests, however, have several scores that tell educators how students compare with a large group of other students in that grade level and can be compared across reading, arithmetic, and other skill areas. In addition, diagnostic subscores are sorted out of the test to indicate on which subscales the child has done well, and not so well.

In Table 16.1 you will find a comparison of commercially printed achievement tests and teacher constructed tests. You can see that they differ in content, in quality of the items used, in test reliability, administration procedures, scoring accuracy, and in interpretation. Standardized tests have some strong features in construction and application but are not as close a match for instruction as are teacher-made tests. Nevertheless, because of their national base and careful construction, achievement tests provide information that the routine teacher-made assessments cannot.

✎ Problems

1. Suppose you were to build an achievement test in your subject matter area. Describe the steps you would go through to build it.
2. How easy, or difficult, is it for a test publisher to get a norms group together? Describe some of the problems involved.
3. What is the intent of item analysis in the construction of an achievement test?
4. You are going to speak to the PTA about why schools need both standardized achievement tests and teacher-made tests. What points would you make in this presentation? How are the tests different and how not different?

Skills Assessed by Achievement Tests

General **achievement tests** are designed to test knowledge of many important aspects of the curriculum. Tests typically provide scores for broad subject areas such as reading and mathematics, but also for several subskills within these areas. Their intent in assessing the subskills that when combined make up the general area of work is to provide diagnostic information. For example, if a teacher sees that Joe's overall reading score is

TABLE 16.1   A Comparison of Teacher-Made and Standardized Test Construction

	Teacher-Made	Standardized
Content sample	Sample of specific content based on local objectives	Content sample covers only general core of most school programs
Quality of items	Quality varies; often undetermined; usually lower than in standardized tests	Generally high; items written by specialists and field tested
Test reliability	Often undetermined; may be high if test is written well, but is often modest	Typically high, often .85 or above
Administration	No set rules; instructions for administration may be written at top of test but not always	Standard procedures given in actual words to be read from the manual
Scoring	Teacher-scored; random errors not uncommon; some subjectivity	Machine scored; errors rare; no subjectivity
Interpretation	Based on percentage right or position in the class	Scores held up to large reference group by use of standard scores; test manual provides advice

poor, and that his score on the subtest that assesses word attack skills is especially low for his grade, the teacher may wish to observe more carefully how Joe is attacking difficult words. In this way, achievement tests are somewhat diagnostic.

When a cluster of tests are assembled for administration as a unit, this cluster is often called a **battery.** Here is a list of skills that achievement tests typically claim to assess in the basic skills area of their test batteries.

- Reading (word attack skills, vocabulary, comprehension)
- Language (grammar and punctuation, expression, spelling)
- Mathematics (computations, concepts, problem solving)
- Reference skills (library and reference book usage, maps and graphs)

In addition to these tests in the basic skills, some publishers include tests in science and social studies. All together this makes up a dozen or more tests to be administered in an achievement test battery. Seven to nine hours are not unusual testing times for the whole battery. Of course, this time should be spread out over more than one testing session.

A word of caution is appropriate here. Just because a test has a title that refers to a given skill does not mean the test actually measures that skill. For example, a test that is called "word attack skills" may focus more on comprehension or on vocabulary. Teachers should look at the test items themselves to determine what the test actually measures. The belief that a test always measures what its title says it does is called the **jangle fallacy.**

Achievement tests at the secondary school level are typically more general than those made for the elementary school. This is in part due to the fact that students in high schools tend to take a basic core of courses, then fan out into different programs such as vocational, business, or college preparatory. This leaves a smaller core of common skills being taught to secondary school students than is true for elementary school pupils.

The *Iowa Test of Educational Development* (ITED) is an example of an achievement test battery for the secondary schools. Its seven tests, that produce eight scores, are as follows:

- Vocabulary
- Ability to Interpret Literary Material
- Correctness and Appropriateness of Expression
- Ability To Do Quantitative Thinking
- Analysis of Social Studies Materials
- Analysis of Science Materials
- Sources of Information
- Content Area Reading Score (derived from items in the literary, social studies, and the science tests)

Achievement tests once had a reputation for dealing primarily with factual content. This is no longer true. For example, in the *Iowa Tests of Basic Skills* items are classified under the mental operations of a) focusing and information gathering, b) remembering, c) organizing, d) analyzing, e) generating, and f) integrating and evaluating. This test, and others in the general achievement area, now include items that require a variety of levels of mental processing.

Achievement Test Scores

There are five different types of scores used to report a child's performance on achievement tests: grade equivalent scores, percentile ranks, standard scores, stanines, and normal curve equivalents. (If you need a review of different types of score conversions, see Chapter 14.) You will see these scores on the student reports that come to your school after the achievement tests have been scored. As a professional you will want to know what these scores tell you, and you will also want to explain the achievement of students to their parents. An example of the scores on a test report of the *Iowa Test of Basic Skills* is given in Figure 16.2 (on page 308). Here you see different types of scores such as grade equivalents, national percentile ranks, and normal curve equivalents. These scores communicate ideas about each child's test performance. What do these data tell us? Let's start by looking at grade-equivalent scores.

Grade-Equivalent Scores

Grade-equivalent scores, usually written in decimal form, tell us the performance level of a child in terms of school grade levels, such as 3.6 or 5.2. The numeral on the

Iowa Tests of Basic Skills

Service 9:
List Report of Student Scores

Class/Group: COOPER
Building: JOHNSON ELEM
Building Code:
System: RIVER FALLS ISD
Norms: SPRING 1992
Order No: 000-005926-001xxx

Grade: 4
Form: 5
Test Date: 05/93
Page: 1

Sample

Student Name / I.D. Number, Other info.	Birth Date / Age	Test (Sex)	Level	Reading Vocabulary	Reading Comprehension	Reading Total	Spelling	Language Capitalization	Language Punctuation	Language Usage/Express	Language Total	Math Concepts/Estim.	Math Probs/Data Interp.	Math Total	Core Total	Social Studies	Science	Sources Maps & Diagrams	Sources Ref. Mat'ls	Sources Total	Composite	Math Computation
ADAMS, LINDA	07/83 09-10	10 (F)	GE	5.8	7.6	6.7	5.8	5.9	8.8	8.2	6.8	5.6	6.7	5.7	6.5	7.3	8.6	6.0	5.3	5.6	6.7	5.4
			NPR	73	86	83	73	67	87	82	79	69	78	72	81	86	90	69	62	65	84	64
			NCE	63	73	70	63	59	74	70	67	61	66	62	68	73	77	61	56	58	71	57
CAMPBELL, BRIAN	09/83 09-08	10 (M)	GE	4.4	4.8	4.6	4.1	4.0	5.4	4.8	4.5	4.3	4.6	4.4	4.5	4.7	4.9	4.1	4.0	4.1	4.5	4.5
			NPR	40	51	47	29	32	59	50	41	33	44	37	40	49	53	39	34	37	42	37
			NCE	45	51	48	38	40	55	50	45	41	47	43	45	49	52	44	41	43	46	43
CASTILLO, DANIEL	10/83 09-07	10 (M)	GE	4.0	4.2	4.1	3.6	3.2	4.4	4.1	3.7	3.6	3.7	3.7	3.8	3.9	4.0	3.8	3.7	3.8	3.9	3.9
			NPR	29	38	34	20	20	42	38	26	23	27	22	26	30	35	30	25	26	27	24
			NCE	38	44	41	32	32	46	44	36	34	37	34	36	39	42	39	36	37	37	35
GRANT, JILL	05/83 10-00	10 (F)	GE	9.9	12.3	8.3	10.8	13.0	13.4	13.4	12.9	11.7	12.0	10.7	11.8	12.1	13.1	12.7	10.4	11.6	12.1	8.8
			NPR	99	99	99	99	99	99	99	99	99	99	99	99	99	99	99	99	99	99	99
			NCE	99	99	99	99	99	99	99	99	99	99	99	99	99	99	99	99	99	99	99
JACKSON, BRYAN	02/83 10-03	10 (M)	GE	K.3	K.4	K.4	1.0	K.6	K.6	K.6	K.6	K.7	K.7	K.7	K.6	K.8	K.6	K.8	1.1	K.9	K.7	K.8
			NPR	1	1	1	1	1	1	1	1	1	1	1	1	1	1	1	1	1	1	1
			NCE	1	1	1	1	1	1	1	1	1	1	1	1	1	1	1	1	1	1	1
LANG, JAMIE	06/83 09-11	10 (M)	GE	7.0	9.3	8.1	6.5	9.2	12.0	11.5	9.4	6.7	9.0	7.4	8.3	9.1	11.0	8.4	6.9	7.6	8.6	6.6
			NPR	90	95	94	80	89	97	96	96	74	94	92	97	96	98	88	83	87	97	85
			NCE	77	85	83	68	76	90	87	86	74	83	80	88	87	98	75	70	74	91	72
RYAN, JENNIFER	11/83 09-06	10 (F)	GE	3.2	3.4	3.3	3.3	2.3	3.6	3.5	3.2	2.9	3.1	3.1	3.6	3.3	3.6	3.0	3.3	3.3	3.3	3.4
			NPR	15	24	19	12	11	26	25	16	9	15	10	13	19	25	16	17	16	15	12
			NCE	28	35	32	25	24	36	36	29	22	28	23	26	31	36	29	30	29	28	25
SHULER, CHRISTOP	12/83 09-05	10 (M)	GE	2.6	2.8	2.7	2.7	1.8	2.9	2.6	2.4	2.4	2.6	2.6	2.6	2.6	2.7	2.2	2.9	2.6	2.5	2.8
			NPR	7	11	8	6	6	16	11	6	3	8	3	4	7	11	6	9	5	3	5
			NCE	19	24	20	17	18	29	24	17	10	20	9	12	19	24	17	22	16	10	16
SOTO, TIM	01/83 10-04	10 (M)	GE	1.2	2.0	1.8	2.1	1.3	1.9	1.5	1.7	1.7	1.8	1.9	1.7	2.1	2.1	1.7	2.6	2.1	1.9	2.3
			NPR	2	3	1	2	2	5	4	1	1	2	1	1	1	3	2	3	1	1	1
			NCE	4	11	1	6	6	15	13	1	1	6	1	1	4	10	6	9	1	1	1
WEAVER, TIMOTHY	08/83 09-09	10 (M)	GE	1.2	2.0	1.8	2.1	1.3	1.9	1.5	1.7	1.7	1.8	1.9	1.7	2.1	2.1	1.7	2.6	2.1	1.9	2.3
			NPR	2	3	1	2	2	5	4	1	1	2	1	1	1	3	2	3	1	1	1
			NCE	4	11	1	6	6	15	13	1	1	6	1	1	4	10	6	9	1	1	1

GE: Grade Equivalent   NPR: National Percentile Rank   NCE: Normal Curve Equivalent

*Includes Mathematics Computation

FIGURE 16.2 A Score Report Provided by the Iowa Test of Basic Skills. (GE = Grade Equivalent, NPR = National Percentile Rank, NCE = Normal Curve Equivalent.) By permission, Riverside Publishing.

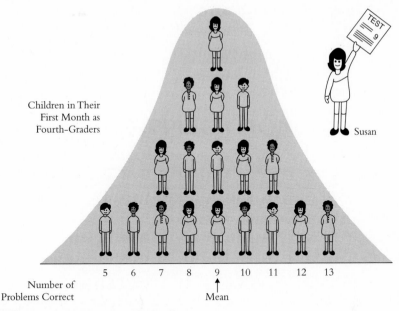

Children in Their
First Month as
Fourth-Graders

Susan

| 5 | 6 | 7 | 8 | 9 | 10 | 11 | 12 | 13 |

Number of
Problems Correct

↑
Mean

FIGURE 16.3   Finding the Grade Norm

left refers to the grade level, and the one on the right to the month within that grade. Figure 16.3 shows how they are derived. Susan got a mathematics grade-equivalent score of 4.1 on her Allschule Achievement Test. Susan got 9 test items correct in mathematics. This number (9) matches the median mathematics score for children in the norms group who were in the first month of the fourth grade. Therefore, Susan placed at the grade level of 4.1, the first month of the fourth grade. Her test score was equal to the median of the children in the norms group who were in the first month of the fourth grade.

Here is another example. Ernesto had a grade-equivalent score of 5.5 on the reading test. This means the number correct on his test was at the median for children in the norms group who were at the fifth month of the fifth grade.

Interpolation and Extrapolation.   Grade-equivalent scores are presumed to be based on the median raw score for children in the norms group who are actually in various months in the school year. This suggests that the test was given to the norms group each month from fall to spring. Of course, it is not. To calculate a median raw score for each month we need data for each month. However, testmakers do not administer the test this often. They may give it once in the fall and once in the spring. Between these two points the expected monthly medians are estimated. This estimation process is called **interpolation.**

Interpolation is illustrated in Figure 16.4 (on page 310). Here you see the median raw scores for September and March. As expected the children did better in March than September. A line has been drawn between the September median and the March median. Medians for months between September and March are expected to lie along

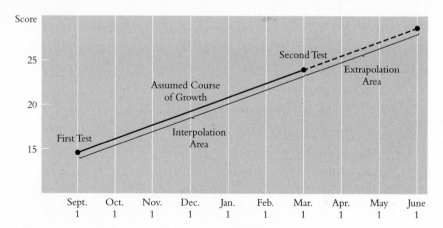

FIGURE 16.4   Interpolating and Extrapolating Scores

the line. For example, the median raw score expected for December is about 20; for February it is about 23. In other words, if I am a fourth-grader and get a raw score of 23, my grade score will be interpolated to be 4.6; February is the sixth month of the school year, so my score of 23 puts me in the fourth-grade, sixth month.

The publisher set September and March as the testing months. March is the seventh month. But what about grade scores for the eighth, ninth, or tenth month of the school year? How do we get grade scores for them? In these situations we assume that the line we drew between September and March continues on in an orderly fashion, something like that shown in Figure 16.4. Therefore, for students with a raw score of 26, the grade equivalent will be 4.8. (April is the eighth month in the Figure.) This process of extending the scores beyond the last actual testing date is called **extrapolation.** This process can also provide norms below the first testing date of the year.

There are some problems with grade norms. Extrapolation and interpolation suggest that achievement may be a straight line function (or nearly so). This is probably not true. Learning may very well take place at different rates during the year. If so the points identified by interpolation and extrapolation may not exactly fit the actual performance level at that point in the year. This is a source of measurement error for grade-equivalent scores.

Also, some students have grade-equivalent scores far above or far below their actual grade. For example, Jessie, a fifth-grade student in the second month of school, may have a grade-equivalent score of 6.9 in total mathematics. This does not mean she can perform all the mathematical processes that the average child in the ninth month of the sixth-grade can. She has not even been introduced to some of the processes that classes study in the last part of the sixth-grade. It simply means that Jessie is a very good student in the fifth-grade. Grade-equivalent scores may be descriptive of achievement for children who are moving along well but not far above or below their grade-level average in the norms group, but grade equivalents begin to lose some of that descriptive quality when students are scoring much above or below their own grade level.

How Not to Misinterpret Grade Equivalents.   Grade equivalents appear simple, but they can be easily misinterpreted. Here are some errors to avoid in their interpretation.

1.   *Grade-level norms must not be seen as standards.* Grade-level norms are the middle scores for students at a given grade in the norms group. This means half of the children in the norms group were below the grade-level norm and half above it. Because of this, you should not consider a grade-level norm as something all children should attain. Whether teachers should expect a child to be at, above, or below the norm depends on many factors besides the grade the child is in. An obvious factor would be academic aptitude. If I am dealing with a class of very bright children, most of them may be expected to be above the middle of the norms group. But for a child who does not have this level of academic aptitude, it may be unreasonable to expect performance even up to the norms-group level. Grade-level norms are not designed to be performance floors for all children.

2.   *Grade-equivalent scores are not estimates of the grade in which a child should be placed.* For example, a grade score of 7.6 in science for a fifth-grade child does not mean that child should be in the seventh-grade science class. As you noted above, this only means the child is doing very well for a fifth-grader.

3.   *Do not assume that the grade-score units are equal at all grades.* For example, the difference in achievement between 4.1 and 4.5 is probably not equal to the difference between 6.1 and 6.5. A half-year of growth at one grade level is probably not equal to a half-year of growth at another, nor are the units that mark off that half-year of growth equal. This fact diminishes our ability to do arithmetic with grade equivalents.

4.   *Do not expect that every child will show one year of growth for each year of school.* Individual children grow at different rates at different times in their development. Also, there is reason to believe that the instructional content is quite different in magnitude and complexity at different ages. Then too, the ability of a given child has something to do with the rate of growth and hence with the change in position in a group. All of this adds up to the inadvisability of assuming that every child should show one year of growth with each year of instruction.

5.   *Be cautious about the accuracy of extreme scores.* There are few children at the extremes of the distribution of the norms group. The fewer people we have at a given point, the more unreliable scores are likely to be. Also, grade norms notably above or below average for a grade level are obtained by extrapolation. Children may grow in a linear mode as shown in the extrapolation, but they may not. The farther the extrapolation gets from the date on which the norming data were collected, the less confidence you may have that the extrapolated score actually indicates the developmental level of a child.

6.   *Do not try to compare grade equivalents from one achievement test to another.* For example, a grade score of 4.3 in mathematics on the *Metropolitan Achievement Tests* probably does not represent the same achievement as 4.3 on the *Stanford Achievement Test.* There will be some differences in content, in defining the curriculum, and in character of a norms group. Comparing grade equivalents across tests probably should not be done.

Other Achievement Test Scores

Besides grade equivalents, achievement tests also report other norms such as percentile ranks. Crissy, a third-grade student, had a score report that showed a percentile rank of 56 in arithmetic computation. This means that her score ranked above 56 percent of the third-graders in the norms group.

In grade equivalents we had the problem of grade scores that placed the child into grades beyond the grade they were actually in. For example, a child in the fourth-grade may have a grade equivalent in science of 5.6. We found this bothersome because it suggested the child knew about topics which she probably did not. However, because percentile ranks are based on children in a given grade, we do not have that difficulty interpreting scores of children at the extremes of the range. These scores simply say that a child in the lower percentile ranks is doing work that is not as good as his other classmates, while a child in the higher percentile ranks is doing work that is better. With higher percentile ranks there is not the suggestion that students can do work at grades somewhat above their actual grade. However, they do show that students here are doing very well within their own grade.

Achievement tests also regularly report standard scores. These are sometimes called **scaled scores.** Recall that standard scores often have a mean of 50 and a standard deviation of 10. An average fifth-grade child in the norms group would have a standard score of 50. (Take another look at the discussion of the normal curve in Chapter 14.) To the extent that a score is below a T-score of 50, it reflects below average work for the grade level in the norms group. To the extent that a score is above 50, it reflects above average work. The middle 68 percent of the norms group will rank between standard scores of 40 and 60, that is, one standard deviation (10 points) below the mean (50) and one standard deviation above it. These are good benchmarks to remember with standard T-scores in interpreting achievement test reports.

Some publishers use standard scores that are different from T-scores. For example, the *California Achievement Tests* used three-digit numbers like 450 or 675. These are based on the same idea as the T-score but have a larger mean and standard deviation. If your test uses a different standard scoring system you can consult the manual that is provided with the test for the interpretation. Most are variations of the T-score idea.

Normal curve equivalents (NCEs) were discussed in Chapter 14. If you take the norms group scores for grade four and put them into a bell-shaped curve, you could tabulate their scores—from low to high—along the baseline of that curve. If you then divide the baseline into 100 equal-sized units, you would have scores running from 1 through 99, inclusive. The average score is 50. With NCEs the middle two-thirds of the group falls roughly between 30 and 70. These are approximate guides for interpreting achievement test scores in normal curve equivalents.

You also saw in Chapter 14 that stanines are based on a division of the baseline of the bell-shaped curve into nine units, all one-half standard deviation in width except the lowest and highest. Recall that you number these units with 1 for the lowest segment of the baseline, 2 for the next lowest, and so on, up to 9 for the highest. A stanine of 5 is the middle or "average" group. The largest clustering of students will fall into sta-nines 4, 5, and 6. Students above 6 are performing quite well compared to the norming group; students below 4 are not doing quite so well. One of the attractive features of the stanine is that it recognizes that all test scores contain a bit of error. Stanines, by pro-viding a general position in the group rather than a specific point, may be the best way to accommodate error in ranking students on achievement test performance. It is also a good score to discuss with parents, because a general placement of their child is usually more easily grasped than a more precise score.

These last score types—percentile ranks, standard scores, NCEs, and stanines—all have the advantage over grade equivalents of showing ranking within the norming group, rather than suggesting a child may be ranking in a class ahead or behind their grade level.

In sum, the information you and I get from achievement tests is useful to the extent that we can make sense out of the scores reported to us. It therefore is important that as potential users of these data we understand the meaning of scores that describe the skills of our students. This information will help us understand the limitations of scores as well as their utility.

Achievement test data are interesting topics to discuss with parents. With one table you can illustrate a child's performance in several areas of instruction. But which of the several scores should you use? The score reported to parents must be descriptive but sometimes not too detailed. Parents seem to grasp grade scores rather well, but make the mistake that a high or low score means the child is actually working beyond his or her grade level. You realize that Jerry, who is in the fifth-grade but gets a mathematics score of 8.6, is not working on eighth-grade topics. And Mabel, a classmate of Jerry's who gets a score of 3.8, is not doing third-grade problems. But Jerry and Mabel's par-ents may not understand this.

However, this confusion does not arise with stanine scores. A stanine for Jerry of 9 does not imply that he is working on topics well above his grade level. It simply says that he is a very capable student within his class. Also, stanines are not so narrow that they place a student at a specific point on a scale that may be notably influenced by error. Many teachers feel that when reporting to parents stanines are very useful because they describe the child's position in the norms group and provide the parent with a meaningful score. When explaining the stanine, begin by asking the parent to imagine that a large group of children in a given grade at a given point in time (such as spring) were divided into nine levels of achievement. The "average" level is 5. From this point parents usually do a fairly good job of understanding their child's achievement relative to his or her status in the group.

✎ Problems

1. Mrs. Jakes, mother of a fourth-grader was heard to say, "My Mabelee made a grade score of 7.1 in science on the Acme Achievement Tests. She's as good in science as a seventh-grader!" How would you respond to this comment?
2. Olivia, a fifth-grade student, has a stanine of 7 on her reading test. Interpret this sta-nine score to Olivia's father.

3. You want to show how students rank among a national sample in their class. What scoring system used by achievement testmakers would you select? Why?

Diagnostic Uses of Achievement Tests

Achievement tests are typically designed to be surveys of children's abilities in the basic curriculum areas. Some achievement tests, however, list in their manuals the items that assess particular subskills that make up a skill area. But this set of items is usually too short to be really diagnostic and contains too few items to be sufficiently reliable. For example, in some tests there may be as few as three or four items that deal with a given subskill. If the student makes a lucky guess, or a careless error, it could make a major difference in the score on this short set of items. Interpreting general achievement test scores must be limited to the primary function of the tests, that is, surveying basic skills.

Noting these problems with tests that attempted to be both surveys of skills as well as diagnostic, some test publishers have developed more reliable approaches to diagnosis. For example, the *Metropolitan Achievement Tests* provide not only a survey test across most curriculum areas, but also a separate set of *Diagnostic Tests* in reading, mathematics, and language. The survey tests provide general achievement scores in the curriculum areas, while the diagnostic tests provide a description of the pupil's strength and weakness in the skill area. This is accomplished by providing more tests in a given skill area (e.g., there are eleven different subtests in reading), and by providing enough test items in a skill area to give the tests some reliability. Also, the tests provide a criterion referenced scoring procedure. A list of the diagnostic tests provided by the *Metropolitan Achievement Tests* is given in Figure 16.5. (The Metropolitan tests are presented as an example of the attempts made by tests publishers to provide more than general survey

Visual Discrimination

Letter Recognition

Auditory Discrimination

Sight Vocabulary

Phoneme/Grapheme: Consonants

Phoneme/Grapheme: Vowel Test

Vocabulary in Contest

Word Part Clue Test

Rate of Comprehension

Skimming and Scanning

Reading Comprehension

FIGURE 16.5 *MAT6 Reading Diagnostic Tests.* There are six overlapping levels spanning kindergarten through grade nine, including 11 tests, though not all are used at all grade levels.

information on student achievement. Other testmakers also provide related assistance to teachers.)

In addition to the diagnostic testing provision, the Metropolitan tests help the teacher with instructional decisions. For example, the Instructional Reading Level can be determined for a child by comparing the criterion referenced reading comprehension score with a list of graded basal readers. The Instructional Mathematic Level can similarly be related to graded levels of mathematics books. Other instructional planning aids are also provided by the test authors. This includes planning not only for students who appear to have difficulty, but also for students who are at or above average levels.

In addition, imbedded in the tests in several subject areas are items that deal with the student's research skills. These items, when grouped together, provide a Research Skills Score. Similarly, a Higher Order Thinking Skills score is derived from items involving critical thinking in several subject-matter tests.

In conclusion, achievement tests in their survey form are not efficient diagnostic tools. However, publishers are providing supplemental tests for diagnosis of skill development problems, and are relating the scores to instructional decisions. Some publishers are recommending procedures that will help teachers deal with identified deficiencies. Additional testing, however, is time consuming and takes away from the hours that teachers would normally use to deal with those very instructional problems they are trying to solve.

The Teacher's Responsibility in Achievement Testing

Teachers must seek an active role in the achievement testing process because they are most qualified to deal with the many topics involved. Here are some areas in which teachers must take responsibility.

Roles for Teachers in Achievement Testing

1. Participate in selection of achievement tests.
2. Prepare the class for the tests.
3. Administer the test responsibly.
4. Debrief the class when all tests are finished.
5. Always be aware of functions for which achievement tests are useful and not useful.
6. Encourage administrators to educate the community about the purpose of achievement testing.

Let's take a closer look at each of these.

Teachers should seek greater involvement in the selection of achievement tests. The appropriateness of content is a fundamental consideration in choosing an achievement test. As a teacher who has been involved in defining objectives and has delivered the instruction to help children reach those objectives, you know best what the content of an achievement test should be.

However, content alone does not make a good achievement test. The care with which the test was constructed weighs heavily on test selection. In this regard, teachers need a more detailed grasp of the how achievement tests are put together, how norms samples are selected, and what the scores tell us. Does a test show such large standard errors of measurement that the scores are untrustworthy? Do the test publishers give the test too much credit for accuracy? Are teachers involved on test selection committees? Be prepared to ask informed questions on these topics.

Be sure that your instructional program prepares students for the tasks the achievement test asks them to perform. Achievement tests will not assess all of the objectives you have for your program. You have an obligation to your students to devote the time to teaching the skills that will be sampled by the test. However, do not concentrate so much on these skills that the test controls your instruction. Follow your table of specifications for your classes.

Days, possibly weeks, before the tests teachers should begin reviews of the subject areas that will be tested—reading skills, mathematics principles and problem solving, and so forth. However, let your objectives be the guide for the review. Intensive reviews are valuable ways to promote retention of subject matter, with or without an impending test. These reviews are designed to consolidate children's skills in the subject matter areas. Teaching specific items on a test probably will not improve a child's skills in general, and is therefore inappropriate as a review technique.

How do we know what skills the test will ask the children to perform? Test publishers routinely list their general objectives at each test level, and cite the items that assess attainment of these objectives. By noting the number of items per objective teachers can decide which general skills will appear prominently in the test and which will not. An example is shown in Figure 16.6, which details the "Usage" subtest in the "Usage and Expression" section of the *Iowa Tests of Basic Skills.* You can see that the usage section focuses more on Verb Forms than any other aspect of usage.

Reviews are presented so that students may approach their examinations confidently. Students should know what to expect in a school-wide testing operation—where they will

Part 1—Usage	Number of items level 10	Number of items level 12
Verb forms	8	7
Pronouns	3	3
Modifiers	0	2
Other linguistic conventions	5	6
Correct usage	3	3

The data reported are from *Guide to Test Content* RIVERSIDE 2000, Integrated Assessment Program, Riverside Publishing Company, Chicago, IL, 1993.

FIGURE 16.6   An illustration of the Content of One Subtest—Usage—Iowa Test of Basic Skills, Form K, Complete Battery

take the examinations, when, and who will administer them. Test-taking techniques should be reviewed along with the subject matter. It is also helpful to advise the children what the results will tell them, their parents, and the school. Briefly describe how the test results are used—program development, individual diagnosis (where feasible), and accountability. Note that motivation is typically stronger when students know how the results are to be applied.

Parental support during achievement testing is important, and parents should know that normal routines are being interrupted by the tests. Elicit their encouragement for their children, but advise them to avoid pressure. Students should be prepared for the examinations, and should take them seriously, but they do not need to be anxious about them.

If you are asked to participate in the administration of the tests, take this responsibility seriously. This means following directions carefully and generally reflecting a serious attitude. Even if you do not like or approve of achievement testing, carry off your duties in a professional manner. To do otherwise may be harming the students and could reflect on the school and on you as a professional. If you have concerns about achievement testing you should bring them to the attention of school officials, but outside the testing situation.

When the tests are over, "debrief" the class. How did they feel about the tests? What was hard? The teacher is looking for skills that may still need work in the next few weeks, skills not taught, or not learned well. What was easy? These topics students probably know well. A debriefing will act also as a closure for the exercise and clear the decks for "normal" classroom routines. Look for content, procedures, and events in the test that can be used as transitions to the class activities you planned for the time following the testing. This will bridge the test activities and the usual class routine.

Always keep in mind the functions for which achievement tests are useful, and the ones for which they are less useful. Achievement tests are broad surveys of some important educational outcomes. They are not intended to match our local program goals perfectly. They do not assess at all the learning outcomes teachers have pursued at the local level. Achievement tests focus on broad domains of content knowledge and their application. This is, of course, crucial material in any school program. For example, students must learn to read, to do mathematics, to know how governments operate. Standardized achievement testmakers have included these general areas in their tests.

But achievement tests are less valuable for measuring how well a student handles complex problems requiring integration of several areas of knowledge and involving work over a longer term. They tell us nothing about efficiency in creating a product, or of how a student contributes to a group solution of a complex problem. In fairness, the trend is to include more of this type of work in achievement tests. However, presently the tests do not target many items for assessing these valued outcomes.

Encourage the school administration to educate community members—people in the media, school board, city and county administrators—as to what achievement tests tell us, and what they do not. These people should be aware that achievement tests cover important knowledge, but are not the "be all and end all" of instructional assessment. These tests do not alone indicate "good" schools (when scores are high) nor "bad" ones (when scores are mediocre). They do not measure the skill of a given teacher. Community leaders should be aware of the purposes for which achievement tests are useful, and strengths in pursuing these purposes.

In sum, teachers have a role in preparing students for achievement tests and in debriefing them afterward. But their most important role is in understanding what an achievement test is and what it actually tells us. Only then can educators strip the unwarranted stature the public awards these tests and appropriately use the information they give us. Teachers must also participate in selecting tests with appropriate content, and should encourage the schools to educate the public what achievement tests can tell us. In the context of these conditions achievement tests can perform their best service.

✎ Problems

1. Jessica, a third-grade student, has a reading grade score of 3.2 and a 2.1 on the items that make up the word attack skills subscore. How much confidence can we have that Jessica has poor word attack skills? Why do you think so?
2. "Look at all these subscores!" said Miss Neumentor. "I don't have to worry about where my third-graders need help; its all right here in this diagnostic profile of this general achievement test." How would you respond to Miss Neumentor?
3. List and describe six responsibilities teachers have in achievement testing.

Applying Test Results

Ms. Harris was in the teachers lounge with Ms. Noteman. "I got my class results on the Iowa test yesterday," said Ms. Noteman. "I've looked them over pretty thoroughly, and I don't see what I can do with them as far as instruction is concerned." Ms. Harris paused, a look of serious concern on her face. "I've stopped trying to work that out," she said. "Honestly, I'm not even sure what all those numbers mean anymore."

This conversation could have taken place in any teacher's lounge across the country. Many teachers, when seeking to find more instructional direction in achievement tests, have been frustrated. Some of the more experienced ones have stopped looking for that kind of information. Although several achievement tests have made efforts to develop special diagnostic tests and have suggested methods for teachers to apply test scores to improving instruction, the fact is that general achievement tests are limited in their instructional orientation. The scores are primarily indicators of status, yet they are not entirely without value for instructional planning.

Achievement test results are reported once a year. This is not frequent enough to use effectively in support of many instructional decisions. However, a score report can guide the teacher in adjusting future emphasis among the various topics of instruction. For example, if my third-grade class average in word attack skills is low, I may wish to review my lesson plans to see if I have been neglecting these skills. I might also see that my class did well in computations, but not so well in problem solving. If so, in the long term I may wish to change my plans to accommodate this disparity in performance.

Although the general skill areas assessed by achievement tests are appropriate for most school programs, the subskill tests are often too short to assess the necessary behaviors or to be reliable for work with an individual child. However, across all children in the class these data may be useful in suggesting subskill areas that should be reviewed for changes in instruction and time allotments. However, keep in mind that general achievement tests are more likely to give you useful information for classwide planning than for use in diagnosing problems for an individual child. This alone is helpful to teachers in laying out instructional strategies.

Also, teachers can capitalize on the availability of achievement test results in their meetings with parents. The profile from a test provides an overview of a child's skills, as compared to a large sample of children in the same grade. Parents often ask, "Are my child's skills what they should be at this age?" A survey achievement test will often help us respond to this question, but we cannot depend on scores alone. In a conference, the teacher should be prepared to support conclusions with other exhibits of the child's work.

For curriculum planning, achievement tests provide the school's administration with useful data for researching program outcomes. Administrators must not only support budgets, personnel assignments, and schedules, but also must justify the school instructional program. Dr. Grosman, the superintendent of Hill County Schools, is appearing before the local school board. They are currently studying the allocation of funds for next year's budget. He is proposing to hire a mathematics curriculum supervisor for the coming biennium. The board president wants to know why he thinks this is needed.

Here is the superintendent's chance to use the achievement test data. He takes the results of the *Iowa Test of Basic Skills* out of his briefcase. The board members do not need a diagnostic profile, nor do they need discussions of instructional applications. They only need a status report of the students at various grade levels. The superintendent puts a transparency on the overhead projector and begins to point out how mathematics scores compare with scores in other subject areas. The board is impressed and agrees with Dr. Grosman that a mathematics curriculum supervisor should be hired.

An example of the use of tests in curriculum planning is given in Figure 16.7 (on page 320). Here we see a profile of the overall results of the achievement test scores. The curriculum supervisors study this profile and see where the low and high points are located. This information raises some questions. What are some viable causes for these lows and highs? What can be done to improve performance in the low ranking skills while maintaining the high ranking ones? The test results identify the problems. The local school must find the solutions in the context of their clientele, their teacher work-force, the parents, and curriculum resources.

Statewide Testing

State Superintendent of Public Education, Dr. Marya Jefe, is preparing to meet with a committee from her state legislature. She turns to her assistant. "On this proposal for change in mathematics curriculum requirements, what kind of statewide data do we have that shows mathematics work is lagging?" she asked. Her assistant shuffled through some papers and replied. "There are seven different achievement tests administered by school districts across the state. The most commonly used test is the *Metropolitan*

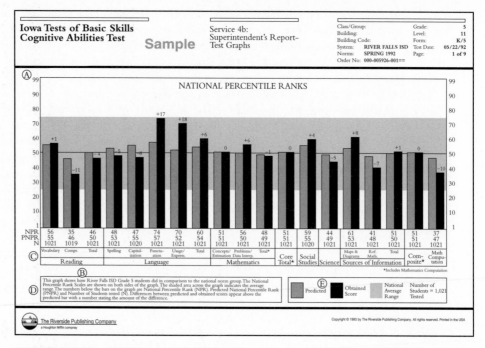

FIGURE 16.7   Profile of a School Based on the *Iowa Tests of Educational Development*

Achievement Tests, used by 41 districts. But 22 of these give it in the fall, 17 give it in the spring and two give it at mid-year. Of the 22 who give it in the fall, eight give it to grades three, six, and nine; ten schools give it to grades two, four, and six, while four districts give it every year through sixth-grade. Of the 17 who give it in the spring we have . . ."

"Yes, yes!" Dr. Jefe interrupted. "I get the point—we really have no test that is used widely across the state at one time of the year in the same grades. In this situation I really have no substantial data to fall back on, do I?"

This story illustrates one major reason states have begun developing testing programs to be applied in all school districts across their commonwealths. Characteristically, state legislatures need data on which to build education programs. However, in most states no such data were available, and consequently, they depended on testimony from different educators. Conclusions from these reports were difficult to use. All educators do not represent the same philosophy about teaching and learning, nor do they look at the same outcomes when evaluating learning. As a result, testimonies presented a collection of opinions, often conflicting in principle and in conclusion. States needed objective data.

By 1993 almost all states were using some form of statewide testing.* Many state legislatures wondered how well students were meeting basic achievement standards, and

---

*The information provided here on statewide testing was taken from Bond, L. and Roeher, E. (1993). 1993 Summary of State Testing Programs, *State Student Assessment Program Database, 1992–1993,* North Central Regional Educational Laboratory, Oakbrook, Il.

this information was not forthcoming from the usual achievement testing programs used by local schools. Hence, statewide testing began to emerge. Because minimum proficiency was the focus, criterion referenced testing was a favored format for a number of states. However, about half of the states have continued to use norm referenced testing in their programs. Some states are using a combination of both.

Because of the volume of tests to be scored, select-type tests were initially chosen. Machine scoring could be applied to speed up the turnaround time in reporting to schools. Some experimentation has been done with performance assessment, and most states have adopted performance approaches as a part of their tests. The most common type of performance assessment is essay writing in response to specific prompts. At this writing, two states, Kentucky and Vermont, have strongly emphasized performance assessment for statewide testing.

The most common statewide testing programs are limited to reading and mathematics. This is followed by reading, mathematics, and writing. Less than half of the states using statewide testing assess skills in as many areas as reading, mathematics, writing, social studies, and science. Clearly, the focus of statewide testing is on the basic skills.

States report a variety of reasons for employing statewide testing. The most common of these reasons are accountability, improvement of instruction, and program evaluation. Some states use statewide testing to provide student or school recognition, and less than half use the data in determining qualifications for graduation.

How states will evaluate their assessment programs is yet to be seen. Is it improving teaching and learning in the states? Only time will tell. In the face of the expense and effort involved, some legislatures are impatient for the verdict.

Constructing Statewide Tests

Every state has worked out a set of curriculum guidelines for each level of the educational ladder. But the items in commercially published tests designed for use across the nation may not closely fit the state guidelines. Historically, local school professionals have differed as to which of the published tests are best for local needs. Because of this, state legislatures have widely endorsed the development of their own tests to assess how well the children in their jurisdictions are meeting the objectives in the state guidelines for achievement. These are known as **statewide tests.**

State curriculum committees typically determine the content objectives for each grade's test. The curriculum experts and psychometrics specialists develop a set of test items in each of the areas to be tested. These items are carefully edited and prepared for field trial. The field trial results suggest some alterations, and the outright elimination of some items. From the items that clear the field trial, the curriculum committees select a set that most closely match the state study guide. These are put into the test to be administered across the state.

Not all states follow this general plan of test development. Some of them take their content objectives to commercial testmakers who have very large banks of test items which can be sorted to approximately fit a given state's guidelines and topical content specifications. The company selects the items to match the state's requirements and arranges them into a test format. These items do not need to be field tested because they have already been used by the company in various circumstances over the years.

Whether tests are totally created by a state, or with the assistance of a commercial test company, one important feature emerges: the statewide test is fitted to the state curriculum guide more closely than any one of the commercial tests on the market. This is the intent of state mandates, and the intent appears to be in the most part achieved. But because curriculum content varies a bit from school district to school district, state tests do not match perfectly the instructional objectives of each school district.

In some states, the legislature only wants to know what portion of children are doing work appropriate for their grade level. This calls for a criterion referenced test, in which test items are selected to represent grade level work and where work notably above or below grade level is not given much attention. The outcome is a statement about what proportion of students are achieving up to the expected level for their grade.

As you review the steps in constructing statewide testing programs, you see a similarity here to standardized achievement tests. They will, for the most part, meet the requirements of standardized tests quite well. However, because of the many variations in state testing procedures it is difficult to make a generalization about the adequacy of all statewide testing.

One further point must be made in reference to state mandated tests. Occasionally a strong political lobby will have an agenda item for public schools. An example of this is the controversy over evolution or creationism. Agenda items may show up in required content for a part of the test. To the extent that test content guides instruction, statewide tests can motivate instruction that involves a political agenda. School professionals, and the public they serve, should be wary of this possibility.

National Testing Plans

Federal policymakers are in the same position as state legislatures. They have no single source of data on national achievement in basic school subjects areas. When policy issues arise, where does a member of Congress go for information? The "Goals 2000" proposal that sets standards to be achieved in schools to be reached by the turn of the century, specifies assessment to ensure that the goals are being reached. As a result national assessment procedures are being developed.

The National Assessment of Educational Progress (NAEP) is a program that selects a sample of schools across the United States, and every two years administers tests at these sites. Tests are given in many learning areas: reading and writing, mathematics, science, citizenship, literature, social studies, career development, art, music, history, geography, computers, life skills, health, and energy. This is a long list of skills, but not all schools will take all tests. Because the federal policymakers want to know how many children have reached a defined criterion of success in these areas, the tests lean heavily on the criterion referenced approach. Most of the testing is done on children who are 9-, 13-, and 17-years-old, with some older students involved, too.

Scores are reported by geographical region, by gender, race, and ethnic background. Some effort is being made to develop state-by-state data. However, because it may lead to gross comparisons between states, reasonable resistance has arisen. Such comparisons could lead to erroneous conclusions unless all factors that contribute to academic success are known and weighted into the comparison. Legislators and educators do not know all these factors, and those that are known are not likely to receive much attention in the comparison.

At this point you might be asking, "What has this to do with me as a teacher?" Well, as a teacher your school could be asked to participate in the NAEP data collection. Do you want to be involved? If you do not know what NAEP is, you may quickly decline. Your state may soon be involved in the state-by-state comparison. Does NAEP data warrant valid conclusions about your state's status among the 49 others? Is such a comparison useful to you as a local teacher in a state system? Some educators believe that tests determine what the curriculum will be. In a nation where states control the education of their citizens, what might be the consequences of a national curriculum springing out of NAEP data?

Schools generally lean toward including in a curriculum the skills on which their children will be tested, hence the saying that "tests lead the curriculum." If a national test begins to define a national curriculum, will the national test support a political agenda? As a professional educator you must be prepared to respond to such questions.

Testing Skills in Special Areas

In this chapter the focus has been on the broad survey-type achievement test. However, there are many tests aimed at achievement in special skills. For example, some schools use reading readiness tests to see if children have the skills believed to be prerequisite to beginning reading instruction. There are achievement tests in the English language, in foreign languages, in mathematics, and in vocational areas. Special tests have been published for the screening of students with special learning problems. For almost any skill area there is an achievement test. For reviews of these, look in the *Mental Measurement Yearbook,* or see publisher's catalogs.

This chapter will not examine these tests because they each have a limited audience. However, at this point you are prepared to do a creditable job of researching and evaluating any type of achievement test. The important thing to remember in dealing with tests of achievement in the special skills areas is that they require evidence of validity and reliability just like other achievement tests. Also, the same basic advantages and limitations apply to these as are true for general achievement tests. Most special skills tests follow the same general procedures in test development, and most use a scoring system like those found in general achievement tests or a variation of it. If you have a good grasp of the ideas that apply to general achievement tests you will be able to evaluate a test in a special achievement area.

Because considerable space would be needed to deal with assessment of skills of special needs children, it is recommended that those who are interested in this area consult books devoted to that topic. Two such books are cited at the end of this chapter in the Additional Reading section.

A REAL CASE NARRATIVE

At Heritage Elementary school, the principal has decided that a committee should look at the findings of their achievement tests and come up with some ideas about program. Here is a narrative taken from the teachers' committee. As a consultant to this committee how would you advise them?

"Well, one thing I know from these printouts on the achievement test—I've got to change a lot of my emphasis in teaching science. My kids did terribly on the test," said Ms. Caldwell.

"I'm with Betty on that one, but in my case it was the Usage test in grammar that took my class down. I've started redoing some lessons in that area already," agreed Mr. Rodman.

"Wait a minute!" broke in Mr. Hight, "These tests aren't that important. I think I know what I should be teaching, and that's how I have been teaching and will continue to do it that way!" he said rapping on the table with each point.

"What gets me is all these numbers they pour on you!" Ms. Estaban said changing the subject. "NCEs, stanines, percentile ranks—what does it say, and why do we need this many scores to tell us how the students did?" She took a deep breath, "I really don't know what any of them tell us, do you?" She glanced around the room for looks of agreement.

After a pause, Mr. Brown said, "We spent three days on these tests—for what? I'd rather be teaching during that time."

"Wait a minute," broke in Dr. Wilcox, the curriculum director. "We are here to come up with some applications, not to trash the tests—let's do it! There's a lot of good stuff in these data sheets, we just have to find out how to get it out."

SUMMARY

1. Constructing an achievement test is a complex process involving an intense review of subject content at each grade level, development of a large item pool, field testing and item analysis, professional editing and formatting, and norming.

2. Standardized tests differ from teacher-made tests in that they involve specialists in content and psychometrics, are fitted to general subject content rather than to specific classroom objectives, and in the extent to which each has trial data for test refinement.

3. General achievement tests used widely in elementary schools survey, at a minimum, reading skills, mathematics, and written expression, while complete batteries also include tests in science, social studies, and occasionally complex reasoning.

4. In secondary schools students diverge into different school programs; therefore students have less specific training in a given skill area than is true in elementary school. For this reason tests in the secondary area are broader in scope.

5. General achievement tests are best used as surveys of skills, not as diagnostic tools.

6. Most achievement tests report grade-equivalent scores, percentile ranks based on students in the norming group, standard scores, normal curve equivalents, and stanines.

7. Although achievement tests are not designed to be diagnostic, publishers are developing tests that can be used to identify a pupil's strengths and weaknesses in skill areas.

8. Teachers should assume responsibility in the selection of achievement tests, should prepare their classes for the test, administer the tests responsibly, debrief the class after testing, be aware of the functions for which the tests are (and are not) useful, and encourage school officials to educate the community members about the meaning of achievement test outcomes.

9. General achievement tests are not well suited to helping teachers in their planning of classroom activities, but they are useful in curriculum planning on a schoolwide basis, adjusting emphasis among subjects, and identifying skill areas that should be the focus of added attention. They also provide information for support of budgetary allocations.

10. Statewide testing has emerged to provide state policymakers information about the status of achievement in school work across their state. Criterion referencing is often used in statewide testing. Statewide tests are constructed much like standardized tests.

11. To provide nationwide information on the achievement of students across the country, a movement for testing at many locations across the nation is forming. Currently, the instrument for this purpose comes from the National Educational Assessment Program.

PROBLEMS

1. How is the creating of an achievement test like that of a teacher-made test? In what ways is it different?

2. List some functions for which an achievement test should be used and some for which it should not.

3. Not all teachers feel the time and effort invested in achievement tests is well spent. What constructive advice would you give these teachers?

4. Katilyn has a grade-equivalent score of 4.7 in mathematics. She is in the third-grade at the eighth month. Can she really do fourth-grade mathematics? What does this grade equivalent tell us about her mathematics ability?

5. George, a sixth-grader, reached the 75th percentile rank in reading. What does this tell us about his reading ability?

6. Marta, a ninth grader, has a stanine score in science of 8. What does this say about her science ability?

7. What was the impetus for developing statewide testing programs? For the emergence of the NAEP? As a local school representative, what is your response to these tests.

KEY TERMS

achievement tests   extrapolation
battery   scaled scores
jangle fallacy   statewide tests
grade equivalent score   NAEP
interpolation

ADDITIONAL READING

Airasian, P. W. (1979). A perspective on the uses and misuses of standardized achievement tests. *NCME Measurement in Education,* 10 (3), 1–12.

Floden, R. E., Porter, A. C., Schmidt, W. H., and Freeman, D. J. (1980). Don't they all measure the same thing? Consequences of selecting standardized tests. In E. Baker and E. Quellmalz (Eds.), *Educational Testing and Evaluation: Design, Analysis and Policy.* Beverly Hills, CA: Sage, pp. 109–120.

Mehrens, W. A. (1984). National tests and local curriculum: Match or mismatch? *Educational Measurement: Issues and practices,* 3 (3), 9–15.

The following two textbooks are recommended for reading about formal assessment with special needs children.

Salvia, J. and Ysseldyke, J. (1991). *Assessment in Special Remedial Education,* 5th ed. Boston: Houghton Mifflin, Chapter 16 for selecting screening devices; Chapters 17, 18, and 21 for diagnostic testing in reading and mathematics.

Taylor, R. L. *Assessment of Exceptional Children: Educational and Psychological Procedures,* 3d ed. Allyn & Bacon, 1993.

CHAPTER 17

ASSESSING GENERAL ACADEMIC AND SPECIAL APTITUDES

"I don't know what to do for Gena!" Ms. Tolivar said to the Irvin Junior High School principal. "She seems sharp enough but keeps falling behind even though she works hard. I have her folder here, but these aptitude scores—what do they tell me? I don't even recognize the names of the tests, leave alone how to interpret their scores!"

This chapter will cover most of what Ms. Tolivar wants to find out about Gena's aptitude test records and what they mean for Gena's instruction.

What This Chapter Will Include. In this chapter you and I will look at the following topics that relate aptitude to educational decisions. You will learn about:

1. The concept of aptitude
2. Aptitude for academic work
3. Achievement and aptitude
4. Uses of academic aptitude tests in school
5. Academic aptitude tests scores and their meaning
6. Types of academic aptitude tests
7. Aptitude tests and teacher responses to students
8. Coaching students to do better on academic aptitude tests
9. Other aptitude assessments for school use
10. A word about college aptitude tests

The Concept of Aptitude

An **aptitude** is the potential for acquiring a skill. For example, you may wish to assess a student's aptitude for mechanical work. In this case, you are not asking how well he or she can overhaul a machine right now, or knowledge of how a motor works, or what the student knows about putting a bridge together. You are asking instead to what extent do you expect that student to profit from a training session in mechanical skills and knowledge. It is this potential for acquiring a particular skill that characterizes aptitude.

Aptitude assessment has long been a goal of psychologists who have studied the educational performance of children. The first successful attempt to put together a set of tasks to show general aptitude for learning was done the Frenchman, **Alfred Binet** (pronounced Bin-AYE). His tasks included comprehension, making judgments, maintaining a mental set, and perceiving and correcting errors. He actually did a rudimentary standardization on his tests and subsequently ranked his items by the difficulty level appropriate for children at various ages (Binet & Simon, 1905).

Lewis Terman brought the Binet scales to America and revised them to fit the American culture. He also incorporated the idea of **IQ** or intelligence quotient.* But these tests could be given to only one person at a time, and are therefore called individual tests. When World War I broke out the federal government needed to classify quickly the aptitudes of many thousands of men. Aptitude tests were at that point converted to group, objectively scored tests. (Currently, both individual and group tests are in use in American schools.)

Early in the century, when intelligence tests came into use, there were two theories of the construct widely seen in the professional literature. The first theory aggregated all of the reasoning and perceptual skills into a single aptitude. This aptitude was called "general intelligence." If you were good in one kind of subskill, you were likely to be good in others. The overriding trait for all cognitive functions was **general intelligence,** or the **"g" factor.**

From this idea, the testmakers built different kinds of items that together produced one score representing general intelligence. This led to the idea that students could be tracked in terms of how quickly they could acquire the necessary academic skills.

Opponents of this idea believed that intelligence was composed of a half-dozen distinct and separate aptitudes for such skills as number, verbal, space, speed of reasoning, and so forth. These separate performance areas were called **group factors.** One could be very good in some skills but not so good in others. Aptitude was specific to the separate mental domains. Tests contained a subtest for each one of the separate aptitudes and produced no overall score, only one score for each subtest. This gave schools a different base for program planning. Tracking was not seen as a logical procedure because the student who was good in number skills may not do so well in verbal skills or in spatial work, such as developing maps and graphs.

Early work on general aptitude tests characterized this trait as a general skill. However, this position regarding general aptitude was described as too simplistic, and a more complex model was proposed (Guilford, 1959) which expanded mental operations to include "three faces of intellect":

1. Content (figural, symbolic, semantic, and behavioral)
2. Product (units classes relations, systems transformations, implications)
3. Operations (evaluations, convergent production, divergent production, memory, cognition)

---

*Tests of mental aptitude are often referred to by laypersons as "IQ" tests. This is technically an error; the IQ is only a number, and as such cannot be tested.

If there is any agreement by psychologists it is in favor of the general, broad aptitude for learning. (Wall Street Journal, 12/13/94).

Additional ideas about the nature of aptitudes have emerged in the last half of the century, but they still do not present procedures that are particularly useful in planning school routines. To complicate the matter, a great debate has evolved over the origin of aptitudes. Are they innate, or do collective experiences play the major role in their development? This query continues to be unresolved. It presses heavily on the question of differences between social classes and between racial groups.

How Should Teachers Deal With the Controversy?

For teachers, these debates about how general aptitudes are constructed are useful only in that they suggest ways to view learning abilities. Teachers cannot spend time pondering whether aptitude is based on heredity or environment. They must deal with children on a daily basis with whatever aptitude each child happens to bring to the class. The basis for a child's aptitude is not something educators can change in the classroom during a day's lessons. Instead, teachers must plan their class's instruction utilizing the current potential of each pupil. Worrying about heredity or environment will not help a teacher in his instruction today.

Without substantial theory, publishers tend to be pragmatic in developing aptitude tests. They begin with questions such as: What ability is required for moving achievement ahead to more advanced levels? Additionally, what test items reflect this ability, and consequently predict success in increasingly complex instruction? Will this set of items help teachers make better instructional decisions? To the extent that these questions have answers that are acceptable to educators, the test will have validity as an academic aptitude test.

Academic Aptitude

The general aptitude tests that first appeared in schools were often referred to as intelligence tests. However, educational psychologists have seen that the broader concepts of intelligence are at present only marginally helpful to teachers. Moreover, since many (if not most) of the tests were validated on school learning, the tests could not be promoted as samples of the broad spectrum of behaviors thought to characterize general intelligence.

As a result, the tests that emerged from this intelligence prototype became identified as **academic aptitude** or equivalently, scholastic aptitude tests. When you look over the content of these aptitude tests it is clear that these names are much better descriptions of the tasks the tests ask students to perform than is "intelligence." Also, descriptions of validation in the test manuals show that testmakers widely use school learning for their criterion of cognitive development. For example, the manuals report the extent to which aptitude test scores correlate with achievement test scores. We find no validation data on how quickly a child acquires "street smarts," or how rapidly the child adapts to new environments, or demonstrates creativity. The tests focus on the ability to acquire academic skills, and items that do not relate to this ability have been eliminated by test publishers. Therefore, the names of academic aptitude or scholastic aptitude are the appropriate titles for these tests.

Achievement vs. Aptitude

Achievement tests are intended to measure what a student has learned, while aptitude tests measure the ability to learn new skills not yet attempted. This distinction, although it appears to separate the two concepts, is in practice too simple. There is an overlap in what the two tests measure. All aptitude tests involve material the student has already learned, and all achievement tests involve aptitude-like tasks, such as abstract reasoning on new problems the student has not faced before. There is a clear overlap in the content of the two types of tests.

The principal difference in aptitude tests and achievement tests is in the performances required by each test. Achievement tests are most likely to ask students to perform tasks related to instructional objectives. Aptitude tests are most likely to involve many problem-solving situations not based on specific instructional programs. Further, they do not purposively sample the instructional content. Aptitude tests do indeed rely on school learning to provide the vehicle for presenting problems. Children who take a typical aptitude test must read, know something about numbers, have had some experience with geometric shapes. But the specific problem-types in aptitude tests are not part of any specific instructional program delivered by schools.

Now, having agreed that this is so, you and I must look at both types of tests and make some further observations. If we should rank aptitude tests in terms of how much they are like achievement tests, we would find that some rely heavily on school learning. Their problems, although more general, are similar to those of achievement tests. An example of this type of test is the *Cognitive Abilities Test* (CogAT). According to the publishers the skills required by the test are "influenced by experiences both in and outside of school," and are "closely related to an individual's success in school. . . "[*] A similar statement is made by the publisher of the *Test of Cognitive Skills* (TCS/2).[†]

Tests, such as the CogAT and the TCS, reflect success in schools because many of their problems are presented in a context of school-like materials and depend on verbal and mathematical reasoning, similar in some ways to problems children have experienced in school.

So aptitude tests seen in schools depend on school learning for context for their problems. Is this entirely bad? Probably not. To the extent that the scores are used for predicting school learning, what will predict Ronald's achievement next year better than a test of general cognitive skills that have something in common with his previous school work?

One way to look at the differences between achievement and aptitude is without focusing on the names of the tests, because the names may not accurately describe what the tests measure. (You will recall from the last chapter that this was called the "jangle

---

[*] *Form 5, CogAT Directions for Administration, Levels A–H,* p. 1. © 1993, by The Riverside Publishing Company. All rights reserved. No part of this work may be reproduced or transmitted in any form or by any means, electronic or mechanical, including photocopying and recording, or by any information storage or retrieval system without the prior written permission of The Riverside Publishing Company unless such copying is expressly permitted by federal copyright law. Address inquiries to Permissions, The Riverside Publishing Company, 425 Spring Lake Drive, Itasca Illinois 60143-2079.
[†] *TCS/2, Test of Cognitive Skills/Second edition, Technical Report,* Monterey, CA: CTB Macmillan McGraw-Hill, 1993, p.5.

fallacy.") Instead, consult the test manual and look at the test items themselves. The point is that achievement and aptitude tests have overlap, but the degree of overlap varies with the nature of the tasks required by the aptitude tests.

Here are illustrations of that point. The *Metropolitan Achievement Tests* assess knowledge of "all areas of the general curriculum—reading, language, mathematics, science, and social studies."[*] Achievement tests, such as the Metropolitan, are intended to assess basic knowledge in the content areas of the "typical" school curriculum.

On the other hand, aptitude tests attempt to assess ability to profit from instruction. For example, the manual that accompanies the *Cognitive Abilities Test* (CogAT)[†] notes that the development of the cognitive abilities measured by this test are influenced by both informal and formally planned experiences. The test has a strong orientation toward reasoning, with tests in analogies, number series, and equation building. One section is "nonverbal," including classification of figures and spatial analogies. Sample items from the CogAT are shown in Figure 17.1 as an example of what you will find in aptitude tests.

The tests in the CogAT do not appear to replicate the content of achievement tests, though much of the context (reading, vocabulary, numbers) is taken out of

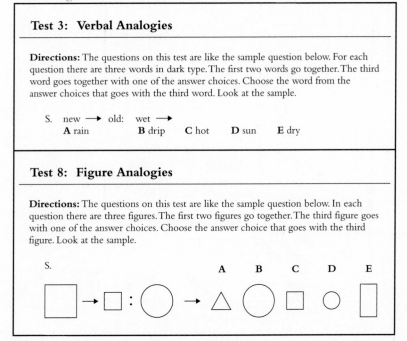

FIGURE 17.1   Sample of a Verbal and a Figural Aptitude Item from the CogAT. (by permission from the Riverside Publishing Co.)

instructional content. It is then put into reasoning-type problems, in part like, and in part unlike, those which children work in school and consequently like those found in achievement tests.

The *Test of Cognitive Skills* (TCS/2) also has some overlap in content with achievement tests. It is made up of sequences, analogies, memory, and verbal reasoning. These are tests that in context of problems are similar to those found in regular school work. However, they do not replicate the material assessed in achievement tests. They are a step away from measuring achievement directly. For example, the memory test uses words, but in some of the test levels the "words" are nonsense, rather than real words. This type of test construction in aptitude tests separates them from any objective of normal classroom work.

A very few aptitude tests have almost no overlap in content with achievement tests. An example of this is the **Culture Fair Intelligence Test.**[*] Here the entire test is presented in geometric figures to manipulate—no reading, vocabulary, or numbers—the purpose of which is to involve exercises that do not require languages so cultural differences are not the source of disparities in test scores. The tasks may assess problem solving and abstract reasoning, but they are a far cry from the exercises that are part of a school instructional program. An example of items from this test is given in Figure 17.2.

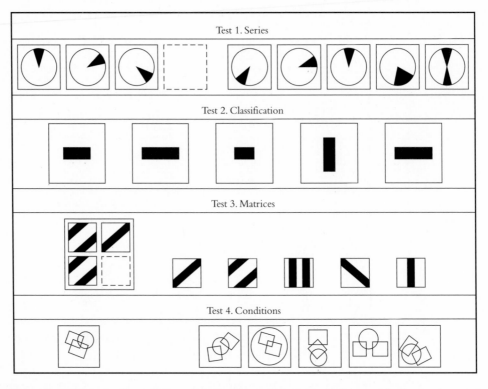

FIGURE 17.2   Sample Items from *Culture Fair Intelligence Test,* Scale 2. (Copyright by Institute of Personality and Ability Testing.)

[*]*Culture Fair Intelligence Test,* Champaign, IL: Institute for Personality and Ability Testing, 1974.

TABLE 17.1   Curriculum Dependence of Achievement and Aptitude Tests

Prototypical test	Curricular dependence
Metropolitan Achievement Tests	Substantial dependence
Cognitive Abilities Test (CogAT)	Moderate dependence
Test of Cognitive Skills/2	Moderate dependence
Culture Fair Intelligence Test	Slight curricular dependence

In sum, there is no clear separation point between achievement and aptitude test-ing. Rather the distinction is one of degree of difference in the operations required by each test. Table 17.1 is an illustration of this. Beginning with the *Metropolitan Achieve-ment Tests* whose content samples the instructional programs of schools, we move on to the CogAT and the TCS/2 aptitude tests. The items in these aptitude tests continue to have some overlap in content with school instruction. But this is much less true of the *Culture Fair Intelligence Test.* This test has almost no school-based tasks in it.

The real value of an aptitude test for educators is its ability to predict achievement in various areas of study. Therefore, the tests that have some overlap with school opera-tions are likely to produce the most impressive results. Some overlap is probably an advantage in this case.

The overlap in the functions measured is shown in correlations between the acad-emic aptitude test and achievement test data. Here are some examples of those correla-tions. The *Test of Cognitive Skills* total score correlates in the .55 to .65 range (for the most part) with the tests in the *California Test of Basic Skills.* The *Otis Lennon School Abil-ity Test* shows similar correlations for many subtests on the *Metropolitan Achievement Tests.* The correlations with total reading and mathematics run a bit higher.

These correlations show that in function the aptitude and achievement tests have a moderate amount of overlap, a point in favor of aptitude tests. If the aptitude scores are to predict achievement, they must show definite correlations with the achievement test data.

✎ Problems

1. Define aptitude and achievement.
2. Suppose you were going to make an academic aptitude test. Would you want it to utilize some academic skills (like reading and numbers), or would you want it to be completely distinct from school-like skills? Explain.
3. Describe the content of a "typical" academic aptitude test and relate this to school instructional content.

Reliability of Academic Aptitude Tests

Ms. Dahlquest is looking over the record folder for Henri and finds an aptitude test score. "Ahh!" she muses, "that's pretty good! I wonder how stable the score is? If we tested him again would he get about the same, or quite a different score?" She scans other data in the folder and comes back to the academic aptitude test. "Unless I can feel confident that the score is stable, I can't put much stock in this estimate of Henri's ability," she thought. "I guess this means a trip to the test manual to look up reliability!"

Ms. Dahlquist is likely to find that academic aptitude tests are characteristically quite reliable. Although some run only in the high .70s to the .80s, others run up into the low .90s. The subtests on an academic aptitude measure will typically have less reliability than the total test. We want the tests we use to have reliabilities into the .80 to .90 range if possible. The higher the reliability, the smaller will be the standard error of measurement (see Chapter 5) and the more confidence I will have that the score for Henri is very close to his true aptitude.

An example of the reliability of an aptitude test is shown in Table 17.2, which presents the data from the manual of the *Test of Cognitive Skills/2.* Because this is a test-retest approach to reliability, the data are given on both the first (pre) and the second (post) tests. The "r" stands for the reliability of the tests. You recall from Chapter 4 that these correlations run from 0.00 to 1.00. The closer the value comes to 1.00, the closer is the relation between the first and second tests. That is, the larger the coefficient, the nearer your position in the group on the first test is to your position on the second test.

Remember that with fairly high reliabilities the student's score gives me a pretty good idea where the student actually stands in the group. The data in Table 17.2 are a typical report by testmakers documenting the reliabilities of their field test.

Applications of Academic Aptitude Tests

Aptitude and achievement tests both can be used to predict success in schoolwork. What data will better predict Jolie's future success than the scores she made on her last achievement tests? Here the prediction is based on the assumption that activities in the next school year will be very much like those of the previous school year. Achievement tests can also provide data in specific content areas such as reading and mathematics.

TABLE 17.2   Two Week Test-Retest Reliabilities for the Total Score on the *Test of Cognitive Skills/2.* (From *TCS/2, Tests of Cognitive Skills/Second Edition, Technical Report,* Monterey, CA: CTB Macmillan/McGraw-Hill, 1993.)

| Grade | Level | N | Pretest | | | Posttest | |
			Mean	SD	$r^\star$	Mean	SD
			Total Test				
2	1	385	402.2	46.7	0.84	419.0	44.7
4	2	346	446.4	50.4	0.90	462.3	50.0
6	3	355	482.9	46.2	0.85	493.4	52.1
8	4	258	496.9	50.5	0.88	514.0	54.4
10	5	555	531.0	56.9	0.83	540.7	61.2
11	6	479	533.5	53.2	0.75	540.8	67.2

*r = test-retest reliability

These scores can be applied to predict success in those same areas for the coming year. Jolie's score in reading achievement is a good indicator of what she will do in reading in the coming months.

The focus of aptitude tests varies from this specific curriculum orientation. Aptitude tests focus on general cognitive skills that are believed to relate to the learning of academic skills. As a result, they tend to be less closely correlated with specific academic subskills than are achievement tests. In this context they have several applications that give them a niche in the collection of information. For example, if you have no achievement history on a given child (e.g., a transfer student), an aptitude test can be administered in a relatively short time—about an hour. The scores can be used to predict a child's achievement and a reasonable placement for that child can be on hand rather quickly.

Aptitude tests can also be used with students who come from a variety of backgrounds and have been taught by widely different methods. The content of aptitude tests tend to contain situations that are not specifically curriculum based. That is, they do not require a good fit with a given school program and therefore can give us the information we need to assist placing the child.

Some academic aptitude tests produce scores on nonverbal as well as verbal subtests. This separation may be helpful for assessing the skill of children who are nonnative speakers or have other language limitations. Their lack of skill in English should not appreciably reduce their ability to perform on the nonverbal subtest. Differences between the verbal and nonverbal subtests are often used to assess just how much language difficulty affects the child's success in different curriculum areas. However, before you and I place too much confidence in this difference between the verbal and nonverbal subtests we should inspect the content of the subtests, especially that of the nonverbal one. In some cases a substantial amount of verbal ability is required to do the so-called nonverbal problems. Teachers should always be sensitive to the jangle fallacy in dealing with all tests.

Aptitude tests have a role in curricular planning in the central school administration. Shall the school devote more money to programs for talented students? Does the school system need more faculty to deal with students who have special learning problems? Are the materials provided appropriately challenging for students? These questions are relevant to the results of achievement as well as aptitude tests.

Aptitude data also have a role in the selection of textbook series and in supporting curricular materials. If the mean aptitude score is below the average of the norms group, educators may wish to look at books that illustrate concrete examples, are more heavily illustrated, and contain more examples of the child's practical experience. On the other hand, if the mean aptitude score is clearly above the average for the norms group, books that are more abstract, that involve more references for additional reading and illustration, and involve more complex examples and problems to solve may be appropriate.

Also, educators and parents are constantly interested in whether their children are working up to their ability. Aptitude test data may provide this information. For parent conferences teachers need corroborating data to support their claims that Kevin is not working up to par, or that it would be inadvisable to place Mai in the accelerated science program. However, advising parents about aptitude data is risky, at best. Leave this to specialists.

It should be noted that in dealing with a single child that the rates at which aptitudes develop are not constant over the years. Think of a bucket whose size and contents vary as the years go by. This is an appropriate analogy for a given child's aptitude (Honzik, Macfarlane, & Allen, 1949). Jona, who is not doing as well this year as last, may do much better next year—or worse. Changes in aptitude are like other human characteristics—they are not as constant from year to year as the general public may believe them to be.

Specialists, such as school psychologists, help teachers diagnose a given child's learning difficulties. These specialists use various assessment procedures including aptitude tests, and will advise the teacher regarding a child's learning skills. To fully capitalize on the information the specialists provide, teachers need a broad grasp of the type of instruments the specialists use. However, the interpretation of diagnostic tests is done by the specialist, not the teacher.

Aptitude tests results are also helpful for counselors in planning programs and in assisting students with career selection. Occasionally, counselors may wish to consult with teachers for corroborating information. Again, it is useful for the teachers to have a grasp of the nature of aptitude tests and the applications for which they are best used.

Aptitude Test Scores

When you looked at achievement tests you found a variety of scores to tell you how well the child performed on the tests. Academic aptitude testmakers provide a similar variety. In fact several closely resemble the scores on achievement tests. For example, the *Cognitive Abilities Test* provides percentile ranks and stanines by age and grade. You interpret these scores essentially the way you interpreted them for achievement tests.

The CogAT also reports a **standard age score** or (SAS) This score is found by converting scores at any given age to standard scores. When you and I discussed standardized scores, it was noted that we could create a standard score scale that would have any mean and standard deviation we wanted. Here the CogAT testmakers converted their scores to a mean of 100, and a standard deviation of 16. This means that on a bell-shaped, normal distribution, Chang, a 9 year old who has a score of 116 (mean plus one standard deviation), ranks above 84 percent of the children at that age in the norms group. This conclusion is the same for any score that is one standard deviation above the mean in a normal distribution. Julian who has a score of 68 (two standard deviations below the mean) will be above about 2 percent of the norms group. (If these figures are not clear please review the discussion of the bell curve in Chapter 14). An example of the scores provided by the CogAT are shown in a score report in Figure 17.3.

The *Test of Cognitive Skills* (TCS/2) also provides several different scores, but a unique addition is their **anticipated achievement score.** This score tells teachers, based on the aptitude test data, what a child's achievement test scores are predicted to be in each of the basic skills. To utilize these anticipated scores, one must use the *California Achievement Tests,* or the *Comprehensive Tests of Basic Skills.* Many teachers will find these anticipated achievement scores useful. However, if you wish to use these scores remember that they are predictions from a test score. All test scores, including predicted

Cognitive Abilities Tests	N Att.	Raw Score	Age Scores		Grade Scores	National Grade Percentile Rank			
			SAS	NPR	NPR	Low 1 10 25	Average 50	75	High 90 99
Verbal	75	56	108	69	71	████████████████			
Quantitative	60	54	126	95	95	████████████████████████			
Nonverbal	65	51	116	84	87	██████████████████████			
Composite	200	161	117	83	84	█████████████████████			

N Att = Number Attempted, SAS = Standard Age Score, NPR = National Percentile Rank.

FIGURE 17.3   Report of One Student's Scores on the *Cognitive Abilities Test/2*. (©1993 by The Riverside Publishing Company. Reproduced from Riverside Publishing Company Catalog, page 134, with permission of the publisher. All rights reserved.)

scores, contain some error. Take them as a general estimate, not as the definite point where the child's achievement should be.

A Word About IQ (Intelligence Quotient)

Academic aptitude tests are not intended to be all encompassing tests of cognitive ability. Therefore, the IQ is not derived out of them. However, teachers hear the term regularly, and will need to be prepared to respond intelligently to ideas, myths, and misinformation about the IQ. The term IQ has itself become a word in American parlance and has come to be synonymous with intelligence, although the psychologists who developed the IQ score never intended it to be. It was a name for a score only.

The IQ was originally an indicator of rate of cognitive development. A child who was developing at an average rate for his or her age had an IQ around 100. If the IQ ranged above 100 the child was developing cognitively more rapidly than its age mates; if the score was below 100 the child was not developing as rapidly as its age mates. The IQ was the ratio of the child's cognitive development age and his actual age in years, multiplied by 100.

However, in recent decades intelligence testing (and its results shown in IQ scores) came under closer scrutiny. It was difficult to define intelligence. Some definitions pointed to relationships between complex abilities that were very complicated to measure. Because good criteria were hard to identify, validation of intelligence tests was very complex to carry off well with less complicated group testing approaches. Further, the assessment devices depended on the assumption that all test-takers had a fairly common background of experiences that promote cognitive growth. This assumption seemed to be true for almost no one, especially not urban minorities and rural children.

As a result testmakers have diverted their attention from overall intelligence to assessing that part of it that appears to be specific to predicting academic success. Consequently, the IQ is now seldom found in school testing materials. Because educators cannot agree on what intelligence is, how it develops, whether its growth is genetically determined or is dependent on environmental stimulation, the IQ has a tenuous role in educational assessment. If educators cannot agree on the construct, a score that reflects the rate of development of the construct cannot be meaningful.

However, educators have not abandoned the idea that some children seem to have more aptitude for learning school subjects than do others. The construct of academic aptitude is still prominent in the literature, in the commercial marketplace, and in conversations in the teachers' lounge. However, academic aptitude test publishers do not claim to be testing something that might be called general intelligence.

Academic aptitude tests do not produce IQ scores. Instead they are likely to produce age-based, or grade-based scores that are intended to reflect aptitude for learning school subjects. They show a child's position among other children at a given age or at a given grade. This information is probably more useful for teachers than an abstract index of general cognitive development such as the IQ came to be.

Types of Academic Aptitude Tests

The aptitude tests used in schools fall into two categories: group administered, in which the same test is given to a whole class at once, and individual administered tests, in which a specialist in psychometrics gives the test to one person at a time.

Group Tests of Academic Aptitude

The majority of academic aptitude tests used in schools are **group tests.** These have convenience and cost-effectiveness on their side. They can be given to large or small groups by an administrator who has very little training in testing. I have already mentioned several group tests, such as the *Cognitive Ability Test,* The *Otis Lennon School Ability Test,* and the *Test of Cognitive Skill.* Like achievement tests, these tests are accompanied by carefully prepared instructions to be read precisely as written. Exact time limits are listed for each subtest. Children who are old enough make their responses to the multiple-choice content on machine-readable answer sheets. These sheets may be scored locally or sent to the publisher for scoring. Group examinations require little time and sophistication to use, a clear advantage for educators.

For decades several popular aptitude tests produced a single score. This score represented general ability to deal with problems in any of the broad skill areas—verbal, number, and so on—sampled by these tests. In recent years, single-score tests have almost disappeared from schools. Now, most tests used in schools produce at least two scores, typically a verbal and nonverbal score. The two scores are especially useful if a child has a language problem. In this case the nonverbal test may be the best indicator of ability. However, both the verbal and nonverbal scores are intended to represent academic aptitude much like that seen in the older, one-score tests. The difference is not so much in the aptitude being assessed, but in the vehicle through which the separate scores are produced, that is, the verbal and nonverbal items.

The claim that subtests of academic aptitude are all assessing the same basic trait is supported by their intercorrelations. For example, in the *Otis-Lennon School Ability Test* the verbal score correlates with the nonverbal score near .90.* This is a substantial relationship and indicates that the two scores are essentially pointing to the same trait.

The conclusion is that group administered academic aptitude tests reflect the belief that aptitude is a unitary trait of children and is related to success in many academic content areas. Different subtests primarily have used different vehicles for getting at that general academic aptitude; a verbal test may depend heavily on vocabulary, a reasoning test on analogies.

Individual Tests of Aptitude

When Dr. Cronen, the school psychologist, arrived Ms. Hacker began, "Tim is just not doing well in my class. He doesn't cause any trouble, is very quiet, so I didn't notice him for awhile. But his academic work is not good at all. I've spent a lot of time with him and we aren't getting anywhere. That's why I called you. I would like to see what you think of his academic aptitude."

Dr. Cronen looked grimly at Tim's record folder. "I'll be in the building on Wednesday morning, and visit with him," she said. "Are you familiar with the Stanford–Binet test or the Wechsler? If I decide testing is in order, I will most likely use one of these to look at Tim's aptitude," she concluded. Because one must have special training to administer and interpret them, individual aptitude tests are usually managed by a school pychometrist or psychologist who has had many hours of training and an internship in their use.

As their name implies, **individually administered tests** are given to one child at a time. The child responds to most questions orally, and the test administrator records answers and other behaviors related to solving the test's problems. Individually administered aptitude tests are reserved for use with children who have special learning problems. However, teachers will be involved in case conferences involving the findings from the tests.

The most commonly used individually administered aptitude tests are the *Stanford–Binet Intelligence Scale* and the *Wechsler Intelligence Scales*. The Stanford–Binet is used from preschool into adult ages. It has four types of subtests—Verbal Reasoning, Quantitative Reasoning, Abstract/Visual Reasoning, and Short-Term Memory. There are 15 subtests to cover these areas. Subtest items are arranged in ascending order of difficulty. No child takes all items; instead, the test administrator terminates a subtest at a point where it appears the child has gone as far as possible.

Scores are available on each subtest, and a standard age score (SAS) is derived from combining all scores. This SAS has a mean of 100, and a standard deviation of 16. This means that the middle 68 percent of a student's age-mates are expected to range between 84 and 116 (see Chapter 14 for a review of the normal curve). Students clearly above 100 SAS are developing cognitively faster than their age-mates; students clearly below 100 are developing slower.

The Wechsler scale includes three separate tests: one for preschoolers, one for first-grade to middle adolescence, and one for older candidates. There are two subtests—the Verbal Scale and the Performance Scale. Each of these is made up of several subtests. The Wechsler scale provides a total score much like the SAS in the Stanford–Binet. It can also provide subscores for diagnostic purposes.

In the interpretation and application of test data consult the school psychologist for answers. Do not hesitate to ask the questions that are on your mind. You, as the teacher, must deal with the child daily, and you must understand what the test scores indicate for making decisions about a child. Ask the psychologist to put the data into detailed operations you can apply in the classroom. Generalizations about the child's aptitudes do not help you plan appropriate lessons. The school psychologist is trained to be of assistance in this matter, so be sure to ask.

Other Aptitude Assessments for School Use

The long list of available aptitude tests and the tests we have already reviewed, along with information in school files, will be sufficient to help us make the decisions we must about children. For example, suppose we want to develop an accelerated mathematics program. Who should be admitted to this special offering? If you have achievement records, teacher testimony and samples of work, and academic aptitude test results, you probably have enough data to make fairly valid placements for the program.

Indeed, there are special mathematics tests that could be used for the purpose of placement, but the time and effort to use them should be weighed against the additional information they would provide. Their main advantages are that all applicants will have scores on a common test that can be compared across all candidates, and that other data need not be collected from your files. But you may be able to do an adequate job with the sources of data you have on hand. Give this approach consideration before seeking a special aptitude test.

Readiness Tests.   One type of test that is often used in schools is the reading readiness test; when to place children in the pre-primer (their first reading book) is an important decision, and reading readiness tests can often help first-grade teachers make this determination. It should be noted that because young children change rapidly, reading readiness tests are at best only modest predictors of the child's ability to start learning to read. These tests may prove to be useful for teachers in primary instruction, but corroborating evidence should be given considerable weight in making placement decisions.

It should also be noted that tests of all types used with young children, including reading readiness, are often not as reliable as users would like them to be. Scores from all tests are best interpreted with the aid of information from other sources; this is especially true of readiness tests. Kindergarten teachers who collect work samples on their children can be a great resource in supplementing reading readiness test data.

The same principle applies with other aptitude tests. They work best as one part of the data on which decisions will be made. Test data may be useful, but if corroborated by supplemental data, it works even better.

College Admissions Tests

Every year newspapers announce that the state ranks at a given level on the recent administration of the *Scholastic Aptitude Tests* (SAT) or the *American College Testing Program* (ACT). Are such rankings legitimate? Probably not. Yet the citizens and policymakers in a state read these rankings and are concerned that the schools are not doing their job.

This concern is based on the idea that college admissions tests are primarily achievement tests. They are not. The SAT and ACT are not designed to survey the high school curriculum. They are aptitude tests designed to predict success, especially in the first year of colleges and universities, and as such should not be interpreted as though they were achievement tests.

In addition, different socio economic constituencies take the SAT in some states than in others. For example, many colleges in the plains states request the *American College Testing Program* (ACT) to be submitted with applications for admission. Many students who are college-bound in those states take the ACT. Similarly, most college-bound students in the New England states take the SAT because their colleges request that test for admissions. As a result, most of the college-bound students in New York will take the SAT. In Iowa, only a relatively few of the college-bound students will take the SAT. A comparison of New York with Iowa on the SAT will be made on two quite different segments of the student population. Situations such as this indicate that direct comparisons of states may lead to erroneous conclusions.

Do college admission tests predict success in higher level education? The answer is yes, but with only modest accuracy. A student's rank in the high school graduating class closely rivals the college admissions test in the prediction of college success. Therefore, admissions officers find a combination of rank in the high school graduating class and college admissions tests works well together.

✎ Problems

1. In your own teaching area describe three situations in which you might benefit from an academic aptitude score on a child.
2. Describe, telling what information we get from each, three scores that might be found on an academic aptitude test report. What is an anticipated achievement score? What cautions do we need to note in its use?
3. Compare and contrast group aptitude tests and individually administered aptitude tests.

Bias in Aptitude Tests

In Chapter 18 a more expansive discussion of bias in testing is presented. However, we may note at this point that one of the criticisms of general intelligence tests that produced IQs is that they favored some segments of the society. During the 1980s a number of research articles, books, and papers presented information on the claim of bias in intelligence tests. Out of all this it became clear that bias could be involved in many aspects of testing and testmaking.

To many educators, bias in tests is represented in one or more of three ways. First, the test produces higher average scores of one designated group than another; second, the content of the test appears to contain situations that are more like those experienced by one designated group than another, and third, the norms group does not proportionately represent the subgroups of the population. Let's take a closer look at these aspects of bias.

Group Averages

Aptitude tests may show bias when one group consistently scores higher than another, but this is not in itself evidence of bias. If you asked all male faculty members and the male seniors in a given school district to run the 100-yard-dash, the mean speed for the seniors will probably be faster than for the faculty. Due to age and agility, the seniors will be odds-on favorites to have the lowest mean time for the race. Is the running of this race a biased assessment? Probably not. It is likely to give a fair (valid) estimate of each group's running ability.

On the other hand, if you could assume that the two groups of males had the same physical skills at the outset, and the younger ones won, then the race may be investigated for bias. Many concerns about bias in tests require the hypothesis that the two groups being compared are at the outset equal in a given trait. To prove or disprove this hypothesis is often a very difficult if not impossible task. If the proof of the hypothesis can be established before the test is made, and the test continues to produce different mean scores (and standard deviations) for each of two or more groups, then the test may well be biased. However, the mere showing of group differences does not in itself show test bias.

Bias in Test Content

The second consideration is a potent one for most school tests. Tests used in schools are often declared biased because subgroups of the society see content to which their constituency has had limited exposure. For example, urban children may know little about characteristics of farm animals. If a test contains content that requires this kind of knowledge, the test may be declared to be biased against urban children. Or suppose a test problem dealt with city bus routing. A rural child may never have ridden on a city bus, and will have little experience with routing. Consequently these children would have limited ability to deal with this problem.

Test companies are aggressively attacking this set of problems by establishing committees, representing ethnic and social class subgroups, whose job it is to thoroughly review the tests and to root out content bias. For example, in writing the *Test of Cognitive Skills* the publisher assembled educators from various ethnic groups. These people reviewed the test content for appropriateness of language, subject matter, and representation of people. Further, the test was taken to schools for pre-testing with different ethnic groups. Items that revealed either advantage or disadvantage for one group were identified. Other testmakers are using similar procedures to eliminate ethnic and gender bias in tests.

Bias in Norms Groups

Bias can also be found in the norms group on which the test is standardized. If, for example, tests were standardized on public school children, and if the schools involved in the data collection have very few Hispanic children, this group may not be appropriately represented in the norms. Consequently, the score conversions of Hispanic students (e.g., raw scores converted to grade scores) may not represent valid placements for these students.

Test companies work diligently to make their norms groups resemble national statistics on the population. They carefully select norms groups so as to sample minority populations and social strata in the percentages shown by national population data. Their data may be a few percentage points off from time to time, but this is probably not enough to change the placement of most students.

Aptitude Scores and Teacher Expectations

There is some evidence that teachers do not treat "low aptitude" children the same as they do "high aptitude" students. This teacher behavior assumes that aptitude is fixed, and that lower aptitude students will not learn well regardless of teacher effort. Such an assumption is difficult to substantiate.

The teacher's expectation for a child's achievement can influence the child's performance (Gronlund & Linn, 1990). Teachers must recognize that all their children are teachable and should have the chance to develop their skills to the utmost. It is wrong to say that Geraldine has only modest academic aptitude and therefore instructional effort to develop her ability is probably not worthwhile. All children should have every opportunity to develop their skills and abilities, and teachers should expect them to do so. This is right for each child, and it is enlightened self-interest for the society that needs the talents of all its citizens developed to their best level. Aptitude scores may help us decide where to start instruction with a child, but they do not indicate where it will end. Test scores should not be allowed to stereotype any child!

Coaching's Effect on Test Scores

"Hey, Dad," called high school junior Mary Louise. "This ad in the paper says they can improve my chances of getting a scholarship-level SAT score if I attend their classes!" Advertisements such as this appear in newspapers all over the nation. The coaching companies claim that students can expect to change their scores, sometimes dramatically. These advertisements catch the eye of students at all ability levels who want to give themselves the best chance to do well.

By coaching, I do not mean teaching the exact content of the test items in an aptitude test. This practice is unethical and is not an advantage for the student; the score will not represent true ability, and students may be placed into work for which they are poorly prepared. Teaching the answers to exact items that will be on the test does not appear to help the student, and erodes test validity.

The evidence provided by testmakers who have studied coaching is unimpressive. The controversy continues, but the hard data appear to favor the conclusion that, for the typical student, short-term intervention does not alter the underlying abilities sufficiently to warrant enthusiasm (Bond, 1989). However, some students, especially those whose school record is inconsistent with their ability to perform on tests and those who use inefficient test-taking procedures, may find special improvement in their test results from taking the coaching.

The areas in which coaching is likely to help include the following:

1. If coaching is extensive enough to improve abilities to perform in academic work, it may also improve ability to perform on the test. If so, the coaching will not only improve student performance on the test, but the increased scores will validly represent ability.

2. Through coaching classes students may gain test-taking strategies. These may allow test-takers to conserve time, become more efficient option selectors in multiple-choice tests, and expand their facility in dealing with several widely used types of test content.

3. The familiarity with different types of test items and content used by a given test publisher may increase the student's feeling of self-confidence and reduce anxiety. This will allow the student to concentrate more intently on the tasks that the test presents and less on introspection and feelings of tension. If a coaching session achieves this it may well improve the students chances to score well.

Is coaching a productive endeavor? That depends. Across the many students who take it, great gains in scores are not likely to appear. However, for some students who are poor test strategists, who may have worked somewhat below par in school but who work hard at the coaching exercises, and for students who lack confidence in test situations, coaching may be of assistance. Only in a very few cases is coaching expected to be highly effective in improving scores.

A REAL CASE NARRATIVE

Below is a conversation among teachers at a high school. If you were one of the teachers in that group what would you say to the group? Relating the content of the SAT to the local school programs is a good place to begin.

Four teachers are seated around a table in the lunch room. Mr. Hedlin, a shop teacher, was reading the news paper. "Whoa!" he called. "This paper is chastising the teachers and the school for the below par scores our seniors got on the SAT!"

"I think some of that is deserved," said Mr. Novelle, an English teacher. "The kids don't come to us as well prepared as they used to. Maybe a little coaching of the seniors on the SAT would be useful in making up the difference," he went on.

Ms. Wesman looked grim. "I've got a point here! Why do we always turn on the schools in these things? Why do we give those tests all that credibility? We used the Skills Aptitude Test last year to select kids for the special math class, and it predicted less accurately than we hoped. These tests don't always do what we expect but we look on them as the authority."

"Right!," Mr. Nieman followed. "I guess every test has some margin of error. I wonder how we find that?"

Ms. Thiagi put down her sandwich to join in the discussion. "That's right! Reading the manual carefully ahead of time could have saved us some embarrassment in math last year," she asserted.

The school counselor, Dr. Genti, looked around the circle getting eye contact. "I think I hear you saying that aptitude tests are used badly by educators and lay people alike." Again she scanned the circle. Momentarily everyone stopped eating and stared intently at her.

SUMMARY

1. An aptitude is the ability to profit from experience in acquiring a given skill.
2. Early in the century most attention was given to general aptitude, a single characteristic referred to as "g." Opponents of this idea believed that intelligence was composed of several distinct aptitudes known as group factors.
3. The general aptitude tests used in schools were rebuilt to focus more on the prediction of achievement in school-related skills and became known as academic or scholastic aptitude tests.
4. Achievement tests usually measure what a student has learned in a specific curriculum, while aptitude tests measure the ability to learn new skills. In practice, the two kinds of tests overlap in what they measure.
5. Aptitude tests are usually quite reliable and must be so for work with individual children.
6. Academic aptitude test scores are useful when a child comes from a nonstandard program, when achievement scores are not available or do not fit a particular curriculum, or in dealing with children who have language problems.
7. Aptitude tests produce several types of scores, including percentile ranks, stanines, and standard age scores (based on a mean of 100 and a standard deviation of 16 points). Some aptitude test publishers provide an anticipated achievement test score which indicates what a child's achievement tests scores are expected to be in the basic skills.
8. There are two main types of academic aptitude tests—group administered (given to a whole class at one time), and individually administered (which must be given by a specialist and to one child at a time). There are also other aptitude tests used in schools; the principal one is the readiness test.
9. College aptitude tests are often mistaken for high school achievement tests. They are not designed to survey the high school curriculum; they are designed to predict success in the first year of college work.

10. Bias is often attributed to aptitude tests when one group has a higher mean than the other. This is true only if both groups can be shown to be the same in the aptitude before the test is administered. Bias is seen when the content of a test favors the experiences of one group over another, or when the norms group disproportionately represents one subgroup over another.

11. For the typical student short-term coaching on taking an aptitude test appears to make only a little difference. However, if the coaching materially alters the student's ability in a skill, or increases one's test-taking skills, some improvement in scores may be seen. Only in a small percentage of cases will scores be improved markedly by coaching.

PROBLEMS

1. Describe why we call tests used in schools academic aptitude rather than general intelligence tests.

2. Compare and contrast achievement and aptitude tests as to purpose and content.

3. Suppose you were to address the PTA, describing the uses of academic aptitude tests in your school. Make an outline for your talk.

4. Mr. Brookstine has heard that his son has a stanine of 7 on the age scale of the CogAT. He wants to know what that means. What would you tell him?

5. You have a child who consistently fails in reading but is doing well in mathematics and science. You would like to have an aptitude score on the child to see if this might help you diagnose the problem. What kind of test would you request—group or individual? Why?

6. Ms. Olgaard was talking with Ms. Neu in the hallway of their school. "You know Arty's a nice boy, but his aptitude test score show he will never burn up the base path. I give him enough to keep him busy, but extra effort will be wasted there, I think," said Ms. Olgaard. How should Ms. Neu respond to her?

7. Mr. Eks is looking at Harman's folder and sees a standard age score of 118. Is Harman average, above average, very much above average? Explain your response.

8. It is time for seniors in your high school to take the *Scholastic Aptitude Test* (SAT). Colynne is considering taking a commercial class in SAT preparation. What would you advise her to do?

9. You are the principal of the middle school in your town. Department heads have submitted budget requests that included $8,000 for purchase and scoring of various aptitude tests in addition to the standard academic aptitude tests on file. For example, Mr. Piper has a request for science aptitude test to be used in selecting science students for the accelerated Space Cadets program. Your discretionary money is limited. What would be your response to the requests for special aptitude tests?

KEY TERMS

aptitude	culture fair tests
Alfred Binet	standard age score (SAS)
Louis Terman	anticipated achievement score
IQ	group tests
general intelligence	individually administered tests
"g" factor	Stanford–Binet Intelligence Scale
group factors	Wechsler Intelligence Scales

ADDITIONAL READING

Gould, S. J., *The Mismeasure of Man.* New York: W. W. Norton & Co, 1981.

Mehrens, W. A. Aptitude measurement. In *Encyclopedia of Educational Research,* 5th ed., vol. 1, New York: Macmillan, 1982, pp. 137–144.

Salvia, J. and Ysseldyke, J. E. *Assessment in Special and Remedial Education,* 4th ed., Boston: Houghton Mifflin, 1988.

Snow, R. E. (1989). Toward assessment of cognitive and conative structures in learning. *Educational Researcher,* 18 (9), 8–14.

CHAPTER 18

LEGAL AND ETHICAL CONSIDERATIONS IN TESTING

The Madison County school board is debating the question of requiring set test scores in reading, language arts, and mathematics for all students before they can graduate. The meeting is packed to standing-room only. "You cannot treat students fairly if you institute set test scores!" asserts Mrs. Johnson, a parent of two high school students. "It is common knowledge that tests do not treat all children fairly," she continued.

"There will be nothing on the test that children have not studied in school," the board chairman replied. "What is unfair about asking children to perform what they have been exposed to in their classes?"

Fairness implies that the devices used by social agencies for selecting candidates for any situation should give equal opportunity to everyone. This principle applies to all types of school assessment. However, disagreements have arisen about how fair some tests have been, and when the disagreement deals with relatively high-stakes decisions, courts are called upon to arbitrate the matter. In addition legislative bodies, in response to public appeal, have acted to establish guidelines for use of tests and similar procedures so that their application can be more fair across all segments of the society.

What This Chapter Will Include. This chapter will present some of the issues and their resolutions as seen by courts and legislatures. Specifically, you will learn about:

1. Legal views of bias in testing
2. Privacy in testing
3. Legal view of tests to assess minimum competencies
4. Legal pronouncements regarding children with disabilities
5. Some ethical considerations for educators

Legal Views of Bias in Testing

Beginning in the years just following World War II cases began appearing in courts requesting resolution of disputes regarding the fairness of education for minority groups in America. These cases not only opened the door to viewing fairness in education as a whole, but also looked at specific educational practices. Among these were the use of tests for admissions, for placement in programs for slower learners, and for people with physical and perceptual handicaps. Out of these cases came some guidelines that now apply to many situations in testing and placement in schools. The overall impact is to make schools and their operations fair and accessible for all segments of the society.

For several decades the development and use of tests have rightly come under the legal magnifying glass. In a dozen or so cases the courts have advised testers on how to run their business in a more fair and orderly fashion. This section summarizes some of the decisions the courts have made.

Placement Bias in Testing

When a test result is influenced by a variable extraneous to the purpose of testing, and this variable gives one socio-economic class, gender, or ethnic group an advantage in achieving a score or in interpretation of the score, the test may be suspected of bias. For example, educators may wish to conclude that males have more exposure to tools, motors, model-making, and so on. If so, males are more likely to see relationships in a mechanical problem than would females. If students are given a mathematics test which is dependent on mechanical knowledge and females do less well in solving these mathematics problems, does it mean that females have poorer mathematics skill? Females' lack of experience with the problem setting may well be the factor that slants the outcome in favor of males. In a setting such as this, bias in the test may be a legitimate conclusion.

This example is a prototype of the problems minority children have faced when taking aptitude tests. Segments of the aptitude tests have been cited as being based on socio-cultural experiences not common to minority students. Because of this, it is asserted that the tests are not fair to this group of children.

As we noted in Chapter 17, bias is often assumed when one identified group has a higher average score on a test than another group. However, differences between means for two defined groups cannot be taken as *prima facia* evidence of bias (Linn & Drasgow, 1987).

For example, imagine testing senior class girls and boys on the amount of weight they can lift. Which group is most likely to have the largest average in bench-pressing weights? It would probably be the boys. This does not mean that the test is biased against girls. If experts in child development can agree that the average American boy is stronger than the average American girl, educators will conclude that the test is not biased. It merely pointed out existing physical differences. Differences in average scores made by two groups may, but do not in themselves, indicate bias in the test.

Most popular concepts of bias depend on the assumption that all groups are equal in the underlying talent being assessed. If this assumption is true, and group differences in test scores appear, they must be due to the features of the test that give one group the advantage. In many cases the assumption of equality cannot be refuted; but in some, such as the weight-lifting example, it is not true. To contend that the test is biased, educators first must show that the assumption of group equality in the relevant variable is in fact true. Bias may not be demonstrated merely by showing that two groups differ in average performance.

However, if interested parties can demonstrate that a test is loaded with problems that require cultural and educational experiences denied a subgroup in society, then they may wish to look at the possibility of bias. Court scrutiny of tests has indeed ruled that some tests are biased based on their social and cultural slant.

Relevant Court Opinions on Testing.   In an important case [*Larry P. v. Wilson Riles* (1979)] the court noted that there was a disproportionate number of African-American children in special education classes, and decided that this disparity had to be due to bias in the test with which children were selected for special classes. The assumption that the test was based on social experiences that were common to all racial groups, and that these experiences equally prepared them to deal with the problems on the test, appeared to the court to be in error. The test, therefore, was believed to be biased against minority children who had not had the relevant experiences. Their chance for success on the test was seen to be curtailed by the lack of socio-cultural opportunities that related to success on the test.

The requirement that everyone have opportunity for success is part of the fairness guaranteed to all students by the Fourteenth Amendment to the Constitution (Phillips, 1994). This amendment guarantees that citizens cannot be deprived of life and liberty without due process of law, and that government cannot deny any person equal protection of the law. The court has interpreted the "equal protection" provision to include many features of social interaction. One such feature is the penalty under which persons work when they take certain tests that in part are based on unique social and cultural events. The guarantee of equal protection invalidates tests that appear to require knowledge or skills that derive out of experiences in which certain ethnic groups have been historically disadvantaged.

The outcome of the Larry P. trial imposed a very large restriction on the use of aptitude tests in California, and to some extent, elsewhere. Test-users have indeed had to abandon the use of some test data because of the findings of the court. Although this has been a limiting feature in some school situations, aptitude test data are only one of the many sources of evidence most schools use in selecting children for special classes.

The court has not always ruled against the use of tests in the classification of minority students. A second case, very much like Larry P., also contested the disproportionate number of minority students in special classes. The use of aptitude tests in assigning minority students to these classes was the focus of the dispute. In this case, *Parents in Action on Special Education v. Hannon* (1980), an Illinois court scrutinized each item in the test used in assignment of students. The conclusion was that the content of items, overall, did not support the claim for bias. Item by item scrutiny was not done in the Larry P. case in California. There the case swung heavily on the disproportionate numbers of minority students assigned to special education classes.

Test construction also came under investigation in the case of *Hobson vs. Hansen* (1967) in the District of Columbia. Noting that minority students were disproportionately assigned to the lower academic tracks, the plaintiff asked whether aptitude and achievement tests were biased tools for placing children in different tracks. The court found that the test had been standardized on a sample of mostly white children and consequently not appropriate for classifying minority children. Therefore, these tests were believed to be an unsatisfactory basis for assigning children to tracks. This signaled all test publishers to study their norming samples to see if they indeed were representing minority groups appropriately.

Two additional cases are of interest because they asked the court to decide whether tests given to students whose first language was other than English presented a bias against these children. The court in *Diana v. California State Board of Education* (1971) looked at bias in terms of children who come from homes where English may not be the first language. These situations appear to be examples of the lack of opportunity requirement, and subsequently would raise the question of bias in scores for the children from those homes. Indeed, in an out-of-court settlement the litigants agreed that to prevent bias, children from non-English speaking homes must be tested in their native language. Also, tests used with non-English speaking children must be normed on culturally and linguistically relevant groups of students and contain no culturally unfair content.

Guadalupe v. Tempe Elementary School District (1972) presented a problem similar to the Diana case. In this case the question also dealt with testing children whose first language was not English. The findings essentially supported those in the Diana case. In assessing the intellectual skills of children whose first language is not English, adaptations must be made so that children can have the advantage of using the language in which they are most fluent.

In allowing the use of tests court orders have mandated that schools ensure that all tests are developed, administered, and scored in a nondiscriminatory manner. This ruling pertains to the assessment activities of teachers in their classrooms as well as to the use of tests made by professional publishers [*Reed v. Rhodes* (1978)].

Reactions to Court Rulings.   The outcomes of court reviews have been important in establishing guidelines for the application of tests. They have also raised the sensitivity of the educational community to the possibility of bias in assessment procedures, and subsequently altered the methods of test construction and recommendations for use. As a result, test publishers are more carefully selecting their norming groups, and are taking steps to review their tests for ethnic and gender bias. For example, the publishers of the *Metropolitan Achievement Tests* describe in detail their efforts to eliminate bias in their tests. A portion of this description (Technical Manual, 1993) states:

> An Advisory Panel of prominent minority-group educators was formed for the purpose of reviewing the MAT7 tryout test for items that inadvertently reflected ethnic, gender, socioeconomic, cultural, or regional bias or stereotyping or content that would disadvantage a group because of differences in culture or familiarity. (p. 17)

In addition to content reviews, some publishers further describe statistical procedures to identify and eliminate items that show disproportionate numbers of one cultural, ethnic, or gender group having an advantage on a test item. These attacks on the bias problem are now used by most large-scale publishers of tests. This extra effort to eliminate unequal opportunity was not commonly seen before the court scrutinized testing procedures.

These measures are indeed helpful, but whether they entirely eliminate bias cannot be decided. The fact is that psychologists have no way of measuring the impact of cultural experiences on cognitive development, and consequently are hard-pressed to identify the differences in experience among subcultures that could make a difference in cognitive functioning. Nevertheless, eliminating test content that clearly relates to differences in experiences of two cultural groups can only improve all types of tests used in schools that are open to all members of a heterogeneous society.

The few cases cited above point to the positive outcomes that emerged from the legal reviews of testing. Both test content and the use of tests are now under greater regulation than before the cases were given review. However, this has not entirely quelled the beliefs that tests are inherently biased and that they deny access of opportunity to some segments of society.

Bias in Classroom Assessment

There is little information on the extent to which bias is a factor in teacher-initiated classroom assessment. Regardless, the court decisions have not only admonished teachers to avoid bias, but also have made all educators much more aware of the possibility of bias in assessment techniques. Within the limits of application, objective tests do not know the ethnic characteristics of the test-taker. They do not notice if the student is male or female. However, since the test's content is selected, and the quality of performances are judged by a human being who may have some preconceptions about race and gender, the questions on which a score is based may give the advantage to members of one gender or ethnic group. The court has cautioned teachers, when making classroom assessments, to avoid this and all other types of bias.

However, the possibility of bias rises with the increased use of subjective techniques by teachers. When a teacher observes a minority student construct the equipment and carry out a science project, does that teacher "find" more deficiencies than when observing a white student? When a teacher assesses an essay written by a female does that teacher "perceive" more expression and sensitivity than when assessing one written by a male? Greater emphasis on performance assessment extends the involvement of judgment in assessment. This expands (possibly without the reader's awareness) the opportunity for bias in evaluation when teachers read reports, themes or student composed stories, or reports on a significant project done outside of class. Because in group work there may be sparse guidelines to assess the differential contributions of students, the teacher may award uneven credit to students for a given project (Phillips, 1994, op. cit.).

The assessment of many performances rely heavily on the teacher's judgment of quality of student products. For example, there is evidence that a number of factors, beside content, influence the scorer of essay tests (see Chapter 10). Could gender or ethnicity become factors that come into play in subjective assessment? To gain the advantage of assigning cooperative group work, or large problem-solving projects for long-term student effort, educators have opportunity to neglect objectivity in evaluating the resulting process or product. This may also allow bias, intentional or not, to slip in undetected. This potential for bias underscores the need for carefully prepared rubrics and the use of checklists and rating scales as assessment aids (see Chapter 12).

Some Conclusions

Our brief review of bias leads to the conclusion that court cases have clearly mandated increased vigilance in detecting and eliminating bias in testing. If not the letter of the decisions, their spirit applies to all teacher-made assessments as well as commercially printed tests. However, in most classroom assessments the teacher may respond to nonachievement variables in the context being observed. This can let bias slip in. This being so, the complete elimination of bias has probably not yet been achieved.

At the present time psychometrics specialists have not established how large the problem of bias toward minorities in educational testing really is (Cole, 1981; Linn, 1982). Also, there is uncertainty as to how well children who might have been tracked into special programs have performed in untracked classrooms. Lambert (1981), responding as a witness for the defense in the Larry P. case, revealed the opposite side of the coin. She speculated about children who were placed in regular classes because of the test, but who without the test may not have been. Incorrect placement of these children could have had a considerable impact on their self-concepts and aspirations. Without testing, she claimed, these children would be deprived of the opportunity to succeed by being erroneously placed in less complex programs.

Research questions on bias in testing continue to call for answers; however, some answers may be beyond the present state of the art.

Rights of Access and Privacy

Further questions in assessment involve an individual's right to inspect his or her own record, and the right to privacy of that record. Here there are two aspects to consider. The first deals with one's right to see what is in his or her file—the right to know if the data are accurate, and to correct them if they are not. The second deals with confidentiality of test data accumulated in the large-scale achievement and aptitude testing which is carried out in many schools; ancillary to this is the management of assessment in the classroom. The Family Education Rights and Privacy Act, often referred to as the "Buckley Amendment" has provided for the access to all records of students in federally funded projects. Since only a portion of the activities in local schools is likely to be federally funded, the right to access principle has not been far reaching. However, its implications have been felt in almost all jurisdictions and have guided many local regulations for managing of records.

The Access Debate

Interesting arguments have been presented on both sides of the access question. Without access errors can appear on records that could be far reaching for a student. Students and parents should be able to see if what is on the record is accurate and is based in fact. On the other hand, some educators argue that more than occasionally data on file can be misinterpreted by the parent or student who is allowed to see it. For example, an achievement test that reports scores in T-scores shows Mary with a 70 in total reading. This in T-scores is two standard deviations above the mean—very high (mean = 50, standard deviation = 10 [see Chapter 14]). However, Mary's mother was very displeased with her daughter because she thought Mary had scored only 70 percent on her reading test. Mary's mother failed to grasp what the score of 70 really meant. Some educators believe that parents and students may not be prepared to read and understand the material on file without considerable assistance. For this reason they feel that the file should probably not be shown to them in the first place.

Both sides in the access argument have good points. What constitutes an equitable resolution is not clear in this controversy, but currently the law is on the side of access, at least where the federal government is involved.

Ensuring Privacy

Another aspect of records is privacy from access by unauthorized persons. Privacy in records has been protected for some time (Hatch Amendment, PL 95–561, Elementary and Secondary Education Act of 1965). Records of children on file in schools must, by law, be kept secure and private. Only parents can release these records to view by anyone other than those who will use them in support of instruction. This means that a teacher may see a student's test scores if it is in the interest of developing instructional procedures. However, without permission of the parent or guardian, a student's file cannot be seen by other persons such as a pastor or rabbi, by a local employer, or by a community agency worker such as a Boy Scout leader. Maintaining privacy in classroom assessment is also important, but this is left mostly to the teacher's own diligence.

Not only must schools protect student records, but additionally information cannot be requested from a student about his or her personal beliefs or affairs unless parental consent is given first. For example, a sociologist cannot ask children about smoking behavior or sexual involvement unless parents agree to the questioning. This rule was established to help people avoid embarrassment or being subjected to stress or psychological or economic harm through the possible exposure of private information.

Privacy at Local Schools

Privacy regulations are as important on the local level as in other settings. However, these regulations are often not carefully managed. For example, a committee of the PTA was assembled in the home of a parent. Three teachers and four parents were in attendance. They were discussing funding for a volunteer parent tutoring group for children who needed some extra assistance in reading. In the course of the evening Mrs. Parsons asked, "Just what is the magnitude of this problem—how many kids are we talking about?"

"Well," began Ms. Worrell, a third-grade teacher, "in my class there is Sandy Brown, Tim Wilson, Harold Grey—at least these."

Mr. Tucker, who had recently looked over files in the principal's office, followed. "Among fourth-graders there is Billy Ammonson reading at 3.2, and Megan Morse at 3.1, and Cheryl Trand at 3.3. All these could use a little extra help." In trying to assess the magnitude of the reading problem among students, they had, probably unwittingly, violated the privacy of several students.

The rules for protection of privacy in classroom assessment are less clear than those for maintaining security of records. Professional integrity suggests that pupil privacy has a place in classrooms as well as in the principal's office. Why? Look at this situation.

Mr. Karls, an instructor in American history, returned a test to the class by placing the stack of papers on a table near the door. Students picked up their papers as they passed out of the room at the end of class.

In the hallway, LaVonne hurried to catch up with Tonya. "Wow!" said LaVonne with her eyes open wide, "Did you see Jane's paper in that stack? She got a D!"

Tonya looked surprised. "I'm going to bring this up at Circle Club—she is coming up for membership, and scholarship is one of the criteria."

In this classroom Mr. Karls has violated Jane's privacy (and probably the privacy of several others). It is no one's business what Jane got on her paper, but by allowing students to shuffle through the stack to find their own papers, they cannot help but see the scores on papers of their classmates. As a result of this lack of protection of privacy, Jane may well suffer a loss of opportunity.

Here is another example. Ms. Harman is returning graded problem sets to the class in algebra. As she hands Jerry his paper she comments, "You and I need to talk! This kind of work won't go far in this class!" Ms. Harman probably intended to motivate Jerry, but how does he feel when he is spoken to in front of the class? Jerry is obviously embarrassed and probably humiliated.

The essence of privacy regulations is to avoid these situations. We must protect students from prying eyes of people who wish to peruse a school file, and we must be sensitive to the situations that expose students to embarrassment or loss in the classroom. The rationale for legal opinions on privacy pertains to students in their classrooms, just as it does for the society at large.

✎ Problems

1. You are a guidance counselor at Attucks High School. A committee of girls comes to you to protest a test used to select students for the special building trades class. They noted that on the mechanical aptitude test the average score for girls was 10 points lower than for boys. As a result, it is very difficult for girls to get into this class. How would you respond to the girls' remonstrance?

2. The Lewiston Public School System has decided to impose minimum competency levels in reading, writing, and mathematics for granting a high school diploma. A group of parents have objected to minimum competencies for several reasons. The principal appointed you to head a committee to respond to this proposition. Write up a five-item agenda with brief explanations for the committee as to why each item is on the agenda.

3. To show students how well they were doing over the semester, Mr. Lentz photocopies his grade book page after each month of the term and posts it on his room's bulletin board. Would you support or oppose this method of reporting? Why?

Minimum Competency Standards

One of the trends in public schools is the setting of minimum levels of achievement for passing from one grade to another, for participation in activities such as sports, and for graduation. Public and political pressures have motivated school boards and state legislatures to impose these minimum competency levels (Jaeger, 1982). Demonstration of competency is typically made by taking a test. Testing on which far-reaching decisions, such as those just mentioned, are referred to as **high stakes testing** (Popham, 1987).

In spite of its problems, many school systems and state legislatures have instituted for each grade level (at least in part) minimum standards of achievement. These standards are called minimum competencies. In some cases parents have taken the matter to court to get a ruling on their legality. The courts have ruled that minimum competency testing is legal as long as no racial biases are evident in the tests, and that schools can show that the tests are valid measures of what is taught in school [*Debra P. v. Turlington* (1981), *Anderson v. Banks* (1982)].

The imposition of minimum standards for promotion and graduation has had some positive effects on schools (Jaeger, 1989). It has required schools to be more specific and detailed about their objectives at each grade level. (Chapter 2 deals with writing assessable objectives.) More attention has had to be given by states to making their certification tests more valid for assessing achievement of the objectives. Also, more care has been given to assure that the curriculum does indeed target the objectives, and that remedial instruction is available for students who fail to reach the minimum standards.

Overall, schools under minimum standards have become more focused on basic skill objectives. All this looks like good pedagogy, and it probably is. However, the opponent to minimum competency programs also have some sound arguments. Minimum competency programs continue to be discussed, often heatedly, among educators as well as among state and local politicians. However, their legal base appears secure.

Children with Disabilities

For many years children with various physical limitations were given very little attention by public institutions. Then the Individuals with Disabilities Education Act required, among other things, that all handicapped students receive "free appropriate public education." [P.L. No. 102–119, 20 U.S.C., W1400 et seq., (1991)]. This act opened the door to education for handicapped children but declared that no single criterion for determining appropriate education be stipulated.

The Individuals with Disabilities Education Act was extended by the Americans with Disabilities Act by requiring that no person with a handicap, who is otherwise qualified, may be excluded from publicly funded services, programs, or activities.

[A.D.A., Pub.L. No. 101–336, 42 U.S.C. S12132 (1990)]. "Otherwise qualified" refers to persons who could profit from a service but cannot obtain the service because its access is designed for persons without physical disabilities. For example, a student who could learn arithmetic is denied instruction because poor vision does not allow reading the printed material involved. Except for the vision limitation, the student is otherwise qualified to learn arithmetic. However, if the handicap itself prevents participation in an activity, the individual is not considered "otherwise qualified." Here, a student with a motor limitation in the lower extremities could not demand access to sports activities requiring the use of one's legs in running or jumping.

How does all of this relate to assessment of the student's progress toward instructional objectives? Otherwise qualified students may not be able to disclose their degree of skill and learning because of the test format (e.g., small print for students with visual difficulties) or the environment (e.g., cement steps into the school for a student in a wheelchair).

Let's see how this works in a school setting. Arthur, a seventh-grade student has mild cerebral palsy. He can write only with great difficulty. He uses a computer to assist himself, but even so his writing is labored and slow. Now it is time to take the Statewide Achievement Test, which requires Arthur to write an essay on local government. Even with a computer Arthur cannot get this job done in the time allowed. Even though he knows the topic well, he will not be able to show his knowledge. This testing, according to the above cited acts, must be deemed as discriminatory in Arthur's case, and a bias against all students with similar impairments.

It should be noted that the disabilities acts do not require that schools lower their standards for acceptable achievement in areas such as awarding diplomas. Nor should the adaptations for handicapped children affect the cognitive function being assessed. For example, if the objective is to make an inference from a reading passage, use of an assistant to read the passage aloud will not affect the mental processes involved in this exercise, that is, interpretation. However, if the objective is just to read the passage, then the use of the reader will alter the mental process involved (unless Braille script is substituted). In using a minimum competency assessment approach to awarding a diploma, schools may have to make adaptations in order to certify that the student has met all qualifications.

Some Ethical Responsibilities in Assessment

Sensitivity to the ethics of assessment is vital to anyone who monitors student progress toward instructional objectives. In this regard, an excellent manual for ethics in assessment can be found in the *Standards for Educational and Psychological Testing* (American Educational Research Association, et al., 1985). This section will examine in some extent a few of the topics dealt with by the Standards.

Ethical Responsibilities in Assessment

Users of assessment procedures of all types have certain responsibilities. Those that apply most to educators are the following:

1. *Users must know how to develop materials for, and evaluate performance on, a variety of assessment methods.* In this statement the salient word is "variety." Because no one method is appropriate for assessing all achievement of instructional outcomes, teachers must be able to select the technique that best moves the class toward the objective. This means not only familiarity with construction techniques, but also applications and interpretation of results for these techniques. Under what circumstances is the assignment of an essay project most appropriate? How do I evaluate the work in a portfolio? How do I write discriminating multiple choice tests? At what stage of learning shall I apply various assessment procedures? Teachers must be able to respond to questions like these, because no one procedure fits all assessment requirements.

2. When published tests are used for schoolwide assessment purposes, *teachers must be knowledgeable about the purposes for the testing, the nature of the tests, proper administration procedures, and the interpretation and the appropriate use of the results.* The tests used in most schools are the achievement tests given usually once a year, and statewide tests. Some schools also use aptitude tests on a regular basis. This means knowing different item types, the test content, how to help students take the test, and what the scores mean when they are returned to you.

3. *Users of assessment materials must be sensitive to security requirements,* including protecting published tests from view until test-time, protecting teacher-made tests from exposure to the class, and monitoring test administrations in such a way as to protect against undue assistance for any student.

4. *Users of assessment procedures must guard the individual's right to privacy.* This means taking care not to reveal to anyone but the individual, or guardian, the results of an assessment, and refrain from making generalizations about a student's status on any assessment procedure.

5. *Take steps to avoid bias in the development and application of assessment procedures.* The most common biases deal with racial and ethnic groups and with gender. Review of all procedures in regard to these groups is essential to ethical use of assessment.

These five guidelines point teachers in the direction of competent assessment. Success in each of them is required for responsible use of appraisal procedures in the advancement of school objectives.

Teaching to the Test

The current atmosphere of education puts pressure on children, teachers, school systems, and states to show clear and regular gains in student achievement. The stakes are high, and the deciding event is an achievement testing program. Failure can mean students' goals are delayed, teachers salaries may be at stake, administrators jobs are threatened, and funding allocations lost.

This high-stakes atmosphere presses teachers to "help" students do better on a specific test. When the stakes are high, schools, like other organizations, may experiment with techniques they would not otherwise consider. For example, teachers may focus on the specific concepts that will be on the test, or in some cases, the exact items on the test (Haladyna, Nolen, & Haas, 1991).

Every teacher, in the daily routine of working with children toward selected objectives, is in a sense teaching to the test. When a child learns how to work a problem involving multiplication of two single-digit numbers, that child has learned a skill that will help on the mathematics section of a statewide test. But routine teaching that is guided by objectives established *a priori* does not violate ethics of assessment. Here teachers have objectives that were constructed aside from whatever the state test includes, and teaching is aimed at these objectives.

Teaching raises ethical questions when students are given practice in the actual exercises that will appear on the test. It does not necessarily mean that the exercises include the exact data given in test problems, but that they include the set of procedures students must implement to get a set of items correct on the test. At its worst, teaching to the test includes the actual exercises from old examinations, or from the current one, whenever available.

Here is an example. During the statewide testing of all students last spring Mr. O'Donnell carefully went through the test and tabulated the processes required for each of the problems in the mathematics section of the test. His hypothesis was that even though next year's test may have new test questions on it the processes involved in solving problems will be the same. This year he is focusing his instruction in mathematics in these skills, giving his classes considerable practice with processes required to solve problems on last spring's test. This is teaching to the test.

Here is yet another example. An elementary school principal was having a teachers' meeting soon after the statewide test had been administered in his school. The topic of discussion was items on the test that were not specifically taught in their school. As the teachers at each grade-level cited topics, processes, and so on that they did not teach—or to which they had given only slight attention—the principal made a list on the blackboard. When teachers from all grades had reported the group discussed topics at grade levels, and across grade levels, to which teachers must give specific attention in the coming year. The principal wrote the conclusions into a formal memo and circulated it at the first teachers meeting in the next school year. Included in the memo was an admonition to be sure these items were covered even if it meant taking time from other curriculum topics not included in the tests.

This is not only teaching to the test, it is also an illustration of test-driven curriculum. It implies that the most important topics to teach are those that are on the statewide test. In such cases the test is given undue authority in establishing school programs.

Does teaching to the test really make a difference? Indeed it does! A child in the middle elementary grades could gain a sizable amount on the norms scale for each additional item correct (Shepard, 1990), and similar effects can be seen at other grade levels.

Teaching to the test also has an unwholesome effect on teaching. Instead of teachers leading their classes to objectives the local schools feel are legitimate and most beneficial for their students, the curriculum is bent to fit the content of the nationally published tests that the school will administer once a year (Hatch & Freeman, 1988). This means the scope of the program will be reduced, and many valuable topics and experiences may be eliminated in favor of extra work on the topics and specific exercises required by the test.

Further, teaching to the test destroys the validity of scores children get in the skill areas. If Germaine has been tutored in the content of the test, his score in reading may have little to do with his actual reading skill. Can he attack a passage in a book and tell what it communicates? Possibly, but the test score cannot be counted on as evidence of this skill. Instead, the test indicates only how well Germaine performed the exercises he practiced for the test; it does not tell us how well this can be generalized to the wide range of performances he has not practiced. The test does not become a random sample of the domain of reading. For this reason, the score does not represent the child's ability to deal with the general skill. Teaching to the test destroys the utility of the test as an aid to instructional decisions.

Clearly, teaching to the test is an important ethical issue for education professionals. But when the stakes are high, the pressures often lead even professionals to bend from the appropriate track. However, the ethics of teaching must direct all educators to resist teaching to the test.

A REAL CASE NARRATIVE

Here is a narrative that involves the ideas of bias and minimum competency levels. If this were your local school board discussing the matter how would you advise them?

The School Board of District 84 is meeting to discuss the matter of setting minimum standards for reading and arithmetic in promoting of students to each grade and for graduation.

"I think this is a good idea," said board member Wicks. "Too many kids coasting through—just putting in time!"

"But wait a minute," interposed member Adkins. "I don't think this has a chance of getting by court rulings. And besides, we'd have to count on test scores for this high-stakes decision, and you know how tests are biased—it's in all the papers!"

"I think we should put in the regulation and if anybody challenges it, we'll see what the court will say. I'll bet they will back us," replied Wicks.

"But Tom, you know that the public thinks tests are biased, and I think the court does, too. And what about the kids with physical handicaps—the test won't fit them and the rest of the kids, too. It just won't fly!" concluded Adkins.

"Well, let's call in the attorney and ask for a review of the cases and see if the court has decided if tests are biased and if minimum competencies will hold up. And the handicapped kids? Add them, too," Wicks replied.

"OK, but it's a waste of taxpayer's money," Adkins complained.

SUMMARY

1. When test scores are influenced by a variable extraneous to the purpose of testing, and this variable gives one group an advantage, the test may be suspected of bias.
2. The fact that one identified group has a higher average score on a test than another is not evidence in itself that the test is biased.
3. Major court rulings declared that tests used in placing children in special classes may have been biased; however courts have not always ruled against tests used for placement

purposes. Court rulings have increased efforts to develop, administer, and interpret scores in a nondiscriminating manner.

4. Bias can also be a concern for classroom testing. This is especially true as teachers turn more to use of subjectively-scored assessments.

5. By law, records of children kept in school files must be secure and private; only parents can release these records.

6. Parents and students must have access to records to see if they are complete and are accurate, but some educators fear that data will be misinterpreted if parents do not understand the meaning of scores.

7. The rules for classroom protection of privacy are not as well defined, but often situations that psychologically impact a student or that artificially subject him or her to loss of opportunity should be strictly avoided.

8. Schools have instituted minimum competency standards for promotion and graduation. Courts have supported this action as long as tests are not discriminating on variables not related to skills being examined.

9. The law requires schools to accommodate children with physical and mental handicaps. Adaptation in mode of instruction and testing is acceptable as long as the adaptation does not alter the type of cognitive function being assessed.

10. Teaching to the test raises ethical questions for educators. Students should not be instructed in actual exercises that will appear on standardized or statewide tests, or in actual processes taken from the tests.

KEY TERMS

high stakes testing
minimum competency

ADDITIONAL READING

Bersdoff, D. N. (1981). Testing and the law. *American Psychologist, 36,* 1047–1056.

Cole, N. S. and Moss, P. A. Bias in test use. In R. L. Linn (Ed.), *Educational Measurement,* 3d ed., London: Collier Macmillan, 1989.

Debra P. v. Turlington

Diana v. State Board of California

Hatch Amendment. PL 95–561.

Jacob-Timm, S. and Hartshorne, T. S. *Ethics and Law for School Psychologists,* 2d ed., Brandon, VT: Clinical Psychology Publishing Co., 1994, especially Chapter 3, Privacy, and pp. 114–117.

Larry P. v. Wilson Riles

Parents in Action v. Hannon

Reed v. Rhodes

SECTION IV

REPORTING ON THE OUTCOMES OF EDUCATION

ASSIGNING GRADES
TELLING PARENTS ABOUT THEIR CHILD'S ACHIEVEMENT
ASSESSING SCHOOL PROGRAMS

This section discusses the methods of summarizing the achievement of teachers and children in the various school programs. In each of the areas the text covers the basic principles and guidelines designed to increase accuracy of your estimates of achievement and to promote communication.

The section begins with a discussion of grading, that process of summarizing a child's work into a single letter or similar symbol. Grades are useful in most school systems but have definite limitations that should be recognized. Grades are most useful if assigned according to a set of guidelines provided in Chapter 19.

Schools are established by the state and local community to fulfill a need for education in the culture. To that end the patrons of our schools deserve a regular report on how well the children are progressing. Chapter 20 emphasizes the importance of increased communication between the parents and school officials, and several types of reporting procedures are discussed.

In addition to students, schools and their programs also need evaluation to see how effectively they are achieving their intended objectives. To provide teachers with the basic concepts of evaluation in school settings, Chapter 21 discusses the topic of school evaluation. The premise of this chapter is that school evaluation is not something educators should leave to someone else to devise and execute. No one knows the school programs as well as the people who are involved daily. This means that teachers should not distance themselves from school evaluation, but rather should seek greater involvement and input into how the evaluation plan is developed, how it is managed, and participate in devising the conclusions that emerge from the study. Chapter 21 helps teachers do this.

CHAPTER 19

ASSIGNING GRADES

Mrs. Pacchioni entered her son's fourth-grade classroom. "What does this 'I' in sight vocabulary mean on Carlo's report card?" she asked Ms. Hopper. "It says here 'I = needs improvement,' but don't we all need that?"

"Well, it is my judgment," replied Ms. Hopper, "that Carlo has trouble with the reading of words that other children are using fairly regularly—he needs to work on this."

"Give me some examples, please," Mrs. Pacchioni asked, an expression of doubt on her face.

"Well, right off hand I haven't got a good example, but I see him reading and reporting on his reading every day, and it is my belief that he just does not have the range of sight vocabulary that many of the other children have—and that he is capable of having," the teacher replied, showing signs of impatience.

"You mean you don't have any papers or tests that show me in what way my boy's reading vocabulary is not good enough?" asked Mrs. Pacchioni. "It's just your impression? That's what you based this grade on, this grade that will be on his record forever?" Now Mrs. Pacchioni was getting impatient, and turned to leave. Ms. Hopper took a deep breath, clearly relieved by the impending departure.

Scenes such as this occur all over the country on a regular basis. What is wrong here? Does the teacher have a well-anchored grading system? Is the grade based on actual records of the child's performance? What are the teacher's criteria for grades? Do the children understand what these criteria are? Do the parents? Can the criteria be communicated to the parents? How will the grade improve instruction?

What This Chapter Will Include. This chapter presents some ideas and operations designed to make grading easier. In it you will learn about:

1. Fundamental principles for grading
2. Why educators grade achievement
3. Types of grades
4. Different bases for arriving at a mark
5. Combining observations into a single mark

6. Inflating grades
7. Some common objections to grading

Teachers spend much time creating grade reports. They hope to communicate to children and parents how well the student is progressing. Grades sometimes carry surprises for the student and have a potential for a large emotional impact. Communication with students and parents, if it is done well, will eliminate surprises and reduce the emotional impact of the marks on the grade card. Following are some ideas that will help simplify the process, reduce the impact of grades, and increase their message value.

For a number of reasons schools find it convenient to condense into one mark a students' achievement in a course of study. These single marks, known as **grades,** are used in communicating with other parts of society ideas the status of a child's skills. Awards, such as valedictory, are most conveniently assigned by use of grade marks. Employers do not want to read a narrative about what a student did during the semester; they want it summarized into one mark. The first thing parents look for on a report card is the grade marks that consolidate their child's work for the term. There is a great deal of support in the culture for grades as a means of compressing the work of students across a period of instruction.

Grades earned in course work act as a cultural passport. If they are high, they open doors to increasing education and to the best employment opportunities. If they are low, these doors may very well be closed (Herrnstein & Murray, 1994). Grades therefore are very serious business.

Principles of Grading

From the outset several axioms of grading should be clear. First, the teacher alone must make the grading decisions. No one knows the child's achievement as well as the teacher. No one knows the instructional objectives and who is making progress toward those objectives like the teacher. No one has access to more assessment data, and is more capable of making a conclusion about the child's progress than the teacher.

Second, judgment is an important factor in all grading. The teacher's selection of materials designed to promote a child's progress is based on a judgment. A part of the decision as to how well the child did the work assigned is a judgment. How much effort the child put into the work is a judgment. The cutoff points for different grades is a judgment. Educators cannot strip judgment out of the grading system.

However, teachers must strive to keep their judgments grounded in tangible evidence—test scores, anecdotal records, work samples—so that they can have faith in the fairness and validity of their judgments and can support them to other people. Ms. Brown is grading her fifth-grade class in arithmetic. Will she likely see the achievement of Tom, a disruptive and often antagonistic boy, the same as she does the congenial and cooperative John? To reduce the impact of the teachers differential responses to various children, **grounding of judgments** should be consciously pursued. This means that judgments should not be made without hard evidence that the judgment addresses achievement in the subject alone, and is not affected by a child's irrelevant behavior.

The third principle of grading is that there are several approaches to reporting a student's achievement, and a combination of approaches may convey the student's achievement better than any single method alone. Grades, such as A, B, C, and so on, project a picture of a student's work. However, they become even more descriptive if accompanied by a parent conference or a letter from the teacher.

Why Educators Grade Achievement

Grades are designed first and foremost to indicate a level of achievement. As such an indicator grades are useful in several areas of the academic endeavor. Here are some important functions of grades.

Functions of Grading

1. Grades indicate how well instructional objectives are being achieved.
2. They describe to children and parents the quality of a child's work.
3. They support administrative functions such as conferring awards, determining eligibility for events, aid in school curriculum planning, are vital in school reports, and help counselors to plan student programs.
4. Grades suggest to potential employers and college admissions professionals the level of the applicant's achievement.

Let's take a closer look at these functions.

Grades Point to Achievement of Instructional Objectives

Grades which are based on evidence of achievement are indicators of what the child has learned and what skills have been acquired. A grade should be based on the achievement objectives of the topic for which the grade is assigned. A grade in spelling should relate to achievement of the objectives of spelling instruction. A grade in history must reflect attainment of the objectives for the class in history. Grades bring objectives to the forefront, because reaching objectives is the yardstick by which we determine grades.

Grades will be most useful as instructional aids if they communicate progress toward a goal. The grade should be identified with the objectives for the marking period. When a student or parent sees the grade, it should be clear what skill it represents, and what the mark indicates in terms of attainment of the skill. This means that behavioral based definitions (see Chapter 2) should underpin a grading procedure.

Grades should also reflect the student's strong and not-so-strong skills and knowledge in regard to reaching the objective. In this way, grades have the potential for being diagnostic. But this information alone is of no value. The teacher, parents, and student must make a plan for acting on the information, something which is too often left undone.

Grades are a reflection of achievement and should not be influenced by personal qualities. However, where aspects of personal and social development are specifically observed to be a hinderance to more rapid achievement the grade report should point this out separately. For example, if the child is getting behind in history because of poor study skills (if specifically observed) this should be reported separately from achievement. Communicating this problem to the child and the parent may be helpful in their work to improve achievement. But it should not be part of the grade in history.

To some extent, grades are a motivator, but motivation is not a purpose of grades. They should not be assigned to spur students on in their work, nor should they be held over the heads of students as an incentive. Grades should reflect achievement, not hard work or lack of it, not neatness or lack of it.

I sat in the back of Mr. George's algebra class on the first day of the semester and listened to his orientation for his students. "And please note this!" he said. "For each day you are absent without a legitimate excuse your grade will be reduced by a half-letter grade level, and for every three tardy days you lose a half grade level." Yes, teachers want their students to attend class and to be on time, but if students are late a third time during the semester does it mean they suddenly know less than they did before that third tardiness? Grades are not intended to be a physical control mechanism. They are intended to report achievement.

Grades as Means of Communication

Parents vary widely in their interest in their child's achievement (Steinberg, 1996). However, more parents will want to see your reports about their child's achievement than will not. Parents have invested a great deal of effort in their child's development and many have definite aspirations for them. They know that one underpinning of success in life is to be "smart" and learn all they can in school. A good report card for the child is to many parents a validation for their work in raising that child.

Parents can be a valuable ally in our efforts to teach children. Some parents will help motivate children, assist with homework, and project the idea that school is important. These parents will want to know how well their children are doing in school. They will appreciate a single summary mark that clearly communicates achievement. Also, they will want to know how this mark can be translated into behaviors they can work on. To do this our reports must identify and evaluate observable behaviors for the parents.

Students also want to know how the teacher evaluates their work. They want to know how they stand in terms of other students or in reference to a criterion of achievement. Grades provide this information. Students also read the teacher's comments and assess them as guides to their future work or they assess them in terms of reality (Ms. Jones says I talk too much in class, but I don't think she is right!). The report card gives the child a basis for discussions with the teacher to plan changes in behavior for the near future.

Use of Grades in Administration

Schools have a need for grades on a broader level than just communicating to students and parents how well the students are doing. Schools must decide who will be promoted from year to year. Prior to graduation schools accumulate for each student credits in curriculum areas such as mathematics, science, social studies, and communication skills. In addition, every student must have a set number of credits in the general studies program. Grades are the deciding factor in granting credit in these curricular areas.

Schools also use grades to plan curricula in various subject areas. Does this school have enough high achieving students to start a special class for accelerated learners? Grade records may help here. In what aspects of our objectives in foreign language do our students do the best? How shall the instructors change their presentation here? A teacher's formative marks will provide data for curriculum planning in all areas of the program.

School administration is also responsible for rewarding high achievement with honor roll selection and scholarships. Grades are the primary vehicle for making these awards. In many schools, grades also are the basis for determining eligibility for extracurricular activities.

Grades have yet another function in the overall administration of a school. They are valuable aids to counseling students in their program and in their personal development. One of the first items a counselor will look for in a student's folder is a report of grades. This record of achievement is used as a clue to future achievement, and as such will help counselors sort out courses that may fit the student's motivation and skill level. It may also be an aid in career planning. For example, if Charlene's marks in mathematics are mediocre, and she is thinking about enrolling in an engineering college, the counselor may wish to suggest some avenues to improving her status in mathematics, or to suggest alternative programs that have a lower demand on quantitative skills. Counselors need grade reports to carry off their jobs well.

Use of Grades by Employers

Much of school learning relates to daily life, for example, knowledge of government, enjoyment of art and literature, the ability to move through a complex quantitative world; but probably no aspect of education gets more attention than how achievement relates to getting a satisfying job. In making hiring decisions some employers want a quick summary of how the applicant has done in academic pursuits, especially in those areas that are most relevant to the job in question. Sadly, fewer employers are now asking for school records, than once was true, projecting a value message to students (Steinberg, 1996, op. cit.).

If grades are to represent student skill in the situations discussed above, they must represent achievement. They cannot represent attitude toward the class, or the difference between aptitude and achievement, or improvement during the term. They must communicate to the employer what skill level the student has in the various areas of the program. To the extent that this is true, grades are useful to employers in fitting students to appropriate jobs. It also tells the student that grade achievement is an important objective if they are to appear attractive in the job market. Motivation to achieve a record that is interesting to employers, as well as communicating skill levels to potential employers are important functions of grades in one's own personal economics.

Types of Grades

There is a wide diversity of opinion among educators as to what a "good" grading system should be. The most common grading systems involve the familiar letter grades: A, B, C, D, F. Some people feel that fewer categories, such as Pass-Fail, are satisfactory. Still others think that schools need to define objectives in greater detail and provide a checklist for each objective. And some teachers feel that no grading system communicates well enough to be useful; they advocate a narrative, written by the teacher, instead of marks.

Each of these systems has advantages and disadvantages in describing what a child is achieving within a set of instructional objectives. Some elaboration of each will identify both the advantages and the problems with these grading practices.

Letter Grades

Almost everyone is familiar with the **letter grade system** (A, B, C, D, F) in which A represents highest achievement and F means failure to make notable progress. It is probably the oldest system still in use and school professionals and parents think they understand it. It is taken as a concise summary of a student's work. Averages based on letter grades predict a student's future academic work about as well as anything we have (including college aptitude tests).

However, the system has limitations. One of its assets is also a liability—it sums an entire term's work with a single grade. Here teachers may look at a student's achievement of objectives, but a single grade cannot describe strengths and weaknesses in the student's performance. Sometimes a more detailed description of work would be informative. For example, Ms. Emptman, a ninth-grade Social Studies teacher recently said, "Sarah works well with the concrete features of history, but has difficulty with making generalizations out of events. I gave her a B because so much of history is knowledge of events, but if we are to profit from history we also need to make some conclusions."

But Mr. Presser, a parent of a fifth-grade boy and a ninth-grade girl, raised the topic of grading in a recent parent-teacher meeting. "With so many variables, such as effort and potential, entering into grades, how do we know what they mean? They not only mean something different to each teacher, they mean something different from child to child within a class!"

There is evidence that teachers do indeed use nonachievement variables in arriving at grades for different students in their classes (Friedman & Manley, 1991). To the extent that teachers do not stick to a clear achievement criterion for grades, Mr. Presser is right. A grade of B for Roger, who achieved it from class test scores and project evaluations alone, does not mean the same as does the B awarded Sarah who got part of her grade because, in spite of modest ability, she worked hard, had a "good" attitude, and a very positive interest in the subject.

In sum, teachers who have no clear set of criteria that apply equally to grading all children are free to grade each child by combining several variables with different weights for each child. Grades recorded with this procedure cannot have the same meaning for any two students. The solution? Base grades on clear indicators of achievement (O'Conner, 1995).

There are adaptations of the letter grading system which some teachers feel fits their interests better than the A, B, C, D, F system. For example, some teachers like to use H (honors), S (satisfactory), and U (unsatisfactory). The categories are wider, and "reward" high achieving students, while raising a flag for children not making adequate progress.

In the primary grades, where finer discriminations among student work is seen as unnecessary by some educators, the H, S, and U system has its greatest following. Young children may well have difficulty understanding a more complex system, but seem to have a grasp of one as simple as H, S, and U, especially if objectives are broken down into component skills and each is graded separately. This will make the system somewhat diagnostic and communicates to parents better than if only one grade is given for each subject area, for example, mathematics. In this case a separate grade in fundamental processes and in application of solving problems in the context of the community might be a bit more diagnostic than one grade in mathematics.

Pass-Fail Grading

Some schools and many colleges have implemented the **Pass-Fail** system of grading, in which all students who show "acceptable" achievement are awarded a Pass and those who do not, a Fail. This system is not intended to discriminate among levels of achievement by students in the class. Rather, it is a system that either gives or withholds credit for a given course.

Pass-Fail has the advantage of allowing students to elect a course, or courses, for which they feel ill-prepared. In the traditional grading systems, students will most often avoid a course in which they may not get an above-average mark because it will erode their grade point average and lower their probability of being accepted at the "best" colleges. With Pass-Fail grading they do not run this risk, and consequently may take courses in which they have some interest, but feel they have little background. This is the greatest advantage of the Pass-Fail system.

There are, as you may have guessed, problems with this system. The very gross markings (only two categories) provides little information about any student's achievement in the class. Therefore, the grading system communicates very little about skills, problem solving, or any other goal. It only shows that the student has received credit, or has not.

This can be turned into a positive aspect in some situations, as is the case with mastery learning. If in Introductory Geology Mr. Erdman requires all students to identify a list of 50 different rocks he has on display, cite their origin, and at least two geographic locations where they are found, he may pass any student who can complete these tasks and fail those who cannot. If the teacher, such as Mr. Erdman, has established a set of criteria that every student must achieve for credit, and reaching these criteria will be granted a Pass grade, then the mark will carry more meaning. However, most applications of Pass-Fail grading are not in mastery courses.

A disadvantage of the Pass-Fail system is the extent to which motivation plays a part. Although motivation is not a focal purpose of grading, many students work harder when they realize their grades are slipping back a tad. The Pass-Fail system has less a motivating quality (Karlins, Kaplan & Stuart, 1969) than do most other systems. Students realize they do not have to do more than is required for the minimum criterion, so they tend to put in less effort.

Although Pass-Fail courses are taken by students to explore work in academic areas in which they may not otherwise enroll, they also use Pass-Fail to take courses they would take anyway. This allows them to take the work in a more casual, less pressured atmosphere (Stallings & Smock, 1971).

Checklist Systems for Grading

In a **checklist system** the report card is a list of objectives, sorted by subject areas. The teacher checks the ones the child has mastered. Often the checklist is altered to make it similar to a rating scale. In this case the objectives are listed, but the teacher's marks show how far along the student is toward achieving the objective. Symbols such as H, S, U (as discussed above) are used, or sometime O (outstanding) is used instead of H (honors). Here is an example of one objective.

Performs one-digit addition with at least 95% accuracy U S O

This system is most often used in the elementary schools, but has application at secondary school levels, also. It is an effective way to communicate with students and parents. Several features must be kept in mind, however, while using the system. The list of objectives must be short or the report becomes cumbersome. The objectives must be written in behavioral terms and in language parents and students can understand. The mark that teachers make must be supported by evidence beyond a hunch; tests and observational records are needed as a basis for the marks. This record-keeping may be time consuming, but it is essential for diagnostic grading.

✎ Problems

1. Compare and contrast the uses of grades by a curriculum coordinator, a local company's personnel director, and a parent.
2. What are the advantages of the A, B, C, D, F system and what are its problems?
3. What is the purpose of Pass-Fail grading? What are its advantages and problems?

The Bases of Grading

"What does this grade of B tell me about my daughter's reading skill," asks Mrs. Quilmer, mother of a nine-year-old fourth-grader.

Ms. Redding, the child's teacher, quickly opened a file with the distribution of class scores on a recent test. "Here is how the class is doing at this point in time in reading comprehension," she said. Your daughter's score puts her right here. That is right in the middle of the B range."

"But how did you decide where the B range is?" asked Mrs. Quilmer.

"Before the term began I decided that, based on my previous classes, the top 15 percent—my very best readers—would get A's. About 25 percent would get the B's. Your daughter fits into that group."

"I get it," replied the mother. "Your grades depend on where my child ranks among her classmates." She paused a moment. "But what if 25 percent of the class is doing very well; does only 15 percent still get A's?"

Mrs. Quilmer has hit upon a problem with a ranking base for grades. Let's explore this a bit further.

Rank Among Peers

A common system for assigning grades is based on where students rank among their peers. Those who rank high get the A's, while those who rank low get the D's and an occasional F. In order to increase objectivity, advocates of this system at one time carried it so far that statisticians were asked to pose the percent of the class that should get an A, the percent that should get a B, and so on. These percentages came from the normal (bell-shaped) curve. This is why the system is often called "curving the class" or "grading on the curve."

If this is your system for determining grades you must establish the grade distribution at the outset, with the percentage of the class that will receive each grade mark. Also you must decide what performances will be considered as part of the grade and how these will be weighted. For example, if you will give three tests, or will require a term paper or major problem solution, these should be cited in your class outline. You should also cite how these components of the grade will be combined into one achievement value, which will be ranked to determine the grade.

When teachers use a system requiring an established setting of percentages for each grade mark based on rank in the class, they assume they know something about the shape of the distribution of skills in the classes. Experienced teachers who have accumulated data over several years may hypothesize that the achievement of the current class will look like the past classes, but most teachers will find it difficult to come up with specific percentages. Certainly it would be a rare class that would fit the normal curve. Also, rank in the class does not tell much about the achievement of objectives for the grading period. An A in your class means a student ranks in the top 15 percent of the class in reading comprehension. Although inferences may be made, the grade does not tell which objectives were achieved. Maybe they are all excellent readers, or maybe they are all terrible readers. The A will surely be more meaningful if it is related to skills.

Performance Criteria

This brings you and me to the next system of assigning grades—established performance criteria. Suppose I have a class in science and I am teaching electricity. I have listed a set of performances for the class to achieve. Some of these require paper and pencil work, some require the solution of laboratory problems, and some require relating work to utilization of electricity in the neighborhood. My grading plan requires the successful demonstration of all listed performances for an A. Then I list a subset of the performances that must be successfully demonstrated for a B, and so on for a C and D. Here a grade more nearly indicates what skills the student in fact has. You and I can interpret the grade in terms of subject-matter content.

Now when a parent says, "My son got a B in spelling, what does this B mean?" the teacher can point to the skills the boy has shown he has acquired. This makes sense to the parent, in most cases.

A variation of this method does not require teachers to list specific performance that must be demonstrated for each grade. Instead, a percentage of the performances is used. For example, the student who demonstrates at least 85 percent of the performances will get an A. This system has much the same effect as listing performances that must be demonstrated, but is far easier to manage. However, the exact performances that are the basis of the grade must be identified and recorded.

In the criterion standard approach to grading, all students can get A's. It is also possible for none of them to get an A. It depends on how many of the criterion performances a student has demonstrated. Under these circumstances the meaning of the grade is constant across classes. For example, suppose you have a very capable class this fall, but had a less capable class last fall. If you graded on the basis of status in the class, the highest ranking students in each class would get the A grades. However, the difference in achievement between students who got A's in the two classes is likely to be quite different. If you used a performance criterion method, this comparison across classes would likely be more equitable. In both classes the students would have to demonstrate ability to complete the same tasks in order to get the same grades.

It should be pointed out that in many classes there will be a positive correlation between grades assigned by the performance criterion and rankings among peers methods. The students who rank highest in the class are very likely to be the ones who can successfully demonstrate the most skills. However, in the ranking system the cutoff point between the grades is not tied to the number of skills demonstrated.

A variation of the performance criterion approach is the **contract plan,** in which the teacher makes a "contract" with each student as to the objectives the student will achieve for various grades by the end of the term. Grades are assigned in reference to fulfilling the contract. The attractiveness of the system is that it individualizes the student work and involves the student in setting the standards for his or her grades. However, grades lose meaning when the definition of achievement varies with each student. Grades based on this system may have meaning for the student, but little meaning for other persons who are interested in the student's achievement; a B for Jerry does not mean the same as a B for Caroline.

Grading on Improvement

There will be a range of aptitudes in any class, and that means some children will not meet all the criterion standards in any given grading period. Because of this, some teachers wish to base all, or at least a part, of their grades on improvements the student has made since the last grade was assigned. This typically requires a pretest and a posttest to show improvement. In this system, even the students with less aptitude have a good chance to get higher grades by showing more improvement over the term, which appeals to the sense of fairness teachers hope to promote in their classes.

However, there are several problems with this method. People who evaluate the grades of a group of students still want to relate them to what the student can or cannot do, and this system cannot provide this type of information. Here is an example. In her instructor's opinion Jessie has "improved" a fair amount this term, and has an A in her computer applications class. But what can she do on the computer? If she started with no skill, maybe she can do a modest amount. But if she started with a modest amount of skill, she now should show considerable skill. Both situations, even though they demonstrate different skill levels, could bring her the same grade.

There is another problem with using improvement as a basis for grading that most teachers fail to consider. How do we put a measurement unit on improvement? How much improvement do I need to make in this term's performance to show twice as much as last term? How do I compare Julie's improvement with Joy's? Improvement is difficult to measure and consequently it is difficult to find a basis for deciding how much is "a lot" and how much is "a modest amount."

As an employer, what should I think? I see the grade of A for Jessie and conclude that she can do very good work on the computer, but the office manager reports that in the interview Jessie was given a computer trial and did quite poorly. In school, she had improved considerably during the grading period, but still may not be at a level where she can manage routine problems without advice.

Another difficulty arises when we grade on improvement. Students are wise enough to know that one way to show improvement is to do poorly on the initial assessment. This puts them at a lower starting point for the term and allows them to show more improvement without unusual effort.

There are some other problems with the improvement criterion for grading that are more complex to explain than we need here, so I will just cite one. Statisticians have advised us that oftentimes people who score very high on one test of a skill tend not to score as high on a retest of the same skill. (The opposite effect is true for the lower end of the score distribution.) Simply, person's scores on either high or low ends of the curve on retesting tend to regress toward the mean. This is called the **regression effect.** If this shift is so, it is much harder for students who score in the upper tail of the distribution to show considerable improvement than it is for students in the lower end of the curve. For this reason most statisticians will caution people who wish to use improvement as a basis for grading.

Achievement Compared to Aptitude

In this grading system students' achievement is compared with their aptitude for learning. More is expected from students with high aptitude than from students with less aptitude. Jayson, who has a high numerical aptitude, must do more to get a B than Gaylan, who has a lower aptitude. In the previous systems we compared students with all others, and teachers compared them with a set of performance criteria. Now we are comparing students with their ability to achieve. This system is different from grading on improvement in that students are compared to the objectively determined expecta-

If your aptitude is:	and your achievement is:	your expected grade should be:
	High	A
High	Average	B
	Low	C
	High	A
Average	Average	A
	Low	B
	High	A
Low	Average	A
	Low	A

FIGURE 19.1   Grading When Aptitude is the Base for Expectation of Achievement

tions of them. Students only have to do what is expected of them, rather than show spectacular gains. The results of this type of system are illustrated in Figure 19.1.

Figure 19.1 shows that the system is likely to lead to many high grades. Of the nine categories of "Grades," six of them are "High." Students in the low aptitude category will automatically get high marks. We have low expectations for their achievement, and they will reach that expectation level or better, leading to "high" grades. However, it is difficult for students with high aptitude to get good grades. Only when they do high quality work will they get a high grade. Neither the average nor the low aptitude students are graded this severely.

This complicates the interpretation of grades. A low aptitude student who is performing at a low level of achievement will get the same grade as a high aptitude student who is performing at a high level. Does this make sense?

This system also suffers from some psychometric problems. Remember the phenomenon, called the regression effect, in which persons on the high end of a distribution of scores tend to drop back to a somewhat lower level on a retest? That phenomenon applies here, too. For this reason, teachers may have unrealistic expectations for students on the high end of the aptitude measurement. The reverse may be true for some students on the low end of the aptitude scale.

There is another problem with the comparison of achievement with aptitude. Users of this system must be very familiar with the aptitude measure to know just how well it can be expected to relate to the achievement that is about to be graded. Some aptitude measures do not correlate particularly well with measures of specific achievement. When this is so, teachers may be determining expectations for achievement based on an aptitude measure which has little validity for doing so.

Indeed, grading students on the basis of how well they do relative to their aptitudes looks intriguing, but in fact has too many drawbacks to be useful.

Other Variables in Grading

This chapter began by stating that grades must reflect achievement. Variables that are not described in our objectives should not be incorporated into the grade. Having said this, I should point out that variables which bear on achievement (effort, attitude, attendance, tardiness, study habits) are legitimate features of a student's behavior that may be reported to parents. These may be related to achievement, but are not achievement and should not be entered into grading. They may, however, be rated separately.

Some basic guidelines for assigning grades are listed in Figure 19.2. They will help you devise your own procedures for grading.

There is one last comment on grades that must be made. Teachers probably grade too many products in the course of a school term. Not everything a child turns in to you needs a grade. Oftentimes some comments on what is done well and how the child might do a better job next time will be more useful than a grade. Do not feel compelled to grade every student effort. Instead, use them as instructional vehicles and let your marks on them be praise for good work and guidelines for improvement. This not only will help the student in acquiring skill, but can also lead the student toward being a better self-evaluator, something a single grade on the paper probably will not do.

✎ Problems

1. Compare the rank-among-peers procedure for grade assignment to the performance criterion approach. Note the logic of each and how they relate to instructional objectives.
2. List the limitations of grading students on their improvement. Can you think of any way to overcome any of these limitations?

---

1. At the outset of instruction provide each student with a description of the basis for grades, when the exercises should be completed, and how they will be weighted in the total grade.
2. Emphasize that grades will be based on achievement of the course objectives and nothing else.
3. Be sure that your evidence is valid for the learning objectives you have outlined for the class.
4. Return all tests, papers, etc. to students promptly and review these with the students to fix appropriate responses in the minds of the students.
5. Do not take away from grades for student tardiness, absence, lack of effort, or other nonachievement behaviors.
6. Grade all students under the same rules.
7. Use a standard method for combining observaiton into a total grade score.

FIGURE 19.2 Guidelines for Appropriate Grading Practice

3. If you wanted to grade on achievement based on aptitude, how would you assess aptitude?

4. Mr. Parmak recently described his grading system to a student teacher. He said, "I look at their test scores, the assessment I make of their lab work, and their group work. Then I go through the class roster and pick out some kids who have worked really hard, and some who have goofed off, or been late to class a lot—that kind of thing. I adjust the grades up if they have been good workers, down if they have been lazy or disruptive." How would you respond to Mr. Parmak's grading plan?

5. Ms. Jennings, a fourth-grade teacher, has assigned Julie a B in mathematics. She makes calculation errors and is not a good problem solver, but she works hard and asks for extra practice. Ms. Jennings wants to reward her for her hard work. Joan also got a B. She finds mathematics fairly easy, but never works at it very intently. She can do calculations quickly and solves problems well and her test scores are high. Ms. Jennings wants to motivate her to work harder. Comment on the teacher's approach to assigning grades.

Combining Marks to Produce Grades

Mr. Gerhardt, a German language teacher, has reached the end of another marking period. His course outline listed four data points for the work of the term. The first is a pretest and used only for advisory purposes in beginning the class. The last three tests would weigh equally in the students' grades. The first test dealt with how to manage parts of speech and sentence structure. His second test included the use of verbs and articles, and would be given a third of the way through the term. A third test, given after two-thirds of the term, would be on vocabulary and sentence translation. And at the end of the term a reading comprehension test would be given. His class results on the last three tests looked like this:

Test	Number of items	Mean	Standard deviation	Range of scores
1	Pretest			
2	40	28	4	14–36
3	30	21	4	9–29
4	70	48	10	26–69

A little arithmetic will help us here. The last of Mr. Gerhardt's tests, having the most items, has the potential for raising or lowering a student's status in the class the most. It has more than twice the test items as Test 3. If Mr. Gerhardt simply adds up the scores for each student, the weighting of the tests in the total will not be equal, as he claims in his outline. Here is an example. Suppose two of Mr. Gerhardt's students received the following scores.

Student test	2	3	4	Sum
Allen	38	26	32	96
Mary	28	21	52	101

These data look curious. Allen, who got the lowest total score, got the highest score on two of the three tests, and was notably above average on each of these (see the previous table). Mary scored only at the mean on two of the tests but got the higher sum. Somehow this doesn't seem right, and maybe it isn't. Let's use a procedure we learned using standard scores (Chapter 14).

Using Standard Scores

In Chapter 14 you saw that both z-scores and T-scores could be used to compare two students' work. Let's assume that Mr. Gerhardt's school has a scoring service, and they converted the scores to T-scores before returning the tests to the teachers. In T-scores the mean is 50 and the standard deviation is 10, and by putting all tests on this same scale, our T-scores came out as follows.

Student test	2	3	4	Sum
Allen	75	62	34	171
Mary	50	50	54	154

Here you see Allen well above 50 (the T-score mean) on tests 2 and 3, but fell below on test 4. Meanwhile, Mary got only average on two of her tests, but a bit above average on the last. Allen's T-scores look like he did the best work across the term. Mary was doing very near average during the term and her T-scores confirm that placement.

What happened here? When we added the raw scores from the tests Mary came out ahead. The tests have very different means and a very different spread of scores. The fourth test had a very large spread of scores and many points (10). Mary's placement on the fourth test pulled her through in raw scores because this test has the most items. Hence, in raw score points the fourth test carries more weight than the other two tests. Even though Mary's raw scores show her doing just average work up to the last test, her raw score on test four pulled her ahead. She did just above average there, but even average resulted in a relatively high raw score. Allen did his worst work on the last test and this dragged him down in raw score totals.

But T-scores convert all scores to the same scale. No matter how many (or few) raw score points are possible on a given test, T-scores convert the distribution to a mean of 50 and a standard deviation of 10 points. This means that scores from each test are put onto the same distribution as all other tests—same average, same spread of scores. This levels the playing field across all tests. No student can benefit, or lose ground, just because a test happens to have a large number of items and a wide spread of scores.

When scores were converted to standard T-scores, Allen came out ahead, the logical result given the tests are equally weighted.

In sum, if your tests or other assessments show a considerable difference among themselves in mean or spread of scores (i.e., in standard deviation), the grades probably will not be entirely fair for all students if they are based on sums across all data points. In such a case, raw scores should be converted to standard scores such as T-scores. The increased effort that you put into your grading may be worth it for the gain in fairness.

Averaging Letter Grades

Some teachers create a frequency distribution for scores, and mark off the ranges in which each letter grade is included. Only the letter grades are recorded in the grade book. Then the letter grades are "averaged" for the final course grade. To do this, an A = 4, B = 3, C = 2, D = 1, and F = 0. This procedure is simple to keep track of. Students only have to remember how many A's they have been awarded, how many B's, and so on.

But a real problem emerges here. Suppose, for simplicity's sake that we have two students—John and Marsha. The teacher is using T-score conversions so that each test has a mean of 50 and a standard deviation of 10 points. Here are the cutoff points between an A and a B, and the actual scores for John and Marsha on each of two tests, converted to T-scores.

		Test 1	Test 2
65 and up = A	John	66 A	56 B
55 through 64 = B	Marsha	70 A	63 B

An averaging of the A's and B's would indicate that the two students are equal. John has an A and a B, and so does Marsha. However, if I add their T-scores, John has 122 and Marsha has 133. Marsha is noticeably above John in total performance. This difference is masked when I merely "sum" the A and B each student received on the separate tests.

Generally, the recording of just A's, B's, and so on is not recommended because it is too gross in its discrimination. The actual T-scores are a preferred basis for the grades.

Grade Inflation

Grade inflation is the process of assigning more A's and B's and fewer C's, D's and F's than a logical view of achievement would call for. For example, if your idea of achievement of all freshmen in our county is something like a normal, bell-shaped curve, you would have more C's than any other grade, about as many B's as D's, and so on. However that distribution in reality is somewhat rare. Instead, teachers tend to be quite generous at grading time. The result is too many A's and B's and too few of the other grades. This is grade inflation.

There is considerable evidence that learners do better under reward than punishment. Teachers take this to mean that giving A's and B's will motivate students to do better than do C's. The level of achievement in schools today probably does not support this argument. Certainly "telling" Paulo that his work is good, when in fact he knows it is mediocre (he sees other students' work) is not providing a service to him.

In part grade inflation comes from not having a defined-by-objectives grading plan set up before the first observation is made in a term. You should know what standard you will use for grading and on what basis student work qualifies for each mark in the system. This takes some of the subjectivity out of grading, and subjectivity contributes to grade inflation about as much as any one single factor. An *a priori* grading plan also reduces some student pressure on the teacher to change grades based on subjective arguments.

Objections to Grades

Not everyone supports the use of grades (Simon & Bellanca, 1976). This section looks at a few arguments made by those persons who oppose the use of grades.

Grades and Motivation

Academics argue that achievement should be based on motivation intrinsic to the learning process—the learning itself should be the motivator; grades introduce a false kind of achievement incentive. If the grading system reduced the sorting of students by achievement, would motivation (as seen by achievement measures) remain the same? In the Pass-Fail system the pressure to achieve a "good grade" is reduced. One need only show evidence of modest achievement to pass. There is some evidence that motivation declines in these classes (Stallings & Smock, 1971), as is the case where liberal grading systems have been imposed. Certainly, to get intrinsic motivation to carry the day will require a vast change in the teaching system and in the societal attitudes toward education than now exist.

Without a graded scale of some kind how do teachers explain the level of achievement to parents, students, or employers? How do schools decide who graduates and who is eligible for activities, and so on?

Grades and Cheating

Some people are opposed to grading because evaluation of any kind encourages cheating. Evaluations carry a possibility of debasing or eroding self-image. To avoid this, people resort to means that may be dishonest. To eliminate cheating you would have to eliminate all evaluation, all assessment; but without these procedures schools would have a difficult time supporting the instructional program. Teachers must know where a child is in a skill to help the child progress. They need diagnostics to decide which skills the child is having difficulty with. Evaluation is not only an important feature of instruction, it also fulfills the many administrative needs for assessment outcomes. However, it does not follow that schools must accept cheating if evaluation is maintained. On the contrary.

Abuse of Grades

Grading meets objections because it is subject to many abuses which reduce its meaningfulness. It is true that grades are used for incentives such as getting to class on time. Also, there is evidence that teachers tend to be more liberal with students they like. Girls tend to get higher grades than boys, even when their achievement tests scores are not different. Many applications of grades are subjectively based and consequently contain some bias and error of measurement.

But because some teachers are careless graders does not mean the system is bad. It means we should help all teachers be better graders. If grades are to reflect achievement, teachers must focus on achievement in as objective a manner as possible, and follow accepted guidelines for arriving at grades. In this manner we can avoid many abuses.

Grades and Self-Esteem

Objections to grades have been made on the argument that grades instill in some less competent children a feeling of failure and lower self-esteem. Children early on identify their classmates who are competent and compare their own performance to them. They see when they do not achieve what other children are achieving. They know how their reading group ranks in the class. They see other children work arithmetic problems on the blackboard, problems that they themselves cannot work. Through all this children develop a concept of their own skills. This concept is based on many experiences. The grade on a report card is a relatively rare experience compared to all the other success-measured experiences the child has. Eliminating grades will not alter self-images to any extent: self-esteem is based on too many everyday events to be influenced greatly by a twice-a-semester report.

In sum, grades are not perfect. Their adequacy varies with the defensibility of their foundation. But there are too many uses for grades to abandon them altogether.

SUMMARY

1. Because grades may have a social and economic impact on a student, it is important for teachers to keep their conclusions about achievement grounded in tangible evidence such as test scores, records of observations, and anecdotal records.
2. Grades serve as guides for instruction, as means of communication with students and parents, and as information to be used in school administration and in employment decisions about students.
3. Types of grades include the familiar letter grades, Pass-Fail grading and checklists.
4. Among the bases for grading are the student's rank among peers, specific performance criteria, the contract plan, the amount of improvement shown by the student, and the student's achievement compared with his or her aptitude.
5. Effort and personal characteristics are not the same as achievement and should not be added into the grading decision.
6. In combining marks to arrive at a letter grade, it is preferable to use standard scores rather than raw scores.

7. Averaging students letter grades tends to obscure important differences among students' actual levels of achievement.
8. Grade inflation occurs when teachers grade too generously, resulting in a disproportionate number of high grades.
9. Among the objections to grades are that grades provide extrinsic motivation, encourage cheating, are subject to abuse that reduces meaningfulness of grades, and can have a negative effect on some children's self-image.

A REAL CASE NARRATIVE

Here is a vignette of an event in a local high school. As you read think how the teacher might have improved his grading procedures, and how could he have responded to the parent.

Mrs. Wilson, mother of Gerald, a tenth-grader, had come to school to discuss Gerald's work in English composition with Mr. Rittel, the English teacher.

"I'm not pleased with Gerald's grade in English," she began. "We expect to send him to college, and he has to be able to write well when he gets there."

"I understand," Mr. Rittel replied benevolently, "Writing is important to success in college!"

"What is this grade based on?" asked Mrs. Wilson, pulling Gerald's report card out of her purse.

"Well, it's a combination of his total work for the semester—themes, a book report, discussion in class, effort, things like that, you know," said Mr. Rittel.

"How much does discussion count? Gerald is shy and doesn't talk much in groups. What characteristics of discussion are graded—quantity, insight, what? And how do you record these?" asked Mrs. Wilson.

"Well, I don't give a score in discussion, but I know good discussion when I hear it; and if a student is on the borderline between two grades I use discussion to help me decide which grade to award. But my emphasis is on themes. Each of them counts for ten points. But I know who is doing a good job in this class and who isn't!" Mr. Rittel said firmly.

Mrs. Wilson thought a minute. "What guide do you use in deciding if a theme gets 7 points or 8 and so on?"

Mr. Rittel became a bit impatient. "I've read a lot of themes in my time and I have a definite feeling for what makes a good theme, a mediocre one, and a poor one!"

But Mrs. Wilson persisted. "If Gerald and I don't know what features influence those judgments, how can I help him improve?"

PROBLEMS

1. You are going to speak to a group of principals, counselors, a student's mother who is president of the Parent Teachers Association, and local company personnel directors. Your topic is "Doing away with letter grades." What do you think will be the response of each of these people to your proposal?

2. You are to be in a debate on the proposition: Resolved: that rank among ones peers is the fairest method of grading.
   a. Jot down some points the affirmative speaker might make.
   b. Jot down some points the negative speaker might make.
3. You are to go to the teachers' meeting at Eisenhower High School today to make a pitch for Pass-Fail grading for elective courses. Make a list of points you would use to sell your proposition. What objections would you expect to get from your colleagues?
4. I am about to "sell" the teachers at your school on a plan for grading students according to their ability. Knowing what my plan is, you have made notes on some reasons you oppose this style of grading. What are the points you would make?
5. Mr. Windgate, a teacher of Earth Science, has given two tests. He will now sum them to get a grade for each student. On the first test the mean was 36, standard deviation 4 score points. On the second test the mean was 28, standard deviation 8 score points. Chang has 40 on the first test, and 28 on the second one. Pei has 36 on the first test, and 36 on the second. In raw scores which has the highest sum across the two tests? In T-scores which one has the highest sum? (Consult Chapter 14 for information on T-scores.)
6. On the same tests as in Problem 5, Sandy has a score of 32 on the first test, and 32 on the second one. Sarah has 38 on the first test, and 23 on the second. In raw scores which one is highest; in T-scores which one is highest?

KEY TERMS

grades

grounding of judgments

letter grade system

pass-fail system

checklist system

contract plan

regression effect

grade inflation

ADDITIONAL READING

Bartlett, L. (1987). Academic evaluation and student discipline don't mix: A critical review. *Journal of Law and Education,* 16 (4), 1555–1565.

Brookhart, S. M. (1993). Teachers' grading practices: Meaning and values. *Journal of Educational Measurement,* 30, 123–142.

Geisinger, G. T., Marking systems. In *Encyclopedia of Educational Research,* 5th ed., vol. 3, pp. 1139–1149. New York: Macmillan, 1982.

Kubiszyn, T. and Borich, G. Marks and marking systems. In L. Kunder (Ed.), *The Effective Teacher,* pp. 365–369. New York: Random House, 1989.

Placer, M. (1995). "But I have to have an A": Probing the cultural meanings and ethical dilemmas of grades in teacher education. *Teacher Education Quarterly,* 22, 45–63.

Stiggins, R. A., Frisbie, D. A., and Griswold, P. A. (1989). Inside high school grading practices: Building a research agenda. *Educational Measurement: Issues and Practices,* 8 (2), 5–14.

Wendel, F. C. and Anderson, K. E. (1994). Grading and marking systems: What are the practices? *NASSP Bulletin,* 78, 79–84.

CHAPTER 20

TELLING PARENTS ABOUT THEIR CHILD'S ACHIEVEMENT

Ms. Lipstein slowly sipped at her coffee as she listened to her neighbor, Ms. Leggit, fuss about her child's achievement report. "I wish I could design a report card!" Ms. Lipstein broke in. "There are things I want to know about—things that the card never includes."

Ms. Leggit thought a moment as she stirred her coffee. "I wish I knew how well my kids are doing compared to what they should know at their age. I have no idea if they are doing what 7 and 10 year olds should be doing."

"I'd like to know what exactly my kid can and can't do in reading, arithmetic, and all that. A report card with a grade of B on it doesn't tell me that!" continued Ms. Lipstein.

Report cards are a common topic at coffee klatsches across the country. There are many views proposed and many ideas suggested for changing the report card. Schools could profit from tapping into these conversations. After all, reports to parents are for the parents. Parents' desire for information is central to developing reporting procedures. Nevertheless, there is some evidence that parents do not dislike the traditional report card (Ohlhausen, 1994).

This chapter is about communicating with parents or other caregivers about how their children are doing in school. Traditionally, the school has devised a system under which the report is produced and is communicated to parents via a "card," in a letter, or in a conference. In this chapter we will look at some procedures for reporting to parents, point to some problems, and to some improvements that can be made. However, no one reporting procedure is satisfactory for all schools. Therefore, teachers need to be familiar with a variety of communication techniques in order to adapt them to their schools needs. In this chapter a number of communication techniques are presented for your consideration.

What This Chapter Will Include.   In this chapter, you will learn about:

1. Report cards' minimal features
2. Guidelines for creating and using report cards
3. Advantages and limitations of report cards
4. How to build a report card for your school
5. Letters to parents
6. Parent conferences

Report Cards

If you send requests for a sample of their report cards to 20 schools across the nation, there will be some differences but also many common features among the cards you receive. Most cards currently break the report into two topics—achievement in academic subjects, and development of personal/social characteristics. This procedure is sometimes referred to as the **dual,** or **multiple marking system.**

Grades in achievement are primary features of a report card. Since it is important that these have meaning, most report cards include definitions of grade marks. However for most cards, reading these descriptions is not very helpful in understanding just what a child has done, or can do. Definitions are nonspecific, partly because many teachers themselves have difficulty stating what their grades mean in terms of achievement.

Personal/social development is also an important citation on report cards. Here the topics listed on the report card are often limited to those that promote order in the classroom, and those that expedite the teacher's work in developing a unit of instruction. This section of the card reports achievement-related items such as, "Follows directions," "Finishes work on time," "Shows good effort," and social development items such as "Is courteous," and "Follows rules."

Report cards should also report days absent and tardy. This is increasingly important in a society in which parents are often working and do not know for sure if the child has actually gone to school every day or even stayed at school all day.

Report cards should also include space for teacher comments to the parent. The space is typically short and allows only a general statement. A review of teachers' comments shows them to be either broad assertions of support for the child or a statement that points to a deficiency already evident in the grade marks. Typical comments by teachers are, "Your son is doing well," "Susan is a pleasure to have in my class," "Jeremy needs a little help with math, but is otherwise up to expectations." Most comments are not diagnostic nor do they prescribe specific ways parents can assist the child. The space on the card is typically too small to allow more than a generalization about the child.

A typical report card is shown in Figure 20.1.

Guidelines for Creating and Using Report Cards

Because the form of the report card has been shown to affect the validity of the assigned grades (Friedman, 1995), some guidelines for structuring of the card are

PARENT OR TEACHER COMMENTS (Please Date)

First Grading Period _____

Second Grading Period _____

Third Grading Period _____

Fourth Grading Period _____

PARENT OR GUARDIAN SIGNATURE

1. _____
2. _____
3. _____

The content of this report is a part of the student's cumulative record and will be forwarded along with all other contents of the cumulative record to any MCCSC school to which the student may transfer, or at the time the student moves into a higher grade situation. Should the student move to another school system, the cumulative record will be transferred to the receiving school, at the request of the parent or the receiving school.

In accordance with the Family Rights and Privacy Act, parents or guardians have the right to review their student's records. Copies of MCCSC Policy and Regulation 5125, outlining these rights and procedures, are available for review in the office of each MCCSC School or the Administration Center, 315 North Drive, Bloomington, IN 47401.

It is the policy of the Monroe County Community School Corporation not to discriminate on the basis of sex in its educational programs, activities, or employment policies as required by Title IX of the 1972 Education Amendments. Inquiries regarding compliance with Title IX may be directed to the Director of Personnel, 315 North Drive, Bloomington, IN 47401 (330-3400) or the Director of the Office for Civil Rights, Department of Health, Education and Welfare, Washington, D.C.

Report to Parents
Templeton Elementary School
1400 S. Brenda Lane
Bloomington, IN 47401
812/330-7735

S.M.I.L.E.

Student _____

School _____

School Year _____ Grade _____

Teacher _____

Teacher _____

Principal _____

The total development of every child's intellectual, emotional, social and physical development is the responsibility of parents, students, teachers and administrators. This report represents an evaluation of your child's progress in school.

Grade Placement for Next Year _____

Reading	1	2	3	4
Reading Level				
Comprehends what is read				
Takes the initiative to read				
Uses strategies when confronted with an unknown word				
Completion of work				

Language Arts				
Uses correct capitalization				
Uses correct punctuation				
Can share ideas through writing				
Displays knowledge of different forms of writing				
Participated in the Author Circle with writing				
Oral presentation of writings				
Writes legibly and neatly				
Learns spelling words				
Completion of work				

Math				
Computes basic facts				
Shows working knowledge of concepts				
Problem solving				
Uses manipulatives appropriately				
Completion of work				

Social Sciences (Science, Social, Health)				
Demonstrates knowledge of content area				
Uses observation skills				
Develops pertinent questions				
Gathers data				
Interprets data				
Meets project requirements				
Works cooperatively				

Technology				
Exhibits proper use of equipment				
Exhibits working knowledge of available software				

Key

(I) Introduce a Skill   (S) Secure in Skill   (N) Not Yet Developing Skill
(D) Developing Skill   (E) Excels Beyond Expectations   (A) Working at Ability Level

An Explanation of the Key

(I) Teacher has introduced the skill but does not feel comfortable evaluating it.
(D) Child is developing in the skill, however, they are not consistent in the use of the skill.
(S) Child shows working knowledge of the skill at least 80% of the time.
(E) Working above classroom expectations using own initiative, developing independent projects
(N) Class has been working on skill but student has not developed the skill yet.
(A) Working at ability level.

Frames				
Participation				
Cooperation				

Social Skills	1	2	3	4
Confidence in self				
Sense of community				
Changes tasks easily				
Takes responsibility for actions				
Works well with others				
Works independently				
Gives personal best				
Willing to take risks				
Uses common sense				
Takes Initiative				
Follows a task to completion				
Plans and uses time effectively				

Music				

Art				

Physical Education				

Attendance				
absent - excused				
absent - unexcused				
present				
tardy				

FIGURE 20.1 A sample report card. No one report card fits all teaching situations. How might you alter this card to fit a situation with which you are familiar?

useful (Mehring & Frisbie, 1991). Following are some things that we can do to make our report cards better communicators.

1. Cards should provide for ratings on progress toward important course objectives.
2. Methods used to translate achievement of course objectives into grades should be clear.
3. Cards should provide for comment on the child's work.
4. Judgments should be grounded in data.
5. Involve students in assessment of their progress.

Let's take a closer look at each of these guidelines.

Cards should provide for ratings on important course objectives. First and foremost report cards should convey the child's status in achieving the objectives of the central subjects of the program. Teachers may also wish to break up goals into elements such as knowledge of the factual base of a subject, skill in the application of knowledge to solving problems, and ability to communicate in the vernacular of the subject. Work habits are also related to achievement, but to what extent do we teach children work habits? If we are going to assign a grade to it, we probably should also give children instruction on how to improve.

Teachers must resist the temptation to mark a child on behavior irrelevant to achievement. For example, in a history class the teacher may wish to rate students on the ability to discuss topics that can be linked to past paradigms of national events. But you must be sure that your rating is based on the student's ability to apply lessons of history, not on his or her conversational skills or extroversion.

Methods by which achievement of course objectives are translated into a grade on the report card must be clear to parents and to students. What instructional objectives are involved, what assessments were included in the grade, and how they are weighted are all relevant questions. Were grades based on rank among peers or on performance criteria? Grades become more meaningful if these questions are answered for parents.

Take advantage of an opportunity to comment on the child's work. Although the space on the card is inadequate for a detailed description of the child's performances (Note the space in Figure 20.1.), a comment not only personalizes the card, but also allows you to point to a feature not listed on the card. Where problems exist, suggest a meeting or a telephone call, but do not leave the comment lines blank. Parents want to feel you prepared this card for them, and a personal comment helps you portray that idea.

Ground your judgments in data such as test scores, performance evaluation records, and anecdotal records. So many variables impinge on the judgments of a teacher—the demeanor of the child, physical appearance, neatness of work, social skills, and so forth. These tend to distract teachers from looking at achievement of instructional objectives. Always give focal attention to hard evidence you have collected on a child before finalizing a grade.

Students should be involved in assessment of their progress. There are two reasons for this. It gives the students a chance to take stock of their work in relation to course objectives, and in relation to their peers. What things do I do well that I want my teacher and parents to note? Where do I do less well? How do I see myself among my peers? In family discussions, parents seldom get this kind of information from their children.

Student input also provides them with an exercise in self-evaluation. This opens avenues for students to see where they can promote their academic status and gives them a chance to relate their views of their activity in the school environment. It teaches them to be better self-evaluators.

Collecting Student Input

How can educators collect student self-evaluation data? One way is to create a rating scale for students to fill in. Another might be a guided short-answer exercise in which the teacher cites topics to which students should respond with a sentence or less. Additional lines that are not labeled should be added so students may make responses on any selected topic. (An example of a self-evaluation form is shown in Figure 20.2.) These procedures should not be used until children are in the upper elementary grades. Many high school students, however, will welcome a chance to comply with self-evaluation requests.

When students use work sheets to submit self-evaluation commentaries, they should be advised that their work in the course is to be viewed aside from how they like or dislike the subject area. Otherwise, they will often report on their feelings and not on their skills.

Look over Figure 20.2 and decide how you might fit it into your subject area.

Advantages and Disadvantages of Report Cards

Report cards are the subject of wide commentary by students and parents, as well as in the comic strips. This is probably because the card fits some objectives better than others. The points made in the section above lead us to some functions that cards may do fairly well, and some that are done not so well. To get at these positive and not so positive qualities of cards we should look more closely at the advantages and disadvantages of report cards.

The principal advantages and disadvantages of cards are listed below.

Advantages and Disadvantages of Report Cards

Advantages

1. Report cards convey general achievement on a range of skills.
2. Parents expect minimal feedback on their children's work, cards provide this, parents believe they understand it.
3. Cards may include comments on study habits and social development.

Disadvantages

1. A single mark disguises details of a child's work.
2. Marks tell nothing about expected levels of achievement.
3. Definition of marks too general to provide meaning.

Student Self-Evaluation Form
Mathematics Grade 5

In the math skills the class has worked on this term, please respond to the following questions by marking how well you believe you are doing in each skill.

Name_____

	Very well	Moderately well	Not well
1. How well do you feel you do in adding simple fractions such as $1/3 + 2/3$ and $1/5 + 3/5$?	_____	_____	_____
2. How well do you feel you can subtract fractions like $4/5 - 2/5$, and $6/7 - 3/7$?	_____	_____	_____
3. How well do you feel you can add fractions such as $3^1/3 + 2/3$?	_____	_____	_____
4. How well do you feel you can subtract fractions such as $4^1/3 - 2/3$?	_____	_____	_____
5. How well do you feel you can apply fractions such as those above in solving word problems in our book?	_____	_____	_____
6. How well do you feel you can apply the fractions like those above in solving the real problems we found in our community?	_____	_____	_____

7. Among the students in this class where do you think you rank in arithmetic skill?

Top third of class _____
Middle third   _____
Lowest third   _____

8. What do you feel is the hardest part of solving problems with fractions?

9. What do you feel is your greatest strength in doing number work?

FIGURE 20.2

We shall first look at the advantages and then turn to the disadvantages.

Report cards convey general achievement on a range of skills. The function of the report card is to convey general information to the parent. They want to see if their sons and daughters are on "track" in their school work, to see what expectations are probably realistic and if expectations are being generally met. To the extent that teachers have followed proper procedures in assigning grades, the marks on cards can communicate quite a lot of information about a student's work. However, when work is condensed into a single mark the description of the students's actual skills may become clouded. If parents want clarification about marks on cards, direct contact with the teacher in person or by telephone may be arranged. *Parents expect a minimum amount of information about a child—report cards provide this information, and parents believe they understand the report.* Parents, for the most part, are interested in getting report cards (Ohlhausen, et al., op. cit.) and have faith that teachers' judgments are sufficiently accurate to warrant the grade marks on the card. Parents expect the school to keep them advised that the child is moving along in the program. The report card communicates a feeling of the child's adequacy as an achiever in the class; the grades on the card says the child is doing well or not so well. The card is not intended to describe what the child's strengths and weaknesses are in a skill area. However, the generalization implied by the checkmark is acceptable for many parents.

The report card can include comments on study habits and social development. Parents look for comments to reveal information about their child. They not only want comments about achievement, but also want the social/behavioral development commentary. Most parents want their children to be good citizens in school, and to work at their assignments. Remarks on these topics are often left to the teacher to devise in a rather small part of the report card, a space that allows for only the most obvious of comments. This is often all parents will want to read. The card is not intended to be diagnostic.

In sum, as a concise summary of a child's performance, the report card does its job. It is especially useful in conveying a general statement about the child's activities in school; less suitable for illustrating skills at which the child is becoming proficient. This is not, however, the intent of the card in the first place, and general statements are sufficient for many parents.

And now what about disadvantages of the report card?

A single grade mark conveys very little about a child's work. One disadvantage of the report card center's on the fact that teachers must distill so much into a small report. The card summarizes hundreds of activities into a single grade. It generalizes into one or two checkmarks the hundreds of behavioral episodes the teacher has observed during the term. By having space for only a single comment about a child, the teacher is unable to elaborate the high and the low points in a student's work. This means the card will carry very little descriptive material.

Report cards tell nothing about the difference between a child's achievement and expectations. Report cards do not communicate some important features to parents. For example, cards reflect what children are doing in general, but fail to note what they may be capable of doing. Neither do they compare a child's achievement with "typical" students in that grade. Parents often ask, "Is this about what my child is capable of doing, or should I expect more?" Cards do not provide the answer to that query. Cards fail to note what children at this age are expected to perform in the context of the present instruction. "Is my child working up to grade level?" parents ask. They will not find this answer on the typical card.

Definitions of marks are too general. As many parents will attest, definitions of the letter grades are often minimally helpful in describing what children are accomplishing. Descriptions such as A = Excellent, B = Good, C = Fair, D = Having difficulty; or C = Commendable, S = Satisfactory, N = Needs improvement, do not indicate skills achieved nor the deficiencies in achievement. If a child has a C, for Fair, what should the child do to improve? Grade marks communicate only the teacher's best estimate of the child's overall adequacy in a subject at a given point in time.

In fairness, this may not be entirely bad. To provide a more complex statement may be an improvement, but still lack definition to the parent, "Cinekwa can do the 100 one-digit multiplication facts with 90 percent accuracy," may appear informative as far as it goes. But it needs to tell parents one more thing. Is this what her teacher expects of a fourth-grader at mid-year? And what should the parents do knowing their child is at the 90 percent accuracy level in multiplication in the fourth-grade?

In sum, grade marks, being very general indicators of achievement, provide nothing that tells parents how the child is learning in relation to potential, nor does it identify strengths and weaknesses that may be guides to helping the child.

Computerized Report Cards

Some schools have computerized their report cards. The card is stored on the computer, filled out with the child's name and other particulars. The teacher's job is to call up each child's card and fill in the remainder on the computer. Space is left for comments and the teacher simply types in descriptions of the child's performance. There is some evidence that teachers do write more comments on the computerized report than when doing it by hand on the standard report card.

Computerized report cards are stored electronically, making them easy to file and to retrieve. In addition they are easily accessed by school officials such as the principal and the school counselor for their professional use. This accessibility, however, does raise the possibility of security problems. Computerized cards must be protected by complex electronic means such as unique codes, or be stored on disks or tape in locked files.

Designing a Report Card

Mrs. Lipstein (from our previous discussion) wanted to be involved in creating the report card, and so would many other parents. Teachers also feel left out of the process when they find an already printed card presented to them. Teachers should demand a role in devising this important tool.

Typically, report cards are designed by someone in the central administrative offices of the school system. But why not involve all interested parties in determining what will be on the report card? No standard report card fits all schools alike: philosophies are different; procedures are different; students and parent clientele are different. We need a card that best fits our needs for communication.

All interested people, of course, cannot conveniently meet to design a report card, but we can seek input from each of these constituencies. What do parents and students want to learn from the card? How can teachers best report this information? What aspects of achievement do teachers most want to communicate to parents? In what form would parents like to receive this information?

A group of your school colleagues might begin with categories of information, such as achievement, motivation, work habits, and interpersonal skills. Next, these educators will break up the categories into subtopics parents want to know about and that teachers can communicate, and symbols will be devised to represent levels of work in each subtopic. When educators have each of these identified, they are ready to format the report card. It should not be cast in stone, but be flexible to accommodate changes as they seem necessary.

Much of the data collection for devising a card can be done by checklists or rating scales (see Chapter 10). If these are used they should include space for parent and student comments. Focus groups can also be used to generate information and consensus. Here a committee of interested persons—teachers, parents students, local personnel officials—is selected, and the problem addressed to them. During a period of open discussion topics of common concern are listed. Then the group is steered toward consensus on the issues and concerns they have generated. The topics in the consensus are used to construct the reporting mechanism—the report card, conference, or combination of several procedures. The next-to-final form can appear in the newspaper and comments invited.

By following the procedures just discussed, we should have a reporting vehicle that periodically tells parents and students what they want to know, and is in a form teachers can efficiently complete. Communication and convenience should be the two top considerations in designing a report card.

✎ Problems

1. What are the advantages and disadvantages of the report card as a communications device?
2. If you alone were creating a report card for the teaching area in which you are working, what would be on the card, and what would be the basis for each "grade" or other mark?
3. No one report card fits all schools equally well. Teachers, parents, and students have different interests in what the report card should communicate. Imagine you were commissioned to develop a new card for your school. What procedures would you go through to develop this card?
4. Some people say that personal/social development is a factor that has some bearing on achievement and should, therefore, be factored into the grade in a class. Others say personal/social development should be assessed separately. What is your position on this controversy?

Letters to Parents

Once a device supported by influential educators, letters to parents have become a relatively uncommon reporting mechanism. Teachers who wish to communicate with parents today are likely to telephone them. However, letters provide a permanent record to which parents and teachers can refer on subsequent meetings.

Letters have some advantages that typical report cards do not have. They can speak in more detail about a subject than report cards do. They can describe things the parent can do to assist in instruction, and samples of typical work can be included with the letter. The letter provides a record for parental and teacher reference. They can describe typical behavior of a child, and extent to which their child deviates from this behavior. Letters can be more specific about learning problems and progress. An example of such a letter is shown in Figure 20.3. As a parent, would you rather get this letter describing your child's work in reading or a single mark on a report card, such as "S" for satisfactory?

These advantages seem to be a substantial endorsement for letters to parents. However, as with other reporting methods, there are some problems. Much of the school's administrative structure operates on grades. Graduation requirements are certified by grades, eligibilities are stated in grades, honors and awards are based on grades. Postgraduation institutions like to have grade reports and so do many employers. Letters do not provide a systematic and cumulative data source needed for these activities. The school would probably have to have grades of some kind, even if teachers used letters to report to parents.

RE: Jeremy

Dear Mrs. Johnson,

Jeremy is doing especially well in mathematics, and is also quite successful in science, social studies (history/government), and art. In these areas he has no problems.

However, he is having some trouble with reading. Specifically, I believe he needs a better understanding of how prefixes and suffixes enlarge the meaning of words. He also needs to expand his sight vocabulary—words we immediately recognize without sounding them out.

I have enclosed several sheets of exercises of the type that would help Jeremy with these problems. You may find these helpful in reviewing work with him. Also, I will be pleased to visit with you at your convenience if you like, so that we may coordinate our work with Jeremy. He is a good worker and a pleasure to have in class.

Sincerely,

J.D. Davis
Teacher

FIGURE 20.3   An Example of a Letter to a Parent

Then, too, writing letters, if done well, is very time consuming for teachers. These letters must be written carefully. They must communicate very precisely, but must not put the school or the teacher in hard-to-defend positions. The tone of the language must be nonconfrontational, nonaggressive, yet must communicate whatever problems are relevant. There must be no errors in letters. An error in spelling or grammar (they do occur) sharply erodes the public image of a teacher and of the school.

Letters should also be comprehensive. They should deal with all work, not just work in which a student may be having a problem. This kind of letter is not easy to write. And imagine a high school teacher with four sections of algebra averaging 25 students each, writing over 100 letters each term! It is not surprising that many teachers have demurred when the topic of letter writing arose.

Letters as sent by teachers have an added complication: they tend to focus more on personality traits than on academic achievement (Geisinger, 1982). The student's instruction has been in academic skills, and consequently that should be the focus of the report.

Generally speaking, letters to parents may convey more information than report cards. However, because they are demanding to complete, they are not in wide use. When special situations arise, the letter may be a good alternative for communicating to parents. But so is the telephone; on the telephone we can mutually give and receive information. But always write a letter to confirm a telephone conversation, because this puts the subject of the call on record, including any agreements that may have been mutually reached.

As a supplement to the report card, letters for some parents may be very useful (Fleming, 1988). In special cases where the child's work needs elaboration, or in cases where the teacher wishes to elicit the parent's assistance, a letter accompanying the report card may make an excellent combination report. However, in this case only a selected few parents would receive these letters, cutting down the chore of writing considerably. With the availability of computers, writing letters has become much easier than it once was.

In your letters be sure to begin with a positive tone, stick to the point, be specific, and include content you can support with observational records and work samples. Avoid labels, especially those that may have a negative connotation.

Parent-Teacher Conferences

The objective of reporting is communication, and the face-to-face encounter is the ideal situation for this to occur. Parent-teacher conferences are such a situation. Teachers discuss the work of a given child; parents respond and provide useful information about the child and the child's interaction with the family. Plans are made for the next reporting period.

But conferences are not a substitute for a report card, and work best when used to supplement cards. Cards carry the estimates of the child's achievement in terms of a given criterion; they are a status report. Conferences, in contrast to cards, cannot accommodate the requirements of managing school administrative functions (e.g., clearing a graduation list). Nor do they help older students in acquiring a job. Conferences communicate best at a different level than report cards do. Conferences communicate to parents the teachers' impressions of a variety of school-related events involving their child. Teachers receive parent reactions, and teachers and parents together structure plans for supporting and promoting a child's skills. Cards do not have these advantages, but there are clear needs for both kinds of reporting in a typical school setting.

Conferences, with their unique forum for parent-teacher communication, are effective at the elementary school level, but almost impossible to carry off at the middle school and senior high school level. In elementary school a teacher may have 20 to 30 parents to schedule. In the upper grades, where one teacher may have over 100 students each day, arranging conferences is next to impossible. Further, to meet each teacher with whom a child has a class, parents of upper level students may have to arrange five conferences each term. This too is a formidable chore for busy parents. In the context of work schedules and arranging child-care for other children in the family, the parent will find it impossible to spend so much time at school. Conferences, as a routine, are for elementary schools, and even here the logistics are difficult.

This does not mean that a conference with a given teacher at the upper level of schools should not occur. Teachers should communicate to parents that they welcome contacts from parents to discuss the program, or the student's progress in the program. Parents should be encouraged to visit whenever they have questions or contributions to make to the school's understanding of a student's problems.

Problems With Parent-Teacher Conferences

Following are some more specific problems of conferences as a reporting method.

Problems With Parent Conferences

1. Timing of conferences—the first conference comes too soon, the last too late.
2. Lack of training and preparation.
3. Availability of parents.
4. Defensiveness of teachers and parents.
5. Time demand takes away from instructional planning and preparation.

Now let's elaborate on each of these problems.

The Timing of Conferences is less than optimal.   In many schools, official conferences are held only twice a year. Providing more meetings becomes unwieldy due to scheduling complications and time required to complete visits. Typically, the first conference is scheduled in the fall of the year, and the other in the spring. The fall conference may come too early into the school term. Teachers do not yet have a fix on each of the students' strengths and weaknesses. They are not far enough into the individualization of instruction for special students.

Also, parents are not ready to ask good questions about their child's progress. At the fall date they have too little feedback from their child, and possibly from the school. For all but a few parents, the first conference is typically not an ideal communication forum.

The second conference comes in the early spring. Ideally, these conferences would come at a time when teachers and parents can make plans designed to promote the child's progress in the instructional program. In the spring of the year, there is probably too little instructional time left to implement a continuing plan. The conference is too late. About all there is to talk about is what has been done.

In sum, conferences scheduled too early in the school year are likely not to come before the participants have the information they need to be effective participants; conferences scheduled too late in the school year do not leave enough time to launch cooperative plans for the child before the end of the term.

Many teachers lack Training and Preparation for conferences.   Teachers are the first to tell you that they feel unprepared to begin conferences with parents. "I really feel nervous about meeting parents," Ms. Newmen says as she prepares to begin conferences with parents of her fourth-graders. "I'm concerned about not being able to deal with their anxieties. I'm sure they will have questions and expect me to have answers, and a lot of things in this business just don't have simple answers."

Feeling anxious is not uncommon even among experienced teachers, because few teachers have had any training in managing conferences. As a result they are ill prepared, have no data—test scores, products, performance assessment records—to ground their comments and opinions about the child. They have no table of specifications to illustrate to the parent what the class is pursuing. They are not ready for the conference because they have not been trained in conferencing.

Availability of Parents complicates scheduling of conferences.   In today's society both parents often are working, and children are supervised by a temporary care-giver. In other homes, there is only one parent, and that parent is working during the day and occupied with household chores in the evening. It is difficult to find a time when a parent can come to school for a conference. Some parents, because of their difficult schedules, decline to come to the conference. Other parents agree to a scheduled time, but then fail to appear. This is not always due to negligence. They have trouble getting sitters to care for young children, transportation is unpredictable, and time off from work may be impossible. We must expect that personal problems will interfere with some parents getting to a conference as scheduled and some will simply not care to attend conferences (Steinberg, 1996). The availability of parents is always a problem in conferencing.

Both parents and teachers may feel defensive in a conference.   As we approach a conference we are often uncertain as to what will take place. We know that some things that do take place could reflect negatively on our professional skill. In these circumstance we tend to be cautiously defensive. However, preparation helps us relieve these feelings of vulnerability. When we have an agenda for our conference and materials to anchor our points on the agenda, we feel more confident, and less defensive.

Parents also feel apprehension in going to conferences. We all like to think our children are models, that they do their work well, and are pleasant students to have in class. Mrs. Ringer, cashier at Super Chain grocery store is heading across the parking lot, where she hears a friend's voice, "Leaving work early? Are you all right?" Mrs.

Ringer turned to see her friend getting out of her car. "It's my conference with Billy's teacher, and I'm a little nervous. You never know what the teacher knows about Billy that I don't," Mrs. Ringer said.

This conversation is typical of the feelings many parents have when they appear at conferences. They do not know what to expect and want to hear the best, but they know that it may not turn out that way. As a result, parents often appear to be on the defensive when the conference begins.

If the entire conference continues with a defensive parent and a defensive teacher, little is likely to be achieved other than passing pleasantries and some safe, objective information. It is probably the responsibility of the teacher to "break the ice." Some friendly conversation will help get the dialogue going, but the teacher must get into describing the student's work—good and bad. That is the purpose of the conference.

Time demands of a conference may cut into preparation of lesson plans, researching class topics, and so on.   Parent conferences take time. We will put in many hours in face-to-face conversation, not to mention organizing materials as exhibits for each parent. This time commitment takes away from other work that teachers routinely do in preparing for class. Conferences are important communications operations, but daily preparations for class work are also important.

Indeed, most schools allow teachers parts of days off to carry out conferences. This eases the time pressure somewhat. But time off takes away from the days of total student-teacher contact. Both teachers and students often need all the days allotted, and more, to arrive at the objectives the school has for the year's work.

Guidelines for Implementing Parent–Teacher Conferences

Conferences can be especially beneficial in both promoting a child's progress, and in selling the school and its program to the public. To achieve these ends, conferences must be well carried out. Here are some guidelines that may help you.

Guidelines for Conferencing

1. Be prepared.
2. Initial contact should be friendly, nonconfrontational.
3. Portray each child as an individual.
4. Retain professional poise.
5. Be a good listener.
6. Keep the conference on the topic.
7. Be flexible in planning for the child.
8. Avoid technical vocabulary.
9. Support generalizations with evidence.
10. Keep notes for the record.

Let's look at each guideline in detail.

Be prepared for the conference. Make an agenda for each conference. Do not be too rigid in following the agenda, but use it as a guide that will remind you to discuss selected topics. Have exhibits on hand that will anchor your comments, including records of observations you have made, test scores, homework, anecdotal records you or someone else may have written, and other relevant materials. Be familiar with each exhibit so that in the conference you can present it as needed.

Parents may ask to see their children's standardized test scores, and they have a legal right to see them. Schools therefore should have a policy on how to manage test scores. How shall we present the scores? Where? And who should present them? Teachers are sometimes charged with the responsibility of conveying this information. They are the only ones who can discuss the scores in terms of classroom instruction. In this case, teachers must know what the scores mean.

If report cards have been issued, be able to explain on what criterion each grade was based. Several exhibits to support the grade will be useful. This is a point at which preparation for conferences pays off. With preparation we have great potential for communication with the parent; without it our comments may well appear to be founded in easily disregarded hunches, biases, and personal sentiments about the child.

The initial conversation is for getting acquainted in a nonconfrontational atmosphere. The first five minutes of a conference are crucial. This is the period that sets the tone of the session. Attempt to sense the parent's feelings about the school and the child. Alleviate apprehension or defensiveness by being friendly. Concentrate on positive features of the school environment and the child's participation. An anecdote about the child is often good to get the conversation going. Wait for the parent to react.

Portray the child as an individual. Talk about the child's skills, activities, and efforts as unique features. Avoid comparing the student to other children. Describe what skills the child has and those on which the child is working at the present time. Knowing the skills the child can perform is often more important to the parent than where the child stands among peers. Focus on the child's progress in his or her development, but make plans for personal growth where indicated.

Maintain professional poise at all times during the conference. This is necessary in order to project confidence in what you wish to communicate. Do not fidget with a pen, bounce your knee up and down, twirl your hair around your finger, or show other signs of impatience or nervousness. Be honest, but tactful in describing a child's work. Be genuinely receptive to the parent's comments. Parents expect to be regarded as an official resource in the child's life, and as such are capable of identifying plans and explanations. Their views are not to be rejected out of hand.

Another guideline of successful conferencing is to *be a good listener.* Let the parent talk, and do not immediately discount a parent's comment. Encourage parents to express themselves by posing questions like "How do you feel when . . . ," or "Is it fair to say that . . . ," or a simple "I see" followed by a longer than average pause. Responses such as these tend to prompt the parent to continue to express themselves. Regular eye contact is also important.

Next, *keep the conference on the topic—the child's work and the school program.* Do put limits on other directions of the conversation; keep it focused on child related topics.

Hearsay typically does not improve the quality of a parent conference, so avoid it. Discussion of local events may be interesting but it does not expand the parent's understanding of the school's program or the child's progress in that program. However, the parent's relating of home situations may well help you respond to the child.

Be flexible in planning for the child's next school term. Without losing control of the direction of the conversation, entertain several ideas about promoting the pupil's progress. Look at them each as having possible value. You and the parent may even wish to make a list of possibilities. Then discuss each possibility, sorting out ones that may be most productive. Let the decision among these be a joint agreement. Parents want to be involved, and this is one way for them to do so. But do not let them avoid the purpose of the conference by taking up the time with irrelevant topics.

Our interest in conferences is to communicate. To this end, *avoid technical vocabulary.* Specialty vocabulary, acronyms for programs, and so forth impede communication. Terms such as percentile rank, the inclusion program, or EMR probably do not mean much to parents. Parents use everyday language and the terms with which they are familiar. We need to put school programs and tools into everyday language. Parents will appreciate it and your communication will be more effective.

Support generalizations with evidence. Stay close to the data and avoid generalizations about the child that cannot be supported by assessment information. In conversations with parents you may wish to describe the pupil's work or behavior in general terms. If you do this have the exhibits that support the generalization. Without them, your observations look like a personal opinion. But if you have evidence to support the generalization it carries weight over sheer opinion.

Make notes during the conference for the record. Records should include plans you and the parent have made, and if discussed, the alternatives to these plans. Records should also list exhibits you showed the parent and contain a general summary of the conference. Share your notes with the parent for verification. Sharing the notes also indicates to the parent that the conference is a cooperative event in which both parties have a role. Some teachers ask the parent to sign the notes as evidence that the content is substantially correct, but because the notes are for your reference, the parent's signature is not necessary.

Guide Sheets for Conferences

Some schools have a standard conference note sheet. This sheet lists topics to be considered in the conference. It also contains a space for comments that summarize the discussion on each topic. A sample of such a sheet is given in Figure 20.4. As you can see in the figure, a sheet like this may increase the probability of touching on the important points in the conference. On the other hand, conferences are not the same from parent to parent, and standard sheets may be too formal to be used with all parents.

Your notes should be filed so that you can refer to them in planning for the child. Also, they are useful in providing continuity for conferences with the child's parents in the future.

In sum, the conference can be an excellent process for communication between a parent and the school staff. However, these meetings must be carried off well if they are

OUTLINE FOR PARENT CONFERENCE

_____ _____ _____ _____ _____
(Pupil)   (Parent)   (Teacher)   (Date)   (Time)

ACADEMIC ACHIEVEMENT
   Discuss: Current performance, evidence, grade, recent
   standardized tests (if any), plans

Reading   (comprehension) _____

              (word attack) _____

English   (composition)_____

              (oral) _____

Mathematics (processes) _____

              (problem solving)_____

Science _____

Social Studies _____

Handwriting _____

Art and Music _____

Physical Development _____

PERSONAL/SOCIAL DEVELOPMENT

Social skills _____

Respects others' rights _____

Effort _____

Time use _____

Attitude toward school _____

OTHER CONCERNS (List)

_____

_____

PLANS

_____

_____

_____

FIGURE 20.4   A Typical Conference Guide Sheet

going to reach their potential. If teachers follow the guidelines we've discussed, the conference has a much better chance of being productive.

✎ Problems

1. Which of the guidelines for conferences do you consider the most important? Why did you select these? Is there another guideline you would like to add? Try it out on a friend to see if other people like it, too.
2. With a friend imagine you are the teacher and the friend is a parent. Begin by each characterizing a child so you have some common ground, and then role-play a conference. Remember the guidelines.
3. Suppose you were assigned to schedule parent-teacher conferences for your elementary school. You may schedule two sets for the year. When would you schedule these, and why then?

SUMMARY

1. The primary purpose of reporting to parents is to communicate the achievement of students.
2. Basic report cards have two components: a section reporting on achievement in the subject areas, and one that reports on the student's personal and social development. This type of card is referred to as the dual or multiple marking system.
3. Report cards have the advantage of compressing a great deal of work into a single symbol; however in the compression the report loses the ability to describe specific skills.
4. Some involvement of students in self-evaluation is instructive for both students and teacher, and helps to develop the students' abilities in being critical of their own work.
5. Computerized report cards expedite the recording process, however they may have some security problems.
6. No report card fits all schools or the information needs of all clientele. To make cards fit the school better a report card should ideally involve all constituents of a school.
7. Letters to parents can go into more detail than report cards, but they will not eliminate the need for grades, are time consuming, and must be written carefully.
8. Parent-teacher conferences have the advantage of face-to-face communication, but do not substitute for a report card. They are most effective at the elementary school level.
9. Problems with parent-teacher conferences include the timing of conferences in the year, lack of preparation, unavailability of parents, defensiveness, and time constraints.
10. In implementing parent-teacher conferences be prepared, begin by getting acquainted, portray the child as an individual, maintain professional poise, listen,

maintain the focus on the child and the program, avoid technical vocabulary, support generalizations with data and work samples, and take notes for the record.

11. To ensure the desired breadth of the conference some schools use a standard conference note sheet that lists topic areas to be considered, with space for comment.

KEY TERMS

dual card
multiple marking system

ADDITIONAL READING

Anderson, K. E. and Wendel, F. C. (1988). Pain relief: Make consistency the corner stone of your policy on grading. *American School Board Journal,* 175 (10), 36–37.

Gronlund, N. E. and Linn, R. L. *Measurement and Evaluation in Teaching,* 6th ed., New York, Macmillan Publishing Company, 1990, Chapter 17.

MacIver, D. J. (1990). A national description of report card entries in middle grades. Center for Research on Effective Schooling for Disadvantaged Students, Baltimore, MD.

Mehring, T., et al., (1991). Report cards: What do they mean during the elementary school years? *Reading Improvement,* 28 (3), 162–168.

Worthen, B. R., Borg, W. R., and White, K. R. *Measurement and Evaluation in the Schools,* White Plains, NY: Longman Publishing Group, 1993, Chapter 14.

CHAPTER 21

ASSESSING SCHOOL PROGRAMS

"I was just reading an article about the Soundout Phonics Approach to beginning instruction in reading," said Ms. Trall, a kindergarten teacher, as she shared a pastry with her colleague, Ms. Longview. "This article says we have been starting children on the wrong exercises in beginning reading, and the authors outline what we should be doing to get kids off on the right foot," she continued enthusiastically.

"How is that different from the Fast Track system we had the workshop on last year?" asked Ms. Longview.

"Well, as I read the article I began to wonder how many of the ideas were the same, but were simply called something different," continued Ms. Trall thoughtfully.

If there is one thing educators can say about their schools it is that new programs and practices are being proposed, and some implemented, all the time. Every year a new way of teaching a basic skill is being discussed in the educational literature. New assessment techniques are sailing on the crest of the wave. New administrative approaches are appearing. Some of these innovations will be accepted; others will be forgotten.

Schools must carefully select the changes they will put into practice. There are many aspects of school operation, of the community, of students, and the economic market that impinge on the decision to make changes in practices and policies. Should we do some evaluation before we decide to retain a current program or institute changes? What sources of information shall we explore? Who wants this information? How will it impact the decision we want to make?

States require all schools to be accredited every few years. This forces educators to look at programs, to find data to support—or refute—the claim that they are doing what they say they are doing. This means schools must implement internal evaluation of programs, procedures, and policies.

Obviously, there are many questions to be explored before educators make conclusions about programs. The ultimate questions will always be: Are the objectives of instructional programs realistic and are the programs meeting the objectives effectively?

To answer this question schools must collect information. Subjective impressions alone will not satisfy the state accreditation, nor will they please the local school personnel. Local educators must plan to tap a variety of sources of information. All of these have a role in evaluation studies.

What This Chapter Will Include.   This chapter will discuss the characteristic of school program evaluation. You will learn:

1. Why teachers should know about evaluating school programs
2. Some reasons for doing evaluations in schools
3. What steps should be taken to evaluate a program
   a. Locating needs to be met by school programs
   b. Inventorying program requirements
   c. Monitoring the program once it is on line
   d. How did the program come out?
4. Who should do the evaluation
5. Some questions to explore before the evaluation
6. Some guidelines for assessing the plausibility of an evaluation plan

Up to now you and I have been looking at assessing the educational growth of individual children. In this chapter we broaden our perspective to look at the success of specific programs. The evaluation of a new program or alteration of a standing program must involve teachers. Teachers implement programs and only they know how programs are actually carried out. Teachers are a resource for data. They should be involved in providing direction, information, and in arriving at conclusions. Teachers are a resource for data. They also are often the ones affected most by alterations in school activities. For these reasons you should have a say in what is evaluated, and how it is done.

Reasons for Doing Program Evaluation

Each year a troop of "experts" march to schools across the nation. They bring with them plans for the "latest" procedure in teaching almost any skill, for doing assessments, for managing school resources, and for operating school support systems. Some of these procedures sound very logical, but schools should evaluate the current local plan before they decide change is advisable.

Educators do not wish to alter programs that are working well. But some study is needed to see if desired outcomes are emerging. If, after careful study, a new idea appears available, they may wish to implement one on a trial basis, and ask, "Did it improve the skill—reading speed, writing, ability to apply science concepts—that they expected it to improve?" These are evaluation questions. Educators must launch a study to collect information to find the answers, and this information should come from many different sources.

Schools should make changes only when dispassionate inquirers have looked at all reasonable information and have decided that the change is supported by the findings. Educators need stability in school programs, but programs must change to increase their efficiency, to adapt to technology, and to adjust to the demands of the social structure they serve. Only a data-oriented study of school programs and other events can tell teachers how appropriate a program is for their system. This indicates evaluation studies that will collect all kinds of relevant "intelligence."

Here is an example. Ms. Allen, Mr. Black, and Ms. Hale, three biological science teachers at Lewis and Clark High School, met to review the school program in biology. Where was it strong, and where was it weak? What criteria could they use to answer these questions? What should they do differently, at what cost in personnel and equipment, at what expected gain in student performance?

"I'm not sure what I am really achieving in my instruction," Mr. Black began. "At the end of our program what do our students really know?"

"I think the first question should be: What are we intending that they be able to do—what are the objectives that we can all agree on? Are we teaching toward different ends?" Ms. Allen replied as she scanned her course outline.

"And maybe it's more than that," interjected Ms. Hale. "How do our objectives undergird the demand for science knowledge in the life of these kids—that's a salient question, I think. Simply put, is our instruction as relevant in a student's world as it was five years ago?"

Concerns like those expressed by these teachers often lead to a request for an evaluation of programs. At this point the teachers have no framework to help them construct the questions in an orderly fashion or to help them decide how to research for the answers. Most important is that people involved with each of the many facets of the educational program feel a need to evaluate their program, its methods of presentation, currency, and relevance of its content. When these situations arise there are systematic approaches that can facilitate the evaluation process. Seeking out these approaches can speed the process and increase the likelihood that the results will be dependable.

Preparing for an Evaluation

In planning for an evaluation educators should ask themselves several questions, among which are the following.

1. *For whom is the evaluation to be done?* The results of the study may be for any number of persons or agencies. This may be a self-study for reaccreditation, it may be a program study for the curriculum department, it may be for the instructional staff who are considering a new textbook series. It may be for school administration in preparing a budget request for the school board. In any case, the kinds of data collected and the decisions made from an evaluation will be, to a considerable extent, defined by whom the study is for.

2. *What is to be evaluated?* Is the innovation in a particular program the focus of the evaluation? Is it the abilities of the instructional staff in carrying off a given innovation? Is it the organizational structure of school departments? Is it the effectiveness of the counseling services in reaching students with problems? Educators must know clearly what the focus of the study is before they begin, and this focus should be apparent to everyone. The clear delineation of teacher objectives is a salient feature of the study from the outset. Human beings have a tendency to wander; in an evaluation educators need focus.

3. *Will the plan for evaluation produce important, valid, and reliable results?* What is the likelihood of the study producing usable findings, findings that can be a firm basis for decision making? Here educators need a plan that describes a systematic data collection. They need to specify the retrieval of data that are replicable and that are tied to the focal variables in the study, and they should have a description of these methods before the evaluation begins.

4. *Will the results of the evaluation have an impact on the program?* Conclusions based on the study should lead to clear directions for the program being evaluated. Plans for implementing the findings of the evaluation should be laid early, or the program may continue with "business as usual." A committee for implementation should be appointed before the evaluation is begun, so that the committee will be ready to proceed when the study is completed. This process will increase the likelihood that the findings will call for changes in the program.

5. *When should the evaluation begin and when will the report be available?* Time lines are simply a part of good planning, and they allow us to do follow-up work in a timely fashion. It allows the staff to coordinate their activities; they start together, provide information at formative points in the study, re-evaluate direction as information becomes available, and end the study at a set date so consumers can know when to expect the results.

The study should be completed at a point in the school year when its findings will be most usable in planning. Educators need the results of the study by a given date because they will want to respond with changes (if required) to be implemented before a specific calendar point, such as before school begins, or before an accreditation review. For example, if teachers are going to institute an integrated approach to teaching science in high school, they must begin before school starts in the fall. Teachers may need workshops, materials must be acquired, classrooms and schedules may need alterations. To implement the findings of a study, lead time is necessary. The evaluation should have deadlines that provide this lead time.

6. *Does the school have a written agreement describing the evaluation plan to all concerned individuals?* Before the evaluation begins educators should prepare (with the evaluator) an agreement that defines the objectives, the procedures, the time line, the data and its analysis, and the costs involved. It is essential that all parties understand what is to be done and in what order. The evaluation will be in trouble if the school administrator, the curriculum director, and teaching staff have different ideas as to what would be done.

Steps in Evaluating a School Program

The essential steps in an evaluation will vary depending on the pervasiveness of the questions involved. The evaluation launched by the Foreign Language department to get answers to a few specific questions will involve fewer steps than would a total school accreditation study. However, the overall procedures are similar.

When an evaluation question comes up educators often turn first to an achievement test to see how well the children did under the present procedures. But in a systematic evaluation, if broad testing is done at all, it will be near the end of the evaluation process. Several other steps must be completed first. This section we will take a look at several of these.

Steps in Evaluation

1. Identify the needs to be met.
2. Inventory the start-up requirements for the program.
3. Monitor the progress of the program.
4. Compare the program results to the objectives.

Identifying Needs

The evaluation begins, in fact, before considering the current program at all. The first step involves a review of the context into which educators will implement a program. This is **context evaluation.** One reason a program may not succeed is that the context into which it was imposed may not indicate a need, acceptance, or grasp of the program. For example, in a suburban school where 90 percent of the students go on to college and the remainder go to technical schools, there may not be much interest in a shop course in carpentry. The context of the school—the community being served and its residents— just did not call for such a course. On the other hand, in a community in which 90 percent of the students go into work situations upon graduating, there may be a real need for training in carpentry and similar skills.

Consider a community in which 25 percent of the adults are functionally illiterate. What portion of the low literate are interested in and capable of attending a program in adult literacy? What level is being required in the local job market? And what circumstances will potential applicants tolerate to acquire the literacy skills? These are questions that precede the development of educational programs; they are typical questions that context evaluation must address.

Evaluations begin with a look at the fabric of the situation into which programs are to be woven. Does the project have a wide base of support in the community into which the instruction is introduced? What needs exist in the clientele? The study of context provides a very strong basis for developing objectives. What objectives should be pursued to meet the needs identified in the context study? It is these kinds of questions with which teachers in all program areas should begin. If the data collected in the evaluation do not positively respond to these questions, the program may well be undermined from the start.

Now let's return to the biology team mentioned earlier. As their evaluation became formulated, they decided first to collect data from published sources about social demands of scientific knowledge, and they related it to their local community. They looked for journals that presented emerging topics in biological sciences. They found the ability levels of students in the community, looked at the percent who continued with post-high-school education and what the requirements of the most commonly attended institutions were. To assess the preparation of students coming into biology they surveyed science work in grades seven and eight. They looked at local industries to see if biology was important knowledge for the job market. Out of all this they developed context for their instruction. Now the objectives for their program offerings could have focus on real world situations.

When this work is complete, it is time to turn to the materials, equipment, and skills required to carry out a program to meet the new objectives.

Identifying Program Requirements

The second question asked during evaluation is, "How will we implement the program?" What kinds of materials, instructional skills, strategies are required to launch or modify the program? These and similar questions deal with establishing procedures for instruction and with the materials out of which educators create instructional supports. Does the school have staff appropriately trained to implement the program? What kinds of materials will they need? How many of these materials are available or can be procured within the budget? Does the physical plant accommodate the required instruction? Does the program require alternative facilities? These are examples of **implementation evaluation** questions.

No matter how well you have established the need for a program in the context of the community and laid down the objectives accordingly, unless you are prepared to support the implementation of the program, you can expect it to be unsuccessful. Looking closely at inputs is an essential part of the evaluation plan.

Now returning to the biology lab we find the teachers looking at the inventory of materials and teaching aids they have on hand. They are reading journals to see what level of training is currently being recommended to carry out instruction in the areas identified by the context survey, and what sequences of activities are being tried by experimenters and curriculum writers. They are finding what it takes to implement a program to meet the objectives they have agreed upon.

Monitoring Progress

At this point you have looked at the need and established the objectives for a program. You have inventoried the tools and resources required for implementing the activities. Instruction is underway. The next task is the monitoring of the ongoing events of the program. This is often called **formative evaluation,** which asks the question, "How well are we carrying out what we planned to do?" Is the staff adequately trained? Are they using the materials in the prescribed manner? Are the materials appropriate for the staff and students? Is the program on schedule? Is the physical plant adequate for the program? Are students adjusting to the demands of instruction? These questions are aimed at monitoring progress.

Formative evaluation provides information for fine-tuning the program at a time when it can still be adjusted. If the staff needs additional training, workshops and seminars can be arranged for them. If the staff sees a need to vary the difficulty level of the reading materials, they still have time to adapt to this need. Formative evaluation checks the procedures and resources as the instruction moves along and provides the staff with an opportunity to make adaptations that keep the program most effectively on track toward the objectives.

Again, let's go back to the biology lab. The teachers found the textbook was increasingly outdated, so as a replacement for the text they began copying materials from magazines, reference books, assigning library reference reading, and increased the number of fields trip and "wild" sample collecting. They found that they, as instructors, were not entirely up-to-date on two topics on the list of objectives and collected several sources to read. Mr. Black attended a weekend workshop at a nearby college to gain some added skill in managing microscopic specimens. In their daily schedule the biology teachers noticed that they were spending too much time teaching equipment operation, and applied for funds to buy some short CD-ROM demonstrations on preparing microscopic slides and using the microscope. All of these events were done because the monitoring of the implementation of the program suggested some needed adaptations to the plan.

Comparing Results With Objectives

The final step in evaluating a program is sometimes called **summative evaluation.** It can take many forms, depending on the objectives you have for your program. If the objective is to have students write better expository themes, you may ask them to compose several of these, to take an objective achievement test involving sentence construction, parts of speech, punctuation, and paragraph construction—the building blocks of writing—or do a critique of themes written by other authors. Possibly, you will ask them to do all of these. In this the last step in the evaluation of a program we ask, "How do the results compare with our objectives?" This is determined by assessing the skills students have relating to the objectives.

Each of the four steps in a program evaluation involve types of assessments which must be performed appropriately. Tests are usually applicable in getting at only a part of the desired information. Evaluators must use other sources of data, such as student-created products, controlled interviews and testimony, financial reports, attendance, post-graduation success, and questionnaires. Teachers must be involved, and sometimes the assessment will include other community residents—parents, law enforcement, local employers, and governmental officials. Educators implement programs so that students can acquire skills that will promote success in their lives outside and beyond school. How well are they doing this? Often educators must go to nonschool agencies to ask how they see the impact.

This may look like a long and complex process, but evaluation procedures are flexible. The biology teachers may be interested in only one phase of the process. They may look only at the context to see how relevant and current their program is. Or they may look at the implementation process as a basis for recommending staff changes or budget allocations. Evaluations are made to attack the questions at hand, but evaluators are always aware that the answer to one question may be found by asking several others. For example, if you are substantiating a budget request, an implementation question the evaluator must also be curious about is the context that says this equipment is no longer used in industry, that teachers need a higher level of training in a specific skill, or that new topics should be added to the syllabus. Any of these could be budget questions.

✎ Problems

1. Take a problem in your field of teaching. Cite specific tasks to be performed during an evaluation in each area: locating needs, inventorying program requirements, monitoring the progress of the program, and finding the results of the program.
2. How would you monitor the progress of the program you outlined in Problem 1? Provide at least four kinds of data you would collect.
3. After attending several workshops on teaching science, the chair of the Science department at James Whitcomb Riley High School decided the department would start teaching by the Lifelong Science Program. In June materials were bought and distributed to the teachers. The program began in the fall. For an evaluation, the department twice discussed the program at a teachers' meeting. They also administered achievement tests in the spring to see how well students were learning science topics. Comment on the appropriateness of the procedures used.

Internal Versus External Evaluators

Evaluations can often be done by staff members of the school or they may be done by special evaluators from outside agencies. There are advantages and disadvantages to using internal and external evaluators, the most important of which are discussed in this section.

Internal Evaluators

We begin with a look at advantages and disadvantages of utilizing internal evaluators.

When someone on your own staff performs the study we call this **internal evaluation.** Members of your staff are assigned to systematically look at one of your own programs.

Advantages and Disadvantages of Internal Evaluators

Advantages of Internal Evaluators

1. Will know the local context.
2. Will know the program.
3. Will be sensitive to local resources.
4. Will know capabilities of local staff.

Disadvantages of Internal Evaluators

1. May have vested interests in the program.
2. May be influenced by acquaintances in program.
3. May feel peer pressure for certain outcomes.
4. May lack sufficient training.

There are clear advantages in following this procedure. Among the advantages is the acquaintanship that local evaluators gain from living in the area and associating with members of the local community and its students. Through conversations with colleagues they are likely to know what the program is about, what the capabilities of the staff are, and what limitations local resources place on the program.

However, there may also be disadvantages in using internal evaluators. Local personnel have vested interests in the success of programs, and may already have an opinion as to whether a program is good or bad. This opinion may be based on their own agenda, rather than success of the program. They may also be influenced by personal acquaintances with central staff members who may approve (or disapprove) of the program being evaluated. This may lead to peer pressure. In addition, local personnel are not likely to be well trained in evaluation. Evaluation is a special area of study, and unique skills are developed in this study, skills that are likely not to be found in a given school.

External Evaluators

If the disadvantages of using internal evaluators outweigh the advantages you must consider an **external evaluator** to review your program. This person might come from the state department of education, from a college or university, from one of the federally-funded regional laboratories, or from one of the many private evaluation services available.

There are several clear advantages of using external evaluators, and also some disadvantages.

External evaluators have the advantage of special training in evaluation. Because of this they will have procedures well organized, and will likely conduct a smooth-running study, and because they have experience with data, will analyze the results quickly.

Advantages and Disadvantages of External Evaluators

Advantages of External Evaluators

1. No personal ties to personnel in the program.
2. No vested interests in outcomes.
3. Likely to be better trained in evaluation.

Disadvantages of External Evaluators

1. May not know program well.
2. Will cost more.
3. May be procedure bound.

They will also have no vested interest in how the program was developed and what it achieved: they have not worked on developing the program, the personnel in the program are not likely to be friends or acquaintances and they owe nothing to the program or its staff. These are real plus signs for outside evaluators. Also, observations made by outside evaluators are likely to be more objective because they do not have to think about friends who may be involved, less limited in the line of questioning that can be developed because they are not influenced by any group, and more focussed on the program. Therefore when tough, summative judgments must be made about programs, external evaluators clearly have the advantage.

Although there are definite advantages for having external evaluators look at your programs, there are also some disadvantages. External evaluators are less likely to be as aware of the objectives, details and context of program activities as would an internal evaluator. Also, external evaluators are not inexpensive and with typical school budgets, this cost-benefit relation is often a complex consideration in that funds spent must often come from programs.

In addition, some external evaluators are very procedure bound. These persons may show more concern for adherence to evaluation procedures than for program implementation, management, and objectives. Evaluation procedures often must be flexible in real settings, and local people may be more ready to accept this than are professional evaluators.

Clearly, use of either internal or external evaluators has certain advantages. However, each has a unique set of disadvantages, too. The selection depends on the situation, with special attention given to local circumstances: finances, trained personnel, and the local interests in certain findings. If there are no finances for an outside evaluator, schools must conduct an internal evaluation. Sometimes workshops can be organized to improve local skills in program evaluation. External evaluators are available to conduct such workshops at a fraction of the cost necessary to employ them to carry out the entire evaluation. After the workshop, teachers may wish to proceed with evaluating their own programs. Many schools find this a productive approach.

However, if finances are available external evaluators are often a good choice to manage your evaluation needs. School personnel must be assured at the outset, though, that external evaluators will utilize the knowledge and skill of school staff in the data collection. This brings the people most familiar with the program into the evaluation process at the point where external evaluators are likely to be least knowledgeable.

✎ Problems

1. List three advantages for using an internal evaluator and three advantages for using an external evaluator.
2. In Klassburg schools the superintendent has two assistant superintendents to help manage the operation of the schools. The school board wants an evaluation of the roles and impact on programs of these assistants. The superintendent has appointed the high school principal to develop a plan for the study and to select the persons who will collect and analyze the data. What is your response to this arrangement, and what, if anything, would you do differently?

Guidelines for Organizing an Evaluation Project

Evaluations range from limited and informal to rather broad and formalized. The three kindergarten teachers at Eisenhower School have decided to meet to assess the quality of the Ginn materials for teaching reading readiness skills. They have invited the reading specialist from the central curriculum office to join them. They look at children's written work collected over the year, at reading readiness test scores, at notes from parent conferences, and each discusses what she believes are the strong and weak parts of the Ginn material. Based on this one of the volunteers, who is not a first-grade teacher, has agreed to summarize their work and to write a set of recommendations for the approval of the group.

This study of the reading readiness materials is an example of an informal evaluation. The problem for study was brought up by teachers, themselves. Teachers were the evaluators, the data providers, and will approve the recommendations. Some informal studies are not even this well organized.

In another example, the Walter Reuther Vocational School wonders why the enrollment in its programs has been only modest and why a fourth of their students drop out the first term. They call for a professional evaluation service to find some answers to these questions. With the service they look at the context for the program, then define objectives, skill of the staff, and material requirements to implement the program. As the program proceeds they look at data collection to respond to each objective, as well as sources of data within the school and in the target industries, and decide what would be observed as summative data to reflect program success. This is a formal evaluation plan. It requires a different type of skill, and the plan of activities must be much more detailed than in the kindergarten study discussed above.

The differences in the complexity of the two projects just described illustrate the fact that organizing an evaluation depends on the expanse of the study and the complexity of the agencies and variables involved. However, formal or informal, complex or simple, there are several general guidelines that should characterize any evaluation study.

1. The focus of the study should be clear at the outset. This includes stating what is to be evaluated, for what purpose, and in regard to what objectives.

2. Persons who will carry out the project should be identified, and time away from normal duties arranged to allow them to work on the evaluation.

3. Some time should be spent brainstorming the multiple sources of data to be collected in the study, and how they will be used in reaching conclusions. Give attention to data that come from different sources, including student products, tests, testimony of persons who can comment from experience, and demographic data sources. Also look for items that corroborate each other (reliability checks).

4. Make an agreement as to what will be done with the results of the evaluation. Unless findings are implemented, the study is merely an exercise. In advance, have a plan to utilize the results of the evaluation. This should be true even if the study is an informal one done by a few teachers (as in the kindergarten study above). Be prepared to take the findings to the next level for action.

5. If the study is a complex, formal one be sure there is an advisory committee to oversee the planning, execution, and interpretation of the findings of the study. Evaluations that range beyond small, informal ones need the guidance of teachers and

administrators in setting the plan, in identifying the principal investigator, and in seeing that it all goes according to plan and that appropriate techniques are followed. This committee should be in force at the outset of the study.

These guidelines are general in that they are intended to advise teachers in assessing the extent to which an evaluation plan is plausible. Additional detail will be needed to support a more formal evaluation, while less detail may suit an informal study.

A REAL CASE NARRATIVE

Here is a conversation which took place among teachers and their principal in an elementary school. Comment on the situation they are discussing and tell how you would manage this problem.

At the end of the teachers' meeting at the Orchard Elementary School the Principal, Ms. Hartman announced that the experimental mathematics program for the primary grades was to be evaluated next month.

"Is this already planned and ready to go?" asked Ms. Thom, a second-grade teacher.

"I don't really know much more than I have told you," replied Ms. Hartman, "but it looks like the plan is set and will be initiated in two weeks."

"But no one has mentioned a thing to us," Mr. Riggle, a third-grade teacher said impatiently. "We are the ones who are carrying out this program. Shouldn't we be involved in the planning of the evaluation?"

Ms. Hartman replied that she had not been consulted and to this point was not involved in the evaluation. She only found out about it in a memorandum two days ago.

"Who is doing this study?" asked Ms. Terry, a second-grade teacher. "Do they expect to appear one day in our classrooms and start poking around? What kind of data will they want?"

"What do they know about how we decided to do this program, or how it has been going?" said Ms. Thom. "I really hate being treated like I'm out of the loop when we are the ones who are supposed to be carrying out the instructional plan that is the heart of the program," she followed a bit in pique. "I wonder, shouldn't we teachers be the evaluators."

SUMMARY

1. The purpose of a program evaluation is to provide data that can be used in deciding whether to initiate, alter, or terminate an activity.
2. In considering an evaluation educators should ask: for whom would the evaluation be done; what is to be evaluated; will the evaluation produce important, valid, and reliable results; will the results have an impact on the program; when should the evaluation begin and when will the report be available; and will the school have a written agreement describing the evaluation in detail?

3. The steps in evaluating a program include: locating needs through a review of the context, identifying program requirements for implementation, monitoring progress after the program is underway, and assessing the outcomes in terms of objectives.

4. Programs may be evaluated by either internal or external evaluators. Internal evaluators are familiar with the program and people involved but less likely to be entirely objective; external evaluators are more likely to be trained in evaluation and be more objective, but will be less familiar with the program history and objectives.

5. The focus of an evaluation should be clear to all parties at the outset, and persons responsible should be identified to interested individuals. There should be an agreement on what will be done with the results, and in the case of formal studies there should be an advisory committee that will oversee the progress of the study and the implementation of findings.

PROBLEMS

1. List and give examples of four phases of activities in an formal evaluation study.
2. List the advantages and disadvantages of using an internal evaluator. Do the same for using an external evaluator.
3. List four aspects of a study that should be clear to all before an evaluation study is done in your school.
4. In my secondary school we are trying out, in four sections of a course, a combination of English composition and literature. At the end of the first year of this trial the principal wants to call in outside evaluators but the teachers want to do the study informally among themselves. Provide pros and cons for each side.

KEY TERMS

context evaluation   summative evaluation
implementation evaluation   internal evaluation
formative evaluation   external evaluation

ADDITIONAL READING

Bogdan, R. C. and Biklen, S. K., *Qualitative Research for Education,* 2d ed., Needham Heights, MA: Allyn & Bacon, 1992, especially Chapters 2 and 7.

Common, D. L. (1985). Curriculum innovation, school improvement, and school evaluation. *Clearinghouse,* 58, 298–304.

Erikson, F. (1990). Qualitative methods. *Research in Teaching and Learning,* vol. 2, 77–194.

APPENDIX A

STATISTICAL PROCEDURES FOR CALCULATING CORRELATION COEFFICIENTS

Overview of Correlation in Education

Correlation is a very useful procedure for persons interested in applying assessment data to educational decision-making. Any time you make a conclusion about a child, you imply a prediction. For example, Clarise is smart—a conclusion; she will be successful in her academic work—a prediction. The closer two variables correlate, the more accurate your prediction will be. Correlation is the procedure that shows you how closely student ranking on one variable correspond with their ranking on another, and hence how accurate your prediction of one of these variables will be based on the other.

Correlation is also important to show how consistent (or reliable) test scores are. If I give parallel forms of a test—each of which purports to assess the same characteristic—the two tests (A and B) should rank students in about the same order. Correlation is the procedure needed to show how close the rank of a student on test A will be to the rank on B.

Procedures

Two correlation procedures are presented here. One is the simplified procedure while the other is the standard exact calculation of the correlation, known as the Pearson method.

The Simplified Method for the Correlation Coefficient.

Step 1. As in all correlation methods, you must have two scores on every student. For example, you could have an aptitude test score and a reading comprehension score for each student in a class. Here is an example.

Student	Scores X	Scores Y
Alfa	15	20
Betty	9	12
Gammi	8	17
Della	10	16
Epstine	7	19
Zeta	12	23

Step 2. Look at the scores on the first test (X). Arrange them in order from high to low. Find the point that cuts the class into two equal-sized groups. This is the mid-point in the score distribution. Now do the same for the second test (Y). The following are the scores on tests X and Y each arranged from high to low. The mid-point is indicated by an underscore.

Test X		Test Y	
Alfa	15	Zeta	23
Zeta	12	Alfa	20
Della	10	Epstine	19
Betty	9	Gammi	17
Gammi	8	Della	16
Epstine	7	Betty	12

Step 3. Now find the number of students who place in the top half of the group on **both** measures you are correlating. In this case Alfa and Zeta are the only ones in the top half on both tests.

Step 4. Calculate the percent of the total group of these students who are in the top half on both tests. Here we have two students out of six, or 33 percent. From the table below, we see that 33 percent is equal to a correlation of .49. The correlation between tests X and Y is .49.

TABLE A   A Conversion Table for Estimating the Value of the Correlation Coefficient

%	r	%	r	%	r	%	r	%	r
45	.95	37	.69	29	.25	21	−.25	13	−.69
44	.93	36	.65	28	19	20	−.31	12	−.73
43	.91	35	60	27	.13	19	−.37	11	−.77
42	.88	34	.55	26	.07	18	−.43	10	−.81
41	.85	33	.49	25	.00	17	−.49	9	−.85
40	.81	32	.43	24	−.07	16	−.55	8	−.88
39	.77	31	.37	23	−.13	15	−.60	7	−.91
38	.73	30	.31	22	−.19	14	−.65	6	−.93

From *Short-Cut Statistics for Teacher-Made Tests,* (1960). Princeton, NJ: The Educational Testing Service, p. 34. The correlation coefficients are tetrachoric coefficient.

The Pearson Product Moment Method of Calculating the Correlation Coefficient.
Step 1. You must have two scores on everyone on whom you will calculate the correlation. This is the same as in the simplified method above, and for this method we will use the data given there.

Step 2. Get out your hand calculator and square each of the scores on test X, then square each of the scores on test Y. Now, for each student, multiply the test X score times the test Y score. Add up all these columns of scores. This is shown in the table below.

Student	X	Y	X²	Y²	XY
Alfa	15	20	225	400	300
Betty	9	12	81	144	108
Gammon	8	17	64	289	136
Della	10	16	100	256	160
Epstine	7	19	49	361	133
Zeta	12	23	144	529	276
Sums	61	107	663	1979	1080

Step 3. Put the sums into the following formula, and solve for the correlation coefficient. Read Σ as "the sum of . .", for example, ΣX = the sum of test X scores. In the above example $\Sigma X = 61$. The n = the number of students. The correlation coefficient is .46, very close to the coefficient found by the short-cut procedure (which was .49).

$$r = \frac{\Sigma XY - \dfrac{(\Sigma X \Sigma Y)}{n}}{\sqrt{\Sigma X^2 - \dfrac{(\Sigma X)^2}{n}}\sqrt{\Sigma Y^2 - \dfrac{(\Sigma Y)^2}{n}}}$$

$$= \frac{1080 - \dfrac{(61 \times 107)}{6}}{\sqrt{663 - \dfrac{(61)^2}{6}}\sqrt{1979 - \dfrac{(107)^2}{6}}}$$

$$= .46$$

APPENDIX B

SELECTED TEST PUBLISHERS AND TESTS

In this Appendix you will find a few test publishers and the well-known group tests of achievement and academic aptitude they publish. It should not be assumed that the tests listed with a given publisher represent their complete catalog. This Appendix identifies widely used or cited tests along with the publishers to contact for information, for ordering specimen sets of the tests for evaluation by local schools, or for ordering catalogs. This listing does not imply that these publishers are superior to publishers not listed here; there are many good tests and competent publishers. These are selected as representative of those whose products are found in many school systems. Their listing here does not imply endorsement.

If an asterisk (*) follows a test name, the test is criterion referenced; two asterisks (**) denote a readiness test.

1. CTB/McGraw-Hill, Del Monte Research Park, Monterey, CA, 93940

   California Achievement Tests, k–12
   School and College Ability Tests, 3–12
   Test of Cognitive Skills, 2–12
   Cooperative Preschool Inventory, P–K**
   DMI Mathematics System, k–8.9*
   PRI Reading System, k–9*

2. Institute for Personality and Ability Testing, P.O. Box 188, Champaign, IL, 61820

   Culture Fair Test, 4–16, A

3. Psychological Corporation, 555 Academic Ct., San Antonio, TX, 78204

   Metropolitan Achievement Tests, k–12
   Stanford Achievement Tests, 1–12
   Otis Lennon School Ability Test, 1–12
   Differential Aptitude Tests, 8–13

Stanford Early School Achievement Tests, k–1
Metropolitan Readiness Test, k–1★★

4. Riverside Publishing 425 Spring Lake Drive, Itasca, IL 60143-2079

Iowa Test of Basic Skills, k–12
Test of Achievement and Proficiency, 9–12
Cognitive Ability Test, k–12
National Proficiency Survey Series★★

5. Science Research Associates, Inc., 155 North Wacker Drive, Chicago, IL, 60606

Iowa Test of Educational Development, 8–12
SRA Achievement Tests, k–12

APPENDIX C

SOURCES OF INFORMATION ON SCHOOL TESTS

A. Books

1. *Mental Measurements Yearbook*. The Buros Institute of Mental Measurement, 135 Bancroft Hall, University of Nebraska, Lincoln, NE 68588. (Contains descriptions and reviews of tests, lists of publishers and addresses, and much more information. Tests are sorted by type of test, e.g., achievement, aptitude, and so forth. Each yearbook contains reviews of new tests and those revised since the date of the last yearbook. You may have to look in several yearbooks to find the test you want.)

2. *Education Index*. Look in your university library for this one. Published annually, it covers the entire field of education. It cites references only, and each edition is for one year only. Begin with the most recent year. Look under "tests," then the type of test you want to find. In some cases the name of the test will be listed in its alphabetical location. This reference provides a list of articles, books, and so forth for further study. It does not provide commentary on specific tests.

B. Journals

Journals in educational assessment tend to be somewhat experimentally oriented. Many of their articles are reports of studies with tests or testing practices. However, most of the journals reported here also accept commentary. Some studies report data on special tests and with special assessment situations. Not every issue will have a section on tests in the market. These journals are available at most university libraries.

Applied Measurement in Education
Applied Psychological Measurement
Educational Measurement: Issues and Practices
Journal of Educational Measurement

C. Test Item Banks Available to Schools

Banks of instructional objectives and test items that assess their attainment are available for almost any subject taught in mainstream public school programs. However, they are offered most commonly as test services tailored to the needs of a specific school. These tailored packages may include tests to fit your objectives, computerized scoring, and interpretation services. If you have a need in your school for this service this may be a productive approach to test construction, but they come at a price. Here are some of the test publishers who have item and objective banks.

1. CTB/McGraw-Hill, Objective-Referenced Bank of Items Tests (ORBIT), Del Monte Research Park, Monterey, CA 93940
2. Riverside Publishing Co., MULTISCORE, 425 Spring Lake Drive, Itasca, IL 60143-2079.
3. Science Research Associates, SRA Objective/Item Bank, 155 North Wacker Drive, Chicago, IL 60606
4. Tescor, Inc., First National Item Bank and Test Development System, Carlisle Drive, Herndon, VA 22070

D. Test Manuals

Each Test publisher will also publish manuals for the tests they sell. Write directly to the test publisher for copies of the manuals. They will come as part of a specimen set but often can be had separately. See the list of test publishers in Appendix B for addresses.

APPENDIX D

A C-LANGUAGE PROGRAM FOR CALCULATION OF DESCRIPTIVE STATISTICS FOR TESTS

This program calculates a mean, standard deviation and Kuder Richards (KR 21) reliability for tests that have ten (10) or more items in them. The initial step is to install the program. This is the most complicated part of using the analysis program. After installation the program can be opened up any time and runs simply and rapidly.

You may set up this program on your personal computer or on the school's local network, whichever is appropriate for you and serves you best. You can then easily open it up and compute the mean, standard deviation, and KR 21 for your test.

There are two steps in utilizing this program: Installation (a one-time operation) and running the program for calculation of the stats. The first step is the most involved but once done the program runs with little effort.

Installation

The program is written in ANSI C-Language. You must have a C or C++ compiler installed on your computer (or on your school's network). A compiler typically comes on a floppy disk. It is simply a set of instructions to the computer that interprets the program written in the compiler's language. Here it could be any of the popular C compilers available on the market (e.g., Microsoft Quick C, Turbo C ++, etc.).

Your school's central computing operation probably has a copy of the C compiler, or can get one for you to use. C language was chosen because it is a fairly portable system and is widely available. The program should run on any IBM-type computer (IBM, Gateway, Del, NCR, and others) and also on Macintosh if a C compiler is available.

After you get a copy of the C language compiler on your computer, call it up by following the instructions that accompany the compiler. Enter the program below exactly as it is shown including all commas, parentheses, semicolons, etc. It is very important that the program be typed exactly as it is written. When you have typed the program SAVE it as a file called "testdat.c". Compile the program using the procedures provided by your C-compiler system. Then Exit the compiler application. What you have done to this point will be done only once. You are now ready for the easy part which you will run each time you wish to get data on a test.

Running the Program on Your Class Data

Once the program is compiled, you may run the program any time you wish. Your computer will give you a C> prompt, then type testdat and hit ENTER. The program will immediately print instructions on the screen. It will ask you how many items (questions) in your test. Type this number in and hit RETURN. Please note that there must be ten or more items. If you enter a number less than ten the instruction will be repeated. (If your test has less than ten, and you "fake it" by saying ten or more, some of your statistics will be incorrect.)

When the number of items in the test is settled, the program will ask you to type in one student score, and hit the ENTER key. Be sure the score is correct before you hit ENTER. You cannot correct that score after hitting ENTER. If before you hit ENTER you notice the score is in error, use the backspace key and correct the score; then hit ENTER.

After the first score is recorded, the prompt will appear for the next score and so on. When all student scores are in, at the next prompt type in a negative number (such as −99). This tells the program that "I have given you all the student scores, so compute my stats." Very quickly the mean, standard deviation, and KR 21 will appear on your screen. (Please note that in rare cases the KR21 will be larger than 1.00. This is due to a peculiarity in the data being run.)

Here is the program that must be put into your computer to get the summary statistics. Be sure to type it EXACTLY as it is written.

```
#include <stdio.h>
#include <math.h>

main( )
{
    float score, sum = 0.0, ssum = 0.0, kr21, std, mean;
    int n = 0, items;

    printf("\t\t\tTEST SUMMARY STATISTICS\n\n");

    printf("How many items in this test? ");
        scanf("%d", &items);
        while (items < 10) {
        printf("Number of items must be greater or equal to 10.\n");
        printf("How many items in this test? ");
        scanf("%d", &items);
}

printf("Enter a score (-99 to quit): ");
scanf("%f", &score);
while (score >= 0) {
```

```
    n++;
    sum += score;
    ssum += score * score;
    printf("Enter a score (-99 to quit): ");
    scanf("%f", &score);
}

mean = sum / n;
std = sqrt(((ssum - (sum*sum)/n) / (n - 1)));
kr21 = ((float)items/(items-1)) *
        (1- ((mean*(items-mean) )/(items*std*std)));
printf("\nnumber of items= %3d\n", items);
printf("number of students= %3d\n", n);
printf("mean= %5.2f\nstandard deviation= %5.2f\n", mean, std);
printf("Reliability= %5.2f\n", kr21);
return 0;
}
```

An Example.   I have given a test to 15 students in my algebra class. I have scored the test and now want the test's descriptive statistics.

At the C> prompt I type in testdat and hit ENTER. The computer responds, TEST SUMMARY STATISTICS, and then, "How many items in this test?"

I have 80 test items, but for the sake of the demonstration I have "accidentally" neglected to input the zero and said I have 8 test items. As you see in the printout below, the program rejected the 8 and does not run until I tell it I have at least 10 items. In this case I have 80. When I have given the computer my items number (80), it then begins to ask for the student scores. Type in one score at a time, check it for accuracy, and follow that with ENTER. (Do not type student names, only their score.) The students' scores are:

Abe 56	Beth 60	Cal 60	Del 76	Fred 50
Gale 67	Hal 68	Irv 75	Jim 65	Lu 66
Mac 70	Nel 68	Orv 60	Eva 55	Kate 57

When all scores are recorded, type a negative number such as -99. The computer quickly puts your test summary statistics on your screen.

Here is the complete sample run:

Test Summary Statistics

```
How many items in this test? 8
Number of items must be greater or equal to 10.
How many items in this test? 80
Enter a score (-99 to quit): 56
```

```
Enter a score (-99 to quit): 67
Enter a score (-99 to quit): 70
Enter a score (-99 to quit): 60
Enter a score (-99 to quit): 68
Enter a score (-99 to quit): 68
Enter a score (-99 to quit): 60
Enter a score (-99 to quit): 75
Enter a score (-99 to quit): 60
Enter a score (-99 to quit): 76
Enter a score (-99 to quit): 65
Enter a score (-99 to quit): 55
Enter a score (-99 to quit): 57
Enter a score (-99 to quit): 50
Enter a score (-99 to quit): 66
Enter a score (-99 to quit): -99

number of items= 80
number of students= 15
mean= 63.53
standard deviation= 7.47
Reliability= 0.78
```